THE EARLY JOURNALS
AND LETTERS OF
FANNY BURNEY

1. Fanny Burney. From a miniature portrait by John Bogle, 1783. This, aside from the well-known Edward Francesco Burney portrait of 1782, is the earliest likeness of Fanny Burney

THE EARLY JOURNALS AND LETTERS OF

FANNY BURNEY

VOLUME I · 1768–1773

Edited by
LARS E. TROIDE

McGILL-QUEEN'S UNIVERSITY PRESS
KINGSTON AND MONTREAL
1988

© Lars E. Troide 1988

First published in 1988 by Oxford University Press

Published simultaneously in Canada and the United States 1988 by
McGill-Queen's University Press
ISBN vol. 1   07735 0538 5
Legal deposit second quarter 1988
Bibliothèque nationale du Québec

This book has been published with the help of a grant from the Canadian
Federation for the Humanities, using funds provided by the Social Sciences and
Humanities Research Council of Canada.

Canadian Cataloguing in Publication Data

Burney, Fanny, 1752–1840
The early journals and letters of Fanny Burney
Partial contents: v. 1. 1768–1773.
Includes index.
ISBN 0–7735–0538–5 (v. 1)
1. Burney, Fanny, 1752–1840—Correspondence.
2. Burney, Fanny, 1752–1840—Diaries.
3. Novelists, English—18th century—Correspondence.
4. Novelists, English—18th century—Diaries.
I. Troide, Lars E. (Lars Eleon), 1942–
II. Title.

PR3316.A4Z48 1988   823'.6   C86–094863–3

To Warren Hunting Smith

PREFACE

THE present volume is intended as the first of ten or twelve that will cover Fanny Burney's journals and letters from 1768 to the middle of 1791. Fanny began her first journal as a shy and precocious girl of 15, '*The silent observant Miss Fanny*'. This edition aims to carry her through the period of her greatest fame as the author of *Evelina* (1778) and *Cecilia* (1782) and will end with her exit from the Court of King George III and Queen Charlotte, after five exhausting years of service to the Queen as Second Keeper of the Robes.

Fanny's later journals have already been edited by Professor Joyce Hemlow and others as *The Journals and Letters of Fanny Burney (Madame d'Arblay), 1791–1840* (12 vols., Oxford, 1972–84). *The Early Journals and Letters* will therefore complete the presentation of Fanny's invaluable seventy-year chronicle in a modern, scholarly format. Dr Hemlow, in the introduction to her masterly edition, has described at length the inadequacies of earlier editions, viz., Charlotte Barrett's seven-volume effort of 1842–6 and Austin Dobson's revision of that work (6 volumes, 1904–5). These begin only with the journals of 1778. By contrast, Mrs Annie Raine Ellis's two-volume edition of *The Early Diary* or 'juvenile journals' (1768–77), first published in 1890, is excellent for its day, but marred none the less by Mrs Ellis's failure to decipher the more than 4,000 obliterated lines in the manuscript, and by her now decidedly antiquated annotations. The present edition will give for the first time, as far as possible, the *full* text of Fanny's early journals, in their original state, with annotations as thorough and accurate as modern scholarship will allow.

ACKNOWLEDGEMENTS

THIS first volume of the present edition is dedicated to Dr Warren Hunting Smith, Associate Editor of *The Yale Edition of Horace Walpole's Correspondence*. Dr Smith was the present editor's mentor in scholarship and the eighteenth century, and this dedication is my long overdue tribute to our friendship and joint labours in the century of Walpole and Fanny Burney.

For assistance on this volume I am indebted to many institutions and individuals. Among institutions and agencies, I first wish to acknowledge my university, McGill, whose administration and English Department granted me two consecutive years of leave from my teaching duties, besides lightening my regular teaching load. The University has also continued to provide the Burney Project with generous and well-furnished working space, first in Morrice Hall and now in the Redpath Undergraduate Library.

I next wish to thank the Social Sciences and Humanities Research Council of Canada. Large grants from the Council paid for the frequent trips I made to Yale and the New York Public Library, in addition to funding three extended visits to England where I explored numerous archives. The grants also funded the 'float-off operation' in the New York Public Library (see below, pp. x, xxix–xxx), made possible a two-month stay in New York by Dr James Neil Waddell to read obliterations in the Berg Collection (pp. x, xxix), paid the salaries of graduate student assistants who helped me with transcriptions and indexing, and covered extensive costs of stationery, microfilming, photocopying, and other miscellaneous items.

A fellowship from the Council paid part of my salary during the second of my leave years, besides providing additional research money. My first leave was made possible by a Fellowship for Independent Study and Research from the National Endowment for the Humanities in Washington, DC. This fellowship paid my whole salary for that year, and I am most grateful to the Endowment.

This book has been published with the help of a grant from

the Canadian Federation for the Humanities, using funds provided by the Social Sciences and Humanities Research Council of Canada.

My labours have taken me to many libraries, archives, and collections. For their help I wish to thank the librarians, archivists, curators, keepers, and support staff of: the McGill University Library (Montreal, Quebec); the Yale University Library (New Haven, Connecticut), in particular its constituents the Sterling Memorial Library and the Beinecke Rare Book and Manuscripts Library; the James M. and Marie-Louise Osborn and Frederick Hilles Collections in the Beinecke Library; the Lewis Walpole Library in Farmington, Connecticut (a special thanks to Assistant Librarians Catherine Jestin, Karen Peltier, and Joan Sussler); the New York Public Library; and the Berg Collection in the New York Public. In England: the Society of Genealogists (London); the British Library; the India Office Library (London); the Greater London Record Office; the Public Record Office (London); the Historical Manuscripts Commission (London); the Guildhall Library (London); the Holborn, Victoria, Chelsea, and Rose Lipman Libraries (London); the National Portrait Gallery, London (special thanks to former Assistant Keeper John Kerslake); the Bodleian Library (Oxford); the Bath Public Library; the Norfolk, Gloucester, and Worcester County Record Offices; the Lynn Public Library; and the Guildhall (Lynn). In Scotland: the Scottish Record Office (Edinburgh). While at Yale I worked in the offices of the Yale Walpole Edition and also made extensive use of research materials of the *Yale Editions of the Private Papers of James Boswell* (chief editors Professors Frederick Pottle and Frank Brady).

A particular debt of gratitude is owed to Dr Lola Szladits, Curator of the Berg Collection, by whose permission the manuscripts of Fanny's early journals, in her care, are here published. Permissions to publish or quote from manuscripts elsewhere have been granted by: the Osborn Collection, Yale (Dr Stephen Parks, Curator); the Houghton Library, Harvard University; the British Library (for materials in the Barrett Collection); the Essex County Record Office, Chelmsford, Essex (Victor Gray, Esq., Archivist); and the estate of Miss D. Viner-Brady, Gloucester. The illustrations in this volume have been kindly provided by Miss Paula F. Peyraud of Chappaqua, New York (the frontispiece of Fanny Burney and the portrait of Garrick); the Osborn Collection (the Nollekens drawing of Dr Burney); and the Berg Collection (illustrations of pages from the early journals manuscripts).

In acknowledging scholarly assistance on this volume I must first thank my colleagues at McGill and on the Burney Project, Professors Joyce Hemlow and Slava Kilma. As I was working on the early journals of Fanny Burney in the Burney Room, Dr Hemlow was concurrently completing there her edition of the later journals, and Dr Klima was editing the letters and fragmentary memoirs of Dr Burney. I was thus able to draw daily, if need be, on their great collective knowledge of the Burneys and their milieu, besides making use of the extensive research archive they have created over the years. The constant presence and advice of these foremost Burney scholars and friends have been invaluable to me.

Next, I am indebted to Mrs Althea Douglas, a sometime collaborator of Professor Hemlow, who performed the essential float-off operation on the manuscripts of the early journals in the bindery of the New York Public Library. This task took several months to complete, and Mrs Douglas did it with the greatest possible care and skill. Another essential service was performed in the New York Public by Dr James Neil Waddell, currently Assistant Master in Bishop's Stortford College, Hertfordshire. For two months Dr Waddell, an expert on Fanny Burney's language, scrutinized the obliterated passages in the journals of 1768 to 1777 in the Berg Collection. By a combination of keen observation and intuition he was able to decipher more than ninety-five per cent of the obliterations, a remarkable achievement.

Professors Philip H. Highfill, Jr., Kalman A. Burnim, and Edward A. Langhans, authors of *A Biographical Dictionary of Actors, Actresses, Musicians, Dancers, Managers and Other Stage Personnel in London, 1660–1800* (Carbondale, 1973–), very generously sent me advance copy of articles to be published in forthcoming volumes of their authoritative work.

Others who helped me with specific problems or queries are: Mr Martin Bowman, Martintown, Ontario; Professor John C.

Riely, Boston University (a former Walpole colleague); Professor John Abbott, University of Connecticut; the late Aleksis Rannit and Mrs Rannit, the Slavic and East European Collection, Yale University Library; Mr Anthony W. Shipps, Indiana University Library; John Kenworthy-Browne, Esq., London; Miss Olwen Hedley, London; Miss Andrea Smith, King's College, Cambridge; B. C. Frith, Esq., Gloucester; the Hon. Victor Montagu, Mapperton near Beaminster, Dorset; Warren Derry, Esq., Bath; F. J. Dallett, Esq., Research Associate, the American Museum in Britain, Bath; Derek M. M. Shorrocks, Esq., Archivist, Somerset County Record Office, Taunton, Somerset; the Revd Arthur E. Green, Vicar of Middleton Church, Norfolk; the Revd Hubert Edward Montague-Youens, Rector of Ribbesford Church, Bewdley, Worcester; and Mrs M. Barrett, Bewdley, Worcester. Professor John Middendorf of the English Department of Columbia University very kindly published queries of mine about unidentified quotations in the June 1982 and March–June 1983 numbers of the *Johnsonian News Letter* which he edits. Responders were: Professor James Woolley, Department of English, Lafayette College, Easton, Pennsylvania; Professor Cedric D. Reverand II, University of Wyoming, Laramie, Wyoming; Professor David M. Vieth, Southern Illinois University, Carbondale, Illinois; Dr Isobel Grundy, Queen Mary College, University of London; Professor Ellen Pollak, University of Pennsylvania, Philadelphia, Pennsylvania; Professor Leland D. Peterson, Old Dominion University, Norfolk, Virginia; and Mr Gary Boire, Lecturer, English, University of Auckland, New Zealand.

The manuscripts of the journals of 1768–77 were transcribed by Mr Marc Cassini, a graduate student in the McGill English Department (MA, 1980), from microfilms and hard copy of the originals in the Berg Collection. The manuscripts of 1778 to 1791 were transcribed by Mr Cassini, Mr Stephen Grasser (MA, McGill, 1980), Mr Roberto Cucci (MA candidate, McGill), and Mr Stewart Cooke (Ph.D. candidate, McGill). I commend their diligence and accuracy. In addition, Ms Phillipa Rispin (MA candidate, McGill) worked on an index of the journals. Students in my 1981 graduate seminar on eighteenth-century editing contributed to the annotations for 1771–3 in this volume. Mrs Frances McCarthy did some of the preliminary research for 1771, Ms Maleka Banu for 1772, and Mr Murray McGillivray for 1773.

In conclusion, I again acknowledge the support of my wife, Teresa, who patiently played the role of single parent during my frequent and long absences on research trips. In a very real sense this book is the child of both of us.

CONTENTS

LIST OF ILLUSTRATIONS

INTRODUCTION

FANNY BURNEY began the composition of her famous journals in March 1768, several months before her sixteenth birthday.[1] A compulsive author, it would seem, almost from the moment she could write, she had marked her fifteenth birthday by ceremoniously burning, in the courtyard of her father's house in Poland Street, London, a great heap of 'Elegies, Odes, Plays, Songs, Stories, Farces—nay, Tragedies and Epic Poems'[2]—all that she had written up to that time. Among the manuscripts consigned to the flames was a novel, 'Caroline Evelyn', the forerunner of *Evelina*, published a decade later (in 1778). This wholesale destruction was prompted in all likelihood by Fanny's stepmother, Mrs Elizabeth (Allen) Burney: Mrs Burney, reflecting the bias of her day, was alarmed over the impropriety of a young girl's dabbling in literature, which was regarded, at best, as a waste of time. Almost a year was to pass before the urge to write became too strong again for Fanny to resist; now it found vent in a secret journal, written 'for my Genuine & most private amusement', and facetiously addressed to 'Miss Nobody' (below, pp. 2, 97).

Fanny's beloved younger sister Susan (later Mrs Phillips), herself a talented writer, was present at the conflagration above and wept over it. Susan has left us a character of Fanny written at this period. Fanny, she observes, is, like their elder sister Hetty (Esther), 'very amiable'. Whereas, however, 'the characteristics of Hetty seem to be wit, generosity, and openness of heart', Fanny's are 'sense, sensibility, and bashfulness, and even a degree of prudery'. Fanny has a 'superior' understanding, 'but her diffidence gives her a bashfulness before company with whom she is not intimate, which is a disadvantage to her'. Hetty shines in conversation; were Fanny as free from *mauvaise honte*, 'she would shine no less'. 'I am afraid', concludes Susan, 'that my eldest sister is too communicative, and that my sister

---

[1] For a definitive life of FB the reader is referred to Joyce Hemlow's *The History of Fanny Burney* (Oxford, 1958).

[2] *Mem.* ii. 124. See also Appendix 1 and FBA's preface to *The Wanderer* (1814), i, pp. xix–xxi.

Fanny is too reserved. They are both charming girls—*des filles comme il y en a peu*'.[3]

Susan's character of Fanny is a shrewd one, remarkable for its precocity (it may have been composed as early as 1767, when Susan was 12), and it is amply borne out by Fanny's journals and other sources from this early period. Fanny's 'sensibility' is attested to by her stepmother's pronouncement, recorded by Fanny in 1768, that she 'possesses perhaps as feeling a Heart as ever Girl had' (below, p. 6). It is to Fanny, rather than to Hetty or Susan, that Mrs Burney appeals later that year when, pregnant and fearful that she might not survive the delivery, she looks for someone to care for the child (see her letter to Fanny of 13 Oct. 1768, below, p. 50). Mrs Sheeles, who took in the Burney children for a time when Fanny's own mother died (in 1762), observed to the Burneys' neighbour, Mrs Pringle, that the 10-year-old Fanny was inconsolable and 'almost killed with Crying', as Fanny notes in her cahier of 1775 (in vol. ii of this edition). Fanny's deep love of her family is evident throughout all her journals and letters. Evident, too, are her feelings for her friends, her ready sharing of their joys and sorrows. Her compassion extends to all living things: she is sickened by a young child's cruelty to a butterfly (the journal for 1770, p. 135) and by the cutting off of a pig's tail for a country 'sport' at Teignmouth (in 1773, p. 290).

Fanny's 'bashfulness' and 'prudery' are also apparent. In a memoir of 1808 her father, Dr Charles Burney, the noted music historian, recalls that Fanny as a child was dubbed 'The Old Lady' by visitors because of the solemn manner she assumed to mask her shyness.[4] Hetty's suitor, Alexander Seton, described her as '*The silent, observant Miss Fanny*'.[5] Fanny's diffidence, as frankly revealed in her journals, sometimes verges on the comical. For example, when asked by Dr Burney to read to the family her witty verses 'To Doctor Last', she runs up the stairs in a panic (but just as characteristically sneaks down again to hear how they are received). Though she confesses to 'thrumming' the harpsichord when by herself, she refuses to play

---

[3] Cited by Mrs Charlotte Barrett in the introduction to her edn. of the *Diary and Letters of Madame d'Arblay* (1842–6), i, p. xi. The manuscript has since disappeared.

[4] *Mem.* ii. 168. CB's memoirs, largely destroyed by FBA, are in the Osborn Collection, Yale University.

[5] FBA to EBB, 21 Oct. 1821, in *JL* xi. 286.

before company, though repeatedly urged and realizing that her behaviour is inexcusably 'hippish'. She consents to perform in home theatricals but suffers severe stage fright in front of her family and friends. Twenty years after one of these amateur performances (of Addison's *The Drummer*) her stepsister Maria (Allen) Rishton reminded her of her prudish refusal, in the role of Lady Truman, to embrace and kiss her husband Sir George Truman (played by the madcap Maria) despite Lady Truman's not having seen her husband for several years and believing him killed in battle. In another performance of her youth Fanny declines to participate in a certain scene because of its impropriety, and elsewhere she rejects an entire role for the same reason.[6]

Fanny's sense of propriety, always strong, is even cruel in one instance, when she publicly cuts her acquaintance, the dancer Miss Lalauze, who is reported to have become the mistress of a Mr Masters.[7] In this case Fanny's concern for form overrides her sensibility.[8] This concern for appearances shows her general (if not always unqualified) acceptance of established norms of behaviour as conducive to the greater social good. On the other hand, it also reflects a realistic appreciation of the very practical risks one runs when flying in the face of convention. Besides being delicate of her own reputation, with her strong 'sense' and 'superior' understanding Fanny must have been aware early of the importance of not doing or saying anything that would compromise the social aspirations and career of her adored father, who had been struggling for years to raise himself from the lowly role of musician to the more elevated status of a man of letters. In this respect she stands in marked contrast to her stepbrother Stephen and her stepsisters Maria and Elizabeth (Bessy) Allen, all of whom would have runaway marriages, and to her brothers James and Charles, who would also later disgrace themselves in various ways.[9]

[6] See below, pp. 116–17, 161, 163, 171.

[7] This occurred in 1775 (vol. ii). FB's behaviour to Miss Lalauze foreshadows her later condemnation of her friend, Mrs Hester Lynch Thrale, for marrying the Italian singing master, Gabriel Piozzi.

[8] FB's prudery does not mean that she was ignorant of sexuality or obscenity. Both her stepmother and her stepsister MA had a coarse sense of humour (see Appendix 3), and FB's echo of Swift's *The Lady's Dressing Room* (below, p. 99) shows that her reading was by no means restricted to the prim and decorous.

[9] CB Jr. was dismissed from Cambridge for stealing books in 1777. JB, a navy

Fanny's keen intelligence is apparent in the many perceptive characters she gives of her family and acquaintances. She herself notes the exceptional memory which allows her to get up dramatic roles with *'utmost facility'* (p. 161). It is this capacious and accurate memory which permits her to recall the gist and spirit (and often the exact words) of extended conversations many weeks after they had taken place. (Fanny's journals were sometimes written the same evening but frequently penned as much as a month later.) It is Fanny's intelligence, coupled with an emotional maturity beyond her years, which probably accounts for her being such a favourite with much older men, the most notable of whom, in the early journals, is Mr Crisp.[10]

An important trait of the young Fanny which Susan does not mention is her sense of humour. Fanny's comic touch is seen, for instance, in her ironic depiction of the marriage of the Burney family cook, Betty Langley, to the 'Glass polisher' (footman) John Hutton, twenty or thirty years her junior (pp. 65–7). Though Fanny's early journals contain many passages of earnest moralizing (as might be expected from the 'Old Lady'), she is very conscious of overinflating her moral balloon and almost invariably pricks it, if necessary, with a self-deprecating quip or joke.[11] This technique of self-deflation, while reflecting that diffidence noticed by Susan, does much to sustain the general freshness and lightness of these journals, that feeling of spontaneity and youthful enthusiasm which was to lessen inevitably with the years.

After Fanny herself, who in this volume at least is more observer than actor, the most important figure by far in the early journals is her father, Dr Charles Burney, the 'author of my being', to whom she was to dedicate *Evelina*. Dr Burney was a man of great talent and charm, author of the seminal *General History of Music* (4 vols. 4to, 1776–89), of whom Dr Johnson said, 'I love Burney: my heart goes out to meet him! . . . I much question if there is, in the world, such another man as Dr.

captain, was forced to resign from active service in 1785 for failing to obey orders. Thirteen years later he ran off with his half-sister Sarah Harriet Burney. See below, *passim*.

[10] Others include the celebrated physician, Dr Fothergill, and the over-playful Mr Crispin of the Teignmouth journal.

[11] See also her parody of the 'sublime' style in the journal for 1768, p. 4.

Burney'.[12] In this volume Fanny records her father's obtaining the degree of Doctor of Music at Oxford in June 1769, and his publication of the journals of his two tours to the Continent in 1770 and 1772, made to gather materials for his great *History* and marking the start of his literary reputation. Her journals here reveal the incredible industry of Dr Burney, who fitted his immense scholarly labours around an exhausting schedule of music lessons and mandatory social engagements. It is evident in everything she wrote that Fanny passionately admired and loved her exceptional father; in one characteristic panegyric she thanks God for giving her 'this treasure which no earthly one can equal' (p. 61).

Almost as adored as her dear 'Papa' was Fanny's virtual second father, Samuel Crisp. 'Daddy' Crisp was an old friend of Dr Burney, a cultivated bachelor who had lived much in Italy and who had written a play, *Virginia*, produced at Drury Lane in 1754. After the failure of the play and his fortune, Crisp retired to the modest house of a friend, Christopher Hamilton, in Chessington, Surrey. Fanny first met Daddy Crisp about 1763, when he was 56 and she was 11, and she promptly lost her heart to him, totally and irrevocably. Dr Burney soon recognized the strength of her attachment, and called Daddy Crisp her 'Flame' (see p. 8). Crisp in his turn became dotingly fond of his 'Fannikin', and the early journals contain many playfully affectionate letters between the two, ending with Crisp's death in 1783. In this initial volume Fanny records with joy Crisp's occasional appearances in London as well as her own visit to Chessington in 1771, after an absence of five years. She also reveals the names of a number of young admirers, among them the polite Captain Blomefield and the witty and entertaining Mr Poggenpohl. None of these young men, however, stood a chance of supplanting Mr Crisp in her heart.

Of the rest of Fanny's immediate family, it is her sister Hetty and her stepsister Maria Allen who figure most prominently in this first volume. Fanny's own life in the years 1768–73 was outwardly uneventful, consisting largely of the inevitable round of social visits with her mother and sisters, of attendance at the theatre and opera, of walks in St James's Park and visits to pleasure grounds such as Ranelagh and Marylebone, and, at

[12] *Diary and Letters of Madame d'Arblay*, i. 184–5.

home, of acting as her father's amanuensis and stealing the occasional hour or half-hour to make entries in her journals. Typical high points during these years were her participation in Mr Lalauze's masquerade in 1770 (probably permitted by her father because of a misunderstanding) and her stay with Maria and Maria's husband Martin Rishton at Teignmouth in the summer of 1773. Far more dramatic, indeed the stuff of romantic fiction, were the lives of Hetty and Maria, whose affairs of the heart make up a common thread running through the journals of 1768 to the middle of 1772.

Fanny's journals of 1768–70 are filled with references to the on-again, off-again romance of Hetty and Alexander Seton, the fourth son of a Scottish baronet. Fanny's first extended set-piece is her transcription of a long conversation she had with Seton one evening late in 1768, when Hetty was out (pp. 44–9). Fanny notes that Seton 'is little, & *far* from handsome, but has a sensible countenance, & appears quite an Adonis, after $\frac{1}{2}$ an Hour's conversation'. She even confesses to being 'half in love with him'. Hetty, on the other hand, is totally smitten by the charming and clever little Scotsman. In the conversation which Fanny records, however, Seton reveals and even flaunts a deep-seated cynicism which Fanny, had she not been blinded by his charm, might have seen as boding ill for her sister. Soon enough Seton shows his true colours, those of a 'fickle' and 'artful' lover who trifles, sometimes brutally, with the suffering Hetty's affections. There is even a hint, in a passage later partly destroyed and obliterated by Fanny, that Seton may have had thoughts of taking Hetty as a mistress (see p. 62 and n. 34). None the less, Seton was evidently shocked when Hetty, no longer able to endure his erratic behaviour, dropped him abruptly and married instead, in September 1770, her relatively dull but safe musician cousin Charles Rousseau Burney, who had been waiting patiently in the wings. The disappointed Seton returned to Edinburgh in 1772 and apparently never married.

In the mean time another hectic romance was developing, this time between Maria Allen and Martin Folkes Rishton, nephew of another baronet and grandson of a president of the Royal Society. The first mention of this affair occurs in an obliterated passage at the end of the journal for 1770 (p. 142), where it is revealed that Rishton, 'whom we all thought a young man of ⟨most⟩ meritorious constancy, after absolutely engaging himself to Miss Allen, whose Heart is devoted to him,—[has] forever abandoned her though he was bound to her, [by] ⟨the ur⟩gent ties of Honour, Gratitude,—I was going [to] say Love—but that would be folly'. The jilt, however, turned out to be temporary, and for the next year and a half Martin carried on a vacillating and covert courtship (both families now being opposed to the match), culminating in the couple's elopement and marriage at Ypres in May 1772. Fanny is fascinated by the '*Novel*' of her stepsister's romance and is properly joyful over its happy conclusion, capped by both families' eventual, if in part still grudging, acceptance of the union. Maria's letters to Fanny in the Berg Collection reveal the first years of the marriage to have been contented enough, but by 1778 the imperious and self-centered Martin had begun an affair with Maria's erstwhile best friend, Mrs Dorothy (Dolly) Hogg. Fanny later attempted to expunge all mentions of Mrs Hogg from her journals. A single reference remains by accident in this volume (in a recovered obliterated passage, p. 9).

Aside from the Burney family, this initial volume is populated by the numerous professional and social acquaintances who visited the Burneys, first in Poland Street and afterwards (from November 1770) in Queen Square, London. There are also the people Fanny meets on her summer trips to Lynn in Norfolk, before her stepmother gave up her dower house there in 1770. (Fanny was born in Lynn, where her father was organist of St Margaret's Church in the 1750s, and the second Mrs Burney was a native of that town and widow of a prominent Lynn merchant, Stephen Allen.) Most notable among Dr Burney's professional acquaintances in these years is the actor David Garrick, manager of the Drury Lane Theatre, whom he had met in 1745 and with whom he collaborated in a number of theatrical ventures. Fanny describes Garrick's visits to the Burney household, when he delighted the children with his humorous antics, and depicts his masterful performances at Drury Lane in a number of famous roles, including Richard III, Bayes, and Abel Drugger. In obliterated passages now recovered (pp. 150, 322), she also alludes to several quarrels

between Garrick and her father, observing that Garrick 'has by
no means the Virtue of *steadiness* in his attachment, &, indeed,
is almost perpetually giving offence to some of his friends'. Dr
Johnson, she adds, 'told my Father, that he attributes almost
all the ill errors of Mr. Garrick's Life, to the . . . *fire* & hastiness
of his Temper, which is continually misleading him'.

On a number of occasions Fanny records visits by Dr
Burney's old friend, the poet Christopher Smart, whom she
portrays in his decline, with 'great wildness in his manner,
looks, & voice'. In an obliterated passage she reports him as
expressing bitter hatred of his estranged wife. Yet Smart still
retains something of his old charm and vivacity, on one occasion presenting Fanny with a rose and fairly overwhelming her
with playful compliments. When he dies in the King's Bench
Prison in 1771, she notes the event with sincere regret (see
pp. 36, 91, 165–6).

A staple of the Burney household in Queen Square were the
Sunday evening musical parties hosted by Dr Burney. A recur-
rent highlight of these gatherings were the harpsichord solos
performed by Hetty's husband Charles Rousseau Burney, who
astounded the guests with his virtuosity. (Hetty herself was a
talented harpsichordist and played duets with her husband.)
The guests included both professional musicians and amateur
performers and lovers of music, such as Sir William Hamilton,
the British minister at Naples, who had greeted Dr Burney on
his visit there in 1770. (Hamilton is best known as the husband
of Lord Nelson's Emma, whom Hamilton married in 1791 after
the death of his first wife.) Among the many professional
musicians were the highly popular and successful composer of
operas, Antonio Sacchini, and the equally popular castrato
singer Giuseppe Millico. Italian castrato singers such as
Farinelli, Tenducci, and Millico himself were the matinée idols
of their day, and Fanny for a time seems to have been infatuated with the 'divine' vocalist (see p. 250).

An important set of acquaintances during the Poland Street
days were the Scottish circle who met at the house of Mrs
Veronica Pringle, the Burneys' next-door neighbour. (Dr
Burney's forebears originally came from Scotland: his father
had shortened the family surname from 'MacBurney'.) It was
through Mrs Pringle that Hetty first met Alexander Seton. One

evening, at a party given at their house by Seton's brother-in-law and sister, the Debbiegs, Fanny made the acquaintance of the noted Scottish architect Robert Adam, who entertained the company with his singing. It was to her great regret that Fanny was forced, in 1770, to give up all connections with Mrs Pringle and her circle, after the break-up between Hetty and Seton. (Dr Burney and Daddy Crisp were now afraid that Seton might have designs on Fanny.)

This introduction has so far dealt with some of the living contemporaries whom Fanny has put into her journals. Also important to the imagination of this born writer were the personalities, past and present, real and fictitious, whom she met in her reading. In the first two of these journals especially (1768 and 1769) Fanny records in detail her encounters with major and minor authors, such as Plutarch, Dr Johnson (*Rasselas*), Goldsmith (*The Vicar of Wakefield*), Mrs Rowe, and Mr and Mrs Griffith. Her taste in reading is moral and sentimental, reflecting both her own temperament and the prevailing fashion of the day. Thus she is shocked by the brutality of Caius Marius ('execrable Wretch!') and falls in love with Prévost's Dean of Coleraine (pp. 26, 60). Moved to tears by the plight of Goldsmith's Vicar, she is filled with admiration for the 'paternal affection' of Paullus Aemilius who, rejecting the 'false notions' the ancient Romans had 'of true greatness & honour', gloried in 'his fondness for his Children' (pp. 12, 25).

The stimulation of these characters met in books soon yields, however, to the fascination of the actual life observed around her. Much of this experience Fanny stored away mentally for eventual use in her own fiction. To take a few instances: Mr Lalauze's masquerade, mentioned above, finds its way (changed, of course) into the second book of *Cecilia* (chapter 3). The character of Evelina's ideal lover, Lord Orville, may be modelled in part on that perfect young gentleman Harry Phipps, later Lord Mulgrave (see p. 119). A new discovery in this volume is the apparent inspiration for the letter to Evelina forged in Lord Orville's name by Sir Clement Willoughby: in an obliterated passage of 1769 (p. 94) Fanny describes an improper letter sent to Hetty and forged in Alexander Seton's name.

More important than any or all of these specific sources,

however, is the detailed sense of contemporary English society which Fanny was absorbing through her artist's temperament, that knowledge of character and place which is essential to the novelist. Fanny's journals for these early years, fascinating for the vivid glimpses they give us of a former age, take on an added interest when seen also as the workbooks of her art.

HISTORY OF THE MANUSCRIPTS
AND EARLIER EDITIONS

In the last decade of her life Fanny Burney (now Madame d'Arblay, widow of the French émigré General Alexandre d'Arblay), having finished her revision of her father's memoirs for publication,[1] turned her attention more exclusively to the 10,000 pages of her own manuscript journals and letters.[2] Her concerns in this massive undertaking were both prudential and artistic. Her primary aim was to excise from the manuscripts any passages that might give offence to persons, or the family of persons, mentioned in them, or that might show herself or her own family in an unfavourable light. A second aim was to cut out material that she judged to be trivial or repetitious or too personal to be of interest to the general public. A final goal, with special regard to the early journals, was to smooth out the occasional bad grammar and stylistic inelegancies of her youth, clarifying the writing where it was needed, tightening or unifying the narrative for greater dramatic effect, and sometimes inserting new passages of fine writing (which as often as not have no real relevance to the original text).

Madame d'Arblay's depredations on the text, though bad throughout, are especially evident in the so-called 'juvenile journals' (her own term) of 1768–77, written before the publication of *Evelina*. The entire journal for 1776 and half or more of 1772 and 1777 have been destroyed totally. The pages remaining from these years, about 800, contain 4,000 lines heavily obliterated by Madame d'Arblay. On the other hand, she has retraced the writing on many pages where the original ink has faded to near-illegibility. In some instances it is evident that the 'retracing' is in fact a substitution for the original writing, which has virtually disappeared. (The present editor has tried to be alert to these deceptive passages, reading beneath the substitutions where possible.)

[1] The *Memoirs of Doctor Burney*, mostly FBA's narrative with excerpts from CB's memoirs, was published in 3 vols., 8vo in 1832.

[2] For a detailed history of the Burney manuscripts and their editing by FBA, Mrs Barrett, and Henry Colburn, the reader is referred to Professor Hemlow's introduction to *JL* i, pp. xxi–lvi.

On her death, in January 1840, Madame d'Arblay left all her own manuscripts to her niece and literary executrix, Mrs Charlotte Barrett.[3] Mrs Barrett soon entered into an agreement with Henry Colburn for their publication and undertook the further editing of them. At first it was intended that the journals and letters be published from the very beginning, that is, from 1768. Editorial notations on the manuscript indicate that the journals for 1768 and 1769 were actually in the printing office, and the rest of the juvenile journals were also marked to be sent there. After a while, however, it became apparent to Colburn and Mrs Barrett that there was far too much material for all of it to be included in the edition. Consequently, as part of a way of reducing this material, the decision was made to drop the juvenile journals entirely. In a note to the *Diary and Letters* (i. 2), Mrs Barrett explained this decision as follows:

... it has been thought right to withhold [the juvenile diary]—at least for the present;—for though it is, to the family and friends of the writer, quite as full of interest as the subsequent portions, the interest is of a more private and personal nature than that which attaches to the Journal after its writer became universally known as the authoress of 'Evelina', 'Cecilia', &c.

Mrs Barrett's edition, focusing largely on the Streatham and Court Journals of 1778 to 1791, came out in seven volumes between 1842 and 1846. Following the death of Colburn, in 1857, Mrs Barrett bought back, at the sale of his stock and copyrights (25 May 1857), 'the original manuscript of Madame d'Arblay's Diary and Correspondence' which she had given to Colburn and which, she claimed, he had kept illegally. She also purchased 'The Juvenile Journal of Miss Fanny Burney, (Madame d'Arblay). A Transcribed Copy, Prepared for the Press: and, also, the original manuscript from which the transcribed copy was made. ...'[4] Upon Mrs Barrett's own death in 1870 these materials passed to her son, the Revd Richard Arthur Francis Barrett (d. 1881), and thence to his niece Mrs Etta Chappel, who turned them over to her sister, Mrs Julia Caroline (Maitland) Wauchope (1843–90), wife of the Revd David Wauchope (1825–1911).[5]

---

[3] CB's manuscripts were left to her nephew Charles Parr Burney. Most of these eventually found their way to the Osborn Collection of Yale University.

[4] Sale catalogue, items 1015 and 1016, cited in *JL* i, p. xlv.

[*See opposite page for n. 5*]

In June 1885 the publisher George Bell approached the Wauchopes about the possibility of publishing the juvenile journals, proposing as editor Mrs Annie Raine Ellis,[6] the author of *Sylvestra*, who had edited *Evelina* and *Cecilia* for him. The Wauchopes, with Mrs Chappell's consent, quickly gave their permission and by September had sent the manuscript of the juvenile journals to Mrs Ellis at her summer home in Berkshire. For the next two years Mrs Ellis worked industriously on the journals, using first the original manuscript and later also the transcribed copy noted above, which she received belatedly from Mrs Chappel. In the course of her labours she consulted the whole range of the Burney materials in the Wauchopes' possession and employed the resources of the Bodleian and British Libraries. In July 1887 she sent to Bell the last of her edited copy, but publication was delayed until January 1890, when *The Early Diary of Frances Burney* appeared in two octavo volumes (with the imprint date of 1889).[7]

In editing the juvenile journals Mrs Ellis ignored the copious deletion marks made by Mrs Barrett, choosing instead to print the entire manuscript as far as possible. In pursuit of this aim she apparently, with the Wauchopes' permission, steamed off a number of blank paste-overs which Mrs Barrett had imposed on the manuscript, though some seventy of these remained for the 'float-off' operation mentioned below. In preparing her copy, however, Mrs Ellis failed to distinguish between the original text and Madame d'Arblay's later additions and substitutions. A later, anonymous editor largely remedied this defect in a 1907 reprint of *The Early Diary* by enclosing Madame d'Arblay's passages in square brackets. Still undeciphered,

---

[5] See Joyce Hemlow, *A Catalogue of the Burney Family Correspondence 1749–1878* (New York, 1971), p. xiii. The story of Mrs Ellis's edition of the juvenile journals is contained in the correspondence between the Wauchopes, Mrs Ellis, and George Bell, 1885–90, in the British Library and the Gloucestershire Record Office (D2227, on deposit from the Viner-Brady family).

[6] Mrs Annie Raine Ellis (*c.*1829–1901) was the eldest daughter of the Revd James Raine (1791–1858), historian of Durham and founder of the Surtees Society. She married Edmund Viner Ellis of Sherborne House, Gloucester. Besides *Sylvestra: Studies of Manners in England from 1770 to 1800* (1881), she was author of *Marie; or, Glimpses of Life in France* (1879). Her editions of *Evelina* and *Cecilia* appeared in 1881 and 1882.

[7] A clipping of a review in *The Saturday Review of Politics, Literature, Science, and Art*, lxix (1 Mar. 1890), 263–5, is with Mrs Ellis's letters to the Wauchopes in the British Library.

however, were the 4,000 lines in the manuscript which had been obliterated by Madame d'Arblay.

The Early Diary was reprinted again, this time without revisions, in 1913.[8] In 1924 the manuscript of the juvenile journals, along with Fanny's later journals and most of the miscellaneous correspondence not inserted by her in the journals, was sold by the Wauchope family to a London bookseller, who in turn sold it to the lawyer-industrialist Mr Owen D. Young of Van Hornesville, New York, and of New York City. These manuscripts were transferred in 1941 to the Berg Collection of the New York Public Library, where they now remain. The residue of Fanny's manuscripts belonging to the Wauchopes was sold in 1952 by Ann Julia Wauchope (1866–1962) to the British Library.

---

[8] As part of Bohn's Popular Library, published by George Bell and Sons. The *Diary* had been printed in 1907 as part of Bohn's Standard Library. It was reprinted once more in 1970, by the Arno Press (New York).

THE PRESENT EDITION

THE main purpose of this new edition of Fanny Burney's early journals and letters is to recover, as far as possible, her original text. Much of it (probably a third at least of the juvenile journals) is gone for ever, burned by Madame d'Arblay. Of the leaves remaining, many are fragments, and sometimes twenty or thirty lines at a stretch have been obliterated by Madame d'Arblay using the dark black ink of her old age (see illustration, p. 263). There are 4,000 such obliterated lines in the juvenile journals alone. Fortunately, traces of the original brown ox-gall ink are still visible beneath the swirling *o*'s, *e*'s, and *m*'s so that with time and the aid of a good light and a magnifying glass it has been possible for Dr James Neil Waddell, working for the editor in the Berg Collection, to decipher more than ninety-five per cent of the obliterated text.

Before the obliterations could be read, however, it was first necessary to remove some seventy paste-overs imposed by Mrs Barrett on the manuscript of the juvenile journals. Most of these were blank pieces of paper covering parts of the original text. Ten of the paste-overs, however, are fragments of journal leaves which were cut away and otherwise destroyed. Once removed, these fragments, often heavily obliterated themselves, had to be placed in proper relationship to the other surviving leaves of the journals.

In the complete run of early journals, from 1768 to 1791, there were over a thousand paste-overs on about five hundred leaves or fragments of leaves (out of 2,500 leaves or 5,000 pages overall). In February and March of 1979 these paste-overs were removed by Mrs Althea Douglas, working in the New York Public Library bindery and repeating an operation that had been performed there on the later journals in the 1960s. The technique which Mrs Douglas used essentially involved floating off the paste-overs by immersing each leaf in a pan of tepid water. The operation, completely successful, is described by Mrs Douglas in her article, 'An Eighteenth-Century Journal, A Twentieth-Century Restoration', published in *The Library Scene*, ix (1980), 8–10. The float-off was feasible because of the good-quality rag paper of the manuscripts, which withstood the soaking, and the equally good quality of the non-acidic inks, which did not run.

The newly recovered obliterations in this first volume constitute about twenty per cent of the total text. There are no major discoveries in them, but much valuable material has been restored. For instance, many of the passages that seemed trivial to Madame d'Arblay will be of interest to students of eighteenth-century manners, customs, and dress, two examples being her descriptions of a wedding reception at Lynn and of the costumes she and Hetty wore to Mr Lalauze's masquerade (pp. 86, 100). The biographer and literary historian will welcome Fanny's and Dr Johnson's observations on David Garrick and the passage about Christopher Smart and his wife, items expunged because of their unflattering nature (pp. 91, 322). Musicologists will be glad to have the overscored passages on concerts and on the musicians who visited Dr Burney; Madame d'Arblay cut these partly because there is already so much on music in the journals, but also because she shared her father's ambivalence towards his profession, preferring to emphasize his literary attainments. Finally, those students of human nature wishing to have the whole truth about Fanny and her family, rather than Madame d'Arblay's whitewash, will approve the recovery of the passages where, for instance, Fanny reveals Martin Rishton's jilt of Maria Allen or where she alludes to her sailor brother James's disgrace upon his return from a voyage in 1769 (foreshadowing his later disgrace and forced retirement from the Navy in 1785; see pp. 83, 142).

At some stage of her editing Madame d'Arblay compiled a 'List of Persons and Things' (after 1768 of persons only) mentioned in the journals from 1768 to 1779, the manuscript of which is with the juvenile journals in the Berg Collection. As she continued to destroy parts of the journals after making this list, it remains an important indicator of what has been lost in these sections. Names in the 'List' which are missing from the extant journals are noted in the headnotes to each year. The greatest number of missing names, 45, occurs in 1772, Madame d'Arblay having ultimately destroyed more than half the journal for that year. Eleven of the persons there are not named elsewhere in the juvenile journals.

This edition of the early journals is intended as a complement to Professor Joyce Hemlow's highly acclaimed one of the later *Journals and Letters of Fanny Burney (Madame d'Arblay), 1791–1840* (12 vols., Oxford, 1972–84). It will, therefore, generally follow the editorial policies and format she devised. The passages obliterated by Madame d'Arblay which have been recovered will continue to be enclosed with the symbols ⌐ and ¬, both to warn the reader of possibly uncertain decipherings and to identify the new material here given. As in Professor Hemlow's edition, the verve and spontaneity of Fanny's original text is preferred to the greater polish of Madame d'Arblay's revisions. The present edition differs, however, from the earlier in that substantive additions (as opposed to purely stylistic changes) have sometimes been retained, either in a bridge passage or set off in editorial brackets. This has been done if the additions are interesting in themselves, needed to clarify the text, or substituted by Madame d'Arblay for passages that have not been recovered.

This edition follows its predecessor in reproducing Fanny's original text literally, for the most part, with retention of her paragraphing, punctuation, archaic spellings and misspellings,[1] and superscripts. Fanny's use of lower-case and capitals is also generally reproduced, though for appearance's sake all proper names and the beginnings of sentences have been capitalized (another departure from Dr Hemlow). The following symbols continue to be employed in the present work:

|	A break in the manuscript pages
⟨ ⟩	Uncertain readings
[ ]	Text or information supplied by the editor; also insertions or substitutions by Madame d'Arblay, identified as such by a footnote
⌐ ¬	Matter overscored by Madame d'Arblay but recovered

---

[1] Only the more glaring anomalies (e.g., 'gaurd' for 'guard' and 'athour' for 'author', which seem to be definite slips of the pen), or spellings which might most easily be mistaken for printer's errors ('wearried', 'dulest') are marked with a *sic* in the text. Consistent oddities, on the other hand, such as 'niether' and 'imagion', have been passed without comment. It is worth noting that some of FB's forms were becoming archaic even as she was writing her first journals. This is indicated by her using both the archaic and modern spellings, for example, 'extreamly' and 'extremely'.

[xxxxx *3 lines*]   Matter overscored by Madame d'Arblay, *not*
[xxxxx *2 words*]   recovered

The head-notes use or reproduce the following bibliographic abbreviations and signs:

AJ	Autograph journal
AL	Autograph letter
ALS	Autograph letter signed
Early Diary	Manuscripts of the Early Diary (Juvenile Journals) of Fanny Burney in the Berg Collection, New York Public Library
pmks	Postmarks, of which only the essential are abstracted, e.g., 23 IV
✲ ⊕	Madame d'Arblay's symbols for manuscripts 'Examined & Amalgamated with others';[2] also, for manuscripts released for publication in a second category of interest
✳	Another symbol of Madame d'Arblay for manuscripts in a second category of interest

In this edition Fanny's own journals and letters are printed as discrete items, with textual head-notes.[3] Letters *to* Fanny which she has copied or inserted into her journals are counted as part of the journals. Where Fanny has copied her own letter into a journal but the original, sent through the post, actually survives, it is the original letter that is reproduced, with textual variants in the copy indicated in the footnotes.

The annotations in this edition are intended, of course, to provide the reader with whatever information (s)he may need to understand the text properly. As far as possible quotations have been identified, obscure allusions and unfamiliar events clarified, and chronology and dates established or confirmed. The editor has attempted to trace all the persons named, however minor they may seem.[4] In one case, at least, an apparent

---

[2] See *JL* i, p. xxxvii.

[3] Full textual notes will eventually be deposited in typescript in the McGill University Library.

[4] It is commonly difficult or impossible to find exact dates of births and deaths in the 18th c., particularly when dealing with minor figures. In order to simplify the vital statistics in identifying notes, the editor has assumed with reasonable confidence, barring specific evidence to the contrary (such as death abroad or litigation of the will), that baptisms took place within two months of birth, burials within a week of death, and that wills were probated within six months of the testator's decease. If the informa-

nobody, Captain 'Bloomfield', one of Fanny's early admirers whom she met at a ball in 1770, turns out to have been none other than Robert Blomefield, later a General of Artillery, who revolutionized the British ordnance and was made a baronet for his services at the Battle of Copenhagen in 1807 (see *DNB*).

As for the number and the length of the annotations, Dr Johnson observed that 'it is impossible for an expositor not to write too little for some and too much for others'.[5] Notwithstanding, the present editor hopes to have manœuvred successfully between Scylla and Charybdis, neither omitting what is necessary nor retaining the superfluous.

---

tion falls near the edge of a year, for instance, a baptism takes place on 23 Jan. 1742, then the year of birth is given as 1741/2. (Years are always given in the new style.)

[5] *Preface to Shakespeare*, 1765.

SHORT TITLES AND ABBREVIATIONS

PERSONS

CB	Charles Burney (Mus.Doc.), 1726–1814
CB Jr.	Charles Burney (DD), 1757–1817
EAB	Elizabeth (Allen) Burney, 1728–96
EB	Esther Burney, 1749–1832
EBB	after 1770 Esther (Burney) Burney
FB	Frances Burney, 1752–1840
FBA	after 1793 Madame d'Arblay
JB	James Burney (Rear-Admiral), 1750–1821
MA	Maria Allen, 1751–1820
MAR	after 1772 Maria (Allen) Rishton
SC	Samuel Crisp, c.1707–83
SEB	Susanna Elizabeth Burney, 1755–1800
SBP	after 1782 Mrs Phillips

WORKS, COLLECTIONS, ETC.

Standard encyclopaedias, biographical dictionaries, peerages, armorials, baronetages, knightages, school and university lists, medical registers, lists of clergy, town and city directories, court registers, army and navy lists, road guides, almanacs, and catalogues of all kinds have been used but will not be cited unless for a particular reason. Most frequently consulted were the many editions of Burke, Lodge, and Debrett. In all works London is assumed to be the place of publication unless otherwise indicated.

Abbott	John Lawrence Abbott, *John Hawkesworth: Eighteenth-Century Man of Letters*, Madison, Wisconsin, 1982.
Add. MSS	Additional Manuscripts, British Library.
AL	Great Britain, War Office, *A List of the General and Field Officers as They Rank in the Army*, 1740–1841.
Alumni Cantab.	John Venn and J. A. Venn, *Alumni Cantabrigienses*, 10 vols., Cambridge, 1922–54.
Alumni Oxon.	Joseph Foster, *Alumni Oxonienses*, 8 vols., 1887–92.
AR	*The Annual Register, or a View of the History, Politics, and Literature* . . ., 1758– .
Barrett	The Barrett Collection of Burney Papers, British Library, 43 vols., Egerton 3690–3708.
Berg	The Henry W. and Albert A. Berg Collection, New York Public Library.
Bibl. Nat. Cat.	*Catalogue générale des livres imprimés de la Bibliothèque nationale*, Paris, 1897– .

BL	The British Library.
BL Cat.	Catalogue of Printed Books in the British Library.
Boswell Papers	*Private Papers of James Boswell from Malahide Castle in the Collection of Lt.-Colonel R. H. Isham*, ed. Geoffrey Scott and F. A. Pottle, 18 vols., New York, 1928–34.
BUCEM	*The British Union-Catalogue of Early Music*, ed. Elizabeth B. Schnapper, 2 vols., 1957.
CCR	*The Court and City Register*.
CJ	*Journals of the House of Commons*.
Commem.	Charles Burney, *An Account of the Musical Performances . . . in Commemoration of Handel*, 1785.
Comyn	The John R. G. Comyn Collection of Burney Papers, The Cross House, Vowchurch, Turnastone, Herefordshire, England.
Daily Adv.	*The Daily Advertiser*, 1731–95.
Delany Corr.	*The Autobiography and Correspondence of Mary Granville, Mrs. Delany: with Interesting Reminiscences of King George the Third and Queen Charlotte*, ed. Lady Llanover, 6 vols., 1861–2.
Dennistoun	James Dennistoun, *Memoirs of Sir Robert Strange, Knt., . . . and of his brother-in-law Andrew Lumisden*, 2 vols., 1855.
DL	*Diary and Letters of Madame d'Arblay (1778–1840)*, ed. Austin Dobson, 6 vols., 1904–5.
DNB	*Dictionary of National Biography*.
DSB	*Dictionary of Scientific Biography*, ed. C. C. Gillispie, 16 vols., New York, 1970–80.
ED	*The Early Diary of Frances Burney, 1768–1778*, ed. Annie Raine Ellis, 2 vols., 1913.
EDD	*The English Dialect Dictionary*, ed. J. Wright, 6 vols., 1898–1905.
Essex	Essex County Record Office, Chelmsford, England.
Garrick, *Letters*	*The Letters of David Garrick*, ed. David M. Little and George M. Kahrl, 3 vols., Cambridge, Massachusetts, 1963.
Gazley	John G. Gazley, *The Life of Arthur Young, 1741–1820*, Philadelphia, 1973.
GEC, *Baronetage*	George Edward Cokayne, *The Complete Baronetage*, 6 vols., Exeter, 1900–9.
GEC, *Peerage*	George Edward Cokayne, *The Complete Peerage*, rev. by Vicary Gibbs *et al.*, 13 vols., 1910–59.
German Tour	Charles Burney, *The Present State of Music in Germany, the Netherlands, and United Provinces*, 2 vols., 1773; 2nd corrected edn., 1775.
GM	*The Gentleman's Magazine*, 1731–1880.
HFB	Joyce Hemlow, *The History of Fanny Burney*, Oxford, 1958.
Highfill	Philip H. Highfill, Jr., Kalman A. Burnim, and

	Edward A. Langhans, *A Biographical Dictionary of Actors, Actresses, Musicians, Dancers, Managers and Other Stage Personnel in London, 1660–1800*, Carbondale, Illinois, 1973– .
Hist. Mus.	Charles Burney, *A General History of Music, from the Earliest Ages to the Present Period*, 4 vols., 1776–89.
HMC	Historical Manuscripts Commission.
Houghton	Houghton Library, Harvard University, Cambridge, Massachusetts.
IGI	International Genealogical Index (formerly the Mormon Computer Index).
Italian Tour	Charles Burney, *The Present State of Music in France and Italy*, 1771; 2nd corrected edn., 1773.
JL	*The Journals and Letters of Fanny Burney (Madame d'Arblay), 1791–1840*, ed. Joyce Hemlow *et al.*, 12 vols., Oxford, 1972–84.
Lib.	Leigh and Sotheby, *A Catalogue of the Miscellaneous Library of the Late Charles Burney*, 9 June 1814, priced copy in the Yale University Library.
Life	*Boswell's Life of Johnson*, ed. George Birkbeck Hill, rev. by L. F. Powell, 6 vols., Oxford, 1934–64.
LJ	*Journals of the House of Lords*.
Lonsdale	Roger Lonsdale, *Dr. Charles Burney: A Literary Biography*, Oxford, 1965.
LS 1, 2, [etc.]	*The London Stage 1660–1800*, Parts 1 to 5 in 11 vols., Carbondale, Illinois, 1960–8. References are to volume and page in each part.
Manwaring	G. E. Manwaring, *My Friend the Admiral: The Life, Letters, and Journals of Rear-Admiral James Burney, F.R.S.*, 1931.
Maxted	Ian Maxted, *The London Book Trades, 1775–1800: A Preliminary Checklist of Members*, Folkestone, Kent, 1977.
Mem.	*Memoirs of Doctor Burney, Arranged from His Own Manuscripts, from Family Papers, and from Personal Recollections*, by his daughter, Madame d'Arblay, 3 vols., 1832.
'Mem.'	'Memoirs of Dr Charles Burney 1726–1769', unpublished edn. by Slava Klima, Garry Bowers, and Kerry Grant of autograph fragments in the Berg Collection, the Osborn Collection, and the British Library, Add. MSS 48345.
Mercer	Charles Burney, *A General History of Music*, ed. Frank Mercer, 2 vols., 1935.
MI	Memorial Inscription(s).
Mus. Lib.	White, *A Catalogue of the . . . Collection of Music . . . of the Late Charles Burney*, 8 August 1814, priced

	copy in the Music Division of the Library of Congress.
Namier	Sir Lewis Namier and John Brooke, *The House of Commons, 1754–1790*, 3 vols., 1964.
Nat. Union Cat.	The National Union Catalogue, Pre-1956 Imprints.
NBG	*Nouvelle biographie générale*, ed. Jean-Chrétien-Ferdinand Hoefer, 46 vols., Paris, 1852–66.
NCBEL	*The New Cambridge Bibliography of English Literature*, ed. George Watson and Ian Willison, 5 vols., Cambridge, 1969–77.
New Grove	*The New Grove Dictionary of Music and Musicians*, ed. Stanley Sadie, 20 vols., 1980.
Nichols, *Lit. Anec.*	John Nichols, *Literary Anecdotes of the Eighteenth Century*, 9 vols., 1812–15.
Nichols, *Lit. Ill.*	John Nichols, *Illustrations of the Literary History of the Eighteenth Century*, 8 vols., 1817–58.
OCD	*The Oxford Classical Dictionary*, ed. N. G. L. Hammond and H. H. Scullard, 2nd edn., Oxford, 1970.
OED	*Oxford English Dictionary*.
Osborn	The James Marshall and Marie-Louise Osborn Collection, Yale University Library, New Haven, Connecticut.
PCC	Prerogative Court of Canterbury.
PRO	Public Record Office, London.
Rees	*The Cyclopaedia; or, Universal Dictionary of Arts, Sciences, and Literature*, ed. Abraham Rees, 45 vols., 1802–20. CB contributed the musical articles in this work.
Rylands	The John Rylands University Library of Manchester, England.
Scholes	Percy A. Scholes, *The Great Dr. Burney*, 2 vols., 1948.
Scots Peerage	*The Scots Peerage*, ed. Sir James Balfour Paul, 9 vols., Edinburgh, 1904–14.
Singh	Prince Frederick Duleep Singh, *Portraits in Norfolk Houses*, 2 vols., Norwich, 1928.
SND	*The Scottish National Dictionary* ed. W. Grant and D. D. Murison, 10 vols., Edinburgh, 1931–76.
Stone	George Winchester Stone, Jr. and George M. Kahrl, *David Garrick: A Critical Biography*, Carbondale, Illinois, 1979.
Survey of London	London County Council, *The Survey of London*, 1900– .
Thieme	Ulrich Thieme and Felix Becker, *Allgemeines Lexikon der bildenden Künstler von der Antike bis zur Gegenwart*, 37 vols., Leipzig, 1907–50.
Thraliana	*Thraliana: The Diary of Mrs. Hester Lynch Thrale (Later Mrs. Piozzi), 1776–1809*, ed. Katharine C. Balderston, 2nd edn., 2 vols., Oxford, 1951.

Tours	*Dr. Burney's Musical Tours in Europe*, ed. Percy A. Scholes, 2 vols., 1959.
Vict. Co. Hist.	*The Victoria History of the Counties of England* [with name of county].
Wheatley	Henry B. Wheatley and Peter Cunningham, *London Past and Present: Its History, Associations, and Traditions*, 3 vols., 1891.
'Worcester Mem.'	'Memoranda of the Burney Family, 1603–1845', typescript of a family chronicle in the Osborn Collection, Yale University Library. The MS is untraced.
Young, *Autobiography*	*The Autobiography of Arthur Young*, ed. M. Betham-Edwards, 1898.
YW	*The Yale Edition of Horace Walpole's Correspondence*, ed. W. S. Lewis *et al.*, 48 vols., New Haven, 1937–83.

BURNEY GENEALOGY

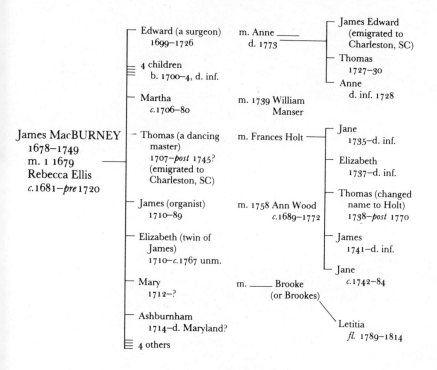

James MacBURNEY
1678–1749
m. 1 1679
Rebecca Ellis
*c.*1681–*pre* 1720

Edward (a surgeon)
1699–1726 — m. Anne ____
d. 1773

- James Edward
  (emigrated to
  Charleston, SC)
- Thomas
  1727–30
- Anne
  d. inf. 1728

4 children
b. 1700–4, d. inf.

Martha
*c.*1706–80 — m. 1739 William
Manser

Thomas (a dancing
master)
1707–*post* 1745?
(emigrated to
Charleston, SC) — m. Frances Holt

- Jane
  1735–d. inf.
- Elizabeth
  1737–d. inf.
- Thomas (changed
  name to Holt)
  1738–*post* 1770
- James
  1741–d. inf.
- Jane
  *c.*1742–84

James (organist)
1710–89 — m. 1758 Ann Wood
*c.*1689–1772

Elizabeth (twin of
James)
1710–*c.*1767 unm.

Mary
1712–? — m. ____ Brooke
(or Brookes)

Letitia
fl. 1789–1814

Ashburnham
1714–d. Maryland?

4 others

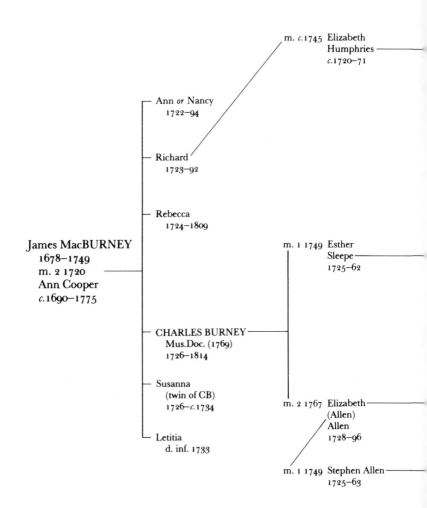

m. *c.*1745 Elizabeth
Humphries
*c.*1720–71

Ann *or* Nancy
1722–94

Richard
1723–92

Rebecca
1724–1809

James MacBURNEY
1678–1749
m. 2 1720
Ann Cooper
*c.*1690–1775

m. 1 1749 Esther
Sleepe
1725–62

CHARLES BURNEY
Mus.Doc. (1769)
1726–1814

Susanna
(twin of CB)
1726–*c.*1734

Letitia
d. inf. 1733

m. 2 1767 Elizabeth
(Allen)
Allen
1728–96

m. 1 1749 Stephen Allen
1725–63

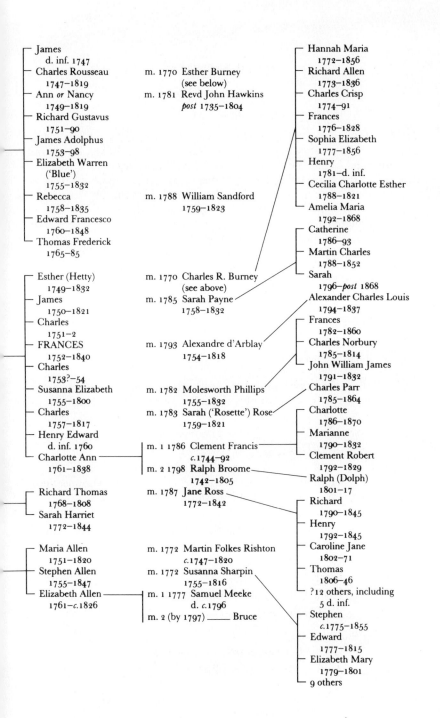

THE BURNEY FAMILY

BIOGRAPHICAL NOTES

CHARLES BURNEY [CB] (1726–1814), Mus.Doc. (1769), FRS (1773), appointed organist at the Royal Hospital, Chelsea (1783). His works are listed by his biographer Percy A. Scholes, *The Great Dr. Burney*, and in the study of his literary career by Roger Lonsdale, *Dr. Charles Burney*. The fragmentary 'Memoirs of Dr Charles Burney' have been edited (to 1769) by Slava Klima, Garry Bowers, and Kerry Grant; these memoirs, along with Madame d'Arblay's *Memoirs of Doctor Burney*, provide biographical reminiscences. Extant also are over a thousand of Dr Burney's letters. The letters to 1784 have been edited by A. F. V. Ribeiro (as a doctoral dissertation at Oxford, 1980); the remainder are being edited by Dr Klima.

On 25 June 1749 Charles Burney married Esther Sleepe (1725–62).

The surviving children of this marriage were:

1. ESTHER BURNEY [EB/EBB] (1749–1832), who married, 20 Sept. 1770, her cousin Charles Rousseau Burney (1747–1819), harpsichordist and music teacher.

   Their children were:

   1. Hannah Maria or 'Marianne' (1772–1856), who married, 30 Oct. 1800, Antoine Bourdois (*c.*1761–1806).
   2. Richard Allen (1773–1836), MA (Oxon.), 1807; divine; Master of St Mary Magdalen Hospital, Winchester (1804). On 10 Oct. 1811 he married Elizabeth Layton Williams (b. 1786).
   3. Charles Crisp (1774–91).
   4. Frances or 'Fanny' (1776–1828).
   5. Sophia Elizabeth (1777–1856).
   6. Henry (1781–d. inf.)
   7. Cecilia Charlotte Esther (1788–1821).
   8. Amelia Maria (1792–1868).

2. JAMES BURNEY [JB] (1750–1821), 2nd Lieutenant, RN (1772), Commander (1780), Captain (1782), retired on half-pay (1785), Rear-Admiral (1821); FRS (1815). His works are listed by Scholes (above) and by his biographer G. E. Manwaring, *My Friend the Admiral* (1938). James married on 6 Sept. 1785, in the parish church of Chessington, Sarah Payne (1758–1832), daughter of Thomas Payne (1719–99), the well-known bookseller.

The children of this marriage were:

1. Catherine (1786–93).

2. Martin Charles (1788–1852), a solicitor, and friend of Charles Lamb. He married (1816) Rebecca Norton (*c.*1799–1868).

3. Sarah (1796–*post* Dec. 1868), who married (1821) her cousin John Payne (*c.*1796–1880).

3. FRANCES BURNEY [FB/FBA] (1752–1840), novelist, journalist, and the subject of a number of biographies including that by Joyce Hemlow, *The History of Fanny Burney* (1958). On 28 July 1793 she married the French émigré chevalier Alexandre-Jean-Baptiste Piochard d'Arblay (1754–1818), an adjutant general in the French army who had been stripped of his commission after fleeing to England. At the restoration he was made a maréchal de camp (1814), given the title of comte d'Arblay (1815), and named a lieutenant-général honoraire (1815).

The d'Arblays had one child:

Alexander Charles Louis Piochard d'Arblay (1794–1837); MA (Cantab.), 1821; divine.

4. SUSANNA ELIZABETH BURNEY [SEB/SBP] (1755–1800), married, 10 Jan. 1782, Molesworth Phillips (1755–1832), 2nd Lieutenant, Royal Marines (1776); Lieutenant–Colonel (1798).

Their children were:

1. Frances (1782–1860), who married (1807) Charles Chamier Raper (*c.*1777–1842).

2. Charles Norbury (1785–1814), BA (Trinity College, Dublin), 1806; divine.

3. John William James (1791–1832), died at sea.

5. CHARLES BURNEY, Jr. [CB Jr.] (1757–1817); MA (Aberdeen), 1781; FRS, 1802; DD (Lambeth), 1812; schoolmaster, classical scholar, and divine. He married on 24 June 1783 Sarah *called* 'Rosette' Rose (1759–1821), daughter of Dr William Rose (1719–86), who kept a school at Chiswick.

> *Their only son was*:
>
> Charles Parr (1785–1864), BA (Oxon.), 1808; DD, 1822; schoolmaster and divine. He married (1810) Frances Bentley Young (*c*.1792–1878).

6. CHARLOTTE ANN BURNEY (1761–1838), who married (1) 11 Feb. 1786 Clement Francis (*c*.1744–92) of Aylsham, Norfolk, a surgeon, and one of the medical officers of the East India Company (1778–85).

   The children of this marriage were:

   1. Charlotte (1786–1870), who married (1807) Henry Barrett (1756–1843); Madame d'Arblay's literary executrix and editor.

   2. Marianne (1790–1832).

   3. Clement Robert (1792–1829), MA (Cantab.), 1820; divine; Fellow of Caius College, Cambridge, 1820–9; Dean, 1821–2; Bursar, 1827–8.

CHARLOTTE ANN married (2) 28 Feb. 1798 Ralph Broome (1742–1805), Captain in the Bengal Army, stockjobber, political satirist, and author of *Simkin's Letters* (1789).

> *The only child of this marriage was*:
>
> Ralph or 'Dolph' (1801–17).

CHARLES BURNEY (CB, above) married (2) on 2 Oct. 1767 Elizabeth née Allen [EAB] (1728–96), widow of Stephen Allen (1725–63), a well-to-do merchant of King's Lynn.

   The surviving children of this second marriage were:

1. RICHARD THOMAS BURNEY (1768–1808), who sailed to India when 18 or 19; headmaster of the Orphan School of Kiddepore (1795–1808). In Calcutta on 9 Nov. 1787 he married Jane Ross

(1772–1842). Of a large family of some ?16 children, those who returned to England and were known to the family included:

1. Richard (1790–1845), MA (Cantab.), 1839; Captain, Bengal Army, 1824–5.

2. Henry (1792–1845), Lt.-Col. in the Bengal Army; one of the executors of Madame d'Arblay's will.

3. Caroline Jane (1802–71).

4. Thomas (1806–46).

2. SARAH HARRIET BURNEY (1772–1844), author of six novels.

Connections by marriage with the Allens

Elizabeth (Allen) BURNEY had three children by her first marriage:

1. MARIA ALLEN [MA/MAR] (1751–1820), who married, at Ypres, 16 May 1772, Martin Folkes Rishton (*c.*1747–1820), grandson of Martin Rishton (1690–1754), sometime President of the Royal Society.

2. STEPHEN ALLEN (1755–1847), divine. He married at Gretna Green on 28 Oct. 1772 (at the age of 17) Susanna Sharpin (1755–1816).

The twelve children of this marriage included:

Stephen (*c.*1775–1855), MA (Cantab.), 1800; divine.

3. ELIZABETH, called 'Bessie', ALLEN (1761–*c.*1826), who married (1) at Ypres on 12 Oct. 1777 Samuel Meeke (d. *c.*1796) and (2) by Dec. 1796 —— Bruce.

The Worcester Burneys

RICHARD BURNEY (1723–92) of Barborne Lodge, Worcester, brother of CB (above) married *c.*1745 Elizabeth Humphries (*c.*1720–71).

Their surviving children, first cousins of Dr Burney's family, were:

1. Charles Rousseau (1747–1819), the harpsichordist and music teacher, who married his cousin EBB (above).

2. Ann or 'Nancy' (1749–1819), married on 27 Jan. 1781 the

Revd John Hawkins (d. 1804), of Nash Court, Kent; divine; Master of Magdalen Hospital, near Winchester (*c.*1796).

3. Richard Gustavus (1751–90), music and dancing master.

4. James Adolphus (1753–98).

5. Elizabeth Warren, called 'Blue' (1755–1832).

6. Rebecca (1758–1835), who married, 24 Mar. 1788, William Sandford (1759–1823), a surgeon.

7. Edward Francesco (1760–1848), an artist.

8. Thomas Frederick (1765–85).

This strange medley of thoughts & facts was written at the age of 15 for my Genuine & most private amusement.

Fanny Burney

(Note I)

Poland Street, London, March 27

To have some account of my thoughts, manners, acquaintance & actions, when the Hour arrives in which time is more nimble than memory, is the reason which induces me to keep a Journal: a Journal in which I must confess my every thought, must open my whole Heart! But a thing of this kind ought to be addressed to somebody—I must imagine myself to be talking—talking to the most intimate of friends—to one in whom I should take delight in confiding, & remorse in concealing:—but who must this friend be?—to make choice of one in whom I can but half rely, would be to frustrate the intention of my plan. The only one I could wholly confide in, lives in the same House with me, & not only never has, but never will, leave me one secret to tell her. To whom, then, must I dedicate my wonderful, surprising & interesting Adventures?—to whom dare I reveal my private opinion of my nearest Relations? my secret thoughts of my dearest friends? my own hopes,

2. The first page of Fanny Burney's Journal for 1768.

JOURNAL 1768

AJ (Early Diary, i, paginated 5–[66], foliated 1–[37], Berg), Journal for 1768. Originally a cahier made of sewn double sheets, but nearly all the leaves have been cut away. Now 28 single sheets and a double sheet 4to, 60 pp., with a blue cover *entitled* (*by FBA*): 1768 | Juvenile | Journal | Nº I *and annotated*: Curtailed & erased of what might be mischievous, from Friendly or—Family considerations I. ✸ ✸

On the verso of the front cover FBA *has written*: original old Juvenile private Journal Nº I Begun at 15. total 66 *Also written above*: 67 68 The figures may refer to the number of leaves or pages originally in the cahier or at some intermediate stage of editing. Also, the first page of the Journal has *FBA's annotation*: This strange medley of Thoughts & Facts was written at the age of 15. for my Genuine & most private amusement.

In her 'List of Persons and Things' for 1768 FBA includes two names not found in the extant journal, 'Miss Jenny Eyres' and 'Miss Dalrymple' (see below, p. 123). Miss Eyres, mentioned nowhere else in FB's correspondence, was possibly a relation of the Revd Venn Eyre (*c*.1712—77), Archdeacon of Carlisle; Lecturer of St Nicholas Chapel, King's Lynn, 1751–77 (H. J. Hillen, *History of the Borough of King's Lynn* (Norwich, 1907), ii. 1023; St Nicholas burial registers, Norfolk Record Office).

Fanny Burney

Poland Street,[1] *London, March 27*[th]

To have some account of my thoughts, manners, acquaintance & actions, when the Hour arrives in which time is more nimble than memory, is the reason which induces me to keep a Journal: a Journal in which I must confess my *every* thought, must open my whole Heart! But a thing of th[is] kind ought to be addressed to somebody—I must imagion myself to be talking—talking to the most intimate of friends—to one in whom I should take delight in confiding, & remorse in concealment: but who must this friend be?—to make choice of one to [*sic*] whom I can but *half* rely, would be to frustrate entirely the

[1] FB lived the first 8 years of her life in King's Lynn where her father, Dr Charles Burney [CB] (1726–1814), was organist of St Margaret's Church. In 1760 the Burney family moved to London, taking up residence in a house at No. 11 (later No. 50) Poland St., St James's, Westminster, then a fashionable neighbourhood, where CB gave music lessons to 'pupils of rank, wealth, and talents' (*Mem.* i. 135; Westminster Rate Books for St James's, Westminster Reference Library). The Burneys were to remain in Poland St. until 1770.

intention of my plan. The only one I could wholly, totally
confide in, lives in the same House with me, & not only never
has, but never *will*, leave me one secret *to* tell her.[2] To whom,
then, *must* I dedicate my wonderful, surprising & interesting
adventures?—to *whom* da[re] I reveal my private opinion of my
nearest Relations? the secret thoughts of my dearest friends?
my own hopes, fears, | reflections & dislikes?—Nobody!

To Nobody, then, will I write my Journal! since To Nobody
can I be wholly unreserved—to Nobody can I reveal every
thought, every wish of my Heart, with the most unlimited
confidence, the most unremitting sincerity to the end of my
Life! For what chance, what accident can end my connections
with Nobody? No secret *can* I conceal from No—body, & to
No—body can I be *ever* unreserved. Disagreement cannot stop
our affection, Time itself has no power to end our friendship.
The love, the esteem I entertain for Nobody, No-body's self has
not power to destroy. From Nobody I have nothing to fear,
⟨the⟩ secrets sacred to friendship, Nobody will not reveal, when
the affair is doubtful, Nobody will not look towards the side
least favourable—.

I will suppose you, then, to be my best friend; tho' God
forbid you ever should! my dearest companion—& a roman-
tick Girl, for mere oddity may perhaps be more sincere—more
tender—than if you were a friend [in] propria personæ [*sic*]—in
as much as imagionation often exceeds reality. In your Breast
my errors may create pity without exciting contempt; may raise
your compassion, without eradicating your love.

From this moment, then, my dear Girl—but why, permit me
to ask, must a *female* be made Nobody? Ah! my dear, what
were this world good for, *were* Nobody a female? And now I
have done with *preambulation*. |

[*At this point perhaps two months of the journal have been cut away and
destroyed.*]

⌐before they bind themselves together, for once engaged they
might as well be married. She is to go to a seat of Lord

---

[2] FB presumably refers to her younger sister Susanna Elizabeth Burney [SEB]
(1755–1800), who married (1782) Molesworth Phillips (1755–1832), a career officer in
the Royal Marines. FB was especially close to SEB, and her journals from 1773 to 1800
are mostly addressed to her.

Eglinton[3] next Tuesday—she was there a little while ago. His Lordship is very fond of seeing them. She declares she shall look about her for conquest—I am very sure, so favourably inclined was she to my *Cousin very* lately, & so Assiduous was he to merit it, that Miss Allen[4] is the sole person who has prevented her betrothing herself to him. But [xxxxx *1 line*] You can not imagion how surprised I am that M^{rs} [xxxxx *1 word*][5] can bear to be so long absented from there. I wish very much to see her; I never have since I was a Child.—I hope I shall after I go to Lynn, as I believe she is not far off. ⌐

Monday Night May 30th

O my dear—such a charming Day!—& then last night— well, you shall have it all in order — — as well as I can re- collect.

Last Night, while Hetty, Susey & myself were at Tea Mama[6] & Miss Allen not being return'd from Harrow[7] & Papa in his study busy[8]—⌐my Cousin,[9] too, was gone,⌐—Mr. Young[10]

---

[3] Alexander Montgomerie (1723–69), 10th E. of Eglinton, Lord of the Bedchamber, 1760–7; a patron of CB. The persons alluded to are probably CB's eldest daughter Esther (Hetty) Burney [EB] (1749–1832), an accomplished harpsichordist, and her cousin Charles Rousseau Burney (1747–1819), music teacher and harpsichordist, who was an even greater virtuoso on the instrument. EB and Charles Rousseau were friends from childhood. Later this year EB met and fell in love with the fickle Alexander Seton (for whom see below, *passim*), but after a troubled courtship she returned in 1770 to Charles Rousseau, and they were married. See Lonsdale, pp. 54–5, 62, 74.

[4] Maria Allen [MA] (1751–1820), FB and EB's stepsister, daughter of CB's second wife (m. 1767) Elizabeth née Allen [EAB] (1728–96) by her first husband (m. 1749) Stephen Allen (1725–63), a well-to-do merchant of King's Lynn. FB's lifelong fondness for the impulsive, emotional but good-hearted MA is indicated by her preservation of all MA's letters to her, despite MA's frequent injunctions to burn them because of their intimate contents. MA evidently carried on many flirtations before her marriage in 1772 to Martin Folkes Rishton (see especially SC to FB, 11 Aug. 1772, Essex).

[5] The name has been totally effaced; not identified.

[6] CB married FB's stepmother EAB on 2 Oct. 1767, 5 years after the death of his 1st wife (FB's mother, m. 1749) Esther née Sleepe (1725–62). EAB and her late husband Stephen Allen had become close friends of the Burneys at Lynn.

[7] Where they had gone to fetch FB's stepbrother Stephen Allen; see below.

[8] FBA has added 'as usual'. CB had already been busy for 15 years collecting materials which were ultimately to form the basis of *Hist. Mus.*, the 1st vol. of which was published in 1776 (see Lonsdale, pp. 43–4 and *passim*; below, *passim*).

[9] Charles Rousseau Burney, who had settled in London to establish himself in his musical career. At this time he was staying with Mrs Gregg and his aunts in York St., Covent Garden.

[10] Arthur Young (1741–1820), the agriculturalist, had married (1765) Martha Allen (1741–1815), a sister of EAB. He and his wife had just moved to Bradmore Farm at

enter'd the Room—O how glad we were to see him!—he was in extreme good spirits—[xxxxx *2 lines*] ⌐ [xxxxx *2 lines*]

Hetty set down to the Harpsichord & sung to him[11]—Mama soon return'd, & then they left it—⌐[xxxxx *1 line*] He run up to me first—Miss Allen assures me I am a favourite of his, an honour for which I am duly gratefull⌐—*well*, *& so*—upon the entrance of fathers & mothers—we departed this life of anguish & misery, & rested our weary souls in the Elysian field—my papa's study—there, freed from the noise & bustle of the World enjoy'd the [xxxxx *1 word*] *harmony* of chattering—& the melody of musick!—there, burying each gloomy thought, each sad reflection in the Hearse of disipation, lost the remembrance of our woes, our cruel misfortunes, our agonising sorrows—& graciously permitted them to glide along the stream of reviving comfort, blown by the gentle gale of new born hopes till they reposed in the bosom of oblivion—then—no! 'tis impossible! this style is too great, too ⌐sublime⌐ to be supported with proper dignity—the sublime & beautifull how charmingly blended!—Yes! I *will* desist—I *will* lay down my pen while I can with ⟨honour⟩—it would be miraculous had I power to maintain the same glowing enthusiasm, the same— ⌐ on my word I can*not* go on—my imagionation is raised *too* high—it soars above this little dirty sphere—it transports me beyond mortality—it conveys me to the Elysian fields—but my ideas grow confused—I fear you cannot comprehend my meaning— all I shall add, is to beg you would please to attribute your not understanding the sublimity of my sentiments to your own stupidity & dullness of apprehension, & not to any want of ˙meaning.

After this beautiful flow of expression, refinement of senti-ment & exaltation of ideas, can I meanly descend to common life?—can I basely stoop to relate the particulars of common

---

North Mimms, Hertfordshire. The proximity of his new home to London made possible frequent visits to the Burneys, whom he charmed by his liveliness and spirits. See *Mem.* i. 202; Gazley, pp. 24, 36–9; below, *passim*.

[11] Young, who was fond of music (and of attractive young ladies), writes in his *Auto-biography*, p. 51, that EB 'entertained, or rather, fascinated me, by her performance on the harpsichord and singing of Italian airs. I was never tired of listening . . . and it is marvellous to me now to recollect that I was thus riveted to her side for six hours together.'

Life?—Can I condescendingly diegn to recapitulate vulgar conversation?—[xxxxx *1 word*] I can!—

O what a falling off is here!—[12]

[xxxxx *1 line*] what a chatter there was!—however, *I* was not engaged in it—[xxxxx ½ *line*] & therefore, on a little considera-tion, a due sense of my own superlative merit, convinces me that to mention more of the ⌐affair,⌐ would be nonsense— |
Adieu, then, most amiable — — who? — —
Nobody!
Not so fast, good Girl!—not so fast—'tis true, I have done with last Night,—but I have all to Day—a Charming one it is, too,—to relate.
Last Night, to my great satisfaction, Mama prevail'd on M^r Y: to promise to be of our party to Day to Greenwich—well, he slept here,—for my part, I could not sleep all Night, & was up before 5 o'clock—Hetty & Susette were before six—& Miss Allen soon after—while we were all ⌐adoring⌐ our sweet Persons,—each at a looking glass—admiring the enchanting object it presented to our view, who should rap at the chamber Door, but—my Cheeks are crimson'd with the flush of indigna-tion ⌐even⌐ while I write it—Mr Young!—I ran into a closet, & lock'd myself up—however, he did not pollute *my* chamber with his unhallow'd feet—but poor Miss Allen was in a miser-able condition.[13] ⌐Mr Young [xxxxx *2 lines*] offered to enter⌐ her Room, & they were a long Time ere they could turn him out of it.
Well but, now for the Greenwich party—we set out at about 10 or 11—the Company was, Mama, Mr Young, Miss Allen, Stephen,[14] & your most obsequious slave— | the Conversation

[12] Cf. *Hamlet*, I. v. 47.
[13] FBA has interpolated: 'her Journal which he wanted to see, in full sight—on her open Bureau. He said he had a right to it as her Uncle. She called Hetty into'. MA frets about her journals being discovered in her letter to FB 15 Oct. [1769] (Berg). They are not extant.
[14] FB's stepbrother Stephen Allen (1755–1847). He was at Harrow School until 1771, when he matriculated at Cambridge. Wild and extravagant as a youth, he reputedly squandered his father's inheritance before coming of age. In 1772 (aged 17) he eloped to Gretna Green with Susanna Sharpin (1755–1816), daughter of Dr Edward Sharpin, a Norfolk physician. His later life was more stable. He settled at Lynn with his wife, where he had 12 children and eventually became Vicar of St Margaret's. FB seems never to have really liked or approved of Stephen Allen, and after his elopement their relationship was uniformly distant and formal. See *JL* iv. 110; below, *passim*.

as we went was such as I would wish to remember—I will *try* if I can, for I think it even worthy the perusal of Nobody!—*what* an honour!—

Well, I have rack'd my brains half an Hour—in vain—& if you imagion I shall trouble myself with racking the dear Creatures any longer, you are under a mistake. One thing, however, which related to myself, I shall mention, as *that* struck me too forcibly to be now, or perhaps *ever* forgot: besides, it has been the occasion of my receiving so much raillery, &c, that it is requisite for You to hear it, in order to observe the decorum due to the Drama. Talking of happiness & misery, sensibility & a total want of feeling, my mama said—turning to me—'Here's a Girl will *never* be happy! *Never* while she Lives! for she possesses perhaps as feeling a Heart as ever Girl had!' Some time after, when we were near the end of our Journey, '& so, said Mʳ Young—my friend Fanny possesses a very feeling Heart?'—He *harp'd* on this some little time, till at last he said he would call me *feeling Fanny*—it was *characteristick*, he said, & a great deal more such nonsense, that put me out of all patience—which same virtue, I have not yet sufficiently recovered to recount any more of our Conversation, charming as part of it was; *which* part you may be sure *I* had my share in, how, else, *could* it be charming? — —

⸙We found the 2 Mʳˢ & Mr. Allen[15] all well, & at the request of the latter, Miss Allen & myself went to an Auction,[16] which was a few Doors off his House. Mr. Young was resting & his lády[17] when we went—we wished him to accompany us, he said it would be very stupid, & so he would stay at Home—on my Word, thought I & I believe Miss A. simpathised, if you was as gallant as you ought to be, not even a Jaunt to Scotland[18]

[15] Presumably the first Mrs Allen was Mary née Maxy (*c.*1705–76), widow of Thomas Allen (*c.*1685–1752) of Lynn, mother of EAB. Mr Allen and the second Mrs Allen would then be either EAB's brother Maxey Allen (*c.*1730–1804), mayor of Lynn, 1771, 1779 and 1792, and his wife Sarah née Bagge (1728–1806); or her other brother Edmund Allen (*c.*1737–72) and his wife (m. 1762) Jane née Wilson (*c.*1721–94) (MI, St Nicholas Chapel, Lynn; 'Mem.' No. 114 n. 2).

[16] 30–1 May 1768, by Abraham Langford and Son, of the lease of the house and garden of Charles Whitworth (*c.*1721–78), MP, Kt. (19 Aug. 1768), at Crooms Hill, Greenwich; also the household furniture 'and several Capital Paintings, by Teniers . . . Rubens . . . and other Masters' (*Daily Adv.* 30 May 1768; see also Lonsdale, pp. 151–2).

[17] Evidently Mrs Young had arrived at Greenwich separately.

[18] i.e., to get married at Gretna Green.

should you think stupid, in our Company—but then, we accounted for his want of taste from his last thought,[19] every thing being *already* [xxxxx *1 word*]: & in this, I think we were not a little govern'd, since possessed of such amiable qualities as *we* are, we might without *much* vanity, have concluded that the man could *never* be ⟨gallant,⟩ who was blind to our graces. But when we Considered fully, spight of our mortified pride, &c—we knew a man might ⟨have⟩ a soul, *though* not at our service—wonderful that!—so we ever gave his mate credit for ⟨having⟩ it in keeping it—you act ⟨astoun⟩ded that we can at all forgive,—even *admire*, a man who is so vulgar, so old fashioned—&c. &c., as to care for his wife[20]—⸜ |

From Lynn Regis

⸝[xxxxx ½ *line*] My dear Papa looks better at present than ever I remember him—but I believe I have told you this before. My Mama too has been better here than she was in Town by much[21] [xxxxx *3 lines*]⸜ I am Reading the 'Letters of Henry & Frances,'[22] & like them prodidgiously. I have Just finish'd M⟨rs⟩ Rowe's Letters from the Dead to the Living—& moral & Entertaining.[23]—I had heard a great deal of them before I saw them, & am sorry to tell you I was much disappointed with them: they are so very enthusiastick, that the religion she preaches

---

[19] To 'stay at Home'.

[20] At this early stage the Youngs' marriage was evidently still a happy one. See below, *passim* for the discord that was to follow.

[21] CB had moved from London to Lynn in 1757 because of a consumptive tendency, forcing him to flee the smoke of the capital. He also suffered periodically from rheumatism which was aggravated by overwork. EAB also suffered chronically from a variety of complaints, some connected with her pregnancies (she was currently pregnant with her and CB's first child, Richard Thomas Burney, born in Nov.), and some probably of psychosomatic origin.

After CB's marriage to EAB in 1767 the Burney and Allen households continued to live apart for several years except for reciprocal visits, the Allens visiting the Burneys in London in the winter, while the Burneys came to Lynn to be with the Allens in the summer. The Allens lived in EAB's dower house opposite St Margaret's Church, where CB had been organist.

[22] *A Series of Genuine Letters between Henry and Frances* (vols. 1–2, 1757; vols. 3–4, 1766) by Mrs Elizabeth Griffith (1727–93), playwright and novelist, and her husband Richard Griffith (1716–88). These were selections from the highly moral and sentimental correspondence of the Griffiths.

[23] Mrs Elizabeth Rowe (1674–1737), *Friendship in Death: in Twenty Letters from the Dead to the Living* (London, 1728), and *Letters Moral and Entertaining, in Prose and Verse* (London, 1729–33).

rather disgusts & cloys than charms & elevates—& so roman-
tick, that every word betrays improbability, instead of disguising fiction, & displays the Author, instead of human nature.
For my own part, I cannot be much pleased without an appearance of truth; at least of possibility—I wish the ⌈history⌉ to be
natural tho' the sentiments are refined; & the Characters to be
probable, tho' their behaviour is excelling. Well, I am going to
Bed—sweet Dreams attend me—& may you simpathise with
me. Heigh ho! I wonder when I shall return to London!—Not
that we are very dull here—no, really—tolerably happy—I
wish Kitty Cooke[24] would write to me—I long to hear how my
dear, dear, beloved Mr Crisp does. My papa always mentions
him by the name of my *Flame* — — Indeed he is not mistaken—himself is the *only* man on Earth I prefer to him. Well I
must write a word more—only to end my paper—so! that's
done—& now good night to you. |

⌈Saturday.

Oh my dear, I have received the *finest* letter that ever was
wrote—sure!—while we were at Dinner, a packet came from
London—papa opened it—& among other Epistles, was the
following to me—

To Miss Frances Burney

When first I saw thee, Fanny, move
Ah me! what meant my throbbing heart?
Tell me—oh tell me—is it Love
That is Lodged here within my Breast?

Incognitus.

Was ever any thing so silly? It is alter'd, much for the worse,
from an old song I have often heard—which runs thus—

---

[24] Papilian Catherine Cooke (1730–97), who with her aunt Sarah Hamilton (*c.*1705–
97) kept Chessington Hall in Chessington, Surrey as a country boarding-place or rest-
home. One of the tenants of Chessington Hall was Samuel Crisp [SC] (*c.*1707–83), an
old friend of CB's who was practically a second father to FB. 'Daddy' Crisp figures
prominently in the early Journals and Letters; over 90 letters of his correspondence
with FB survive. No letters survive between FB and Kitty Cooke, whom FB loved for
her 'honest' and 'worthy' heart, though dismayed and amused by her comically vulgar
speech and manners (see below, p. 158 and *passim*).

'When first I saw thee graceful move
Ah me! what meant my throbbing breast?
Say—soft confusion!—art thou Love?
If Love thou art—then fare well rest!'—[25]

I burst into a violent fit of laughter — — & Read it aloud—
as soon as Mama saw it she immediately knew the Hand—it
was Stephen's—I am sure *I* should never have suspected it was
by the same Hand came to Hetty—but the letter was a blank—
not one line in it. I am resolved to send him a Letter in return[26]
[xxxxx $\frac{1}{2}$ *line*] What a trick! I vow I'll be even with him.
We expect 2 young Ladies to Tea this afternoon—Miss
Turner,[27] & Miss Tayler.[28] The former is the most agreeable
Girl in all Lynn—& the latter is the greatest beauty here⌐ |

[*The top line at least of the next page has been cut away. FB's would-be 'tor-
menter' in the first paragraph was perhaps Stephen Allen, who joined his
family at Lynn after term's end at Harrow. Whoever the speaker may have
been, he seems to be contemplating a creative piece (a poem?) in which he playfully pillories FB and presumably her sisters as well.*]

⌐[xxxxx 2 *words*] or at least, that he will leave *me* unmention'd,
that he would torment *not*—Indeed, *I* have little to fear, as I

[25] A song by Caterina Ruini Galli (*c.*1723–1804), Italian mezzo-soprano in England,
first published about 1750. See *GM* xxv (1755), 515; *BUCEM*; Highfill; *New Grove*; FB
to SC 30 Oct. 1775, in vol. ii.

[26] If written, this letter is missing.

[27] Mary ('Pow') Turner (*c.*1745–1815), daughter of Charles Turner (d. 1792), Mayor
of Lynn, 1759, 1767, later Collector of Customs there, and Catharine or Catherine (née
Allen) Turner (d. 1796). According to a letter of Mary Harwood to Charlotte Barrett,
[Oct. 1826] (Barrett), Miss Turner's mother was a sister either of EAB or of EAB's 1st
husband Stephen Allen. In Feb. 1773 Mary Turner m. (at Lynn) the Revd John Towers
Allen (*c.*1744–87) of Wiggenhall St German, Norfolk. See below, p. 244; *JL* iv. 163 n. 5;
H. L. Bradfer-Lawrence, 'The Merchants of Lynn', in *A Supplement to Blomefield's
Norfolk*, ed. C. Ingleby (1929), Turner pedigree opp. p. 160; Mrs Turner's will, PCC,
prob. 16 Nov. 1796.

[28] Dorothy Tayler (1751–1828), daughter of Joseph Tayler (1719–71), MD, physician of Lynn, and Ann (née Wilson) Tayler (*c.*1727–90). She m. (23 Oct. 1769, at Lynn)
George Hogg (*c.*1748–1811) (MI and registers of St Margaret and St Nicholas, Lynn).
The beautiful Miss Tayler was a close friend of MA. The two continued close friends
after both their marriages until 1798, when MA discovered that Mrs Hogg had been
carrying on a 20-year liaison with her husband Martin Folkes Rishton. This liaison
resulted in an illegitimate child, Edward Hogg (1784-*post* 1869), who became Rector of
Fornham St Martin, Suffolk and who was Martin Rishton's residuary legatee (will,
PCC, prob. 17 Jan. 1821). The present mention of Dorothy Tayler is the only one
recovered from FBA's journals and letters; she probably destroyed all other references
to her. Revelation of the liaison is in MAR's letters to FBA, 1798–1800 (Barrett).

was so ⟨maide⟩nly demure & prudish & shy, that he can not, I will be answerable, know any thing of me—& so I told him—& he gave a tacit acknowledgement—but then, he said, I should appear as a *shade*—thank him kindly!—& then, I am to be made [xxxxx *2 words*] the *blacker* for advising Hetty to [xxxxx *1½ lines*]

I am now writing in the pleasantest place belonging to this House—It is called some times the *Look out*—as ships are observed from hence—& at other times the Cabbin—It is at the farthest end of a long yard that runs along the House & beyond it—the windows look into the River Bend[29]—there are⁷ |

[*The top of the next page, which is the verso of the preceding, has been cut away.*]

spent there. I am going to tell you something concerning myself, which, if I have not chanced to mention it before will I believe a little surprise you—it is, that I scarse wish for any thing so truly, really & greatly, as to be *in love*—upon my word I am serious—& very *gravely* & *sedately*, assure you it is a real & *true* wish. I cannot help thinking it is a great happiness to have a strong & particular attachment to some *one* person, independent of duty, interest, relationship or pleasure: but I carry not my wish so far as a *mutual tendresse*—⌜God⌝ no, I should be contented to love *sola*—& let *Duets* be reserved for those who have a proper sense of their superiourity. For my own part I vow & declare that the mere pleasure of | having a great affection for some one person to which I was niether guided by fear, hope of profit, gratitude, respect—or any motive but mere *fancy* would sufficiently satisfy me, & I should not at all wish a return. Lord Bless me—how I run in! foolish & ill-Judged!—how despicable a picture have I drawn of an object of Love!—mere giddiness, not inclination, I am sure, penn'd it—Love without respect or gratitude!—that could only

[29] MAR recalls the 'Lookout', or 'Cabbin' in a letter to FB 3 Sept. [1780] (Berg). She and her husband have just moved back to Lynn, into a house which belongs to Charles Turner. The house has 'a very large Lookout . . . which overlooks the River that I pass many hours in and which often brings back past scenes to my view when I think of the Hours we used to spend in that little Cabbin of my Mothers—but this overlooks a much pleasanter part of the River as we never have any ships Laying Against our Watergate at least very Seldom to what we had there by which means we escape the Oath[s] & Ribald'ry of the Sailors and porters which used often to drive us from thence.'

be felt for a person wholly undeserving—but indeed I write so
much at random that it is much more a chance if I know what I
am saying, than if I do not. I have n⟨ot⟩ ˈ

[bottom of page cut away]

ᴨsome time—they had amused themselves with railing against
Lynn, every thing, every body in it, & praising to adulation
London—*I offered some few words* in favour of my poor old
abused Town—the land of *my* Nativity[30]—& the worlds happiness. We disputed a little time & Hetty suddenly cried—
'Hush—hush—Mama's in the next Room—if she hears
us—we two shall be whipt—& Fanny will have a *sugar plumb*.'
'Ay, cried A. 'tis her defending Lynn which makes Mama—&
my Grandmama so fond of her. 'Fond of me! cried I—what
makes you imagion Mrs. Allen fond of me?' 'What she said of
youᴨ ˈ

[bottom of page cut away]

I have just finished 'Henry & Frances'—They have left me in a
very serious, very grave mood—almost melancholy—a Bell is
now tolling, most dreadfully loud & solemn, for the Death of
s[om]e Person of this Town, which contributes not a little to
add to my seriousness—indeed I never heard any thing so
dismal—this Bell is sufficient to lower the highest spirits—&
more than sufficient to quite subdue those which are already
low. The greatest part of the last volume of Henry & Frances, is
writ by Henry—& on the gravest of grave subjects, & that
which is most dreadful to our thoughts—Eternal misery—Religion in general is the subject to all the latter part of these
Letters, & this is particularly treated on. I don't know that I
ever Read finer sentiments on piety & Christianity, than the 2ᵈ
vol. abounds with—indeed, most of the Letters might be call'd,
with very little alteration, Essays on Religion. I own I differ
from him in many of his thoughts, but in far many more I am
delighted with him—his sentiments shew him to be a man
possess'd of all the humanity which dignifies his sex; his
observations, of all the penetration and Judgement which
improves it, & his expressions, of all the ability, capacity &
power which adorns it. I cannot express how infinitely more I

---

[30] FB was born in King's Lynn on 13 June 1752 and baptized there in the Chapel of
St Nicholas on 7 July.

am charm'd with him at the conclusion than beginning. Some of his opinions—I might say many of them—on divine subjects, I think, would be worthy a sermon—& an excellent one too.—'tis a sweet, mild Evening—I will take a turn in the Garden, & re-peruse, in my thoughts these genuine, interesting Letters—this Garden is very small, but very, very prettily laid out—greatest part is quite a grove, & 3 people might be wholly concealed from each other, with ease, in it—I scarse ever walk in it, without becoming grave | for it has the most private, lonely, shady, *melancholy* look in the world.

Tuesday—Cabin

I have this very moment finish'd Reading a Novel call'd the Vicar of Wakefield.[31] It was wrote by Dr Goldsmith, Athour [*sic*] of the Comedy of the Good-natured Man—& several Essays. His style is ⌐prudent¬ & I knew it again immediately. This Book is of a very singular kind—I own I began it with distaste & disrelish, having Just Read the elegant Letters of Henry—the beginning of it, even disgusted me—he mentions his wife with such indifference—such contempt—the contrast of Henry's treatment of Frances struck me—the more so, as it is real—while this tale is fictitious—& then the style of the latter is so elegantly natural, so tenderly manly, so unassumingly rational!—I own, I was tempted to thro' the Book aside—but there was something in the situation of his Family, which ⌐if it did not interest me, at least¬ drew me on—& as I proceeded, I was better pleased—the description of his rural felicity, his simple, unaffected contentment—& family domestic happiness, gave me much pleasure—but still, I was not *satisfied* as a *something* was wanting to make the Book ⌐please¬ me—⌐to make me *feel* for the vicar in every line he writes¬—nevertheless, before I was half thro' the 1st volume, I was, as I may truly express myself, *surprised into Tears*—& in the 2^d Volume, I really sobb'd. It appears to me, to be impossible any person could Read this Book thro' with a dry Eye ⌐& yet, I don't much like it—my sensations on reading it were ⟨woful and tender⟩—but it is an inconsistent performance ⟨all the same⟩—I was

---

[31] *The Vicar of Wakefield* (2 vols., 1766), by Oliver Goldsmith (*c.*1730–74). *The Good Natured Man* was produced at Covent Garden 29 Jan. 1768 and published 5 Feb. (*LS 4* iii. 1308). *Essays by Mr. Goldsmith* appeared in 1765.

affected without being interested, I was moved without being pleased, which I might not [xxxxx *1 line*]⁷ ˡ [He advances][32] many very bold & singular opinions—for example, he avers that murder is the sole Crime for which Death ought to be the punishment[33]—he goes even farther, & ventures to affirm that our laws in regard to penaltys & punishment are *all* too severe. This Doctrine might be contradicted from the very essence of our religion—Scripture—for [xxxxx *3–4 words*] in the Bible— in Exodus particularly,[34] Death is commanded by God himself for many Crimes besides murder. But this Author shews in all his works a love of peculiarity & of making originality of Character in others; & therefore I am not surprised he possesses it himself. This vicar is a very venerable old man—his distresses *must* move you ⁷tho' the ⟨Tale⟩ in itself may fail to please.⁷ There is but very little story, the plot is thin, the incidents very rare, the sentiments uncommon, the vicar is contented, humble, pious, virtuous—but upon the whole ⁷the Book has not at all satisfied my expectations—⁷ how far more was I pleased with the genuine productions of Mʳ Griffith's pen—for that is the real name of Henry.—⁷I hear that 2 more volumes are lately published[35]—I wish I could get them—I have read but 2—⁷ the elegance & delicacy of the manner—expressions— style—of that Book are so superiour!—How much I should like to be Acquainted with the Writers of it![36]—those Letters are doubly pleasing, charming to me, for being genuine—⁷of which, if their own authors left no record, I have *proof positive* from my Mama, who saw the original Letters, with the post marks on them all, at the Publisher's Shop.[37] That Book has⁷ encreased my relish for minute, heartfelt writing, and ˡ encouraged me in my attempts to give an opinion of the Books I Read. ⁷[xxxxx *1½ lines*] letters—a propos to that, I wish my dear Kitty Cooke would write, as I long for any word of my dear *Grandaddy*—a propos to Letters a few Days since—Miss Allen has wrote Mʳ Young—& among other things which she wrote, she was pleased to say of me 'the *feeling Fanny* longs to

---

[32] Inserted by FBA.   [33] See chap. 27.

[34] See Exodus 21–2.   [35] See above, n. 22.

[36] FB and the Griffiths apparently never met.

[37] The publisher, William Johnston (d. 1804), had shops at the Golden Ball, St Paul's Churchyard, 1748–73, and in Ludgate Street, 1759–75 (Maxted).

be friendly and kind to *you*.'[38] I saw it before it went, & ⟨added at the end⟩—'It is a hateful untruth upon my honour F. B.' He has not yet answered her—& perhaps will not at all,[39] for now I recollect she sent her Letter long ago when Mrs Young went to Bradmore, who took it with her.⌐

Cabin—Wednesday afternoon.

I always spend the Evening, sometimes all the afternoon, in this sweet Cabin—except sometimes, when unusually thoughtful, I prefer the Garden.—I cannot express the pleasure I have in writing down my thoughts, at the very moment—my opinion of people when I first see them, & *how* I alter, or *how* confirm myself in it—& I am much deceived in my *fore sight*, if I shall not have very great delight in reading this *living proof* of my manner of passing my time, my sentiments, my thoughts of people I know, & a thousand other things in future.—there is something to me very Unsatisfactory in passing year after year without even a memorandum of what you did, &c. And then, all the happy Hours I spend with particular Friends and Favourites, would fade from my recollection.—

⌐Sunday⌐ July 17

Such a set of tittle tattle, prittle prattle visitants! Oh Dear! I am so sick of the ceremony & fuss of these fall lall people! So much dressing—chit chat—complimentary nonsense—In short, a Country Town is my detestation. All the conversation is scandal, all the Attention, Dress, and *almost* all the Heart, folly, envy, & censoriousness. A City or a village are the only places which, I think, can be comfortable, for a Country Town ⌐has but⌐ the bad qualities, without one of the good ones, of both. We Live here, generally speaking, in a very [re]gular way—we Breakfast always at 10, & rise as much before as we please—we Dine precisely at 2 Drink Tea about 6—& sup exactly at 9 ⌐&⌐ I make a kind of rule never to indulge myself in my two *most* favourite persuits, [r]eading & writing, in the morning—No, like a good Girl I give that up wholly, Accidental occasions & preventions excepted, to [needle][40] work, by which means my Reading & writing in the afternoon is a

---

[38] See above, p. 6.   [39] See below, p. 20.   [40] Inserted by FBA.

pleasure I ⌜am not⌝ blamed for, ⌜& does me no harm,⌝ as it does not take up the Time I ought to spend otherwise. I never pretend to be so superiour a Being as to be above having and indulging a *Hobby Horse*,[41] & while I keep mine within due bounds & limits, Nobody, I flatter myself, would wish to deprive me of the poor Animal: to be sure, he is not form'd for labour, & is rather lame & weak, but then the dear Creature is faithful, constant, & loving, & tho' he sometimes prances, would not kick any one into the mire, or hurt a single soul for the world—& I would not part with him for one who could win the greatest prize that ever *was* won at any Races. Alas, alas! my poor Journal!—how dull, unentertaining, uninteresting thou art!—oh what would I give for some Adventure ⌞ worthy reciting—for something which would surprise—astonish you!—⌜Would to Cupid I was in love!—Shall I never feel that so much desired passion—& are you not sick, my dear, at so ⟨foolish⟩ a wish? Even myself I ⟨bal⟩k at writing will⟨ful midd⟩l-ing nonsense. I have very⌝ lately Read the Prince of Abyssinia[42]—I am almost equally charm'd & shock'd at it—the style, the sentiments are inimitable—but the subject is dread-ful—&, handled as it is by Dr. Johnson, might make *any* young, perhaps old, person tremble—O ⌜heavens!⌝ how dreadful, how terrible is it to be told by a man of his genius and knowledge, in so affectingly probable a manner, that true, real happiness is ever unattainable in this world!—Thro' all the scenes, publick or private, domestick or solitary, that Nekaya or Rasselas pass, real felicity eludes their pursuit & mocks their solicitude. In high Life, superiority, envy & haughtiness battle the power of preferment, favour & greatness—⌜and with or without⌝ them, all is Animosity, suspicion, apprehension, & misery—in Private familys, disagreement, Jealousy & partial-ity, destroy all domestick felicity & all social chearfulness, & all

---

[41] The term *hobby horse*, in the sense of a favourite pastime or diversion, goes back at least to the 17th c., but FB's humorous flight here was probably inspired by Laurence Sterne's famous ruminations on hobby horses in *Tristram Shandy* (9 vols., 1760–7). She mentions Sterne's *Sentimental Journey* below, p. 65; see also the reference to 'scattered spirits', p. 34.

[42] *The History of Rasselas, Prince of Abissinia* (1759), by Dr Samuel Johnson. FB's father had known Dr Johnson since the 1750s, but the period of their real friendship dates from 1773, after the publication of the 2nd vol. of his *Tours*, which Johnson greatly admired. Similarly, FB was to meet Dr Johnson in 1777 but became a great favourite of his after the publication of *Evelina*. See below, *passim*.

is peevishness, contradiction, ill will & wretchedness!—And in solitude, Imagination paints the World in a new light, every bliss which was wanting when in it, appears easily attained when away from it, but the ⌐universal¬ loneliness of retirement seems unsocial dreary, ⌐misanthropical¬ & melancholy—& all is anxiety, doubt, fear & anguish! In this manner does Dr. Johnson proceed in his melancholy conviction of the impossibility of all human enjoyments, & the impossibility of all earthly happiness. One thing during the Course of the successless enquiry struck me, which gave me much comfort, which is, that those who wander in the world avowedly & purposely in search of happiness, who view every scene of present Joy with an Eye to what may succeed, certainly are more liable to disappointment, misfortune & unhappiness, than those who give up their fate to chance ¦ and take the goods & evils of fortune as they come, without making happiness their study, or misery their foresight.

Wednesday, July [20]
10 in the morning.

We have Just had a Wedding—a *publick* wedding—& very fine it was I assure you. The Bride is Miss Case,[43] Daughter of an alderman of Lynn,[44] with a great fortune—the Bridegroom, Mr Bagg,—the affair has long been in *agitation*, ⌐above 2 years,¬ on account of Mr Bagg's inferiority of Fortune.—Our House, ⌐very ⟨conveniently⟩¬ is in the Church Yard, & exactly opposite the great Door—so that we had a very good view of the *procession*. There was ⟨musick⟩ & [xxxxx *1 word*] & Bridesmaids, [xxxxx *1–2 words*]—The Bride is about 30 & is pretty & gentle,

---

[43] Pleasance Case (1737–90), daughter and coheiress of Philip Case (see next note), m. (20 July 1768, in St Margaret's Church, Lynn) Thomas Bagge (1740–1807), third son of William Bagge (1700–62) of Islington Hall, Norfolk (see H. L. Bradfer-Lawrence, 'The Merchants of Lynn', Bagge pedigree opp. p. 176).

[44] Philip Case (1712–92) of Gaywood Hall; lawyer; Comptroller of the Customs at Lynn, Wisbech, and Wells, 1754, Clerk of the Peace for Norfolk, 1760, Mayor of Lynn, 1745, 1764, 1777, 1786. Case amassed a great fortune (at his death he owned considerable detached properties and reportedly over £100,000 in the Funds) and for half a century 'virtually controlled the public and social life of King's Lynn' (Bradfer-Lawrence, p. 200 and *passim*). According to Bradfer-Lawrence, who cites this passage in FB's Journal, the reluctance of Philip Case to consent to the marriage 'arose doubtless from political reasons'; the Bagges were an ancient Tory family 'naturally opposed to the Whig interest in the town' (p. 177).

very agreeable—the bridegroom about 28, a very good figure & handsome. In the Bridegrooms new chariot—went the Bridegroom & Mr. Case. Next Mr. Case's own Coach—& in this was the Bride, Mrs. Case,[45] & a Dowager ⟨ma⟩id[46] whom I know not. Then, followed the rest of the Bridesmaids, Miss Case's Ladies & some other ladies both old & young.ꝿ The Walk that leads up to the Church was Crowded almost incredibly a prodidgious mob indeed!—I'm sure I trembled for the Bride. O what a *Gauntlet* for any woman of delicacy to run!—Mʳ Bagg handed the Bride & her Company out of their Coach, & then Mʳ Case took her Hand & lead [*sic*] her to the Church Door, & the Bridegroom follow'd handing Mʳˢ Case. O ꝿ⟨heavens⟩ꝿ! how short a time does it take to put an eternal end to a Woman's liberty! I don't think they were a ¼ of an Hour in the Church altogether—lord bless me! it can not be time enough, I should think, for a poor Creature to see where she was—I verily believe I should insist on sitting an Hour or two to recover my spirits—I declare my Heart ach'd to think how terrible the poor bride's feelings must be to walk by such Crowd's of people the occasion in itself so awful!—How little does it need the addition of that frightful mob! In my conscience I fear that if it had been me, I should not have ˡ had courage to get out of the Coach—Indeed I feel I should behave very foolishly. When they had been in the Church about a ¼ of an Hour, the Bells began to ring, so merrily—so loud—& the Doors open'd. We saw them walk down the Isle—the Bride & Bridegroom first, Hand in Hand. ꝿ—I forgot their Dresses—the Bride, as usual, all white—the groom in a light blue suit of Cloaths, lightly trim'd with silver, & [xxxxx *1 word*] Purple—his Hair well Dress'd [xxxxx *1 line*] On their return,ꝿ the Bridegroom look'd *so* gay, *so* happy—Surely it must be grateful to her Heart to see his Joy!—it would to *mine* I know. She look'd grave, but not sad—& in short all was happy & charming. Well

[45] Pleasance Clough (*c.*1707–77), m. (*c.*1733) Philip Case. Bradfer-Lawrence, p. 192, argues that Mrs Case was a daughter of George Hepburn (1668–1759), MD of Lynn, physician to Sir Robert Walpole, basing his claim on a passage in Joseph Farington's *Diary*, ed. J. Greig (1923–8), iii. 123. As Bradfer-Lawrence admits, however, 'the printed pedigrees say she was a Clough of Feltwell', and George Hepburn's daughter Pleasance in fact died a spinster at Lynn in 1797, aged 77 (MI, St Nicholas Chapel, Lynn).

[46] Presumably the mother of the bridegroom, viz., Jane née Dixon (d. 1790), widow of William Bagge.

of all things in the World, I don't suppose any thing can be so dreadful [xxxxx ½ *line*] as a publick Wedding—my stars!—I should never be able to support it! we ʳhave several Chairs here, all came to see the procession from our House—Miss Turner among them She is a charming Girl.ˈ Mʳ Bewly,[47] a great and particular friend of my papa's, & a very ingenious, clever man, is now here.—ʳHe is just come from his own House which is a few miles off this Town.ˈ At Breakfast time we had, as you may imagion, a long conversation on matrimony— Every body spoke against a *publick* wedding, as the most shocking thing in the world—papa said he woud not have gone thro' those people in such a manner for 5000 a Year—Mʳ Bewly said that when *he* was married, his lady[48] & self *stole* into the church, privately as possible, ashamed of every step they took. [xxxxx *5 lines*]

Friday.

I have a surprise to communicate to you, ⟨which is⟩ that ᴵ

Cabin. Saturday, July [30]

And so I suppose you are staring at the torn paper, & unconnected sentences—I don't much wonder—I'll tell you how it happen'd. Last Monday I was in the little parlour, which Room my papa generally dresses in—& writing a Letter to my Grand mama ʳSleepeˈ[49]—You must know I always have the last sheet of my Journal in my pocket, & when I have wrote it

---

[47] William Bewley (1726–83), surgeon and apothecary of Great Massingham, Norfolk. A man of wide scholarly interests but chiefly skilled in scientific subjects, he was principal scientific and medical writer for the *Monthly Review* (Lonsdale, p. 82 n. 4). He and CB became close friends while CB was at Lynn, and the two continued to correspond and visit after CB's move to London in 1760. Bewley died at CB's house in St Martin's St. while on a visit to London in 1783.

[48] Barbara Green (d. 1798), m. (1749) William Bewley. The place of their wedding has not been ascertained (her will PCC, prob. 20 Apr. 1798).

[49] The mother of CB's first wife, Esther Sleepe (1725–62). 'Daughter of a M. Dubois, [who] kept ⟨a⟩ Fan Shop in Cheapside', she was probably the Frances Wood (anglicized from Dubois?) who m. (1705) Richard Sleepe (d. 1758), a player in the Lord Mayor's band. Mrs Sleepe had been 'from some unknown cause—probably of maternal education . . . brought up a Roman Catholic', and both FB and SEB describe her as 'a real fine lady, of other days'. No letters survive between FB and Mrs Sleepe, who was dead by 1775. See 'Mem.' No. 49 and nn. 3, 4; D. Dawe, *Organists of the City of London, 1666–1850* (1983), pp. 12, 85; Boyd's Marriage Index, Society of Genealogists, London; below, p. 60.

half full—I Join it to the rest, & take another sheet—& so on.
Now I happen'd unluckily, to take the last sheet out of my
pocket with my Letter—& laid it on the piano forte, & there,
negligent fool!—I left it. ⌐Unfortunately while we were at Mrs.
Allen's on Sunday Evening, I wrote about half a page in which
I mention'd poor Susan [xxxxx *2 words*] teazing me with *particular* questions, on a *particular* subject, which related to a *particular* case, concerning Mama—Can you not guess
what?[50]—[xxxxx *1 line*] & besides this, I mentioned several
other little ⟨matters⟩—¬ Well, as ill fortune would have it, papa
went into the Room—took my poor Journal—Read & pock-
etted it! Mama came up to me & told me of it. O Dear! I was in
a sad distress—I could not for the Life of me ask for it—& so
dawdled & fretted the time away till Tuesday Evening. Then,
gathering courage—'Pray, papa—have you got—any *papers* of
mine?—' 'Papers of yours?—said he—how should *I* come by
papers of yours?—' 'I'm sure—I don't know—but'—'Why do
you leave your papers about the House?' asked he, gravely—I
could not say another word—& he went on playing on the
piano forte. Well, to be sure, thought I, these same dear
Journals are most shocking plaguing things—I've a good mind
to resolve never ⌐ to write a word more.—However, I stayed still
in the Room, working & looking wistfully at him for about an
Hour & half. At last, he rose to Dress—Again I look'd wistfully
at him—he laugh'd—'what, Fanny, s^d he, kindly—are you in
sad distress?—' I half laugh'd—'well—I'll give it you, now I see
you are in such distress — — but take care, my dear, of leaving
your writings about the House again—Suppose Any body else
had found it—I declare I was going to Read it loud—Here—
take it—but if ever I find any more of your Journals, I vow I'll
stick them up in the market place!' And then he kiss'd me *so*
kindly—Never was parent so *properly*, so *well-Judged* affectionate.

I was so frightened that I have not had the Heart to write
since, till now, I should not but that — — in short, but that I
cannot help it!—As to the *paper*, [xxxxx ½ *line*] [I destroyed it
the][51] moment I got it. We have had several little partys of
pleasure since I wrote last but they are not worth mentioning.
My papa went on Thursday to Massingham to Mr Bewlys—

[50] Presumably EAB's pregnancy.   [51] Inserted by FBA.

ᵣ[xxxxx *3 lines*] O—Mr. Young has Answer'd Miss Allen's Letter[52]—never sure, was *such* an Answer! Seriously 'tis hardly intelligible—he either is, or, pretends to be the vainest mortal under the sun—He tells her that he expected a dear Letter from her, but she—he found—'a poor modest common wofull affair—' said He—he tells her she may direct to him at the Marquess of Rockinghams[53]—he is set out in his Tour—*if* she will, or can, write any thing worth reading—but says he—'no more of your wofulls'—Did you ever hear the like? In another place he says 'So Fanny *says* 'tis an untruth—[xxxxx *1 line*]ⁿ |

[*The following conversation between FB and Dorothy Young is not in the extant Journal but is reprinted from* ED *i. 19–21, where Mrs Ellis says it has been reproduced from 'a transcript of selections from these diaries made about forty years ago'* (ED *i. 21, n. 1). This was presumably part of the transcribed copy prepared for the press in the 1840s when Charlotte Barrett and her publisher Henry Colburn were considering bringing out the 'juvenile journals' as well as the journals from 1778. The transcribed copy, which Mrs Barrett bought back with the original manuscript at the auction of Colburn's stock and copyrights in 1857, was used by Mrs Ellis's publisher George Bell in the preparation of her edition and was presumably destroyed after the edition's publication (in 1890). Mrs Ellis mentions 'the conversation with Miss Young' in a letter to the Revd David Wauchope, 10 Apr. 1886 (BL), where she remarks that it 'is in print', probably referring to proofsheets prepared in the 1840s by Colburn, who Mrs Ellis conjectures 'began printing, but lost courage, and stopped about the end of the 2nd Diary'. She adds that 1768 and 1769 'have actually been in the printing-office'.*

In the extant Journal the leaf numbering jumps from 23/10 to 27/12 at this point, which suggests that the conversation was originally recorded on a missing leaf 25/11.]

I have been having a long conversation with Miss Young[54] on journals. She has very seriously and earnestly advised me to

---

[52] See above, p. 13. Young's reply shows again his penchant for gallantry, which, however, he seems to have always kept within the bounds of decency (see *Mem.* i. 202–3).

[53] Charles Watson Wentworth (1730–82), 2nd M. of Rockingham, 1750; First Lord of the Treasury (Prime Minister), 1765–6, 1782. Young spent the latter half of 1768 on a 6-month agricultural tour of the northern counties of England in which he was accompanied by Mrs Young. His account of the tour was published late in 1769 as *A Six Months Tour through the North of England*, 4 vols. One of his stops was Wentworth House, Ld. Rockingham's seat in Yorkshire. See Gazley, pp. 39–40, 57; *A Six Months Tour . . .* (2nd edn., 1771), i. 269–316.

[54] Dorothy ('Dolly') Young (*c.*1721–1805) of Lynn, a granddaughter of Dr George Hepburn, physician to Sir Robert Walpole, was an amiable and intelligent spinster

give mine up—heigho-ho! Do you think I can bring myself to oblige her? What she says has great weight with me; but, indeed, I should be very loath to *quite* give my poor friend up. She says that it is the most dangerous employment young persons can have—it makes them often record things which ought *not* to be recorded, but instantly forgot. I told her, that as *my* Journal was *solely* for my own perusal, nobody could in justice, or even in sense, be angry or displeased at my writing any thing.

'But how can you answer,' said she, 'that it *is* only for your perusal? That very circumstance of your papa's finding it, shows you are not so very careful as is necessary for such a work. And if you drop it, and any improper person finds it, you know not the uneasiness it may cost you.'

'Well but, dear ma'am, this is an "if" that may not happen once in a century.'

'I beg your pardon; I know not how often it may happen; and even *once* might prove enough to give you more pain than you are aware of.'

'Why, dear ma'am, papa never prohibited my writing, and he knows that I *do* write, and *what* I do write.'

'I question that. However, 'tis impossible for you to answer for the curiosity of others. And suppose any body finds a part in which they are extremely censured.'

'Why then, they must take it for their pains. It was not wrote for *them*, but *me*, and I cannot see any harm in writing to *myself*.'

'It was very well whilst there were only your sisters with you to do anything of this kind; but, depend upon it, when your connections are enlarged, your family increased, your acquaintance multiplied, young and old *so* apt to be curious—depend

who had been the closest friend of CB's first wife Esther. Esther Burney in fact on her death-bed had recommended Miss Young to CB as a suitable second wife, but CB was unable to overlook Miss Young's extremely unattractive physical appearance (see *Mem.* i. 97–9, 192–3). FBA remarks, ibid. i. 99 n., that it was Miss Young's 'kind arms' that first welcomed her into the world, and she always held her in affectionate esteem.

Miss Young in her last years was living with Stephen Allen and his family (she made him her residuary legatee). She died at Haslingfield in Cambridgeshire (one of Stephen Allen's livings), 31 Jan., and was buried at Middleton near Lynn, Norfolk, 8 Feb. 1805 (H. J. Hillen, *History of . . . Lynn* (Norwich, 1907), ii. 1031; *GM* lxxv[1] (1805), 187; MAR to FBA 12 Jan. 1803, Berg; D. Young's will, PCC, prob. 18 Feb. 1805; Middleton burial registers).

upon it, Fanny, 'tis the most dangerous employment you can have. Suppose now, for example, your favourite wish were granted, and you were *to fall in love*, and then the object of your passion were to get sight of some part which related to himself?'

'Why then, Miss Young, I must make a little trip to Rosamond's Pond.'[55]

'Why, ay, I doubt it would be all you would have left.'

'Dear Miss Young!—But I'm sure, by your earnestness, that you think worse of my poor Journal than it deserves.'

'I know very well the nature of these things. I know that in journals, thoughts, actions, looks, conversations—*all* go down; do they not?'

The conclusion of our debate was, that if I would show her some part of what I had wrote she should be a better judge, and would then give me her best advice whether to proceed or not. I believe I shall accept her condition; though I own I shall show it with shame and fear, for such nonsense is *so* unworthy her perusal.

I'm sure, besides, I know not what part to choose. Shall I take at random?

[*The conversation reprinted from* ED *ends here*.]

Wednesday, August the 10th

ᴦOur Family is very much adored at present—[xxxxx *3 words*] large party, that we appear now *the thing*. Stephen left about a week ago, & went to Thetford, at a Mr. Wright's,[56] who keeps a farm at that village. Miss Allen left us at the same time, to meet & spend some time there with him. This morning my papa, Mama, Hettina & Bessy[57] went in the Coach to join

---

[55] i.e., to drown herself. Rosamond's Pond, in St James's Park, was a favourite trysting place as well as the scene of suicides of distraught lovers till it was filled in in 1770 (Wheatley, iii. 168–9; see also the *Oxford Journal*, 24 June 1769, s.v. 'London, June 20').

[56] Perhaps the Thomas Wright, freeholder of Thetford, listed in *The Poll for Knights of the Shire for . . . Norfolk . . . March 23, 1768* (Norwich, 1768), p. 55; not further identified.

[57] FB's stepsister Elizabeth ('Bessie' or 'Bessy') Allen (1761–*c.*1826), who m. 1 (1777) Samuel Meeke (d. *c.*1796); m. 2 (by Dec. 1796) —— Bruce. In a letter to FB, 8 Mar. 1786 (Berg), MAR describes Bessy Allen as a child as having been 'spoiled', 'conceited', and 'pert'. Sent to Paris in 1775 to refine her 'unformed & backward' manners, she responded by eloping to Ypres in 1777 with Mr Meeke, an adventurer. By all accounts she was blatantly unfaithful to Meeke. Her last years were spent under close confinement by a husband (Mr Bruce or a 3rd spouse) who had reportedly married her for her

them. We expect them Home, however, &—I believe & hope—Stephen with them. Miss Young, Susette, Charlotte[58] & your humble [servant] make up our present Family. We have had a great deal of visiting lately, both at Home & abroad— Mama & papa together are acquainted with every Family, I believe, in the Town, which is by no means a small one.[59] I believe I have not told you that Mr. Edmund Allen[60] is at Lynn—he is at Mrs. Allens, from whence I am but just return'd.⁊ Well, my Nobody, I *have* read part of my Journal to Miss Young—& what's more, let her chuse the Day herself, which was our Journey, & the Day in which I have mention'd our arrival, &c.[61] I assure you I quite triumph!—prejudic'd as she was, she is pleasd [*sic*] to give it her sanction,—*if it is equally harmless every where*—nay, says she even approves of it. ⁊ & Mrs. Allen has received a Letter to Day from Mrs. Young—she & her sposa are [xxxxx *1 line*]⁊ For some time past, I have taken a walk in the fields near Lynn of about an Hour every morning before Breakfast—I have never got out before 6, & never after 7—The fields are, in my Eyes, particularly charming at that time in the morning—the sun is warm & not sultry—& there is scarse a soul to be seen. Near the Capital I should not dare indulge myself in this delightful ⁱ manner, for fear of [xxxxx *1 word*] [Robbers][62]—but here, every body is known, one has nothing to apprehend. I am Reading Plutarch's Lives—his own, wrote by Dryden has charm'd me beyond expression[63]—I have Just finish'd Lycurgus[64]—& am as much *pleased* with all

money and deprived her of every comfort. See *JL* iii. 4 n. 12; xi. 447 n. 5; below, vol. ii and *passim*.

⁵⁸ FB's sister Charlotte Ann Burney (1761–1838), who m. 1 (1786) Clement Francis (*c.*1744–92), a surgeon in the East India Company; m. 2 (1798) Ralph Broome (1742– 1805), Captain in the Bengal Army and author. See below, *passim*.

⁵⁹ Lynn in the later 18th c. had a population of about 10,000 (see *Encyclopedia Britannica* (2nd edn., Edinburgh, 1778–83), s.v. Lynn Regis; Rees, s.v. Lynn-Regis).

⁶⁰ See above, p. 6, n. 15. He and his wife lived at Bristol.

⁶¹ Not in the extant Journal.

⁶² Substituted by FBA.

⁶³ FB's quotation below from 'The Life of Caius Marius' confirms that she was reading the so-called 'Dryden translation' of Plutarch, i.e., *Plutarch's Lives, Translated from the Greek by Several Hands* (5 vols., 1683–6), to which John Dryden (1631–1700) contributed the opening 'Life of Plutarch'. The exact wording which FB quotes first appears in the London edition of 1727. An extensively revised edn. in 6 vols. was published by Jacob Tonson in 1758; this edn., which retains the 1727 wording of the passage she cites, may have been the one read by FB.

⁶⁴ 'The Life of Lycurgus', translated by Knightly Chetwood. Lycurgus was the

his publick Laws, as *dis*pleased with his private ones. There is scarce *one* in the former which is not noble & praiseworthy—&, as *I* think, *very* few of the latter which are not the contrary—the custom of only preserving healthy Children, & destroying weak ones—how barbarous![65]—besides, *all* his domestic family duties appear strange to me!—but you must consider how very, very, very bad a Judge I am, as I read with nobody, & consequently have nobody to correct or guide my opinion: nevertheless, I cannot forbear sometimes writing what it is. [xxxxx *5 lines*] Adieu, my fairest!—Miss Young is [xxxxx *4–5 words*], & I am going to read the way to Keep him[66] to bed.

8 o'clock

It is provoking—here the only time Mama has slept out, and then—this happens! Mrs. Lidderdale & her Daughter[67] are come Home—& Mr. Bewley is come to Lynn—I vow & declare if it was not for the sage Miss Young's being here, I should be troubled to Death: for being the Head of the House requires a much *better* Head than my poor shoulders support. There are very few things which [xxxxx *1 line*]

[top of page cut away]

traditional founder of the Spartan constitution and social and military systems (*OCD* s.v. Lycurgus 2).

[65] 'It was not in the power of the father to dispose of the child as he thought fit, but he was obliged to carry it to the place called *Lesche*, where some of the oldest men of the tribe were assembled . . . if they found it deformed, and sickly, they ordered it to be cast into the place called *Apothetæ*, which was a deep cavern in the earth near the mountain *Taygetus* . . .' ('Dryden translation', 1758 edn., i. 126).

[66] A comedy by Arthur Murphy (1727–1805). FB took part in an amateur performance at Barborne Lodge in 1777, playing Mrs Lovemore (see vol. ii), and she was to meet Murphy at Streatham in 1779. See J. P. Emery, *Arthur Murphy* (Philadelphia, 1946), pp. 54–62, 213; *DL* i. 202 and *passim*; *LS 4* ii. 836–7, iii. 1319–20, 1331, and *passim*.

[67] Susan Hepburn (*c.*1704–96), 3rd daughter of Dr George Hepburn, who m. (1738) Thomas Lidderdale (1706–66), MD; and her daughter Maria Georgina Lidderdale (1742–87), called 'Liddy'. Mrs Lidderdale's husband shared her father's medical practice at Lynn and inherited it all upon Dr Hepburn's death (in 1759). Miss Lidderdale, who never married, is variously described by MAR as 'ceremonious', 'moralizing', and 'prosing', but also as 'obliging' and 'good natured'. In a letter to FB this year she says that 'Liddy raves about Mr. Gresham', perhaps a suitor who had dropped her (see Appendix 3). Miss Lidderdale was buried at Middleton near Lynn on 10 Jan. 1787 (Middleton registers). See also MAR to FB 25 Nov. 1772 and 26 Oct. 1775 (Berg); *GM* lxvi¹ (1796), 356; R. W. Ketton-Cremer, *Country Neighbourhood* (1951), p. 203; J. Chambers, *A General History of the County of Norfolk* (Norwich, 1829), i. 461.

I read Plutarch's Lives with more pleasure than I can express. I am charmed with them & rejoice exceedingly that I did not Read them ere now; as I every Day, certainly, am more able to enjoy them. I have Just finish'd Paulus Amilius,[68] whom I love & honour, most particularly, for his fondness for his Children, which instead of blushing at, he avows & glories in: and ⌐that at⌐ an Age, when almost all the heros & great men thought that to make their Children & Family a secondary concern, was the first proof of their superiority & greatness of soul, & when, like Brutus,[69] they co'ld stand with Countenance firm and unmoved & see their sons cxecution—At such an Age, I say, I think the paternal affection of Paulus Amilius his first & principle [*sic*] glory. Insensibility, of all kinds, & on all occasions, most *moves my imperial displeasure*[70] — — however, that of the Ancient Romans was acquired by the false notions they had of true greatness & honour. Well, rest their souls!—& mine—for I am now going to commit it to Morpheus.

Saturday August ⟨13⟩ ¹

[*bottom of page cut away*]

What Beauties rare have met me!—
How often have I, sighing said
Poor Hetty's charms are now quite Dead
Nor dare they vie with Fanny.

Melidorus.

Your servant, Mʳ Melidorus, I am much obliged to you— Who would not be proud to have such verses made on them? ⌐Mrs. Allen, who is now down stairs, has presented Hetty, Mary, Susette & myself with Tickets — — Mama talks of *chaproning* us. I never was at a publick assembly in my Life, at

---

[68] 'The Life of Paulus Æmilius', translated by Joseph Arrowsmith. Lucius Aemilius Paullus Macedonicus (d. 160 BC), Roman general and consul, publicly avowed his sorrow over the loss of 2 sons in an oration to the Roman people ('Dryden translation', ii. 279–81; see also *OCD* s.v. Paullus 2 Macedonicus).

[69] Lucius Iunius Brutus, the traditional founder of the Roman Republic. The story of the capital conviction he inflicted on his sons Titus and Tiberius (for conspiracy) is probably apocryphal. See 'The Life of Poplicola', translated by 'Mr. Dodswell' [?Henry Dodwell], 'Dryden translation', i. 252–3; also *OCD* s.v. Brutus 1.

[70] If a quotation, not found. Here as elsewhere FB may simply be waxing literary and calling attention to it by the underlining.

⟨school⟩ balls I've been often, & once at a private Ball at an Acquaintance, where I danced till late in the morning—I was in a slip, & a very [xxxxx *5 lines*]ⁿ

[*The bottom of the page has been cut off. Some isolated words and phrases have been recovered from the last 5 lines, which suggest that Miss Lidderdale came to FB with word that her mother Mrs Lidderdale had suddenly fallen very ill. See immediately below.*]

Wednesday—August [?17]

ᴴMʳˢ Lidderdale continues mending in her Health—Hetty & Miss Allen are Just come Home from Mrs. Allen'sᴴ—We had a large party to the Assembly on Monday, which was *so—so—so*—I danced but one Country Dance—the Room was so hot 'twas really fatiguing. Don't you laugh to hear a Girl of ᴴsixᴴteen complain of the *fatigue* of Dancing?—Can't be help'd!—if you will laugh, you must, I think. My Partner was a pretty youth enough—& *quite* a youth—Younger than myself—poor dear Creature, I really pitied him, for he seem'd to *long* for another caper—in vain—I was inexorable—not that he quite *knelt* for my Hand—if he had I *might* have been *moved*—for I have an uncommonly soft Heart—I am interrupted, or else I am in an excellent humour to scribble nonsence—

Evening.

I have this moment finish'd the Life of Caius Marius[71] &, being quite alone, cannot for my life forbear writing a word or two merely to vent my rage at him—brutal! inhuman! savage! execrable Wretch!—*Man* I cannot write—ᴴGood Godᴴ! how shock'd, how unaffectedly shock'd I am to find that such a *human* brute could ever really exist!—I would give the world to be assured the story was fabulous—of *what*, let me ask—of what *could* the Heart of that Creature be made of?—from the moment I read his inhumanly cruel & insulting speech to the injured Metellus,[72] after having forced him to put Turpilius to

---

[71] 'The Life of Caius Marius', translated by Miles Stapleton. Caius or Gaius Marius (*c.*157–86 BC), Roman consul and military leader (see *OCD* s.v. Marius 1).

[72] Quintus Caecilius Metellus Numidicus (*fl.* 109–98 BC), Roman consul and general. According to Plutarch, Marius forced Metellus to put his friend Turpillius to death for having allegedly betrayed the city of Vacca to Jugurtha, the warring King of

Death—viz 'that he had lodged a vengeful fury in Metellus' Breast, which would be continually tormenting him, for having put to Death Turpilius, his most intimate friend & hereditary guest'—from that moment, I was so warmly irritated against him, I had scarse patience to read another line but there is *something*, a *Je ne scais quoi* in Plutarch's Lives, that draws one's attention, & absolutely prevents one's leaving off—& then, when I found how great, how very great a General he was,[73] I was half reconciled to him—But when, in his old Age he was reduced to wander from place to place, insulted, persued, half famished & every way miserable, vilely as he had behaved & contemptible as he appear'd, I could not help shuddering at his dangers, & most earnestly wished his safety—for there is something in Age that ever, even in it's *own* despight, *must* be venerable, *must* create respect—& to have it ill treated, is to me worse, more cruel & wicked than any thing on Earth—*But*—when he entered Rome — — I really trembled—shudder'd at the recital of his actions—so *old* a man to have the *Heart* to be so enormously vicious—Indeed, I did hope that scenes of such extreme cruelty & inhumanity were confined to fable & romance—But I cannot help taking notice how interesting, how entertaining— | sensible—*irresistably* pleasing this incomparable Plutarch is,—you *see*, I am as much engaged in the fate of his Heros, as if they were all men of my Acquaintance. But you may have perceived before now that I am very earnest & warm in whatever interests me—not of a philosophick—or phlegmatick turn.—But this is between friends.— |

[The rest of the page is cut off and missing. The following, on the verso, seems to begin with the conclusion of a draft of a letter, otherwise missing, to FB's

Numidia, and then gloated over the deed after the accusation against Turpillius proved false ('Dryden translation', iii. 112–13; *OCD* s.v. Metellus 6 Numidicus). FB's quotation of the passage from Plutarch, which occurs at iii. 113, is exact except for the interpolation of 'Turpilius' and 'most' in the phrase 'Turpilius, his most intimate friend'.

[73] Besides concluding the war against Jugurtha (106 BC), Marius was responsible for important military victories over the Teutones at Aquae Sextiae (102) and over the Cimbri at the Vercellae (101). In 88 BC the armed usurpation of Sulla forced him to flee Rome; Plutarch gives a much embroidered account of his wanderings and hardships ('Dryden translation', iii. 146–54). In 86 BC he recaptured Rome with Cinna and became consul again. His return to power was marked by a general slaughter of his enemies; in particular, treacherous friends like Antonius, Catulus, Caesar, and Crassus were cruelly executed or forced to kill themselves (ibid., iii. 154–8; *OCD* s.v. Marius 1).

sister Charlotte. The identity of the good-natured person referred to is not clear.]

ᴿthat he's vastly good natured I am tired of writing to you. Poor Mrs. Lidderdale is very ill. Adieu, dear, dear Charly.

Charlotte Burney

Friday morn. [August ?19]

We expect an immensity of Company this afternoon—ᴺ ᴵ

2   St Margaret's Churchyard, Lynn Regis,
                        [?27] August 1768
To Mrs Gregg,[74] Rebecca Burney, Ann Burney,
Mrs Ann (Cooper) Burney,[75] and Charles
Rousseau Burney[76]

ALS (in verse) (Berg), August 1768
Double sheet folio, 4 pp. *pmks* LYNN 2⟨7⟩ AV wafer mark
Addressed: To │ Mʳˢ Gregg, │ At her House, │ York Street, │ Covent Garden, │ London.

August 1768
Sᵗ Margᵗˢ church yard
Lynn Regis.

Ah! where shall I expression find
To soften my Aunt Becky's mind?

[74] Mrs Gregg, who here makes her only apearance in FB's writings, was probably the 'Elizabeth Gregg, Widow', who died later this year and was buried in St Paul's Churchyard, Covent Garden, 11 Dec. 1768 (*The Registers of St. Paul's Church, Covent Garden*, ed. W. H. Hunt (1906–9), v. 75). Mrs Gregg was the widow of one Francis Gregg, who lived in York St. from 1730 to 1742 and again from 1749 (Rate Books). FB calls Mrs Gregg 'Cousin', but her exact relationship to the Burneys has not been determined, and nothing further has been found of her.

[75] Ann Cooper (*c.*1690–1775), m. (1720, as his 2nd wife) James MacBurney (1678–1749), father of CB. Apparently from Shrewsbury originally, she was 'daughter to a Herald painter. She had a small Fortune, & had received an offer of marriage from the celebrated Wycherly the Poet' ('Worcester Mem.'). FB was apparently fond of the old lady, but much later in life learned from her father's memoirs of her grandmother's 'niggardly unfeelingness' towards CB as a youth (FBA to EBB [25]–8 Nov. 1820, *JL* xi.

[*See opposite page for n. 75 cont. and n. 76*]

And how, Alas! shall I essay
To sooth my Cousin[77] by my lay?
O dearest ladies!—did you know
With what true penitential woe
I sue for mercy, wish[78] for grace,
You soon would pity my sad Case.
I know you both so good and kind
That malice dwells not in your mind,
And therefore 'tis I humbly hope
The Door of mercy you will ope!
And that your Hearts will each relent
And shame be my sole punishment.

    And now you're [*sic*] anger you disperse
You stare to see me aim at Verse:
Cries Mrs Gregg—'Why Fanny!—Child!
My dear!—you're frantic—mad—quite wild!
I'm[79] lost in wonder and amaze,
Ah! things were diff'rent in MY Days!
When *I* was young, to Hem & sow
Was almost all I wish'd to know: |
But as to writing *Verse* & *Rhimes* — —
O Dear! oh Dear!—how changed the Times!'

    'True, cries my Aunt, She might as well
In better prose her nonsence tell
I affectation can't endure;
But 'tis too late to hope a cure.'

    If my Aunt Nanny should be by
She'll laugh—perhaps frown—& look *so* sly!—
But not a single word she says,
Or yet of flatt'ry, or dispraise,

---

189). Widowed in 1749, by 1764 she was living in London, where she and her spinster daughters Ann Burney (1722–94) and Rebecca (1724–1809), FB's aunts, resided in the house of Mrs Gregg. FB's grandmother and aunts continued to live in the Gregg house after Mrs Gregg's demise; possibly Mrs Gregg bequeathed the house to Rebecca, who is listed as paying the poor rate from 1769. In 1775 FB's grandmother died and, like Mrs Gregg, was buried in St Paul's Churchyard (see vol. ii).

[76] Charles Rousseau was evidently staying with Mrs Gregg and his aunts at this time. Ann Burney was one of the witnesses at his wedding to EB in 1770.

[77] Mrs Gregg.
[78] Written over 'hop[e]' in the MS.
[79] Written over 'Please' and also above the line in the MS.

But well I know 'tis her design
To hear you first Read ev'ry Line,
And then she better will know what
To say to this, reply to that.
    And when my scrawl you read to Granny,—
'Pure free & easy, Madam Fanny!—
And so you re'ly condescend
To name *your Granny* at the *End?*'
    Ah, hold your Anger, dearest Ma'am
And, credit me!—I mean no harm
Only with patience wait a minute,
Something, you'll see, will happen in it;
Think not to name you last I meant;
Far from my Heart be the intent!
Now Cousin Charles, with solemn face,
Diegns to *look over* at this place,
(Three Times he reads, or I'm mistaken
The lines where he in Hand is taken)
'I cannot for my Life find out
What 'tis that she would *be about*;
Surely she writes with *some* intention,
For something of us all makes mention—
But, whatso'er she did intend
Folly & nonsence is the End!'
    Hold, hold! good Critics, not so quick,
I vow you turn my Heart quite sick;
Upon my word you are too hard,
Consider, I am off my gaurd [*sic*]:
How'er, I must confess you're right
To humble one who aims to Write
So much above her skill & power—
So set my Peg a little lower.
    But, truce to nonsence, let me beg
To know how does my Cousin Gregg?
And greatly do I wish to hear
How fares the Health of my Aunt dear.
Present my duty to my Granny
And with it, Love, to dear Aunt Nanny.—
We all at Lynn are very well,
But when we leave it, cannot tell;

As *Papilons*[80] waits to hear
From Worcester, from his Brother dear
When he my Cousin Charles will want
Ere he shall fix his London Jaunt. |
My Compliments to Cousin give:
And now I humbly take my leave.
I wish you happiness and peace,
And am your ever duteous Niece. *F. Burney*.

I wish you *Readers* by the dozen,[81]
And am your most obedient Cousin F. Burney.

[*The Journal for 1768 continues*]

[Poland Street][82]

[Mr. Greville[83] supped here, & talked of][82] the *Book fight*
between Mr Sharpe[84] and Signor Barretti—concerning Italy, of
which Country the former has wrote an Account; which the

[80] FB's playful name here for her 'Papa' CB; perhaps suggested by a character in Samuel Foote's comedy *The Lyar* (see *LS 4* iii. 1331; Highfill). 'Brother dear' in the next line would be CB's brother Richard Burney (1723–92) of Barborne Lodge, Worcester, cousin Charles Rousseau's father.

[81] Unexplained. Perhaps cousin Charles was trying his hand at something literary.

[82] Inserted by FBA.

[83] Fulke Greville (*c*.1716–1806), wealthy and elegant grandson of the 5th B. Brooke, befriended CB in 1746 when CB was a struggling young musician indentured to the composer Thomas Arne. Impressed by CB's intelligence and charm as well as by his musical skills, Greville took him on part-time as a domestic musician and companion and in 1748 purchased the remaining years of CB's indenture to Arne. He generously released him from service, however, after only 9 months when CB married Esther Sleepe and Greville left on an extended tour of Europe.
Prior to purchasing CB's indenture Greville had CB give away the bride at his clandestine wedding to Frances Macartney (*c*.1730–89), a celebrated beauty who was daughter to a wealthy Irish landowner. The new Mrs Greville was later to stand godmother to FB. The Grevilles' daughter Frances Anne (1748–1818) also became a noted beauty and was a lifelong friend of the Burneys; in 1766 she married John Crewe (1742–1829), MP, cr. (1806) B. Crewe. See Lonsdale, pp. 14–22; *Mem*. i. 24–81 *passim*.

[84] Samuel Sharp (?1700–78), surgeon. Following a trip to Italy the winter of 1765–6, he published *Letters from Italy, Describing the Customs and Manners of that Country*, which appeared in 1766. Sharp's work motivated Giuseppe Marco Antonio Baretti (1719–89), the miscellaneous writer and friend of Dr Johnson, to publish *An Account of the Manners and Customs of Italy; with Observations on the Mistakes of Some Travellers, with Regard to that Country* (2 vols., London, 1768). Sharp responded with *A View of the Customs, Manners, Drama, &c. of Italy, as They Are Described in the. . . Account of Italy . . . by Mr. Baretti* (London, 1768), but Baretti appears to have had the last word in the controversy with *An Appendix to the Account of Italy, in Answer to Samuel Sharp* (London, 1768). FB was to meet Baretti in 1772 and knew him thereafter as a friend of her father and Dr Johnson.

latter has absolutely confuted. 'I wish, said Mr Greville, men would not pretend to write of what they cannot be masters of, Another Country—It is impossible they can be Judges; and they ought not to aim at it—for they have different sensations, are used to different laws, manners and things, & consequently are habituated to different thoughts and ideas—'tis the same as if a Cow was to write of a Horse—or a Horse of a Cow—why they would proceed on quite different principles, and therefore certainly could be no Judge of one Another.'

He ask'd Papa if he play'd much on Piano Fortes,[85]—'If I was to be in Town this winter, s^d he, I should cultivate my acquaintance with old Crisp—' 'Ah, said papa, he's truly worth it.' 'Ay indeed is he, Answered Mr Greville, he's a most superiour man.'

This one speech has gain'd him my Heart for ever. This man is exceeding fond of my father, before he went to Germany,[86] he used to sup with $^|$ him perpetually, in the most familiar & comfortable style—& now again, he resumes this freedom $^\ulcorner$notwithstanding$^\urcorner$ [xxxxx $\frac{1}{2}$ *line*] His Wife and Daughter are the two greatest beautys in England.[87]

$^\ulcorner$I wrote yesterday to Mr. Crisp—Hetty has had a long Letter & pressing invitation from him[88]—I am fishing & Angling to move papa to let me go to Chesington for some time—I fear I

---

[85] The pianoforte was still something of a novelty in England at this time. In fact, as Mrs Ellis points out (*ED* i, pp. lv–lvi n. 1), Greville here mentions the pianoforte and SC together since it was SC who had brought the first pianoforte into England (from Rome, *c*.1740?) and Greville had bought this instrument from SC for 100 guineas (see Rees, 1, s.v. Harpsichord). SC had been a close companion of Greville in the 1740s but became progressively estranged from him because of what he called Greville's 'constitutional inconstancy' (SC to FB ?Aug. 1779, Berg, printed *DL* i. 261–4). FBA states (*Mem.* i. 182) that SC refused to let Greville know the directions to Chessington Hall. See also 'Mem.' Nos. 41–4; Scholes, i. 189–90.

[86] Greville had gone to Germany in 1766 as British Minister to the Imperial Diet and Envoy Extraordinary to Bavaria. He continued in the latter post officially till 1770 but had returned to England on leave in Apr. of this year (D. B. Horn, *British Diplomatic Representatives 1689–1789* (1932), pp. 42, 46). Greville's 'freedom' with CB was to turn sour in 1771 when, oppressed by chronic gambling debts, he asked CB to pay back the £300 he had spent to purchase his indenture in 1748.

[87] In an insertion here FBA praises Mrs Greville's 'ode to Indifference' ('A Prayer for Indifference'), a much admired poem first published in *The Edinburgh Chronicle*, 14–19 Apr. 1759. It is included by David Nichol Smith in *The Oxford Book of Eighteenth-Century Verse* (Oxford, 1926), pp. 426–8 and by Roger Lonsdale in *The New Oxford Book of Eighteenth-Century Verse* (Oxford, 1984), pp. 483–5.

[88] Both letters are missing. FB did not visit Chessington until 1771, when she noted that it had been 'almost 5 Years' since her last journey there (below, p. 157).

shall not succeed—but I can but try, which I shall pretty boldly to night at supper—Stephen will go to Harrow School to morrow. Adieu pour le present. ⌐

Sunday Night Septr 11

I have Just finish'd the Life of the great—the unfortunate Pompey.[89] He was certainly an imperfect being—but all in all, a most wonderful man. His Death, treacherous, cruel,—has made me melancholy—Alas the poor Cornelia!—How deserving of pity. My sweet ⌐baby⌐ Charles[90] is come home— ⌐he is well, hearty, &⌐ full of spirits, mirth & good-humour. My Aunt Nanny who went lately to see him at the Charter House, was assured there that he was the sweetest temper'd Boy in the school. ⌐We have heard from | Mama—she is well, & Mrs. Lidderdale is better. [xxxxx *1 line*]⌐ Papa is gone to supper with Mr Greville. You must know that this Gentleman is the Author of a Book called—*Characters—Maxims and reflections—Serious—Moral & entertaining*.[91] I never read it thro', but what I have pleased me extremely.

Septr 12th

I am prodidgiously surprised, immensely astonish'd indeed—absolutely petrified with amazement—And what do

[89] 'The Life of Pompey', translated by William Oldys. Gnaeus Pompeius (106–48 BC), called Magnus after 81, Roman general and triumvir along with Crassus and Julius Caesar, fled to Egypt after the annihilation of his army by Caesar's forces at the Battle of Pharsalus (48 BC). As he was landing in a small boat he was treacherously stabbed to death by one of his old centurions. Cornelia, his latest wife, witnessed the murder from Pompey's galley. She 'gave such a shriek, that it was heard to the shore', and fled ('Dryden translation', iv. 215; *OCD* s.v. Cornelia 2, Pompeius 4).

[90] FB's younger brother Charles Burney Jr. [CB Jr.] (1757–1817), 10 years old at this time, who was to become a schoolmaster, a noted classical scholar, and a divine (the last belatedly, because of a theft of books which caused his expulsion from Cambridge in 1777; see vol. ii). CB Jr. had the previous Feb. been admitted to the Charterhouse 'at the nomination of his Grace the Duke of Marlborough' (MS document on CB Jr.'s academic career, Osborn, quoted Scholes, i. 344; Keane Fitzgerald to CB 9 May 1767, Osborn).

Three letters survive from CB Jr. at the Charterhouse to FB in Poland St., one undated and the other two dated 13 Dec. 1768 and 11 Oct. 1769 (Osborn). These and two others written to FB from the Charterhouse in 1774 (also Osborn) are all that remain of CB Jr.'s correspondence before 1778.

[91] Greville's *Maxims, Characters, and Reflections, Critical, Satyrical, and Moral* (1756), co-authored by his wife and with possible assistance from Dr John Hawkesworth. CB owned a copy of the 2nd edn. of 1757 (*Lib.* p. 22; see also Abbott, p. 67).

you imagion the cause?—You can never guess—I shall pity your ignorance & incapacity, &, generous noble minded as I am, keep you no longer in suspense—Know then—Ha!—this frightful old ʳfellow—ᵀ⁹² how he has startled me—past Eleven O'clock!—bless you, friend, don't bawl so loud—My nerves can't possibly bear it—no—I shall expire—this robust, gross creature will be the Death of me—Yes—I feel myself going— my spirits fail—my blood chills—I am gone!—

To my eternal astonishment, I am recovered!— | Ay, 'tis true, I really am alive—I have actually & truly survived this bawling. Well, & now that I have in some measure *recollected my scatter'd spirits*,⁹³ I will endeavour sufficiently to compose myself to relate the Cause of Wonder the first. Would you believe it— but now I think of it you can't well tell till you hear—well, have patience—all in good Time—Don't imagion I intend to cheat you—no—no—Now attend.

Miss Tillson,⁹⁴ a young lady of fashion, fortune, education, birth, accomplishments & beauty, has fallen in love with my Cousin Charles Burney!—ʳthere's for you.—[xxxxx *1 line*] She is but 17—she has Just left Blackland school⁹⁵ at Chealsea [*sic*].

⁹² FBA has substituted 'watchman'.

⁹³ Probably an allusion to *Tristram Shandy*, i.e., to the animal spirits of Walter Shandy which are scattered by an irrelevant remark of Mrs Shandy at the moment of Tristram's conception. Cf. the passage on 'Hobby Horse' above, p. 15.

⁹⁴ Gertrude Tilson (?1752–*post* 1808), daughter of James Tilson (*c.*1709–64) of Pallas, King's County and Bolesworth Castle, Cheshire, sometime Consul at Cadiz who m. (1750) Gertrude Lambart (d. 1775), eldest daughter of Richard, 4th E. of Cavan and widow of William Fitzmaurice (1694–1747), 2nd E. of Kerry. At this time Miss Tilson was living with her mother in Wigmore St., Cavendish Square. Spurned by Charles Rousseau, the spoiled and capricious girl eloped the following year with Gilbreath Mahon, an Irish musician and adventurer who deserted her in 1774. After her mother's death in 1775 she became a noted courtesan dubbed 'The Bird of Paradise' in London circles because of her love of brightly-coloured finery. With the wane of her beauty she gradually sank from view, and she is last heard of in some spurious memoirs of the D. of Queensbury, published in 1808, which describe her as then living in the Isle of Man 'under the protection of a Hibernian refugee' (J. P. Hurstone, *The Piccadilly Ambulator; or, Old Q.* (1808), ii. 59). See H. Bleackley, *Ladies Fair and Frail* (1909), pp. 245–94, 308–9, and sources there cited.

⁹⁵ From the 17th c. Chelsea was noted for its ladies' boarding-schools, 'for which it rivalled Hackney at the other end of London' (Wheatley, i. 376). Blackland School presumably had its origin *c.*1705 when Blacklands House, belonging to William Cheyne, 2nd Visc. Newhaven, was let to a French boarding school (J. Bowack, *The Antiquities of Middlesex* (1705), p. 14). MA attended the school for a time, being placed there by her mother in 1765 ('Mem.' No. 111). See also A. Beaver, *Memorials of Old Chelsea* (1892), pp. 343–4; *Boswell Papers*, xvii. 118, xviii. 255.

[xxxxx *3–4 words*] where Charles taught [xxxxx ½ *line*] for she boards there for about a week together for her Health.[96] Well, I'm so sleepy, I must begon[e]—you may hear more anon— |

Wednesday, Sept[r] [?21]

I have not wrote you a line this Age, my sweet Journal— indeed, I have no wonderful matters to scrawl now—Is it not very perverse in Dame Fortune to deny me the least share in any of her so much talk'd of tricks? especially as I should by means of my inimitable Pen immortalize every favour she honour'd me with: but so it is, & so it seems likely to be;—that I am to pass my Days in the dulest [*sic*] of dull things insipid, calm, uninterrupted quiet. This Life is by many desired—so be it—but it surely was design'd to give happiness after—& not one ounce before twenty *full* years are pass'd—but till then— no matter what happens—the spirits—the health—the never dying *hope* are too strong to be *much* affected by whatever Comes to pass—Supper Bell as ⟨I Live.⟩ |

10 o'clock—

⌐I left them the moment I had Eat my Potatoe—their Insight obliged my Charming Nobody with the use of my right Hand—*And so* I will now tell you briefly a few things.⌐

I left off with a little acc[t] of Miss Tilson—I shall only tell you that I heard of her passion & the amiable object by Hetty; who was told it by ⌐the school misses⌐[97] & afterwards confirm'd by the fair one's one [*sic*] mouth. ⌐She at first insisted on Hetty's being engaged to the fair youth, for that report reached farther than Chelsea—namely to Lynn—but on Hetty's opening her mind, & assuring her that she was mistaken, Miss Tilson own'd her partiality. Hetty has seen him too, and ⟨he assures

---

[96] Miss Tilson perhaps had a consumptive complaint. Bowack, p. 13, comments on the 'Sweetness of . . . Air' at Chelsea, which is perhaps why it was a favourite place of residence with physicians (Wheatley, i. 379).

FBA has added that Miss Tilson 'wrote her declaration to [Charles Rousseau] on her Glove, which she dropt for him to pick up', and that she 'has a Portion in her own hands of several thousands—'.

[97] FBA has substituted 'Miss Sheffield'. This was probably either Alicia Caroline Sheffield or Sophia Maria Sheffield, the younger daughters of Sir Charles Sheffield (*c.*1706–74), cr. (1755) Bt. See *GM* xciii[1] (1823), 189–90; Sir Charles Sheffield's will, PCC, prob. 19 July 1775.

his in⟩difference & she still remains constant—she left school yesterday—she only boarded there for the month. She has promised to write to Hettina[98]—⌐ ⌐ [Her mother married Mr. Tilson on the][99] Death of the Earl of Kerry. She is very short—but Hetty says very pretty. [xxxxx *1 line*]

Mr Smart[1] the poet was here yesterday. He is the Author of the 'Old Woman's Magazine ⌐or Midwife'⌐ & of several poetical productions, some of which are sweetly elegant & pretty—for example—'Harriet's Birth Day'—'Care and Generosity'—& many more. This ingenius [*sic*] Writer is one of the most unfortunate of men—he has been twice confined in a mad H[o]use—& but last year sent a most affecting Epistle to papa, to entreat him to lend him ½ a Guinea!—How great a pity so clever, so ingenius [*sic*] a man should be reduced to such shocking circumstances. He is extremely grave, & has still great wildness in his manner, looks & voice—'tis impossible to *see* him & to *think* of his works, without ⌐ feeling the utmost pity & concern for him.

Well, I shall have to undress in the Dark if I scribble any longer—& so I must petition for leave to bid you adieu: Granted.

Certainly I have the most complaisant friend in the world—ever ready to comply with my wishes—never hesitating to oblige, never averse to any concluding, yet never wearried [*sic*] with my beginning—charming Creature.

And pray, my dear Miss Fanny, *who* is this?—Nobody.

---

[98] The letter, if written, is missing.

[99] Inserted by FBA.

[1] Christopher Smart (1722–71). CB had been a friend of Smart since 1744 and had introduced him to the bookseller John Newbery, who became Smart's publisher and whose stepdaughter Smart married in 1752. From 1750 to 1753 Smart directed, under Newbery's auspices, *The Midwife, or The Old Woman's Magazine*, a threepenny journal which ran to 3 vols. In this journal there first appeared Smart's poem 'Care and Generosity; A Fable' (*The Midwife*, ii. 277–8, Sept. 1751). There is apparently no poem by Smart entitled 'Harriet's Birthday'; FB probably refers to 'Ode On the Fifth of December, Being the Birth-Day of a Very Beautiful Young Lady' (first published in *The Student, or the Oxford and Cambridge Monthly Miscellany*, No. 6 (30 June 1750), i. 225). A MS copy of this poem was given to CB by Smart (see Lonsdale, pp. 26–7).

Smart was confined in St Luke's Hospital, 1757–8, and in Potter's madhouse, Bethnal Green, 1759–63. The letter FB here mentions is missing. See Lonsdale, pp. 25–8, 66–8; A. Sherbo, *Christopher Smart: Scholar of the University* (East Lansing, 1967), pp. 46–9, 111–12, 164, and *passim*; also below, pp. 91, 165.

Alas alas! what then is to become of Every body?

How should I know? let every body manage themselves & others as well as I do Nobody, & they will be 'Much the same as God made them!'[2]—And now, Adieu my charmer—[xxxxx 7 *lines*] Adieu then—my fair friend—that's one comfort that I can make you fair or brown at pleasure—Just what I will—a creature of my own forming—I am now ⌐going to⌐ Read[3] the Illiad [*sic*][4]—I cannot help taking notice of one thing in the 3ᵈ Book—which has provoked me for the honour of the sex: Venus tempts Hellen [*sic*] ⌐ [with every][5] delusion in favour of her Darling,—in vain—Riches—power—honour—Love—all in vain — — the enraged Deity threatens to deprive her of her own beauty, & render her to the level with the most common of her sex—blushing & trembling—Hellen immediately yields her Hand.

Thus has Homer proved his opinion of our poor sex—that the Love of Beauty is our most prevailing passion. It really grieves me to think that there certainly must be reason for the insignificant opinion the greatest men have of Women—At least I *fear* there must.—But I don't in fact *believe* it—⌐thank God!⌐

Saturday morn. Septʳ 24 ⌐

[*bottom of page cut away*]

Dinner Bell I declare—

Tuesday—Octʳ 4ᵗʰ

O dear, O dear, the kindest Letter from Mʳ Crisp[6]—if my papa has not the most obdurate, barbarous & inhuman Heart

---

[2] Apparently a quotation, but not certainly identified. Perhaps FB is echoing a sentence from Goldsmith's *Vicar of Wakefield*, chap. 1: 'They are as Heaven made them'.

[3] 'Going to Read' emended to 'Read[in]g' by FBA.

[4] Presumably the trans. (1715–20) by Alexander Pope (1688–1744). CB owned a set of an edn. which was sold at the auction of his library along with a set of Pope's 'Works ... 1751', presumably William Warburton's edn. of that year, and a set of Pope's trans. (with William Broome and Elijah Fenton) of the *Odyssey* (1725–6). The passage FB refers to is at iii. 473–524. See *Lib.*, p. 43.

[5] The bottom of the preceding page has been cut away and 'with every' supplied by FBA for continuity.

[6] Missing.

in the world, he *must* be moved by it to permit some of us to accept his invitation. We are all in Agonies of fear & suspence—waiting with much impatience for papa's return [xxxxx *3 words*] *If* he should refuse us!—I verily believe I shall play truant!—I wish he'd come Home—I shall be *so* happy to see that dearest of men again!—& then Miss Cooke—the good Mrs Hamilton[7] too—*in short*, Chesington all in all. I am going to console myself with reading the Illiad till his return — — Achilles has Just relented, & hastes to the Assistance & succour of the Grecians[8]—is it not a fortunate part?—if only dear papa would *Just so* relent too, I could almost aver that he would give us equal Joy, to that felt by the Greeks at the yielding of Achilles. To be sure the simile is not at all superior. Who will scruple to compare my papa to the *god-like* Achilles?—& who his Daughters to the ⌐valiant¬ Grecians?—'*Long famed for* ⌐*warriors*,¬ *for Beauty more!*'[9] Homer | himself would approve the justice of this Comparison, for Homer himself—was blind!—

⌐Wednesday morn.
Oct. 5th

Papa came in late last Night, we produced the sweet Letter at super & when he had Read it, urged his [SC's] request with all our might—but he gravely & thoughtfully began to talk of the loss he must sustain in business, & the impossibility of his leaving Town when he had so many engagements in it, & so we were obliged to be silent!—

All in the dumps, to Bed we went—very early this morning, Hetty was resolved to make ⟨the attempt⟩ once more, & implore for 2 of us—*She* ⟨urged⟩ us—to go together—it was a long time ere she had Courage to speak—but Just after Breakfast, 'Do you think, sir, said she, that 2 of us could go for a Day or two to Chesington?' 'And pray, said papa, how am I to spare you[10] [xxxxx *3 lines*] 'Sir, answered she, I could go on Friday morn & return ⟨very early⟩ on Monday [xxxxx *2–3 words*]

---

[7] See above, p. 8, n. 24.

[8] This occurs in Bks. xviii and xix.

[9] Probably FB's adaptation of Paris's words to Hector: 'Thus may the *Greeks* review their native Shore, / Much fam'd for gen'rous Steeds, for Beauty more' (iii. 107–8; cf. also iii. 328–9).

[10] With EAB at Lynn EB would be needed to direct the household, and she and FB were also on call as CB's amanuenses.

Papa said nothing [xxxxx *1 line*]—& soon after went out, without another word. So you see we are still in suspense— Papa Dined at Home—I hope to God he means to let us go—if I *am* disappointed at last, I shall entirely give up all⌐ |

[*At this point an undetermined number of pages have been destroyed. The top of the next page has been cut off.*]

We all honour him[11] for his noble openness of heart, sincerity & manly friendliness. I'm sure there is not any thing in the world, I would wish to conceal from him. ⌐Papa has not seen him yet, as he [SC] could not stay late. I am horridly afraid we shall lose him again soon, for Mr. Greville ⟨presses⟩ him to pay a visit at Willbury, in Wiltshire, where his own affairs detain him.

Papa has had a Letter[12] from my Brother[13]—he has wrote a few Lines to us all, he gives us hope of seeing him very soon, I hope to God we shall, for it is long since we have.⌐

Hetty & I are going out to Tea this afternoon, to Mrs Pringle,[14] a widow lady who lives in this street. She is a most sensible, entertaining, clever |

[11] SC. Evidently when he learned that the Burneys could not visit him, he determined to come to London instead.

[12] Missing.

[13] James Burney [JB] (1750–1821), FB's elder brother, had been at sea since Sept. 1760 when, aged 10, he went on board a man-of-war, the *Princess Amelia*, Capt. John Montagu, as a captain's servant. He subsequently served on the *Magnanime*, Capt. Montagu (June–Sept. 1762) and the *Boston* and *Niger*, Capt. Sir Thomas Adams (Sept. 1762–June 1765). In Feb. 1766 he embarked again, this time as a midshipman on the *Aquilon* frigate of 28 guns, Capt. Richard Onslow. The *Aquilon* was to serve principally in the Mediterranean, and returned to England in July 1769.

JB eventually attained the rank of captain (in 1782), but his career was effectively terminated that year when he disobeyed orders in convoying the outward-bound East India fleet. Retired on half-pay in 1785, he never saw active service again. He was to make himself even more of an outcast by his political liberalism, but repeated petitions finally bore fruit, and he was promoted to rear-admiral on the retired list in the last year of his life (1821).

Always of a somewhat reckless nature, JB scandalized his family and acquaintance in 1798 by leaving his wife Sarah and 2 children (see vol. ii) and running off with his half-sister Sarah Harriet Burney. He returned to his wife in 1803. The same year saw the publication of the 1st vol. of his authoritative 5-vol. *Chronological History of the Voyages and Discoveries in the South Sea or Pacific Ocean* (1803–17). This work, still the standard on its subject, goes up to but does not include the voyages of Capt. Cook, though JB accompanied Cook on his 2nd and 3rd voyages (1772–5 and 1776–80). See below, *passim*; *JL* i. 119 n. 11; iv. 204–6; v. 521 n. 10; Manwaring, pp. 4–7 and *passim*; 'Mem.' No. 88.

[14] Veronica née Rennie, widow of Mark Pringle (d. 1761) of Crichton, Midlothian;

[*top of next page cut off*]

[Mrs. Colman][15] wife of the celebrated Author, who is also chief manager of that House, is extremely kind & friendly to us all— we are to Dine at her House on Tuesday. Well, adieu for the present, if I pass an Agreeable Evening, I shall write again at night—or early to morrow—if not—your most obedient, very humble servant to command.

O lord—I've finish'd the Illiad this Age—I never was so charm'd with a poem in my life—I've Read the Odyssey[16] since—& Mr. Hawkesworth's[17] [xxxxx *1 word*] translation of Telemachus—rto which papa subscribed.7 I am going now to Read rMr.7 Hume's[18] History of England, which rI shall begin to read to morrow—well, now adieu at once.7

sometime British Consul at Seville and San Lucar. Veronica Pringle was Mark Pringle's 2nd wife, and his estate went to his eldest son by his 1st wife, John Pringle (d. 1782). Mrs Pringle had 3 sons of her own, for whom see below, *passim*. She and her family continued to live in Poland St. until the end of 1771. FB last saw her in 1775, and she was apparently dead by 1791, as there is no mention of her in the will of her son Robert Pringle, dated 1 Feb. 1791 (PCC, prob. 30 Nov. 1793). See A. Pringle, *The Records of the Pringles or Hoppringills of the Scottish Border* (Edinburgh, 1933), pp. 176–8; *Scots Magazine*, xxiii (1761), 335; Westminster Rate Books for St James's, Westminster Reference Library; below, *passim* and vol. ii.

[15] Sarah Ford (d. 1771), m. (1768) George Colman the elder (1732–94), dramatist, manager of Covent Garden Theatre, 1767–74. Mrs Colman, sometimes described as an actress, had met Colman in 1760 shortly after being deserted by Henry Mossop, an Irish actor, to whom she bore a daughter Harriet (the 'Miss Ford' whom FB mentions below, *passim*). She and Colman began living together about 1761, and in 1762 she bore him a son, George Colman the younger. It was presumably about this time that CB met Colman through their mutual friend, David Garrick. Colman had only recently legitimized his relationship with Miss Ford; they were married by the Revd Richard Penneck on 12 July 1768 at St John's, Southwark. See Highfill, iii. 405–6, 409, 420; Lonsdale, pp. 57–60; *Mem*. i. 204.

[16] See above, p. 37, n. 4.

[17] John Hawkesworth (1720–73), LLD, miscellaneous writer. CB was a subscriber to his translation of *The Adventures of Telemachus, the Son of Ulysses . . . from the French of . . . de la Mothe-Fénelon* (London, 1768). Hawkesworth and CB had been friends since *c*.1748. See Abbott, pp. 132–6 and *passim*; *Mem*. i. 59; below, p. 62 and *passim*.

[18] David Hume (1711–76), the philosopher and historian. His *The History of England, from the Invasion of Julius Caesar to the Revolution in 1688* was published in 6 vols. from 1754 to 1762. CB, whose copy is listed in *Lib.*, p. 32, was a fervent admirer of the work and had contrived to meet Hume when he visited Paris in 1764. Hume afterwards wrote a letter to Ld. Eglinton requesting a musical post for CB (see Lonsdale, pp. 49, 62, 74–5).

Sunday Noon.

We pass'd a very Agreeable Evening at Mrs Pringle's yesterday—Mr Seaton,[19] a very sensible & clever man, & a pro-
didgious admirer of Hetty's, |

[*At this point some pages have been destroyed*.]

^[xxxxx *3–4 words*] He [Seton] is fonder than ever of Hetty, &
amused himself with pressing her fair Hand every other word
while we were in the Coach—perhaps he thought it was too
Dark for *me* to see him. I had a Letter[20] from Miss Lidderdale
yesterday. All charmingly well at Lynn—I couldn't help hearing some thing [xxxxx *2 lines*]^

Tuesday Novr 15

^Sun^day morning, Mrs Pringle called here to invite me to
tea in the afternoon, to meet *the Emperor Tamerlane*;[21] however,
I excused myself on the score of having a little Concert at
night—'Well then, said she, shall he come here!' There was no
saying No—so she agreed that he should be introduced by her
son[22] in the Evening. ^My Cousin [Charles Rousseau Burney]

[19] Alexander Seton (1743–1801), 4th son of Sir Henry Seton (1703–51), 3rd Bt., of
Abercorn, brewer, of Edinburgh. Seton seems to have been in London on business
until 1772 when he returned to Edinburgh upon being given a sublease of the family
brewery. While in London he stayed mostly with his brother-in-law and sister, Capt.
and Mrs Hugh Debbieg (see below). FB's initial good opinion of Seton was to alter
drastically as for the next 2 years she watched the 'fickle' and 'artful' young man dally
with her sister's affections. See the Introduction and below, *passim*; *Roll of Edinburgh
Burgesses and Guild-Brethren, 1761–1841*, ed. C. B. Boog Watson (Edinburgh, 1933),
p. 143; B. G. Seton, *The House of Seton: A Study of Lost Causes* (Edinburgh, 1939), ii. 520–
2 (which erroneously calls Seton the 3rd son and gives his year of birth as 1741;
corrected against Edinburgh parish registers).
[20] Missing.
[21] Played by Mr Mackenzie (below, n. 26). *Tamerlane*, a tragedy by Nicholas Rowe
(1674–1718), poet laureate and dramatist, was first produced in 1701. It was customary
for the play to be performed annually on the 4th or 5th of Nov.; in 1768 it was performed at the Drury Lane Theatre on 4 Nov., besides the amateur production FB here
describes. See *LS 2*, i. 17; *LS 4*, iii. 1365: L. C. Burns, ed., *Tamerlane, a Tragedy by
Nicholas Rowe* (Philadelphia, 1966), pp. 6–7.
[22] Andrew Pringle (d. 1803), Mrs Pringle's second son. He entered the Bengal Army
as a cadet in 1770, attaining the rank of captain in 1781 and resigning in 1792. After
resigning the Service Andrew Pringle became a merchant at Lucknow. He died in
Argyle Street, London, 5 Oct. 1803. See Pringle's will, PCC, prob. Nov. 1803;
A. Pringle, *The Records of the Pringles* . . ., pp. 177, 320, 333; *Scots Magazine*, lxv (1803),
739; V. C. P. Hodson, *List of the Officers of the Bengal Army 1758–1834* (1927–47), ii. 209;
iii. 575, 577.

Dined with us—I really think he improves. In the Evening, Mr.⌐ Cerveto,[23] who plays the Base [very finely][24] [xxxxx *3–4 words*] | [xxxxx *1–2 words*] & his son, came in—&, to grace the whole set, Mr Crisp. We had a charming Concert — — Hetty play'd the piano Forte—Charles the violin, the two Cerveto's the Base, & papa the Organ: & afterwards, we had two solos on the violin cello by young Cerveto, who [xxxxx *1 line*] plays delightfully—&, ⌐my Cousin⌐ shone in a Lesson of papas on the Harpsichord.[25] Mr Pringle & Mr Mackenzie (you must know he is Grandson to the unfortunate Earl of Cromartie,[26] who lost his Estates, &c, in the [xxxxx *1 word*] Rebellion) came in during the performance, drank a dish of Tea—& away again. ⌐The dear Mr. Crisp sup'd with us—or rather, saw us sup, for he never Eat any himself.⌐ Well, now we come to ⌐Monday,⌐ that is, Yesterday. At about 5 o'clock, Hetty & I went to Mrs Pringle's—where we found to our great Joy, Mr Seaton was to be of the party—he is a charming man. |We went ⌐in our Coach, Mrs Pringle, her son, Mr Seaton, & our Lady-ship's [to see the play of Tamerlane acted by young gentlemen at an Academy in Soho Square.]⌐[27] The play was much better

[23] Giacobbe Basevi Cervetto (*c.*1682–1783), Italian composer and violoncellist. By 'base' FB means *basso continuo* or thoroughbass, played by the cello. Upon his arrival in London about 1738 Cervetto, according to CB, 'brought the violoncello into favour, and made us nice judges of that instrument'. Cervetto became solo cellist at Drury Lane, and CB met him when he joined the Drury Lane orchestra in 1744/5. Cervetto's natural son James Cervetto (1747 or 1749–1837) was also a composer and a noted cellist who already 'during childhood surpassed his father in tone and expression'. In 1760 he had appeared at London with EB in a recital of young prodigies. See Mercer, ii, frontis-piece; also ibid. ii. 1005, 1012; *Hist. Mus.* iv. 660, 669; Rees, s.v. Cervetto; *New Grove*; Lonsdale, pp. 10–11, 54; Scholes, i. 98.

[24] Inserted by FBA.

[25] Perhaps one of CB's *Six Sonatas or Lessons for the Harpsichord*, pub. in 1761 (see Scholes, i. 101, ii. 344, 345).

[26] George Mackenzie (*c.*1703–66), 3rd E. of Cromartie or Cromarty, 1731. For his part in the Rising of 1745 he was in 1746 sentenced to death for high treason, whereby his estates and peerage became forfeited; he received, however, a conditional pardon in 1749. The Earl, much impoverished in his later years, died at No. 7 Poland St. on 28 Sept. 1766.

The 3rd Earl seems to have had no legitimate (or illegitimate) grandson named Mackenzie. Probably the person in question was Kenneth Mackenzie (d. 1796), grand-son of the 2nd Earl, who in 1789 inherited the Cromartie estates (since restored to the family). See *Scots Peerage*, iii. 77–8, 82–3.

[27] Inserted by FBA. Soho Academy, at No. 8 Soho Square, was founded in 1717 by Martin Clare. Currently run by Dr Cuthbert Barwis (d. 1782), it was 'one of the most celebrated and successful of [18th-c.] private boarding schools'. The Academy was particularly known for its performances of Shakespeare's plays, which were regularly

perform'd than I expected, and the Dresses were superb—
made new for the purpose, by the members of the society, and
proper for the Characters & Country—that is after the Turkish
manner. The Farce too was very well done. ⌐I'm sure,¬ we
were much entertain'd—Mr Seaton was so very clever—droll,
& entertaining, you can't imagion. When the performance was
over, *Tamerlane* came to me, to open the Ball!—⌐God,¬ I was
frighten'd to Death—I beg'd & besought him not [to begin]²⁸—
he said one of the members always did—however, I prevail'd,
after much fuss, to put Hetty & Andrew first, & we were
second. I assure you, I danced *like any thing*—& call'd the
second Dance—[xxxxx *2–3 words*] after which, I hopped about
with the utmost ease and chearfulness. ⌐Every now & then ˡ [I]
stole a word or two with Mr. Seaton—you can't imagion how
much he admires Hetty—he followed her up & down the
Room, & chatted at every interval of Dancing. All in all, we
spent a very agreeable Evening. We came in just before 2 in the
morn. Mr. Seaton & Andrew walk'd after the Chair.

This morning, [xxxxx ½ *line*] Mr. Mackenzie, *my Emperor*, as
Mrs. Pringle calls him, came to *know if I caught cold*, sat about
half an Hour, & away again.¬

They were very perfect in the play, except in one speech; the
young Gentleman who perform'd Selima, stopt short, & forgot
himself—it was in a Love scene—between her — — him I
mean & Axalla—who was very tender²⁹—She—he—soon
recover'd tho'—Andrew whisper'd us, that when it was over—
'*He'd lick her*!—' St[r]atocles, amused himself with no other
action ˡ ⌐at all,¬ but beating, with one Hand, his Breast, & with
the other, held his Hat. I'm sure, I was ready to die with
laughter at some of them. Arpatia & Moneses We all thought
were best perform'd. Tamerlane was *midling*. he seems to be
about 20—niether handsome or ugly, Agreeable or disagreeable, & on the whole, very tolerable.

---

presented by the boys. It remained at No. 8 Soho Square till 1805, when it either closed
or moved to premises elsewhere. See *Survey of London*, xxxiii. 61.

²⁸ Inserted by FBA.

²⁹ This love scene occurs at the end of Act I. Stratocles appears immediately after in
the first scene of Act II; presumably the actor beat his breast as Stratocles describes the
captive Bajazet to Moneses: '. . . but oh! to speak / The Rage, the Fierceness, and the
Indignation!— / It bars all Words, and cuts Description short' (Rowe, *Tamerlane*, 1757
edn., p. 29).

Thursday Nov[r] [17][30]

┌I find that the play we saw at the Academy was performed once before, & again yesterday, in tolerable ⟨manner⟩—Mrs. Pringle, who was her chaperon, presented Hetty with a Ticket, who had the pleasure of Dancing with Mr. Seaton, with whom she was in raptures. Tamerlane enquired much, she says after me. [xxxxx 2½ *lines*] He [Seton] admires her [EB] of all things and they chatted much more than they Danced, & he was not a little gallant┐ | ┌&┐ she, ┌in return,┐ is quite charm'd with him. [He called with a message from Mrs. Pringle this morning][31] and I had the pleasure of a delightful *Tete a Tete* with him—for Hetty was out, & Susette kept up stairs. I am really half in love with him. He is so sensible, clever, entertaining.—His person is very far from recommending him to favour—he is little, & *far* from handsome, but has a sensible Countenance, & appears quite an Adonis, after ½ an Hours conversation. Do you know, he actually stay'd above 3 Hours with me?—┌[xxxxx 2 *lines*] I own to you [xxxxx 3 *words*] that my vanity is in some measure flatter'd by his Company, that a man┐ of his superior sense & cleverness, should think me worth so much of his time is much more than ever I had reason to | expect. He ask'd me, if my sister & self were engaged to M[rs] Pringle's this Afternoon?

'No—not that I know of, at least.'

'No?—why M[rs] Pringle promised me I should meet Miss Burney & you there this Evening. But she's a strange Woman;—┌that she is indeed—┐she has an excellent Heart, & understanding, but she is not well versed in ┌politeness.┐ But however, I wish I could know if you ladies were to be there—because if I go at a venture, I may be disappointed, & then so much time is thrown Away. I hope Miss Burney caught no Cold last night, ┌for she came away, Just after a Dance?┐'

F. 'No, Sir, I believe not. But you fared worse, I fear, it rain'd very hard, & Hetty says you could not get a Chair or Coach.'

M[r] S. 'Why I could have managed that better! There were but 2 Chairs to be had—Miss Crawford,[32] a young Lady who was with M[rs] Pringle, offer'd to go | in the same Chair with

---

[30] FB has incorrectly written '16'. Cf. below, p. 50.

[31] Inserted by FBA.

[32] Spelled 'Craufurd' in FBA's 'List of Persons and Things' for 1768 and 1769; sister of EB's admirer Mr Crawford or Craufurd. Not further identified.

herself—& then Miss Burney could have taken me into her's. But she would not consent to it at all—& I see you Laugh too! I am afraid I made an improper proposal—'

F. 'Improper! why surely you only ⌐rallied.'¬

Mʳ S. 'No indeed. It is very common in Scotland, & in truth I know nothing of the English punctilios. Perhaps it was wrong. I fear'd so at the Time, when Miss Burney refused me, & you can't imagion how much it chagrined me. But I see few young ladies, & often fear I make myself either particular³³ or ridiculous.'

F. 'Indeed, when my sister told me of it, I very naturally concluded you could only have made such a proposal in Jest.'

He caught up the words—*when my sister told me of it*—'O, said he, how much I would give to hear some of your private Conversations! I dare say they are very ⌐ curious; & the remarks you each make, I am sure must be very clever. I don't doubt but you sometimes take me to task!'

F. 'I see you are now *fishing*, to draw out our sentiments: but I shall be on my gaurd [*sic*]!'

⌐Mr. S. 'Ay, now I see at once! I am sure I am rather disliked, by your Care to conceal from me your opinion.'

F. 'O but my concealing it, tells you nothing, for if we dislike you, politeness occasions it, & if, on the contrary, we praise you, we would fear raising your vanity, to *tell* you of it!'

Mr. S. 'O how slyly you escaped!¬ I hesitated some time, to know whether I should call ⌐here¬ or not, for it is customary in my Country to do so many things which appear singular here, that I am continually at a loss, & should esteem it a most particular favour, if you would have the goodness to tell me honestly at once, when you see me making any of these gross mistakes.' ⌐

F. 'I'm sure it would be highly vain & conceited in *us* to pretend to Advise *you*.'

Mʳ S. 'Quite the Contrary. And if I had the pleasure of hearing some of your private Chats, I doubt not I should make myself quite another Creature: for then, what you blamed, I would amend, & what you were pleased to be contented with, I would confirm myself in.'

F. 'But *correction* should come from a superior—in Character I

³³ i.e., peculiar, singular, odd, strange; an obsolete usage (*OED* s.v. Particular *a.* 7c).

mean—for merely to hear that *we* either approved or con-
demn'd does not make you either better or worse, as it may
most likely, proceed from caprice, fancy, or want of Judgement.'

Mr S. 'I beg your pardon—I doubt not your capacity to amend
me at all: And as I am really a stranger to the manners of the
English, it would be great goodness. I am so little in Company
with young Ladies (scarce know 5) that I have not observed
their little peculiaritys, &c. The truth is, the young women
here, are so mortally silly & insipid, that I cannot bear them.
Upon my word, except you & your sister, I have scarse met
with one worthy being spoke to. Their Chat is | All on Caps—
Balls—Cards—Dress—nonsense.'

F. 'Upon *my* word, you are unmercifully severe.

Mr S. 'Nay, it's truth. You have sensible Women here but then,
they are very Devils—Censorious, uncharitable, sarcastick—
The women in Scotland, have twice—thrice their freedom,
with *all* their virtue—& are very conversable & agreeable—
their educations are more finish'd: In England, I was quite
struck to see how forward the Girls are made—A Child of 10
years old, will chat & keep you Company, while her parents are
busy or out &c—with the ease of a woman of 26. But then, how
does this education go on?—Not at all: it absolutely stops
short. Perhaps, I have been very unfortunate in my Acquaintance but so it is, that you & your sister are almost the only
"Girls" I have met who could keep up any Conversation—& I
vow, if I had gone into almost any other House, & talk'd at this
rate to a young lady, she would have been sound a sleep by this
Time; Or at least, she would have | amused me with gaping &
yawning, "all the time," & certainly, she would not have understood a word I had utter'd.

F. 'And so, this is your opinion of our sex?—'

Mr S. 'Ay;—& of *mine*, too.'

F. 'Why you are absolutely a man Hater, a misanthrope.'

Mr S. 'Quite the contrary. Nobody enjoys better spirits—or
more happiness—'

F. 'Then assuredly you have advanced most of these severe
Judgements, merely for Argument, & not as your real thoughts.
You know, we continually say things to support an Opinion,
which we have given, that in reality we don't above half mean.'

Mr S. 'I grant you I may have exaggerated—but nothing more. Look at your Ladies of Quality—Are they not forever parting with their Husbands—forfeiting their reputations—& is their life aught but disipation? In common genteel Life, indeed, you may now & then meet with very fine Girls—who have politeness, sense & conversation—but *these* are few—& then look at your Trademen's Daughters—what ¹ are they?—poor Creatures indeed! all pertness, imitation & folly.'

I said a great deal in *defence* of our poor sex—& *all* I could say—but It sounds so poor compared to my *opponent*, that I dare not write it.

Mr S. 'And what are you studying here? said he—O ho, "Marianne?"³⁴ And did you ever Read "le paysan parvenu?" There are the two best novels that ever were wrote, for they are pictures of nature, and therefore excell your Clarissas & Grandison's far away. Now Sir Charles Grandison is all perfection, & consequently, the last Character we find in real Life. In truth there's no such thing.

F. 'Indeed! do you really think a Sir Charles Grandison *never* existed?'

Mr S. 'Certainly not. He's too perfect for human Nature.

F. 'It quite hurts me to hear any body declare a really & throughly good man never Lived. It is so *much* to the disgrace of mankind.'

Mr S. 'Ay, you are too young to conceive it's truth. I own to you, you are therefore more happy. I would give all I am worth to have the ¹ same innocence & credulity of Heart, I had some years since; & to be able to go thro' Life with it.'

F. 'But if, as you assert, nobody around you would be the same, would not *that* innocence rather expose you to danger, than encrease your happiness.

Mr S. 'Faith I don't know; since you *must* be exposed to it at all events. Besides, when once—which *every* body must be—you are convinced of the wickedness & deceit of men, it is impossible to preserve untainted your *own* innocence of Heart. Experience *will* prove the depravity of mankind, & the

³⁴ *La Vie de Marianne, ou les Aventures de Madame la comtesse de* * * * (Paris and The Hague, 1731–41), by Pierre Carlet de Chamberlain de Marivaux (1688–1763). His *Le Paysan parvenu, ou les Mémoires de M* * * *, appeared at Paris, 1734–5. *Clarissa, or the History of a Young Lady*, by Samuel Richardson (1689–1761) was published at London, 1747–8, and his *The History of Sir Charles Grandison* in 1753–4. See *Lib.*, p. 31.

conviction of it only serves to Create distrust, suspicion—caution:—& sometimes causelessly.'

F. 'But surely this experience has it's advantages as well as inconveniences, since without it you are liable to be ensnared in every trap which, according to *your* Account of mankind, they put in your way.'

Mr S. 'Assuredly. But depend upon it, no one need fear missing this experience!'

F. 'You seem to have a most shocking opinion of the world in general.'

Mr S. 'Because the world in General merits it. The *most* innocent time must be the Rise of any state, when they are unacquainted with vice. Now Rome, in it's infancy—'

F. 'O *that* was not the most florishing time of Rome, for in it's infancy it was inhabited merely by villains & Ruffians.'

Mr S. 'O but they soon forgot that, in forming their state; & established excellent Laws, & became models of morality, liberty, virtue.'

F. 'Yes; & the first proof they gave of their virtue, was to murder their founder,[35] to whom they were indebted for every thing—& farther to rob the nieghbouring states of their wives & Daughters, whom they forcibly detain'd. I can't say you have hit on the best Country to shew the innocence of it's first state.

Mr S. 'O, you are too hard upon me! Well then, the rise of the Grecian Cities—they certainly were virtuous in their Infancy. And so are all nations in proportion to their poverty; for money is the source of the greatest vice, & that Nation which is most rich, is most wicked.

F. 'But, Sir, this is saying, in reality, Nothing for virtue; since if these people you mention were only virtuous thro' necessity, & as wicked as they could be, they are in fact full as vicious as *any* Country whatever.'

Mr S. 'That's very true. In short I believe there was always the

---

[35] FB presumably refers to Romulus, the mythical founder of Rome with his brother Remus. Plutarch in his life of Romulus recounts the legend of Romulus's mysterious disappearance in the thirty-eighth year of his reign, which led to the suspicion that he had been murdered by the Roman senators who cut up his body and took away the pieces. He also tells the familiar story of the Rape of the Sabine Women. See Plutarch's 'Life of Romulus', translated by James Smalwood, 'Dryden translation', 1758 edn., i. 66–70, 89, 95.

same degree of real (tho' there could not be of practical) vice in all mankind, in all Countrys, & at all Ages, as at present.'

F. 'You must give me leave again to repeat that I fancy you inveigh this violently against the world *partly* at least in order to support your own side of the question: for surely any person who really & truly *thought* so like a misanthrope as you *talk*, must abhor mankind, & shut themselves up in a Cave, away from them all. You absolutely appear to be the greatest satirist, & most severe Judger of the world—'

Mʳ S. 'O no. I assure you, nobody Lives happier in it—or Can have greater or more equal spirits. But I can see the faults of people nevertheless.' ⌐

F. 'Permit me to say one thing, Sir: You tell me that you are a stranger ⌐here,⌐ that you know not the manners of the Ladies here; that you don't know *this*—are ignorant of *that* — — a Lady's going Home after a Ball, for example!—well Sir, give me leave to ask what you *have* observed? why even all our faults! you have not been very blind to *them*, or taken much Time to find them Out! You seem to have taken the ⌐bad⌐ side of the question all the way.'

Mʳ S. 'O Ma'am, your most obedient. — — But ⌐good God⌐ (looking at his Watch) what a Time have I detained you from your employments by my tongue! But it is so seldom I can find Ladies who, like you & your sister, can keep up a Conversation, that I am loath to lose them when I do: & I do protest, that to talk with a young lady who will answer me with the sense & reason that you do now, gives me far more pleasure than all the plays, operas or diversions in the world: for none of them can be compared to a sensible, spirited Conversation.'

I should be ashamed to write down these ⟨mu⟩ch un-deserved, *outré* compliments, but ⌐ that they are made, as you see, only when they were unavoidable, & consequently become no compliment at all. I am quite surprised to find how much of his Conversation I have remembered but as there was only him & myself, it was not very difficult.

⌐12 o'clock [midnight]

Waiting for papa to come Home, who is gone to see the Hip-pocrite,[36] ⟨a new⟩ play. We have not been to Mrs. Pringle's, but

[36] *The Hypocrite*, by Isaac Bickerstaffe (d. ?1812), based on Colley Cibber's *The*

are to go to morrow to meet Mr. Seaton there, who, she says, is *quite* in Love with Hetty. Mr. Crisp has been here this Evening. He looks vastly well, & was so kind and as amiable as ever. Well, I think I have wrote enough in Conscience for one Day. ⌐

Saturday—Nov^r [19]^37

⌐We passed the most curious Evening yesterday, to be sure, that can be imagioned: never, sure, did any Conversation seem more like a scene in a Comedy. But in order to give you any idea of it, I must tell you some thing of what pass'd on Wednesday, when Hetty was at the Play & Ball again in Soho Square.

You must know, Mrs. Pringle had engaged her, ⟨when⟩ she went, to Dance with Mr. Crawford,^38 a young⌐ |

[*The extant Journal for 1768 breaks off here. The day after the last entry, 20 Nov., FB's stepmother gave birth at Lynn to FB's half-brother Richard Thomas Burney. On 13 Oct. EAB had written a letter to FB (Berg) commending the unborn infant to FB's care in case she should die: 'Allow me my dear Fanny to take this moment (if there proves occasion) to recommend a helpless Infant to your Pity and Protection, you will ev'ry day become more and more Capable of the Task— & you will, I do trust you will, for your same dear Father's sake, cherish & support His Innocent Child—'tho but half allied to you—My Weak Heart speaks in Tears to you my Love, . . .' The letter shows again EAB's appreciation of FB's 'feeling heart' and also her sense of distance from CB's children. This estrangement, due in part at least to EAB's emotional and domineering nature, was to worsen as time went on.*

In her letter EAB also mention's a 'Cap' from FB for the unborn child as well as a letter FB has addressed to it. There exists in the Berg a comical letter written by MA as if in reply from FB's new brother. MA has the new-born child acknowledge FB's letter and gift, putting in his mouth the phrases of broken English spoken by the foreign musicians and singers who came to CB's house: 'Master Newcome's Affectionate Lov[e] to his sister Fanny is Extremely obliged to her for kind Letter which was delivered to him the minute he made his first Appearance in the World. . . . She likevise do him grate honour to send him de Joli Bonnet which was de first he did port on his tete . . . As he is one man of Business he hope She will Excuse de long lettre from him . . . her affectionate Broter Bernai.']

Non-Juror. It was premièred at Drury Lane on Thursday, 17 Nov. 1768, and was performed 15 more times during the season (*LS 4* iii. 1368 and *passim*).

^37 FB has incorrectly written '18th'.

^38 Also spelled 'Craufurd' in FBA's 'List of Persons and Things' for 1768. Mr Crawford was an 'Admirer' of EB, who did not return his admiration. He has not been further identified. See below, *passim*, and vol. ii.

AJ (Early Diary, ii, paginated 67--[112], foliated 1–47, Berg), Journal for
1769.
Originally probably a cahier of double sheets sewn through spines. In
general the first leaves seem to have been cut out, some discarded or 'burnt',
and some preserved with the second leaves (or second half of the cahier) discarded. Now 35 single sheets 4to, 70 pp., with 7 paste-overs. A light blue
folder has replaced an earlier dark blue one; the second leaf of the dark blue
remains, attached to the back flyleaf of the original cahier. *Entitled* (*by FBA*):
Juvenile Diary | N° 2 | 1769
   In her 'List of Persons' for 1769 FBA includes three names not in the extant
journal: 'Dr. Bagge', 'Capt. Pringle' (see below, p. 99), and the 'Rev^d Mr.
Pugh' (below, p. 107). The first is Charles Bagge (1715–91), DD, Vicar of St
Margaret and St Nicholas, Lynn, 1755–91, who officiated at the wedding of
Brigg Fountaine and Mary Hogg on 29 June 1769 (below, p. 78).

[Sa]turday, Jany 7th

O dear! O dear! how melancholy has been to us this last
week, the first of this year! never during my life have I suffer'd
more severely in my mind, I do verily believe.—But God be
praised! I hope it is now over!
   The poor Susette, who I told you was disappointed of her
Lynn Journey by a violent cold, was Just put to bed somewhat
better when I wrote to you this Day se'night—I soon after went
to her, & found her considerably worse, she talk'd to me in a
most affecting style, her voice & manner were peculiarly
touching[1] — — 'My dear Fanny, cried she, I love you dearly
— — my *dear* sister!—have I any *more* sisters?—' O how I was
terrified—shock'd—surpris'd!—'O yes! continued she, I have
sister Hetty—but I don't wish her to come to me now, because
she'll want me to Drink—& I can't—but I will if *you* want
me—& where's papa?' For my Life I could not speak a word, &
almost choak'd myself¹ to prevent my sobbing [½ *line torn away*]
O dear!—I shall die! — —' 'My *dear* Gi[rl] [?you *can't*!—']² 'O
but I must though!—But I can't help it—it is not my fault you

¹ The apothecary Heckford diagnosed SEB's illness as 'an Inflammation of the
Breast' (below, p. 53). SEB from childhood had 'a fearful tendency to a consumptive
habit', and CB had taken her with her sister EB to France in 1764 partly in hopes that
the change of climate would do her good (*Mem.* i. 154).
² Two or three words have been torn away here.

know!—' Tho' I almost suffocated myself with smothering my grief, I believe she perceived it, for she kiss'd me, & again said 'How I love you! my *dear* Fanny!—I love you dearly!' 'My sweet Girl! cried I—you—you *can't* love me so much as I do you!—' 'If I was Charly[3] I should love you.—indeed I should — — Oh!—I shall die!—' 'But not *yet*, my dear Love—not *yet*!—' 'O yes. I shall!—I should like to see papa first tho'!'

In short, she talk'd in a manner *inconceivably* affecting—& how greatly I was shock'd, *no* words can express—My dear Papa out of Town too!—we sent immediately for Mr Heckford,[4] an excellent Apothecary, who has attended Our Family many years—He bled her immediately, & said it would not be safe to omit it—She continued much the same some Hours—between 1 & 2 I went to Bed, as she was sleeping, & Hetty & the [m]aid[5] sat up all night, for Hetty was very urgen[t] ¦ that I should.—She had a shocking night!—at 7 o'clock Mr Heckford was again call'd—she had a blister put on her Back, & he beg'd that a physician might be directly applied to, as she was in a very dangerous way!—O my good God! what did poor Hetty & myself suffer!—Dr. Armstrong[6] was sent for—& my good Aunt Nanny, who is the best Nurse in England, tender, careful & affectionate & but too well experienced in illness[7] — — we were much inclined to send an express after my dear Papa to

[3] FB's youngest sister Charlotte. If SEB died FB would take her place as Charlotte's next older sister and female companion and guide in the family.

[4] William Heckford (d. 1797), apothecary. At this time he lived in Broad St. near Poland St. Heckford became well-to-do by his practice and had a residence in Twickenham, where he was a Justice of the Peace. Master of the Society of Apothecaries in 1792–3, he was buried at Twickenham, 25 Nov. 1797. See C. R. B. Barrett, *The History of the Society of Apothecaries of London* (1905), pp. 150, 159–60; E. Ironside, *The History and Antiquities of Twickenham* (1797), p. 149; R. S. Cobbett, *Memorials of Twickenham* (1872), p. 74; Heckford's will, PCC, prob. 23 Dec. 1797; Westminster Rate Books for St James's, Westminster Reference Library; Twickenham Rate Books; MS 'Registers of Freedom Admissions', Guildhall Library; Thomas Mortimer, *Universal Director* (1763), p. 58.

[5] Not further identified.

[6] John Armstrong (*c.*1709–79), MD, poet, physician, and essayist; author of a celebrated didactic poem, *The Art of Preserving Health* (1744). CB had met Armstrong in London *c.*1747, and it was Armstrong who in 1751 advised CB to go to the country for his health, advice which led to CB's accepting the post of organist at Lynn, where he remained until 1760. See Lonsdale, pp. 29, 36—7; also W. J. Maloney, *George and John Armstrong of Castleton* (Edinburgh, 1954), *passim*.

[7] Perhaps an allusion to the last illness of Mrs Gregg, who had been buried only the previous Dec. Ann Burney and her sister Rebecca also had an elderly mother (Mrs Ann [Cooper] Burney) to care for in York St.

Lynn, but resolved to wait while we possibly could. Unfortunately, M^r, M^rs & ⌐little Miss⌐ Young[8] all came very early to spend the Day here—I never went *to* them, or *from* Susy, till Dinner, & then I could Eat none. Never, I believe, shall I forget the shock I received that Night—her Fever increased—she could not swallow her medicines, she was quite delirious—Mr Heckford said indeed she had a *very* poor chance of recovery! — — — He endeavour'd himself to give her physick, which he said was *absolutely* necessary, but in vain—she rambled—Breath'd short, & was terribly suffering—her disorder | he pronounced an Inflammation of the Breast—when he found it impossible to give her any thing—'I am sorry to say it, said he, but indeed at *best* she stands a *very* poor chance!' I felt my Blood freeze—I ran out of the Room in an anguish beyond *thought* — — & all I could do was to almost rave—& pray,—in such an Agony!—O what a night she had! We all sat up—she slept perpetually without being at all refresh'd, & now was *so* light-Headed!—I kept behind her pillow, & fed her with Barly water in a Tea spoon the whole Night, without her knowing of it at all—indeed she was dreadfully bad! On Monday however, the Dr. & Apothecary thought her *somewhat* better, tho' in great danger—we all sat up again—⌐We⌐ wrote to papa,[9] not daring to conceal the News, while her Life was thus uncertain—on Tuesday, they ventured to pronounce her out of danger—We made Hetty go to Bed, & my Aunt & I sat up again—& on Wednesday, we two went to Bed, the dear Girl continuing to mend, which she has, tho' very slowly, ever since. My beloved Papa & mama have both wrote to us quite, kindly— |

[*Possibly some pages have been discarded here. For the following passage FBA has substituted another, dated 'Jan' — Tuesday' and 'Wednesday', and mentioning SEB's continuing recovery and CB's return from Lynn.*]

⌐O my dear, I have heard of a Gentleman who walk'd in the Park[10] on Sunday [?15 Jan.] *purposely* to look out for Hetty the fair, & Fanny the Brown—he kept so earnestly on the *watch*,

---

[8] Emended by FBA to 'Miss Mary Young', i.e., Mary Young (1766—1851), eldest daughter of Arthur and Martha (Allen) Young, sister of EAB (see above, p. 3; n. 10; Gazley, p. 24; *AR*, xciii. 333).

[9] This letter and the replies from CB and EAB are all missing.

[10] Probably St James's Park, the most fashionable of the day.

that he was suspected to be seeking for a *mistress* — — this Gentleman, my dear, is Mr. S — —

Nay, my child, who are you thinking of? Why it was only papa's old friend Mr. Sheperd."[11]

Thursday, Jan. 19th

Well, my dear Creature, we have great hopes & expectations of happiness to-morrow—Susette is *quite* [?well]—"Letters from Lynn speak them the same[12] — — I wonder what Company Mrs. Pringle will have—Well I shall soon know"— Adieu *pour le present*.

Saturday, Jan[y] 21st

There was a very great Party at M[rs] Pringle's, "all the Company who were present at our last visit, except one, & several others. This one] was Mr. Seton. Mrs. Pringle told to do that *her Beau*, as she calls him, call'd here just before, but she would not let him in. You are sure, she *but* thank'd her kindly!—She gave for reason want of room—Want of non-sence? [xxxxx *4 words*] or if not, why not dispence with some other? If she had left out half a dozen of her Gentlemen, & invited him, I dare answer they Would not have been miss'd."

We Danced till 2 o'clock this morning. M[r] Crawford with Hetty, & a M[r] Armstrong[13] with me who made me Laugh to

---

[11] Probably Antony Shepherd (1721–96); DD (Cantab.), 1766; Plumian Professor of Astronomy at Cambridge. CB's friendship with Shepherd, of which this is the earliest mention, reflects his lifelong interest in astronomy. He may have consulted Shepherd while preparing *An Essay towards a History of the Principal Comets that have appeared since the year 1742*, published later this year. Shepherd later became a Canon of Windsor and showed FB some unwelcome attentions while she was at Court. See Lonsdale, pp. 80–3, 497–8; below, *passim*; *DL* iii. 316 and *passim*.

[12] FBA has inserted that SEB is 'to go to Lynn where Mama & Charttie & Bessy & Miss Allen will pass the Winter'. 'Charttie' is either a slip or another nickname for Charlotte Ann Burney. CB and EAB probably agreed to keep Charlotte at Lynn as a playmate for Bessy Allen, since she and Bessy were almost exactly the same age and much younger than their brothers and sisters. Years later, however, MAR recalled EAB's favouritism towards Bessy and 'severity' towards Charlotte, that 'frightend her either into sulleness or made her guilty of Falsehood', while MAR was 'the only one who took notice of her' (MAR to FB 8 Mar. 1786, Berg). In 1771 Charlotte was 'put to school in the neighbourhood' of Lynn (below, p. 170).

[13] FBA has added 'a young man with a fine person, & a handsome face'. Apparently no relation to Dr Armstrong, the young Mr Armstrong may have been a connection of the 'William Armstrong, Esq.' (not further traced) who in 1768 lived around the corner

so immoderate a degree that I was quite ashamed; for he aim'd
at being a wit, & yet kept so settled a solemn Countenance,
with languishing Eyes that he made himself quite ridiculous.
⌐There was one Gentleman,[14] a Cousin of Mr. Crawford's,¬ |

*[At the end of the page FBA has noted 'P./4. & 5. Burnt', i.e., fos. 4 and 5.
The foliation jumps from 3 to 6.]*

[Dr Armstrong I see now—at last, with][15] real pleasure—for I
have seen him lately with a very contrary feeling. He ask'd
Susette many questions concerning her Health—'I can tell
you, said he, you have had a very narrow escape!—you was
Just gone!—the Gates of Heaven were in view—' 'O, cried I,
they shut them on her—I fancy she was not good enough to
enter!—' 'O yes, answered he, they were very ready to receive
her there—but I would not let her depart,—I thought she
might as well stay here a little while longer.' |

[bottom of page cut away]

⌐[xxxxx *2 lines*] we left the Park early—I was some steps behind
the rest but as we came out suddenly who should accost me
but Mr. Seton—who I imagion'd was at the End of the world.
He accompanied us Home—He again lamented with prodidgious civility His long absence—& other speeches to that
purport—Mrs. Pringle I doubt not has quite given *him up*—we
ask'd about her, he said, with a significant sort of smile, that he
had call'd on her, he believed, a hundred times, but *never found
her at Home*.¬ |[16]

[bottom of page cut away]

Thursday Feb[y] 9th

⌐We Drank Tea at Mrs. Strange's[17] & pass'd a very agreeable
Evening—Their acquaintance, Mr. Seton,[18] was there—he is
from the Burneys in Great Marlborough St. (Westminster Rate Books for St James's,
Westminster Reference Library).

[14] Probably the 'Mr. Craufurd, Cousin of Hetty's old Admirer', mentioned below,
p. 243. Not identified.

[15] Inserted by FBA.

[16] This apparent fall from favour (for reasons unknown) was only temporary.

[17] Isabella Lumisden (1719–1806), sister of Andrew Lumisden (see vol. ii), secretary
to the Old Pretender at Rome; m. (1747) Robert Strange (1721–92), the engraver,
knighted 1787. Mrs Strange's fervent Jacobitism long stood in the way of her husband's

[See p. 56 for n. 17 cont. and n. 18]

no Relation, I believe, to Mrs. Pringle's 'squire—he doats on music—of which we had a great deal. Hetty play'd & sang almost every song in the buona Figliuola[19]—he is really an agreeable man. Mrs. Strange is remarkably [xxxxx *1 word*], entertaining & witty—her *sposa* does not shine much in Conversation, charming as his Points all are—but I believe is a good natured & sensible man—His Daughter[20] too possesses no very striking accomplishments, but is very talented—there was more Company, but as they had not the honour of engaging *my* attention, I shall not let them ⟨spirit out⟩ yours.ᵀ

Monday—Febʸ 13ᵗʰ

The ever charming—engaging—beloved Mʳ Crisp spent the whole Day with us Yesterday—I love him more than [ev]er—every Time I see him I cannot help saying so—Never¹ can there have been a more truly amiable man—he appears [to] take a

advancement at home. From 1760 to 1765 Strange was studying and working in France and Italy, and it was during this absence from England that CB probably undertook the musical instruction of his eldest daughter Mary Bruce (see below), who with her brothers and sister was being reared by Mrs Strange. Mrs Strange, whose 'powerful understanding', 'goodness', and 'wit' are extolled by both CB and FB, witnessed the marriage of CB and his 2nd wife in 1767, and the Burneys and Stranges remained firm friends for the rest of their lives. From 1767 to 1775 the Stranges lived at No. 14 Castle Street, Leicester Fields. See *Mem.* i. 195, 205, 293; 'Mem.' No. 113; *JL* i. 142 n. 13; Dennistoun, ii. 69, 179, and *passim*; below, *passim*.

¹⁸ Probably Strange's fellow Scot and artist John Thomas Seaton (*c.*1738–living 1806). Seaton exhibited portrait paintings at the Society of Artists, London from 1761 to 1777, and at the Royal Academy in 1774. From 1776 to 1785 he practised successfully in India. See D. Foskett, *A Dictionary of British Miniature Painters* (1972), i. 499; Thieme; E. Waterhouse, *The Dictionary of British 18th Century Painters in Oils and Crayons* (1981), p. 340.

¹⁹ *La Cecchina, ossia La buona figliuola*, comic opera by Niccolò Piccinni (1728–1800), libretto by Carlo Goldoni (1707–93). The opera was premièred with great success at Rome in 1760, and became the most popular comic opera of the mid-century. CB was to meet Piccinni at Naples in 1770. A copy of 'La Buona Figliuola, *Piccini*', perhaps the arrangement for voice and harpsichord used by EB, is listed in *Mus. Lib.*, p. 7. See *New Grove*; *LS 4* ii. 1199, iii. 1381; *Tours*, i. 245–6; Mercer, ii. 974.

²⁰ Mary Bruce Strange (1748–84). She alone of the Stranges' 5 children inherited some of the father's artistic talent; in 1764–5 she competed for the drawing prize of the Society for the Encouragement of Arts. FB described her in 1775 as 'far from a shining character' but 'estimable', and 'improved much on acquaintance' (vol. ii). In 1770 she and her father witnessed the wedding of EB and Charles Rousseau Burney. Though courted by a Dr Craufurd in 1777–8, Miss Strange died unmarried in 1784 (coincidentally on the same day as Dr Johnson). Two letters survive from her to FB, dated Paris, 7 Aug. 1776 and 25 Jan. 1778 (Barrett). See Dennistoun, ii. 199 and *passim*; *DL* ii. 282–3; *JL* i. 142 n. 13.

parental interest in our affairs, & I do believe ⟨loves⟩ us all with a really fatherly affection—the frankness—the sincerity with which he corrects & reproves us, is more grateful to me, than the most flattering professions could be, because it is far, far more seriously & really kind and ⌐friendly⌐—He protests he will take no denial from Papa for Hetty & me to go to Chesington this summer ⌐*approchant*,⌐ & told Papa to remember that he had *bespoke* us: I fancy he is wearied of asking almost, & I am sure my dear papa is tired of refusing—for what in the world can be more disagreeable, more painful to a mind generous & good as his? — — I declare I am almost ashamed to hear Chesington mention'd before him, & cannot for my life Join in intreaties to go; tho' my Heart prompts me most *furiously*, ⌐but I can say nothing more—⌐

⟨Valentine's⟩ Day
Feby 14

⌐[xxxxx *3 lines*] | [xxxxx ½ *line*] pass our Window this morning before I was up.—Don't you imagion I was prodidgious Curious to know his Christian Name? that so important a thing should be denied to me! [xxxxx *1 line*] a Pair of Gloves & a Copy of verses, the most passionate & tender imagionable on this occasion. Notwithstanding the Hand, &c, are apparently disguised, I am almost certain it is Mr. Seton's contrivance,—for the last Time we saw him, we talk'd of these very kind of Gloves, which are a particular sort.[21] Hetty vows she will wear them next Monday in the Park if possible—

The dear Susy & all at Lynn are well—I saw my grand Daddy Crisp for a moment to Day—it is late, & I must haste to Bed, as Papa will want a very early breakfast to morrow.⌐

Poland Street Feby 16.

How delightful, how enviable a tranquility and content do I at present enjoy!—I have scarse a wish, ⌐and am happy & easy as my Heart can desire. ⌐My Papa has more Business of late than ever, [& he is] almost always out[22]—[xxxxx 2½ *lines*] Hetty

---

[21] i.e., fur-lined. See below, p. 58.

[22] A fragment of CB's Baldwin Diary for early 1768 (Berg) shows that he was giving as many as 55 lessons a week, besides teaching in Mrs Sheeles's boarding-school in Queen Square ('Mem.' No. 113 and n. 3; below, p. 147).

has perpetually visits to pay—so that I amⁿ very much alone, but to that I have no objection[—]I pass my time in Working, Reading, & *thrumming* the Harpsichord, ʳwhich I play so badly, that I never dare touch a note, when any living soul is present, but which notwithstanding I amuse myself with often when alone.ⁿ I am now Reading Stanyan's Grecian History[23]— [xxxxx *1 line*] tho' the *words* are not obsolete, the style & expressions are not at all familiar, & many of the latter what at present, I believe, would not be reckon'd extremely elegant.— But it is nevertheless a very clever Book; which *I* need not say, since it is generally approved; but that's no matter. | Susy[24] & I correspond constantly—her Letters would not disgrace a Woman of 40 years of age.—My dear Papa is in charming Health & good humour, tho' hurried to Death—you will perhaps admire the consistency of my expressions, & allow most cordially that *I* have a right to Criticize others—Prithee, my good friend, don't trouble me with any impertinant remarks.—past 12 o'clock!—& I [m]ust rise at 7 to-morrow! — — I must to [Be]d immediately.—I write now from a pretty ⟨ne⟩at little Closet of mine that is in the [Be]d Chamber, where I keep all *my* affairs—[Te]ll me, my dear, what Heroine ever yet ⟨exis⟩ted without her own Closet?— |

[*The bottom of this page has been cut off. The next passage describes EB's meeting with Mr Seton, presumably on Monday, 20 Feb., in St James's Park.*]

ʳ[xxxxx *3 lines*] He [Seton] said not a word which alluded to the Gloves, tho' she had them on, but I don't much wonder at his silence on this Head, since the *Verses* are such as he cannot well own, I mean the Conclusion of them, the beginning is very allowable & really extremely pretty but he Ends with these words—after telling her that these Gloves, which are lined with a sort of *fur*, will defend her skin from all Cold, &c, he says

> O could I learn that happy art
> With equal warmth to touch thy Heart:

[23] Temple Stanyan (*c.*1677–1752), *The Grecian History* (2 vols.; 1707, 1739). This work was the standard in schools until superseded by William Mitford's *History of Greece* (5 vols.; 1784–1818). CB owned two copies of the 1751 edn. (*Lib.*, p. 52).

[24] Now at Lynn. The earliest extant letter of their correspondence is FB to SEB *c.*15 July 1774 (vol. ii). Before that FB had addressed to SEB her Teignmouth Journal of 1773 (below, pp. 274–311).

No Cold should ever reach thy charms
Secured within my eager Arms!

[I cannot say this conclusion is perfectly⌐ [?gentlemanly]²⁵ |

[*The bottom of the page has been cut away. At the top of the next FBA has noted: '9. 10. 11. 12. Burnt', i.e., fos. 9–12.*]

⌐Hetty walk'd in the Park this morning, I did not refuse to go: Mr. Seton was there. We Join'd them, for he had Miss & Young Mr. Deage²⁶ with him, but [he] did not as usual accompany her Home, being engaged to a Party in the Park. He asked if I was recover'd from the little illness I had, which he had heard of at Mrs. Pringle's. He told her that he wanted to have sent to know how I did, in *her* and *his* Name, but Mrs. Pringle beg'd him to send without mentioning her!—No wonder, I'm sure, such a message would have rather surprised me. It is above 2 months since I have seen Mr. Seton, & indeed, it may be 3 before I do, as I go out so seldom.

Mr. Crawford call'd here this Evening; having foresight that he would, we were both denied. I don't think his friend²⁷ need be apprehensive that he will ever suffer from excess of modesty.⌐

Sunday night

My Grand daddy [SC] is here to night, to the *very* great satisfaction of us all. ⌐I perceived by his countenance an equal Joy at hearing Mr. Seton was *not* at Mrs. Pringle's, as vexation that he *was* in⌐ the Park, tho' he has again resumed with Hetty a sort of reserve which prevented his saying so. However, he⌐ told us very gravely this—'Experience is never good till 'tis *bought*!'²⁸ Hetty, in a very gay & flighty manner assented, & added that every body should have experience of their own, not follow

²⁵ Conjecturally supplied as the first word of the next line, which has been cut off.

²⁶ This seems the correct reading, but probably FB's slip for 'Debbieg'. While in London Seton was staying with his sister and brother-in-law Capt. and Mrs Debbieg, whom FB mentions below as having three children. 'Miss' Debbieg, a daughter, has not been further traced, while 'Young Mr' Debbieg would be the elder son Clement. See below, pp. 71, 117 and *passim*.

²⁷ It is not clear who is meant.

²⁸ Cf. the old proverb, 'Experience is good, if not (or but often) bought too dear' (*Oxford Dictionary of English Proverbs*, 3rd edn. rev. by F. P. Wilson (Oxford, 1970), p. 234).

advice from other People's.—'Ay, returned he, let them have it!—& it must be *paid* for too!—yes, *well* paid for!'

＂[xxxxx *1 line*] All well at Lynn, but no prospect, I believe, of any Journey to Town [xxxxx *2–3 words*] especially as in less than 3 months papa proposes our Journey there.＂

O! I must tell you that I have fallen in Love with a Gentleman whom I have lately come acquainted with: he is about 60 or 70—has the misfortune to be Hump back'd, crooked Leg'd, & rather deform'd in his Face.—But, in sober sadness, I am delighted with the Dean of Coleraine,[29] who's picture this is, & which I have very lately Read. The Piety, the Zeal, the humanity, goodness & humility of this charming Old man have won my Heart. Ah! who will not envy him the invaluable treasure? |

[*Some pages seem to have been discarded here.*]

[?Only the][30] ＂thought of the veil, or a wounded Heart would occasion my constant keeping at Home, as either would so much engage my attention, & occupy my whole mind, as to prevent the intrusion of any other idea.＂

Saturday

＂La belle Passion!—what notions people entertain of it! But does Mr. Seton think I never stir out because *he* never sees me? To be sure I am not frequently from Home, on the contrary,＂ I seldom quit ＂it,＂ considering my ＂Age＂ & opportunities; but why should I, when I am so happy in it? ＂I never＂ [can[31] ?want] employment, nor sigh for amusement—we have a Library which is an ever lasting resource when attack'd by the spleen—I have always a sufficiency of work to spend, if I

---

[29] *The Dean of Coleraine; a Moral History, founded on the Memoirs of an Illustrious Family in Ireland* (3 vols., London, 1742–3), a translation of *Le Doyen de Killerine* (Paris and The Hague, 1735–40), by Antoine François Prévost, known as Abbé Prévost (1697–1763), author of *Manon Lescaut*.

[30] Conjecturally supplied from the preceding line, which is missing. FB's 'thought of the veil' here suggests the influence of her Catholic grandmother Sleepe, whom she greatly loved and admired. One of the reasons for CB's leaving FB in England when he took EB and SEB to France in 1764 was that he feared the additional influence of a Catholic environment on FB. In any event FB remained in the Church of England, though she eventually married the Catholic emigré Gen. d'Arblay. See *ED* i, p. xlix n. 3.

[31] Inserted by FBA.

pleased, my whole Time at it—musick is a Feast which can
never grow insipid—& in short, I have all the reason that ever
mortal had to be contented with my lot—and I *am* contented
with, I *am* grateful for it! If few people are more happy, few are
more sensible *of* their happiness. But what of ⌐ that?—is thêre
any merit in paying the small tribute of gratitude, where bless-
ings such as I have received compel it from me?—How
strongly, how forcibly do I feel to whom I owe All the happiness
I enjoy!—it is to my Father! to this dearest, most amiable, this
best beloved—most worthy of men!—it is his goodness to me
which makes all appear so gay, it is his affection which makes
my sun shine. But if to this Parent I owe all my comfort— it is to
my God I owe *him*! and that God who hath given to me this
treasure which no earthly one can equal, alone knows the value
I set on it. Yet what value can compare with [it's] worth?—the
worth of *such* a treasure? A Parent who makes the happiness of
his Children!

I am in a moralising humour.—How truly does this Journal
contain my real & undisguised thoughts—I always write in it
according to the humour I am in, & if any stranger was ⌐to
think it worth⌐ reading, how capricious—insolent & whimsical
I must appear!—one moment flighty & half mad,—the next
sad & melancholy. No matter! it's truth & simplicity ⌐ are[32] it's
sole recommendations, & I doubt not but I shall hereafter
receive great pleasure from *reviewing* and almost *renewing* my
youth & my former sentiments. Unless, indeed, the latter part
of my Life is doom'd to be as miserable as the beginning is the
reverse, & then indeed, every Line here will rend my Heart—I
sigh from the bottom of it at this dreadful idea—I think I am in
a humour to write a funeral sermon—Hetty is gone to
Ranelagh, & I fancy does not *simpathise* with me!

I went to [*rest of line cut off*]

[*The page has been cut in half, and the middle of the page is missing. The first
paragraph following apparently refers to EB's despondency over Alexander
Seton's fickleness.*]

⌐*would* be herself. I *do* love her, most affectionately & sincerely
love her, & my very Heart is grieved when I see her give way to
this strange dejection, which however I hope will now wear off.

---

[32] At the top of this page FBA has noted, '15 Burnt. to . . . 21', i.e., fos. 15–20.

Eh bien—now for *Autres choses*.

I have received 2 very entertaining Letters from sweet Mary[33]—she is a *very* clever Girl, and writes amazingly well. She tells me that Mrs. Young is at Lynn—[xxxxx *1 line*] her Cara sposa has paid her a visit—[xxxxx *1 line*]⌐ |

⌐Saturday, April

I may be perhaps foolishly & causelessly apprehensive— may the Event prove thus!—but certain it is I *am* apprehensive of the consequence of my sister's attachment to Mr. Seton. He joined her last night at [xxxxx *1 word*], & walked & conversed with her the whole Evening, *that* is no matter: but he told her he had wrote some verses on Henry & Emma,[34] which he should be happy to have her opinion of; she expressed great eagerness to see them—then could he give them to her? Should she be in the Park on⌐

[*middle of page cut away*]

Our Party last ⌐Sunday⌐ was large & *brilliant*. Mr Greville, the celebrated Dr Hawkesworth,[35] Mr Crisp and my Cousin [Charles Rousseau Burney] Dined with us. In the Evening, M^rs and Miss Turner[36] of Lynn, two Gentlemen Named Vincent,[37]

---

[33] Presumably MA. The letters are missing.

[34] 'Henry and Emma; a Poem, upon the Model of the Nut-Brown Maid' (1708), by Matthew Prior (1664–1721). Henry tests the constancy of Emma's love by pretending to be a fugitive wanted for murder; Emma says that she will follow him into hiding (Matthew Prior, *Literary Works*, ed. H. B. Wright and M. K. Spears (2nd edn., Oxford, 1971), i. 278–300, ii. 909–10). FB may have feared that Seton was planning similarly to test EB's constancy, presumably by challenging her to go off with him. If he did so, no evidence remains of it.

[35] See above, p. 40 n. 17. Hawkesworth was editor of *The Adventurer*, published from 1752 to 1754, to which he contributed about 70 of the 140 numbers; the other major contributors were Samuel Johnson and Joseph Warton. About this time CB was prevailed upon by Greville to set an ode by Hawkesworth for the dedication of a new chapel of the Dublin Foundling Hospital (Hawkesworth to CB, 2 Apr. 1769, Comyn). As for Hawkesworth's 'affectation', Edmond Malone later reported that 'Johnson was fond of him, but . . . owned that Hawkesworth—who had set out a modest, humble man—was one of the many whom success in the world had spoiled. He was latterly, as Sir Joshua Reynolds told me, an affected, insincere man, and a great coxcomb in his dress. He had no literature whatever' (J. Prior, *Life of Edmond Malone* (1860), pp. 441–2, cited in *Life*, i. 253 n. 1; see also L. F. Powell, 'Introduction [to *The Adventurer*]' in Samuel Johnson, *The Idler and the Adventurer*, ed. W. J. Bate, J. M. Bullitt, and L. F. Powell (New Haven, 1963), p. 336 and *passim*).

[36] See above, p. 9 n. 27.

[37] Perhaps Richard Vincent (*c*.1701–83), instrumentalist and composer, and

& M[r] Partridge[38] made a very agreeable addition to our Company.

Dr. Hawkesworth does not shine in Conversation so much superior to others, as from his writings might be expected. Papa calls his Talking Book Language—for I never heard a man speak [in a style][39] which so much resembles [writing.][39] He has an amazing flow of choice words & expressions—'twould be nonsense to say he is extremely ˡ clever & sensible; while the Adventurers exist, that must be universally aknowledged [*sic*],—but his talents seem to consist rather in the solid than the splendid.—All he says is just,—proper, & better express'd than most *written* language; but he does not appear to me to be at all what is call'd a wit—neither is his conversation sprightly or brilliant. He is *remarkably* well bred & attentive, considering how great an Author he is; for without that consideration, he would be reckon'd so. He has a small tincture of affectation, I believe;—but I have quite forgot the wise resolution I so often make of never Judging of people by first sight!—Pity! that we have all the power of *making* resolutions so readily, & so properly, & that few or none are capable of *keeping* them!—but here again am I Judging of other's fortitude by my own weakness!—O dear, I am always to be wrong?—However, I think I may ˡ prevail on myself not to be my *own* Judge too rashly— why should I think I am *always* to be wrong?—I know not I am sure; certain it is I have hitherto never been otherwise; but *that* ought not to discourage me, since so inconsistent is Human nature allow'd to be, that for that very reason 'tis impossible I should be the same Creature at the conclusion as at the beginning of my life: ˹But how I trifle!—is not that, too, astonishing, considering how seldom I do˺ turn out to be a Wiseacre?

˹Mrs. Turner & her Daughter are extremely agreeable—the

Thomas Vincent (*c.*1720–?83), oboist and composer, possibly Richard Vincent's nephew (*New Grove*).

According to FBA, *Mem.* i. 173, CB and SC 'after a separation of very many years [*c.*1748–63], accidentally met at the house of Mr. Vincent, a mutual acquaintance', probably one of these Vincents. See also Rees, s.v. Vincent; Mercer, ii. 870, 1011; D. Nalbach, *The King's Theatre 1704–1867* (1972), pp. 46–7; *LS 4* i, p. lxix; Highfill, iv. 33, vi. 275.

[38] Henry Partridge (1746–1803), eldest son of Henry Partridge, Recorder of Lynn; a lawyer (Middle Temple, 1770; KC and a bencher, 1787). He witnessed the will of Mrs Turner in 1795. See Singh, i. 257.

[39] Inserted by FBA, the second because of a tear in the page.

Vincents are tolerable—Messrs Greville & Crisp I need not
mention—my Cousin was not remarkably in spirits[40]—but
now for the Lynn man, Mr. Partridge.

He is very short, but well made, & really handsome, with
much expression & sweetness in his Face. Indeed I am
extremely pleased with him, & honour Miss Allen for her
choice, as I hope in Time I shall him for his.[41] He is very⌐ |

[*Some pages have been discarded here. The first sentence following is of course
ironical.*]

⌐to be sure it would be very proper to take a chance Partner at
such a publick place as *Vauxhall*!—We could not find our
Coach on account of the great quantity of carriages till four
o'clock: but indeed I paid for this rioting, for I caught a very
bad Cold, & have been very indifferent, tho' I am now well
again. [xxxxx *3 lines*] We are much surprised at niether seeing
or hearing from my eldest Brother as we have long expected
him & are quite impatient for his arrival.[42] My dear Susy writes
to me by all opportunities, as I do to her in return—Every Body
well at Lynn.

My sister [EB] has had a Letter[43] from Richard Burney,[44]
Brother to our Cousin in town. He talks too of writing to
Susette & to me, & so he has some time, but perhaps expects to

---

[40] FB may have assumed, quite reasonably, that Charles Rousseau was dejected
about EB.

[41] Mr Partridge is the first known suitor of MA. FB, though fond of her stepsister,
evidently had doubts about her wifely potential. The cynical and world-weary SC, who
disliked MA, later recounted to FB MA's string of flirtations and lovers (including
Partridge), accusing her of wild, childish, trifling conduct and of lusting after men in
general (letter of 11 Aug. 1772, Essex). Partridge had evidently already begun to have
second thoughts by the autumn of this year, as MA writes to FB (15 Oct. 1769, Berg)
about her uncertainty whether he will come to see her at Lynn, adding 'Well we shall
see I suppose this youth's intentions in time'. Despite FB's forebodings, MA did
eventually prove a constant and affectionate wife to Martin Rishton.

[42] See below, p. 83 and *seq*.

[43] Missing. Nothing survives of the correspondence of Richard Gustavus Burney.

[44] Richard Gustavus Burney (1751–90), 2nd son of CB's brother Richard Burney of
Barborne Lodge, Worcester. Another of the musical Burneys, he followed his father's
profession of dancing master and was also a singing instructor, besides playing several
musical instruments; Daniel Lysons, in *Origin and Progress of the Meeting of the Three
Choirs of Gloucester, Worcester and Hereford* (Gloucester, 1895), p. 47, calls him 'a
performer of much taste, both on the violin and violoncello'. His gaiety, wit, and
foppery alternately charmed and exasperated FB. He had been in London in Apr. 1767
when SEB mentions 'Cousin Dick' as seeing her off to Chessington (fragment of SEB's
journal for 1767, McGill University Library).

be *intreated* first. I wish him to come to London extremely, he has been absent now near two years, he was at ⌐ that Time remarkably sensible & clever.⌐

O! I am to go to a Wedding to-morrow—the partys—one Mr John Hutton, Glass polisher, & Mrs Betty Langely [*sic*]⁴⁵ spinster, our ⌐Allen family Cook—⌐perhaps I may give you, Miss Nobody, an account of this affair to-morrow. I never had the honour of being at a Wedding in my life—but tho' this will be the first, I fancy it will not be the last too.

I am vastly sorry Mr Crisp is gone—I shall think of him every Sunday at least, all my life I believe.—I am now going to *charm* myself for the third time with poor Sterne's Sentimental Journey,⁴⁶ ⌐2 more volumes, by another person, are lately published [xxxxx *1 line*] by the original Author.⌐

Monday Eve. May 15th

Well, the wedding is over, the good folks are Join'd for better for worse — — A shocking Clause that!—'tis preparing one to lead a long Journey, and to know the path is not altogether strew'd with Roses—This same marriage Ceremony is so short, I really should have doubted it's validity had *I* been the ⌐ Bride; though perhaps she may not find the Road it leads her to very short; be that as it may, she must now trudge on, she can only return with her wishes, be she ever so wearied.

We have spent an exceeding agreeable Day. I speak for myself & a few more at least, I will not answer for the Bride & the Groom's feelings, at least not for the latter—tho' they niether of them appeared miserable; but had I been that *latter*,

---

⁴⁵ Elizabeth Langley (*c.*1719–*post* 1780), m. (15 May 1769) John Hutton, footman. Hutton is presumably the Burneys' manservant John mentioned in FB's journals through 1775. Betty Hutton is mentioned again by SEB to FB, 19 June 1780 (Barrett), where SEB reports that EBB has been ill, but was 'much better than could have been expected as Betty Hutton told me—I am sure you will rejoice to hear that good Creature is with her'.

⁴⁶ *A Sentimental Journey through France and Italy, by Mr. Yorick* (2 vols., 1768) by Laurence Sterne (1713–68), was published less than a month before the author's death. *Yorick's Sentimental Journey, Continued* (2 vols.), by 'Eugenius', was published 11 May 1769 (*Daily Adv.*). Usually attributed to Sterne's friend John Hall Stevenson (1715–85), the anonymous writer for the *Monthly Review*, xl (1769), 428, describes it as 'like the Sentimental Journey of Yorick, in nothing but the shortness of the chapters, the abrupt transitions, and the whimsical digressions. There is nothing to touch the heart, or delight the imagination.' CB owned a copy of the 'Sentimental Journey, 4 vol. in 2 . . . 1769' (*Lib.*, p. 52).

I fear I could not have said so much for myself.—As to the Bride, she is blythe as the month; if one can compare in any degree a weed of December, with the fragrance of May; for a weed in truth it is, & a weed not in it's first prime. But ⌜as⌝ some account of the *wedding* ⌜may be expected from my Girl, rather than disappoint *you*, my love, I will give a sheet or 2. I⌝ begin with the Company, first, |

The Bride. A maiden of about fifty, short, thick, clumsy, vulgar; her complection the finest saffron, & her Features suited to it: she was Dress'd in a white Linnen Gown, & with all the elegance which *marks* her character & station, having the honour to be Cook to Mʳ Burney.

The Bridegroom. A young man who had the appearance of being her son. A good modest sober and decent youth. Every body must allow this Couple to be exceeding well and very properly match'd. He was in Blue, trim'd with Red: N:B: the choice of these Colours are suited to the choice of the partys.[47]

The Father—(of the Day) Mʳ Charles Burney Junʳ [Charles Rousseau Burney]. It must be acknowledged that this accomplish'd virgin was determin'd to have every thing in Character; as not meerly her Husband, but her Father too was young enough to own her for a mother. It is generally allow'd | Originality displays genius.

The Bride's maids. Miss Anne Burney, a Virgin who may count years with the Bride herself,[48] though I fear she would not pretend to equal her in accomplishments: Miss Esther Burney, who, more modest still, pretends not to equal her in *any* thing;—not even in her wishes, except it be this last step she has taken: and Miss Frances Burney, who in *nothing* [xxxxx *2–3 words*] can equal ⌜any of them—at least not⌝ the Bride.

The rest of the Company—a Mʳˢ Ritson[49] and a Mʳ Somebody, no matter what,—Betty's friends—

And thus the Train closed.

We went in Papa's Coach, as many as it would hold,—the *Gentlemen* were obliged to walk—which condescendsion is not inconsiderable, for the Mʳ *Somebody*, & the Bridegroom too, have the honour of being Footman to very *topping* people! The Bride supported her spirits amazingly. |

[47] White of course = virginity. Blue and red may stand for hope and martyrdom.
[48] Ann Burney, FB's 'Aunt Nanny', born in 1722, was 46 or 47 at this time.
[49] Not identified; presumably a servant.

Sunday Night, May 21

Papa & my sister have Dined & spent the Evening at M^rs^
Pleydell's,[50] ᴿso our Family has been very small; however, we
have not lacked either good humour or wit—my Cousin
[Charles Rousseau], Charles [CB Jr.] & self have contrived to
pass a very agreeable Evening together: [xxxxx *1–2 words*]
Lord,ᴺ 'tis past one o'clock! & papa not come Home!—I must
run to Bed—Of what little consequence are late or early Hours
at Night? ᴿwhy should I be thus eager after nothing?ᴺ at best I
can but prolong a life which *must* be spent, & which one Day
will little remember the few years which care [xxxxx *1 word*]
may give it.—My Throat is sore—that one circumstance
answers all this pretty, stupid common place stuff in a
moment—*That* tells me the difference of ease & pain, and that
tells me that rest & good Hours, by mending the Health, contribute to the happiness;—And that tells me to leave idle and
affected moralising; to leave my Journal;—to put out my
Candle—And to hie to Bed:—where by reflecting on the folly,
stupidity & inconsistency of what is here ᴵ written, I may so
much improve that for the future I shall—not learn to write
better; but cease to write at all!—If so—Adieu—My Journal—
my Nobody—Adieu—adieu!—

Monday, May 22^d^

Well—I *have* slept, & perhaps *have* reflected—but as the
sleep came last, it has drove all reflections away which at all
tended to the detriment of this little Employment; & therefore,
once more welcome my Pen! my Nobody! my dear faithful
Journal!—

[50] Elizabeth Holwell, daughter of John Zephaniah Holwell (1711–98), temporary
Governor of Bengal, 1760, and a survivor of the 'Black Hole' of Calcutta; married (1759,
in India) Charles Stafford Playdell or Pleydell (d. 1779). In 1768 the Playdells returned
to England, where Mrs Playdell became a scholar of CB. Mrs Playdell, whom both CB
and FB thought beautiful, charming, and talented, departed again for Calcutta with
her husband and children in May 1771, but had returned to England by 1776; her
husband remained at Calcutta where he served as Superintendent of Police and as a
member of the Board of Trade, dying there in 1779. Mrs Playdell was apparently dead
by 1798. See *Asiatic Annual Register* (1799), 'Characters', p. 30; Great Britain, *Report on
the Palk Manuscripts* (1922), p. 252 n. 4; J. M. Holzman, *The Nabobs in England* (New
York, 1926), pp. 10, 40, 157; *GM* l (1780), 394; *Mem.* i. 203–4; CB, pocket book memorandum for 1776, Berg; below, *passim*.

A droll mistake happen'd to me to Day—We Live in a Parlour which is forwards, & I saw a Gentleman walking at the other side of the street who stopt before our House, & look'd at the Window some time—& then cross'd the way & knock'd at the Door: Papa happen'd to be at Home—'who is it?'—said he—I told him I did not know, but I believed some man who had a tolerable assurance by his staring.—He came immediately into the Parlour, & after asking Papa how he did, came up to me, & said—'I have call'd in, ma'am, on purpose to pay my respects to you—and—' I stared, & could not imagion who it was, but, was quite at a loss what to do, but my papa relieved me by saying—'O!—*this* is not your Acquaintance—this is her sister—' 'No! cried he—well, I never saw any thing so like!—I really thought it was Miss Burney!' Helas! what flattery! But still I was puzzled to think who it was, till by papa's Conversation I discover'd at last he was Lord Pigot,[51] ⌜a stupid man⌝ who I had heard was of the Party yesterday at Mʳˢ Pleydall's.

But how fortunate it was for me that papa chanced to be at Home—I should have been horridly confused at his mistake else, for nothing on Earth is so disagreeable as to be obliged to tell any body *you don't know them*;—it is mortifiing [*sic*] on both sides. His Lordship did Papa the honour to call to invite him & Hetty to spend the Evening at his House.[52] ⌜As Papa's time is not at present taken up with business as it has been, they both are gone; he very politely invited *me* too—[?but to accept][53] of what mere politeness offers would not be to display a great share of it myself.⌝ *Younger* sisters are almost different Beings from Elder one's, but thank god it is quite & unaffectedly without repining or envy that I see *my* elder sister Gad about & visit, &c—when I rest at Home—

I fancy Lord Pigot is a very agreeable man—he is undoubtedly polite & ⌜well bred—⌝Charles & I sup alone—I am Reading that satirical, entertaining poem the new Bath

[51] George Pigot (1719–77), cr. (1766) Baron Pigot; Governor and Commander-in-Chief of Fort St George, Madras, 1755–63 and 1775–7; MP. FB's opinion of him as 'stupid' is perhaps too strong (her later comments are more approving), but a visitor to Madras in 1776 described him as 'a man of shallow abilities, [though] of great spirit, and I believe in general honourable . . .' (J. Stewart to W. Hastings, 13 Feb.1776, cited Namier, ii. 280).

[52] Ld. Pigot occupied two houses at Nos. 25 and 26 Soho Square until 1775, when he returned to India (*Survey of London*, xxxiii. 85).

[53] The end of the line has been cut away.

Guide[54]—but I have Read very little lately, tho' I doat on nothing equally, but I have had sufficient employment in working.

⌐To morrow we shall spend the Evening at Mr. Robinson,[55] a Lynn Gentleman who with his Family are come to Town for a month or so. I am almost sure we shall pass a most insipid Evening, for tho' the Family are all *good sort of people*, like other *good sort of people*, they are rather dull and ⟨?cloy⟩. We were observing once to Mr. Crisp that the *good* & the *agreeable* were seldom united—'ay ⟨begad⟩ cried he, 'tis rare enough to meet with the one or the other—⌐ |

[*The top and bottom of the next 2 pages have been cut off. The following insert by FBA was probably copied from the preceding line.*]

[In speaking of Lord Pigot's taking me for] ⌐Hetty⌐ my Papa accounted for the mistake by saying ⌐They are both of a size, &⌐ you may have observed, my Lord, that People who Live together, naturally catch the looks & air of one another & without having one Feature alike, they contract a *something* in the whole Countenance which strikes one as a resemblance. There are two Ladies who your Lordship very likely ⌐knows,⌐ M[rs] Greville & M[rs] Crewe, mother & Daughter;[56]—in examining their Faces, they are as different as one Face can be from another; yet by Living together, they have accustom'd themselves so much to the same habits & manners, that I never see ⌐the⌐ one, without thinking of the other.' |

[*The following fragment of a quotation is perhaps the close of a medical anecdote by Dr Armstrong or the apothecary William Heckford.*]

⌐to squint, & to my great surprise, the Boy when I took him Home ⟨found that⟩ he can; by attending to it early, his Eyes are now quite well again.'

[54] Christopher Anstey (1724–1805), *The New Bath Guide: or, Memoirs of the B——R—[Blunderhead] Family, in a Series of Poetical Epistles* (1766). FB was to meet Anstey at Bath in 1780 (*DL* i. 353 and *seq.*).

[55] Alderman Walter Robertson (*c.*1703–72), Scottish wine-merchant of Lynn; mayor of Lynn, 1747 and 1761. Phonetic spellings in the Lynn rate books show that both 'Robinson' and 'Robertson' were pronounced 'Roberson'; hence FB's slip. CB writes in 'Mem.' No. 69 that 'Walther Robinson, Aldn' was one of 'the most intimate & affectionate friends' he had at Lynn, where Robertson's daughter Dorothy was one of his scholars (Young, *Autobiography*, p. 23); Robertson married (1740) Alice née Holly (*c.*1708–72), widow of Simon Tayler (1703–38). Perhaps they were accompanied to London by their son Walter Robertson (d. 1808), who married Ann née Haylett (d. 1774).   [56] See above, p. 31.

Sunday morn. May 28th

I am a week in arrears.

On Tuesday Evening, as I before mentioned, we Drank Tea, supp'd with Mr. & Mrs. Robinson, &c. and also, as I before mentioned, we were tolerably insipid & dull: after supper, we were a little enliven'd by the entrance of Mr. Young, who came from the Opera[57]—He had Dined with them, & left them for the Hay market. How odd, that every where there is the least probability we should, we meet with him!⌐ |

[*bottom of page cut away*]

⌐ Tuesday, May 30th

My dear Papa & Hetty are come Home loaded with favours from that sweet woman Mrs. Pleydell who sent me her love, & a high and full apron & muffler of finest India muslin, with a most charming Nosegay. My Papa observes that the East India People (Mrs. Pleydell was Born there) are all remarkable for generosity—& indeed all we have ever known fully Justify the observation.⌐

Thursday—June [15]

What an Age since I last wrote!—I have been wavering in my mind whether I should ever again touch this Journal, unless it were to commit it to the Flames—for this same *mind* of mine, would fain persuade me that this same *Journal* of mine is a very ridiculous—trifling & useless affair; & as such, would wisely advise me to part with it for ever—but I felt at the same Time, a regret, a loss of something in forbearing to *here unburthen* myself—the | pleasure which (in imagination at least) awaits me in the perusal of these sheets hereafter, pleaded strongly in favour of continuing to encrease them—& now that I once more have taken Courage to begin, I think I already feel twice the Content I did while this dear little Book was neglected—

I have much to write, & as I am to Day entirely alone, Why I have both Time and opportunity, but as I am not at present

---

[57] Where he had attended the final performance of the season of *La Buona Figliuola* (see *LS 4* iii. 1411). Young had been apprenticed to Robertson at Lynn, from 1758 to 1761, and had been romantically interested in his daughter. See Gazley, pp. 5–7, 24.

much inclined to be particular—I shall only mention a few ⌐circumstances⌐ that are past.—

In the first place, my sister & self lately spent the Evening at Mrs Pringle's.—Her party was—Mr Scot,[58] Preceptor to the King when Prince of Wales—Mr Seton, & M^{rs} & Mr Debbieg[59] his sister & Brother in Law, who are a very polite, sensible Couple.

The Company divided into little Partys immediately—Mr. Debbieg—his Lady, Mrs Pringle & Andrew went to Cards—a *Diversion* I always avoid—Mr Seton & Hetty amused them-selves very comfortably ⌐ together, ⌐at no time did I see either join in the general Conversation, but they chatted most comfortably⌐ in an uninterrupted Tete a Tete.—if Mr Scot had not been there, I should have made some excuse for coming Home; but as he was, I was extremely well contented to stay for he disliked Cards as much as myself, & very good naturedly devoted the whole Evening—(till supper seperated *parties*) to me.—That he is very clever, his office of Preceptor *ought* to make undoubted—he is very sociable & facetious too, & enter-tain'd me extremely with droll anecdotes & storys among the Great & Court. ⌐I was call'd Home early to Papa, who was not well—but is since, thank God, recovered.⌐

[58] George Lewis Scott (1708–80), mathematician; sub-preceptor to Prince George (afterwards George III), 1750; a commissioner of Excise, 1758–80. CB described him as 'not only an able mathematician, but an excellent musician . . . a performer on the harpsichord'. He also praised Scott's contributions to the *Supplement* to Chambers' *Cyclopaedia* (2 vols., 1753): 'Whatever articles he furnished . . . concerning harmonics or the ratio of sounds, may be depended on' (Rees, s.v. Scott, George Lewis).

[59] Hugh Debbieg (*c*.1732–1810), engineer in ordinary and captain in the Corps of Engineers, 1759; Maj. (army), 1772; Col., 1782; Gen., 1803. He married (1763) Janet Seton (1736–1801), daughter of Sir Henry Seton, 3rd Bt., sister of Alexander Seton. Debbieg was trained as an army engineer at Woolwich, first seeing active service in 1746 when only 14 years old. In 1772 he went to Newfoundland as commanding officer of engineers, and during the American war he was employed at home in constructing fortifications and making military surveys.

An otherwise distinguished military career was blemished in 1784 when Debbieg was courtmartialled for writing several 'disrespectful and injurious' letters to the Duke of Richmond, who as Master General of the Ordnance was his commanding officer; however, though found guilty on all counts, because of his 'high character' and 'meritorious services' he received merely a reprimand. He retired from active service at this time and was invalided in 1796, but continued to be promoted, eventually attaining the rank of general (1803). See *AL*, 1769, p. 175 and subsequent years; T. W. J. Conolly and R. F. Edwards, *Roll of Officers of the Corps of Royal Engineers, from 1760 to 1898* (Chatham, 1898), pp. 4, 7; *GM* lxxi[1] (1801), 379; lxxiii[2] (1803), 1080; lxxx[1] (1810), 595; *AR* xxvii (1784), 289–90; lii (1810), 388; Edinburgh parish registers.

Not long after, Mʳˢ Debbieg & Mʳ Seton call'd here—⌜we were denied but it was⌝ to invite Hetty & me to Drink Tea & spend the Evening with the former.—Hetty Joyfully ⌐ accepted the invitation—it was not convenient to me to go, & so she made my excuses—She spent an exceeding agreeable Evening—they all made very civil enquirys about me, & ⌜were *vastly sorry* I could not come.⌝ Mʳ Seton offer'd to fetch me— so did Andrew—& ⌜Mʳ⌝ Debbieg himself—but Hetty, who knew I should not be delighted to see them all here, made excuses for me.

⌜Nothing still of the *serious kind* has happened between Hetty & Mr. Seton—I wish, for her peace, there had, for she absolutely doats on him. We expect the same party to meet at this House soon.

The Thirteenth of the month was my Birth Day—when— horrid to tell! I was turn'd of seventeen!—how much do I regret every year that passes at present! 'tis folly—but I cannot help it—⌝

Miss Crawford[60] call'd here lately—she is very earnest for us to visit her—but *we* are not very earnest about the matter:— however, ⌐ the laws of custom make our spending one Eveᵍ with her necessary. O how I hate this vile custom which obliges us to make slaves of ourselves! to sell the most precious property we boast, our Time;—& to sacrifice it to every prattling impertinent who chuses to demand it!—yet those who shall pretend to defy this irksome confinement of our happiness, must stand accused of incivility,—breach of manners—love of originality,—& ⌜God knows⌝ what not—nevertheless, they who will nobly dare to be above submitting to Chains their reason disapproves, they shall I always honour—if that will be of any service to them!—

For why should we not be permitted to be masters of our Time?—why may ⌐ we not venture to love, & to dislike—and why, if we do, may we not give to those we love the richest Jewel we own, our Time? what is it can stimulate us to bestow *that* on all alike?—'tis not affection—'tis not a desire of pleasing—or if

---

[60] See above, p. 44. Mrs Pringle revealed to FB in 1775 that Miss Craufurd's brother, EB's admirer, having failed to enlist Mrs Pringle as a '*match maker*', 'made his sister visit You, but her Visit was never returned,—& then he offered Tickets for a Concert—but they were not accepted' (vol. ii).

it is, 'tis a very weak one;—no! 'tis indolence—'tis Custom— Custom—which is so woven around us—which so universally commands us—which we all blame—and all obey, without knowing why or w[h]erefore—which keeps our better Reason, ⌐which⌐ sometimes dares to shew it's folly, in subjection—

And which, in short, is a very ridiculous affair, more particularly as it hath kept me writing on it till I have forgot what introduced it — — I feel myself in no excellent mood—I will walk out & give my spirits another *turn*, & then resume my Pen. |

Sunday afternoon
June [25]

Now don't imagion that because I have not wrote sooner since the Walk I proposed taking in order to amend my spirits & Temper; I have so ill succeeded as not to have gain'd the desired point till now — — no, no, I have been in most *exceeding good humour*, I assure you, tho' not at all inclined to Write: nor indeed am I at present, but as I believe I shall not have Time to employ myself in this *pretty manner* again soon, and as I have a most remarkable & very *interesting* affair to relate, I have resolved, neck or nothing, to take the Pen once again in Hand! This same affair is that—

My Papa went last Monday to Oxford, in order to take a Doctor's Degree in Musick:[61] Is not *that* a grand affair?—He composed an Anthem,[62] by way of Exercise, to be perform'd on the Occasion, in which Miss Barsanti[63] was to be the principle

[61] CB matriculated from University College on Tuesday, 20 June 1769, directed a performance of his anthem on 22 June, and took the degrees of Mus.B. and Mus.D. on 23 June. He had originally intended to take the degrees at Cambridge after composing the setting of the Installation Ode, to be written by Thomas Gray, the new Professor of History at Cambridge, for the installation of the D. of Grafton as Chancellor of Cambridge University. Frustrated in this design, CB turned to Oxford for his degrees instead. See Scholes, i. 140–6; Lonsdale, pp. 77–9; *Mem.* i. 210–14; below, pp. 73–81 *passim*.

[62] 'I will love Thee, O Lord, my Strength', a setting of Psalm 18 for solo voices, quartet, chorus, and orchestra. The MS of CB's work, never published, is in the Bodleian (MS. Mus. Sch. Ex. c. 15). It contains 177 pages of orchestral score.

[63] Jane (or 'Jenny') Barsanti (d. 1795), soprano singer and actress; m. 1 (1777) John Richard Kirwan Lyster (d. 1779); m. 2 (1779) Richard Daly (d. 1813), actor and later manager of the Theatre Royal, Dublin. Her father was Francesco Barsanti (1690–1775), an Italian instrumentalist and composer, who came to London in 1714. Her mother (see below) was a Scotswoman, not further identified (but see Laetitia Hawkins, *Memoirs* (1822–4), i.222). Miss Barsanti, who first studied under her father and then became CB's favourite pupil, made her début as a singer on this occasion, performing

[*sic*] singer, & make her first appearance in Publick. ⌐Niether
Hetty or myself went— ¦ but Papa took my Cousin [Charles
Rousseau Burney] with him, to play the Harpsichord, & two of
his Brothers, Richard and James,[64] met them at Oxford & were
both employ'd—the one on the violin cello, the other on the
Fidle. He took other Performers with him,[65] & had the best
assistance the Town could give.⌐

His Anthem was ⌐played⌐ last Thursday, & gave much satisfaction—indeed the musick of it is delightful—poor Barsanti
was terrified to Death, & her mother, who was among the
Audience, was so much affected, that she fainted away, but by
immediate assistance soon revived. However, notwithstanding
her fears & apprehensions, Barsanti came off with *flying
Colours*, met with great applause, ⌐& so much exerted herself
when encouraged that she sung much better than ever in her
Life. I am quite happy to hear this—⌐my dear, kind Papa wrote
us a short note to let us know all was well over the moment the
Performance was finish'd—The very great kindness of his
thinking of us at so busy a Time, I shall remember with the
most grateful pleasure all my Life. ⌐At Night, the oratorio of
Athaliah[66] was performed, & Barsanti ¦ sung again, with
amazing Success, in so much, that when the university, &c,

---

three airs and three recitatives to great acclaim. By 1771 she had lost her singing voice
through illness and turned to acting instead, in which career she also enjoyed great
success. In 1775 FB wrote of her: 'Independent of her talents, I love her for her Character & Disposition. Indeed she is a very charming Girl.' See *New Grove*; Highfill; Rees,
s.v. Barsanti; below, *passim*, and vol. ii.

[64] Richard Gustavus Burney and James Adolphus Burney (1753–98), dancing
master and musician, whom FB later describes as 'all good humour', and 'a very
manly, good natured, unaffected, & good Hearted young man' (below, p. 131 and
vol. ii). Scholes (i. 144) points out that Dr Hayes, as conductor (see below), would have
sat at the harpsichord, in which case Charles Rousseau Burney presumably would have
played the violin.

[65] See below, pp. 79–80.

[66] *Athalia*, by George Frederick Handel (1685–1759), libretto by Samuel
Humphreys (*c.*1698–1738), after Racine; first performed, under the composer's direction, in the Sheldonian Theatre, Oxford, in 1733. 'Yesterday [Friday, 23 June] the
Anniversary Commemoration of Founders and Benefactors to this University . . . was
celebrated in the [Sheldonian] Theatre . . . In the Evening the Masque of Acis and
Galatea was performed, in the Musick Room, to a most numerous and brilliant
Audience: As was the Oratorio of Athalia on Thursday Evening, as the Choral Musick
for this Term' (*Oxford Journal*, 24 June 1769). Handel's masque of *Acis and Galatea*,
libretto by John Gay and others, after Ovid's *Metamorphoses*, xiii, received its first
performance at Cannons, Edgware, in 1718. See *New Grove*.

understood that she did *not* perform in Acis & Galatea which was to be done on Friday night, they beg'd the favour of papa to let her sing an Italian song between the acts in which she was greatly applauded, & encored. I wish I had been there. Mrs. & Mr. Pleydel payed Papa the Compliment of going to Oxford purposely to hear his Anthem."ᵉ As Hetty keeps the Letter, ʳor rather Note, my Papa wrote to me,ᵉ I will Copy it here, for I shall always love to Read it: ʳHe was in so much haste, he has not even sign'd it.ᵉ

[*The original of this letter is missing. FB's copy is on fo. 33ʳ and ᵛ of the Journal for 1769.*]

Oxford, Thursday June 22ᵈ
past 2 o'clock

My dear Girls,

I know it will please you much to hear that the Performance of my Anthem is just very well over, not one mistake of consequence—Barsanti did extreamly well, & all was much applauded—I shall to-morrow have both my Degrees; (for I must first take that of Batchelor of musick) with great unanimity & reputation—Dʳ Hayes⁶⁷ | is very civil; & lends me his Robe with a very good Grace—Adieu—I know not when I shall get Home. — — ʳMr. & Mrs. Pleydel are here, & your three Cousins—Park⁶⁸ & Pasquali⁶⁹ and all—ᵉ

⁶⁷ William Hayes (1708–77), D.Mus., 1749; Heather Professor of Music at Oxford, 1742–77. Hayes had been an early stimulus to CB's musical ambition. In 1742 or 1743 'the Celebrated [Revd William] Felton, from Hereford, & after him the 1st Dr. Hayes, from Oxford, came to Shrewsbury on a Tour while I was studying so hard without Instructions or example, and struck & stimulated me so forcibly by their performance on the Organ as well as encouragem[en]t that I went to work with an ambition & fury that wd. hardly allow me to eat or sleep' ('Mem.' No. 16). Hayes conducted the performance of CB's doctoral exercise (below, p. 80).

⁶⁸ John Parke (1745–1829), oboist and composer. In 1768 he had been appointed principal oboist at the Opera. By 1771 he was playing at Vauxhall Gardens, and a year or two later he became first oboist at Drury Lane Theatre. He retired about 1815 (*New Grove*). Of his playing CB wrote, 'No tone approaches so near to that of Fischer [Johann Christian Fischer (1733–1800)], in richness and power, as that of . . . Park' (Rees, s.v. Fischer, John Christian).

⁶⁹ Francisco Pasquali, a leading double-bass player, was a neighbour of the Burneys in Poland Street. In 1772 he built a concert room in Tottenham St. which he and his partner, the architect Michael Novosielski, leased to the E. of Sandwich and his friends in 1786 for the Concerts of Ancient Music. Pasquali was one of the principal double-bassists in the Handel commemoration of 1784 (*Commem.*, p. 19). See R. Elkin, *The Old Concert Rooms of London* (1955), pp. 82–3, 86; *Survey of London*, xxi. 38; *New Grove*; Westminster Rate Books for St James's, Westminster Reference Library.

This made us extreamly happy—we have pass'd this week quite alone, but very comfortably & chearfully. & now for something concerning myself, at which I am a little uneasy. As I found Friday was to be the *Day of Days* that my Father took his Degrees, as soon as we had Read this Letter, I ran up stairs & wrote one to him in Verse—which I am horidly afraid he will think impertinant—I Read it to Hetty before I sent it, & she persuaded me it would meerly have the effect I intended, namely to make him Laugh—I wish ⌜to God⌝ it may, but I shan't be happy till he comes Home, ⌜which is to be to night, as we hear from my Cousin [Charles Rousseau Burney] & Barsanti who came yesterday:⌝ I will Copy from memory the foolish thing I sent. 'tis an attempt at Cranbo[70]—& a poor one enough.

4   Poland Street,
                                          23 June [1769]

To Doctor Burney

AL (in verse) (Osborn), 23 June 1769
Folio, 2 pp. *pmK* 23 IV
Addressed: To | Mr Burney | At Mr Mathew's[71] | Stationer | Oxford.
The verse letter actually sent is here substituted for FB's copy in the Journal for 1769, fo. 34^r & ^v. Variant readings are indicated in the footnotes. Another copy in FB's hand, 2 pp. folio, addressed 'To | Doctor Burney | Oxford', is in the Berg. This fair copy, with minor variations in punctuation, was probably made later from the letter actually sent, which CB brought back with him from Oxford.

Poland Street
Friday, June 23^d

To Doctor Last[72]

O aid me, ye muses of ev'ry Degree,
O give me the standish[73] of Mulberry Tree

[70] So in the MS, a slip for 'Crambo'. The term refers originally to 'a game in which one player gives a word or line of verse to which each of the others has to find a rime' (*OED* s.v. Crambo 1). In 1750 CB published a setting of *Lovely Harriote, a Crambo Song*, the words by Christopher Smart, where the humour lay in finding numerous amusing rhymes for 'Harriote' (see Scholes, ii. 342). In 1789 FB mentions a crambo song on the name of Dr Willis, the physician who treated George III during his attack of 'insanity' at that time (*DL* iv. 262).

[*See opposite page for nn. 71–3*]

Which was cut for the Author of Ferney;
O give me a Quil to the stump worn[74] by Gray,
And Paper which cut was on Milton's Birth Day
  To write to the great Doctor Burney!
O Doctor! of Doctor's the Last & the Best
By Fortune most honour'd, distinguish'd & blest
  And may you for ever be her nigh!
O smile (if a Doctor's permitted to smile)
And your natural[75] gravity lessen a while
  To Read this, O dread Doctor Burney!
For the Letter most kind we to Day did receive
With grateful affection our Bosom's do heave
  And to see you, O grave sir! how yern I!
'Tis true the Time's short since you last was in Town
Yet both fatter & Taller you doubtless are grown
  Or you'll make but a poor Doctor Burney.
For I never can think of a Doctor, not big
As a Falstaf, [*sic*] or without a full bottom'd wig[76]

[71] William Mathews or Matthews (d. 1791), stationer and music-seller in Catte St. and later in the High opposite All Saints' Church, Oxford. Mathews was also a noted bass singer and participated in the performance of CB's anthem (see below, p. 79). He was a clerk of Magdalen College. See John H. Mee, *The Oldest Music Room in Europe* (1911), pp. 74, 130, 137; *Oxford Journal*, 16 Dec. 1769.

[72] 'A Pun, alluding to the character in the Devil on 2 sticks' (FBA's note in the Journal for 1769). *The Devil upon Two Sticks*, a 3-act comedy by Samuel Foote (1721–77), was first performed at the Haymarket in 1768. The most recent performance prior to FB's verse letter was on 19 June 1769. 'Doctor Last' in the comedy is a shoemaker who gets a physician's license. He appears again in *The Doctor Last in His Chariot*, a farce by Isaac Bickerstaffe, first played at the Haymarket, 21 June 1769. This piece is mentioned below, p. 81. See Highfill, v. 324, 344–5; *LS 4* iii. 1336–45, 1407–17 ff.

[73] 'An Ink Standish cut out of a mulberry Tree planted by Shakespear for Mr. Keate, author of Ferney an Epistle to Voltaire' (FBA's note in Journal for 1769). George Keate (1730–97), miscellaneous writer, in 1768 publ. 'Ferney: An Epistle to . . . Voltaire', a poem in praise of Voltaire and his works but containing a tribute to Shakespeare. In recognition of his tribute Keate was commissioned by the Mayor and Corporation of Stratford-upon-Avon to present to David Garrick the freedom of the town, which they had agreed to confer upon the actor for his services to Shakespeare. The freedom was presented in May 1769 in a casket made from a mulberry tree traditionally held to have been planted by Shakespeare himself. For fulfilling this commission Keate in turn was presented with an ink standish made from the same tree. Later in the year Garrick directed the famous Shakespeare Jubilee at Stratford. FB was to meet Keate in 1774. See Garrick, *Letters*, ii. 651–2 and n. 7; K. G. Dapp, *George Keate* (Philadelphia, 1939), pp. 3, 66–8; vol. ii.

[74] Altered from 'wore' by FB in Journal for 1769.

[75] 'And' omitted by FB in the Journal; 'natural' changed to 'new acquir'd' by FBA.

[76] 'As a Falstaff, & not with a full bottom'd wig' (Journal).

And the slyness[77] Fame gives an Attorney;
Not more at the Bag did the Citizen's stare
Of Harley,[78] when Harley was made a Lord Mayor
Than I shall at thin Doctor Burney.[79]

May[80] Wisdom, which still to good humour gives Birth
May fatness with dignity, goodness with mirth
    Still attend you, & speed your Town Journey;
And O till the Hour when[81] Death us shall part
May Fanny a Corner possess of the Heart
    Of the owner of her's, Doctor Burney!

[*The Journal for 1769 continues.*]

Mersh[82]—June 29th
Thursday Night

We are arrived thus far on our Journey—to ⌐morrow we
shall reach dear Lynn, tho' we have hopes of being met by my
Mama & Susette at Wisbech, which is our next stage, & where
we shall Breakfast. Miss Allen cannot meet us, as she will be
engaged at a Wedding[83]—but of these affairs ⟨anon⟩—I want
now to mention a few things which passed before we set off.⌐

Papa came Home from Oxford on Sunday Night, as we
expected—We ran to meet him with as much joy as if instead of
a Week's, we had *groan'd* at a years absence—I had frighten'd

---

⁷⁷ 'sly air' (Journal).
⁷⁸ Hon. Thomas Harley (1730–1804), of Berrington, Herefordshire; Lord Mayor of
London, 1767–8; MP (Namier). Harley became Lord Mayor on Michaelmas day
(29 Sept.) 1767. Evidently he scandalized some onlookers at the installation ceremony
by wearing the informal bag-wig instead of the more customary full-bottomed wig.
⁷⁹ 'Than I at the thin Doctor Burney' (Journal). This is also the original version in
FB's letter, but altered by her before the letter was sent.
⁸⁰ 'O! may' (Journal).
⁸¹ 'That' (Journal).
⁸² March or Mersh, a town in Cambridgeshire 81 miles from London via St Ives and
Hoddesdon, and 8 miles SW of Wisbech, the Burneys' next stop. Lynn lies another 15
miles to the NE of Wisbech.
⁸³ Brigg Fountaine (*c.*1745–1825) of Narford, Norfolk, whose granduncle, Sir
Andrew Fountaine, was one of CB's early Norfolk patrons; m. (29 June 1769, in St
Margaret's Church, Lynn) Mary Hogg (*c.*1724–72), only daughter of George Hogg (*c.*1724–72),
Mayor of Lynn, 1770. The service was performed by the Revd Dr Charles Bagge, Vicar
of St Margaret's, and the witnesses were MA and Dorothy Tayler, who later in the year
was to become the bride's sister-in-law (MI and registers, St Margaret's; Stephen
Allen's will, PCC, prob. 19 May 1763; *GM* xcv¹. 477; Lonsdale, p. 41).

myself not a little before he came lest he should be angry at my
pert verses—but the moment he arriv'd, I forgot every thing but
the pleasure of seeing him—he was more kind—more affectionate than ever; if possible—tho' he two or three Times called
me 'sawcy Girl!'—of which however, I wisely chose to take no
notice, rather prefering to drop the subject. Notwithstanding
his extreme hurry & business, he had thought of us when at
Woodstock,[84] & most kindly brought us both presents from
that place—but the best ᴵ thing he shewed us was the Oxford
Journal, in which his affair was mentioned—who wrote it we
know not,[85] but I will Copy the paragraph.

Oxford Journal, June 23ᵈ [86]

On Thursday last was performed in the Musick School an
Anthem[87] Composed by Mʳ Charles Burney of Poland Street
London, as an Exercise for the Degree of Doctor in Musick:
which was received with Universal applause, & allow'd by the
Judges of musical merit to be the most elegant & ingenious
Performance that was ever exhibited here on the like occasion.
The vocal parts were performed by Miss Barsanti (being the
first Time of her appearance in Publick) Messʳˢ Norris,[88]
Mathews,[89] Price[90] Millar,[91] &c: the Instrumental by Mr.

[84] 8 miles NW of Oxford. Blenheim, seat of the D. of Marlborough, adjoins the town
on the south, and CB may have visited Blenheim as the guest of James Lates, violinist,
who played in CB's exercise and who was connected with the Duke's musical establishment. It is also possible that CB paid his respects to the Duke himself, who had
nominated CB Jr. to the Charterhouse the previous year.

[85] The author had not been identified. The publisher of the *Oxford Journal* was
William Jackson (d. 1795) (*GM* lxv¹ (1795), 359).

[86] So in MS; correctly 'June 24'. The original notice is in two paragraphs. FB has
condensed and embellished it somewhat, besides transposing certain words and
sentences. Verbal omissions, changes, and additions by FB are indicated in the notes
following.

[87] 'in the Music School before a numerous Audience an Anthem'.

[88] Thomas Norris (1741–90), English tenor singer, organist, and composer. He was
appointed organist of St John's College, Oxford, in 1766; in 1776 he became organist of
Christ Church Cathedral (*New Grove*). He had an extensive singing career in and out of
London, and in 1784 sang to great acclaim in the Handel commemoration. Norris sang
two solo airs and a recitative in CB's exercise, besides participating in the piece for
quartet (along with Price, Millard, and Mathews).

Norris, whom in later years CB referred to as 'old Norey', seems to have been
another of EB's early admirers. See *JL* iv. 490; CB to Charlotte Burney Francis,
25 Feb. 1786, Barrett; and CB and JB to FBA, 22–4 July 1797, Berg.

[89] William Mathews, music-seller and bass singer (see above, p. 77 n. 71). Mathews
was a principal bass in the Handel commemoration (*Commem.*, p. 20). Besides taking
part in the quartet, he sang a recitative and air for bass solo.

[*See p. 80 for nn. 90–1*]

Burney the Composer[92]—Mess[rs] Malchair,[93] Charles Burney Jun[r], Richard Burney, Parks, Pasquali,[94] Lates,[95] &c.—And Yesterday M[r] Burney was admitted to his Degree,[96] to which he was introduced *ex officio* by the Rev. Mr. Hornsby,[97] Savilian Professor of Astronomy: the whole of the musical Performance[98] was conducted by our Professor, D[r] Hayes.

[90] John Price (d. 1784), counter-tenor. Price was a chorister in Gloucester Cathedral, 1739–44, and singing man, 1745–84, and also a lay clerk and verger there. In 1762 he succeeded Thomas Baildon as one of the choir of St Paul's Cathedral, London. From 1760 till his death he sang at the Meetings of the Three Choirs of Gloucester, Worcester, and Hereford. 'He had a fine counter-tenor voice, and was particularly remarkable for singing the air in Milton's *L'Allegro* which describes Laughter "holding both his sides"' (D. Lysons *et al.*, *Origin and Progress of the Meeting of the Three Choirs . . .*, p. 38). He sang with Norris and Mathews at the Meeting at Gloucester in 1769 and presumably sang the alto part in the quartet in CB's exercise. See ibid., pp. 38–63 *passim*; *Gloucester Journal*, 8 Nov. 1762, 20 Dec. 1784; Gloucester Cathedral Treasurer's Account Books, 1721–86.

[91] Spelled 'Millard' in the printed programme of CB's exercise. Millard presumably sang the second tenor part in the quartet, and was undoubtedly Charles Millard (*c*.1748–1814), nephew of Dr William Hayes, who matriculated at Magdalen College, 1766; chorister, 1761–7; clerk, 1767–72; BA, 1770; MA, 1773; divine. As a boy Millard was selected to sing a duet with the Italian prima donna Giulia Frasi (a one-time scholar of CB's), probably at the Gloucester Music Meeting in 1763 (Lonsdale, p. 24). In 1771 he became a Minor Canon of Norwich Cathedral, afterwards becoming Chancellor (1809). An ear-witness recollects 'the delight with which I used to listen to the service in Norwich Cathedral, when the Minor Canons, eight in number, filed off to their stalls, Precentor Millard at their head, whose admirable style and correct taste as a singer I have never heard surpassed . . .' (E. Taylor, *The English Cathedral Service, Its Glory, Its Decline* (1845), p. 30).

[92] CB probably played the violin since Dr Hayes, as conductor, would have sat at the harpsichord (Scholes, i. 144).

[93] John (Johann-Baptist) Malchair (Malscher) (1730–1812), German violinist, composer, and watercolour artist; leader of the Oxford Music Room band, 1760–92 (*New Grove*; J. H. Mee, *The Oldest Music Room in Europe*, pp. 78–85).

[94] Not in the original account; inserted by FB.

[95] James Lates (d. 1777), English violinist and composer. A son of David Francisco Lates, who taught modern languages at Oxford University, he played in the Oxford Music Room band and in other concerts in the vicinity of Oxford from about 1759 until his death, and he was connected with the D. of Marlborough's musical establishment at Blenheim (*New Grove*).

[96] 'his Doctor's Degree'.

[97] Thomas Hornsby (1733–1810), BA, 1753, MA, 1757, DD, 1785 (Oxon.); Savilian Professor of Astronomy, 1763–1810; Sedleian Professor of Natural Philosophy, 1782–1810. According to the Oxford statutes of 1636, a candidate for 'a degree in music . . . shall perform one or more cantilenas of six or eight parts, with harmony of voices and instruments. This being finished, he shall receive from the Savilian professors the solemnities of his creation.' The two Savilian professors held the chairs in geometry and astronomy established by Sir Henry Savile in 1619 (Scholes, pp. 144–5; *Corpus Statutorum Universitatis Oxoniensis* (Oxford, 1768), p. 54).

[98] FB has inserted 'of the musical Performance'.

Miss Barsanti's Voice & manner of singing were greatly admired, both in the above performance,[99] in the musick Room on Thursday & Friday Nights: and this young Lady, who is a scholar of Doctor Burney,[1] will, if we mistake not, in Time amply repay the Publick any indulgence with which they may be[2] disposed to encourage the becoming diffidence of modest merit.

There's for you!—think of that Master Brooke.[3]

Well,—when Papa had been ⌐in⌐ a short Time, unfortunately a ⌐new⌐ play called Dr. Last in his Chariot,[4] was mentioned ⌐by my Cousin, who was with us—⌐Papa looked at me—I looked any other way—'O you sawcy Girl!' cried he— Charles appeared curious, I was horidly ashamed—'What do you think, continued papa ⌐to my Cousin—⌐do you know this abominable girl calls *me* Dr. Last?—'

Charles & Hetty both Laughed, & papa took out the Letter, & holding it out to me said 'come, do me the favour of Reading this!—' I would fain have torn it, but papa drew it back, & was going to Read it—I beg'd him not—but *in vain*, & so I ran out of the Room—but to own the truth, my curiosity prevail'd so far, that I could not forbear running down stairs again with more speed than up, & into the next Room ⌐to hear these comments.⌐ I found, by papa's voice & manner, that he did not appear displeased—tho' he half affected to be so—he Read it loud—⌐they all Laughed very much—⌐'I assure you, said Papa, 'tis very *good stuff*!—I Read it to Mrs Playdel, & she was much pleased—particularly with the last stanza—& to one or two of my new Oxford friends at Breakfast, & we had a very hearty Laugh.—'

This was enough—I ran once more up stairs, & lighter than a Feather felt my Heart!

⌐I was monstrously ashamed of appearing at supper—Papa *sawced* me not a little, but as I found he was not at all sincerely angry, I bore it very tolerably.

[99] 'likewise' deleted.

[1] FB has deleted 'and not above fourteen Years of Age'. Miss Barsanti's date of birth has not been found, but this estimate seems a bit low.   [2] 'are'.

[3] Words of Sir John Falstaff to the disguised Master Ford in *The Merry Wives of Windsor*, III. v. The Burney family adopted them as a humorous catch-phrase for calling attention to something noteworthy or extraordinary. Cf. *JL* iii. 63, iv. 312.

[4] See above, p. 77 n. 72.

Monday & Tuesday we spent in the melancholy task of *leave taking*—I went to almost all my Relations & acquaintance ⟨in Poland Street—⟩to grandmama Burney, aunt Beckey, Miss Pascalls[5] &c. Mrs. Pringle—&c.⌐

O—but one thing has very much vexed me—my Papa has Read my nonsense to M⌐ʳˢ⌐ Skinner,[6] an intimate acquaintance & a very clever woman, & she insisted on having a Copy, which papa desired me to write—. I was horid mad, & beg'd most earnestly to be excused, for such trash, however it may serve to Read at the moment, must be shocking a second Time but Papa would take no denial—'It's very sufficient, said he for the occasion, and for your Age.' However, I am as much mortified at doing this, as if my first fear had been verified, for I cannot at all relish being thus exposed to a *deliberate* examination.—

⌐O how I long to see my Lynn friends—my Susette [xxxxx ½ *line*] we 3 travel very comfortably, having 2 additional Horses to the Coach—but Hetty calls me to Bed.—⌐

Lynn Regis
Sᵗ Marg⌐ᵗˢ⌐ Church Yard, July [?21]

Once more I take up a Pen to write to my Journal, which I thought I never again should.—⌐⌐I don't mean that any particular event or occurrence⌐ |

[*top of page cut away*]

We found every Body here well—my mama is in better Health than ever [xxxxx 1½ *lines*] Miss Allen is the same gener-

[5] Mary Pascall (b. 1736), Ann Pascall (b. 1739), and Elizabeth Pascall (b. 1742), daughters of James Pascall of St Giles-in-the-Fields, Middlesex, who m. (1724) Anne née Gondouin of St Anne, Westminster. James Pascall was dead by 19 Feb. 1755 when his widow remarried a widower, Aaron Lambe (d. 1777), auctioneer, the Pascall sisters' stepfather, who is mentioned below, p. 100. Lambe and his family were neighbours of the Burneys in Poland St. See IGI; Marriage Licences, Bishop of London's Registry, copy in Society of Genealogists, London; Aaron Lambe's will, PCC, prob. 16 Dec. 1777; *DL* ii. 387; Thomas Mortimer, *Universal Director* (1763), pt. iii, p. 92.

[6] Probably Sarah née Lancaster (d. 1808), m. (1764) the Revd John Skinner or Skynner (*c.*1724–1805), MA (Cantab.), 1748, BD, 1756; Chaplain to the Archbishop of York, 1761; Subdean of York, 1762–1805. FB's copy for Mrs Skinner of her verse letter is missing. See A. Sherbo, *Christopher Smart: Scholar of the University* (East Lansing, 1967), pp. 202, 244–5; J. E. B. Mayor and R. F. Scott, *Admissions to the College of St John the Evangelist in the University of Cambridge* (Cambridge, 1882–1931), iv. 478; *GM* lxxviii¹ (1808), 463.

[7] Presumably because of the distractions of a full household and the constant visiting at Lynn (see below).

ous, unaffected, lively Girl as ever—Susette seems much improved in every particular,—Charlotte ⌐has lost part of that Beauty she had, she is thinner, pale, & every way altered in her person for the worse; but she is still⌐ mighty pretty, & ⌐in every thing⌐ also improved, indeed she is a sweet good Girl, ⌐& as I attribute her alteration meerly to her growing very fast, I have much hope she will soon recover it all.⌐[8] [Bess]y is more graceful & more handsome than ever, |

[*top of page cut away*]

But I am extremely uneasy at present on the account of my elder Brother [JB]—so are we All. He told us in his last Letter, which we had above ½ a year ago,[9] that he expected to be Home this last spring—we have long been impatient for his arrival—& we find by the News paper that the Aquillon, his ship, was paid off last week:[10] what can be the meaning of his not writing to us then?—we know not how to enquire for him, nor where to direct to him—dear dear fellow! how much do I wish to see him—My Papa I perceive is very anxious—he has wrote to Town with directions for his Journey hither in case of his going there. |

[*some pages discarded here*]

[We have nothing but visiting here, & this perpetual][11] Round of constrained Civilities to Persons quite indifferent to us, is the most provoking and tiresome thing in the World, but it is unavoidable in a Country Town, where every body is

[8] Besides rapid growth, Charlotte's 'alteration' may well have been due to her step-mother's 'severity' towards her at Lynn. See above, p. 54 n. 12.

[9] See above, p. 39.

[10] '*Gosport, July* 17. On Thursday [13 July] his Majesty's Ship Aquilon was paid [at Portsmouth Harbour]' (*Daily Adv.*, Friday 21 July 1769). JB, however, along with several other members of the crew, did not receive his full wages until Nov. (*Aquilon* pay books, ADM 33/472, PRO). FB later noted in an obliterated passage in her Journal for 1773 (below, p. 310), that Capt. Onslow of the *Aquilon* 'was formerly so obliging as to disgrace my Brother!' JB had evidently been guilty of some insubordination or other offence, which may have led to his being detained and the £20 withheld. Whether detained or not, he was obviously for several months too ashamed to rejoin his family or even write to them. When he did reappear (apparently by early Oct.; see CB Jr. to FB 11 Oct. 1769, Osborn, and MA to FB 15 Oct. 1769, Berg), it is likely that an irate CB, angered by his son's disgrace and his thoughtlessness, temporarily forbad him from coming home. JB seems to have moved in with his family again at the end of Nov. See below, *passim*.

[11] Inserted by FBA.

known, as here. 'Tis a most shocking & unworthy way of spending our precious irrecoverable Time, to devote it to those who know not it's value—why are we not permitted to *decline* as well as *accept* visits &· acquaintance? It is not that we are ignorant of means to better employ ourselves, but that we dare not persue them. However, restraint of this kind is much much less practiced or necessary in London than else where—excuses there are no sooner made than admitted—acquaintance as easily drop'd as courted—& Company chose or rejected at pleasure—undoubtedly the same plan *might* be persued here but how? with breaking the customs of the place, disobliging the Inhabitants, & incurring the censure of the Town in general as ⌜insolent &⌝ unsociable, proud, or impertinant Innovators. Seeing therefore what must be submitted to, 'tis best to assume a good grace.— ˌ [xxxxx *14 lines*]

Saturday morn, Aug: [?26]

How strange, how unaccountable, yet how ⌜powerful⌝ & irresistable is the power of Time! We have not yet heard a word of my Brother, but nevertheless I find my uneasiness & grief on his account abate & subside insensibly:—I know not how to account for this, for doubtless I could have no fears formerly that are not now equally Just, niether is my affection for this dear Brother at all diminished, no indeed! I love him as tenderly, & as truely as ever, & I cannot ˌ well say more—but still does every morning Wake with lessened affliction, it's Edge is blunted, it's very name often forgot—the general ease & chearfulness that I see in others not a little contributes to banish my grief—'tis this same Time which has insensibly stolen away *my* unhappiness, that has, & I believe still sooner, robbed them of their's:—most welcome Thief!

Yet far, far from my Heart is forgetfulness—My Brother is inexpressibly dear to me, & my concern at his absence though ⌜⟨much⟩ & imperceptibly⌝ abated, is not extinct—nor ever, without happy news, will be! But sorrow is so unavailing, so useless, that the moment it sufficiently subsides to give Reason for fair play, I shall ever listen with pleasure to her exhortations.—Misery is a guest that we are glad to part with, however certain of her speedy return.

It is with great satisfaction I observe in Hetty (who sometime

before we left Town grew melancholy & sad)[12] the same constant flow of spirits & gaiety she inherited from Nature. Few
things, I think, are more dispiriting than perceiving a disposition alter from liveliness to dejection,—nothing so much
saddens me.

Would ⌐to God⌐ we could hear good News of my Brother.
Even now, that I confess my Affliction so much & insensibly
lessened, I never see a stormy Night without shuddering nor a
Letter without trembling— |

⌐11 at night—Monday—Aug. 28th

Happily I am out of the Parlour, which is full of Company,
some of whom being young & remarkably agreeable, 'tis with
no small ⟨stir⟩ I am alone again. Our Party has been Mr. &
Mrs. Partridge[13] the parents of Miss Allen's beloved; Mr. &
Mrs. Robinson,[14] *their* Parents; the first is an exceedingly
sensible, sagacious, & benevolent old man, a favourite & friend
of Papa's, & I really believe the most superior man in Lynn;
Mrs. Lidderdale, her sister—Mrs. Hepburn,[15] Mrs. Edmund
Allen,[16] and Mrs. Allen—senior—& these with our own very
large Family make a very formidable set: but this, however, is
the last *fuss* of this kind we shall have at Home, for we quit
Lynn next Wednesday [30 Aug.]. [xxxxx $3\frac{1}{2}$ *lines*]⌐ |

[12] Presumably because of Alexander Seton's noncommital courtship.

[13] Henry Partridge (1711–93) of Northwold, Norfolk, and Lowbrooks, Berkshire;
lawyer; Recorder of Lynn, 1745–69 (see H. Le Strange, *Norfolk Official Lists* (Norwich,
1890), p. 200). He married 1 (1745) Mary Say (1728–48); and 2 (1751) Alice Tayler (d.
1797). By his 1st wife he had Henry Partridge, 'Miss Allen's beloved' (see above, p. 64;
portraits in Singh, i, facing p. 256).

[14] i.e., Robertson; see above, p. 69 n. 55. The current Mrs Partridge was daughter of
Mrs Robertson by her 1st husband Simon Tayler (1703–38), merchant at Lynn; hence
'*their* Parents'.

[15] Probably Maria (Mary) Hepburn (*c.*1701–83), the unmarried 2nd daughter of Dr
George Hepburn of Lynn by his 1st wife Maria (*c.*1677–1707), whom he married
*c.*1693. Mrs Lidderdale, the 3rd daughter, also had two spinster half-sisters living in
Lynn, viz., Isabell Hepburn (*c.*1714–1802) and Pleasance Hepburn (*c.*1720–97),
daughters of Dr Hepburn by his 2nd wife Pleasance (*c.*1679–1736) (MI, St Nicholas
Chapel, Lynn). According to H. J. Hillen, *History of . . . Lynn* (Norwich, 1907), ii. 1031–
2, Mary Hepburn 'was a very extraordinary character, and stood unrivalled all her life
time among wits of [Lynn]. Her keen sayings, and stinging repartee are still fresh in the
recollection of her surviving contemporaries.' Isabell and Pleasance, on the other hand,
were 'vastly inferior' to the children of Dr Hepburn's first marriage, 'being but little
distant from idiocy'.

[16] See above, p. 6 n. 15.

Poland Street, London
Sunday, Sept[r] [10][17]

We have been at this ever dear House, in charming London,
above a week—I am now in my little Closet, and intend writing
the memoirs of the past 10 Days for the perusal of my *dear friend*
whose gratitude I doubt not will be as great as the obligation
requires.

⌐Let me see—'twas last Monday sennight in the little bay at
Lynn that I wrote last—To that Day then will I return.
Mama, Miss Allen, Hetty & my ⟨Papa⟩ [?din]ed at Mr.
Turners[18]—in the Evening Susette & myself went [?to] them;
& from thence¬ |

[*The end of the last line and the bottom of the page have been cut away. Prob-*
ably the Burneys or the whole company went to the wedding reception, described
on the verso.]

⌐The Bride[19] received us in [?full majesty at the] End of the
room, attended by her Father, mother & sister, & the *Groom*
accompanied us all to her, and then saluting us himself seated
us—which same Ceremony is preserved with all its forms in
Lynn tho' I believe pretty near abolished everywhere else; at
least for the Honour of the Nation I will hope so.

Having Drank Tea & sit till we were heartily tired & very
near asleep (for the Conversation, or rather the attempt at it,
was insufferably dull) we all return'd again to Mr. Turner's—&

---

[17] FB has incorrectly written '8th'.

[18] Charles Turner (d. 1792), sometime Mayor of Lynn and Collector of Customs
there (see above, p. 9 n. 27), was, with Walter Robertson and Stephen Allen (d. 1763),
CB's 'most intimate & affectionate' friend at Lynn ('Mem.' No. 69). A cousin of Sir
John Turner (vol. ii), who had procured for CB the post of organist at Lynn, FB calls
him 'a very *Jocular* man' (ibid.), but MAR mentions his 'Bronze' (MAR to FB *pre*
28 April 1775, Berg), and Bradfer-Lawrence describes him as 'an extremely unpopular
official, & the chief cause of the wane of his family's influence in Lynn' (H. L. Bradfer-
Lawrence, 'The Merchants of Lynn', in *A Supplement to Blomefield's Norfolk*, ed.
C. Ingleby (1929), p. 160).

[19] Probably Mary Cowen, who on Sunday 27 Aug. 1769 was married, by the Revd
Dr Charles Bagge in St Nicholas Chapel, to John Goddard (St Nicholas registers). The
groom was perhaps the 'Jn. Goddard, esq' of Elm, near Wisbech, who died in 1787
(*GM* lvii[2] (1787), 1024). Neither family is mentioned elsewhere in the Burney papers;
attending this reception was evidently one of the 'constrained Civilities' lamented by
FB above (p. 83).

then, being join'd by the third Miss Turner,[20] we proceeded to the hall[21] to[n] |

[*The bottom of the page has been cut away. On the next page FB describes her departure from Lynn with her father and EB. It appears that they were accompanied for several miles by SEB and Mrs Allen and as far as Thetford by MA .*]

[n][?Charlotte stayed] in Bed to indulge her sorrow at the loss of Papa, for I have not the vanity to go farther, tho' I beg Hetty's pardon—the dear Susan and [?Mrs.] Allen went in the Coach with us for above 2 mile, & then took a weeping leave—we saw then Mr. King,[22] very much to our happiness—he is a sensible, a very elegant man, I have seen nobody in Norfolk with whom I have been more pleased—Miss Allen & I stroled about the Fields & Churchyard & read the Epitaphs on Tomb stones till Dinner was ready—Mr. Green[23] had provided us an excellent Repast of Fruit—and he gave also what was still more acceptable, his Conversation. I cannot think of him without pity or regret of his unhappy marriage—the poor Woman too is much to be compassionated—how mortifying must it be to her that she was not included in the Invitation given to her Husband by papa to meet us!—& how many similar mortifications must she meet with!

We proceeded in about 2 Hours & ½ to Thetford, to Farmer Wright[24]—We *misses* choose [*sic*] to be set down in the Town, which we walked[n] | [?through looking at the remains of][25]

---

[20] Presumably one of the daughters of Sir John Turner, cousins of Mary ('Pow') Turner. The elder, Anne Turner (d. 1822), m. (1772) Robert Hales (d. *pre* 1822), Collector of the Customs for Lynn. The younger, Frances ('Fanny') Turner (d. 1813), m. (1775) Sir Martin Browne Folkes, 1st Bt. (*AR* xv. 158; *GM* xcii[2] (1822), 190; below, p. 109).

[21] Perhaps the Lynn Guildhall is meant, though for what function is unknown.

[22] Perhaps the 'Henry King, formerly an officer of the customs at Lynn', who died on 19 Oct.1800 (*GM* lxx[2] (1800), 1108; see also *Universal British Directory* (1798), iii. 761; 'The Poll for Members of Parliament . . . Lynn-Regis . . . 1768', MS B.L.I.c., Norfolk Record Office; Guildhall Meetings 1729–82, MS vol. in Lynn Public Library).

[23] Presumably a Lynn fruit-seller. Nothing has been found of the Greens or the reason for the wife's disgrace. The passage suggests, however, that Mrs Green may have fallen into adultery, been forgiven by her husband, but remained of course an outcast to everyone else.

[24] See above, p. 22.

[25] Conjecturally supplied; the bottom of the page has been cut away.

monasteries & abbeys, very curious & very *antique*.[26] Then
call'd to supper—

12 o'clock—

There is something in the sight of the ruins of Antiquity
which always inspires me with melancholy, & yet gives me a
pleasure which compensates for the pain—'tis dreadful to see
the ravage of Time & the fury of War, which are the joint causes
of the destruction of Cities &c—And yet 'tis pleasing to discover
the taste of former ages by the remains of their Works, and to
endeavour to trace the rise & progress we have made in improv-
ing or altering the fabricks, laws, & customs of our fore fathers;
& we can form no opinion, with equal certainty of truth, by any
other means than by the *relicks* We have preserved—

Tuesday, Sept[r] [12]

Again interrupted—& every Day my subject *grows upon
me*—I must be more concise, or I shall never come to the
present moment—which God bless it is more precious than all
the past put together.

At Thetford we ⌐saw Bessy, who is very well, & pretty, &
then we sup'd & slept—in the⌐ [?morning we separated. Miss
Allen and Bessy looked weeping][27] after us till the Road
turned: our first stage was very gloomy—we spent it in regretting the absence of those who had so much contributed to
enliven our first Days Journey, which was really delightful—
but we recovered our spirits afterwards, & were very comfortable—we slept at Hockrel[28] that night & on Friday Evening

---

[26] Thetford, 30 miles by coach from Lynn, had been a major ecclesiastic centre in the
Middle Ages. The ruins there included remains of the Cluniac Priory or Abbey of St
Mary (12th c.); the monastery (later nunnery) of St George (11th c.); the priory of the
Canons of the Holy Sepulchre (12th c.); a monastery of the Dominicans (14th c., earlier
occupied by the Cluniac monks); and another of the Augustine Friars (14th c.). See
Thomas Martin, *The History of the Town of Thetford* (1779), pp. 98–202; A. Leigh Hunt,
The Capital of the Ancient Kingdom of East Anglia (1870), pp. 62–83; W. G. Clarke, *A Short
Historical Guide to the Ancient Borough of Thetford* (Thetford, 1908), pp. 20, 23–4, 27,
29, 40.
[27] Conjecturally supplied; the bottom of the page is missing. For the obliterated
passage FBA has substituted 'slept, & the next morning separated. Miss Allen & sweet
Susette looked weeping.' From the obliterated passage above, p. 87, however, it is clear
that SEB had left the travellers earlier.
[28] Hockerill in Hertfordshire lay another 50 miles S. by coach from Thetford via

[1 Sept.] got to Town—rather slow travelling, but the same Horses with our heavy large Coach could not go faster—We Dined that Day on Epping Forest[29]—what a delightful spot!— we almost always go different Roads to Lynn, which makes a variety of prospect & novelty of view highly preferable to the [high Road][30] sameness.

Hetty was charmed even with the smoak of [*2 lines cut out*] [London],[30] but [I] ᴦwould willingly dispence with passing the summer here, & would joyfully have remained another month or two in Lynn.ᴨ

Here however, we are & with as much happiness both in present possession and in | prospect for the future as can possibly fall to a mortal's lot:—if my dear James would write!—ᴦbut I am willing to hope he is well settled on board some ship, & at the end of another voyage, will fly to his friends with all that ardour which nothing I am convinced but his shame & apprehension have hitherto repelled & which will then of course give way to his joy of every thing being forgot & forgiven.

The first intelligence we received from Betty, who, with her *sposa*,[31] has kept home during our absence, was such as gave Hetty extreme pleasure, namely that Mr. Seton has two or three times been here to enquire after her & the Family—& another which g⟨ave⟩ [*3 lines cut out*] for half the old acquaintance I know.ᴨ—There is a *something*, a *je ne sai quoi* in the really admirable or agreeable which does not need intimacy or Time to create esteem & admiration for them: for | my own part, I love many people with sincere affection whom I have not seen above half an Hour—of this number, is Mʳˢ Pleydel, who has something in her manners which engages the Heart as effectually immediately, as many thousand people would be able to do in years—I hear she is now at Tunbridge— |

[*The bottom of the page has been cut away. The following fragment is on the verso*.]

Newmarket. It was the second stopping place for coaches travelling from London to Newmarket. See *Vict. Co. Hist. Hertford*, iii. 296.

[29] Epping in Essex lies 14 miles S. of Hockerill and 17 miles from London. Philip Luckombe, *English Gazeteer* (1790), s.v. Epping, describes the Forest as 'a royal chace' that 'reaches from the town almost to London'.

[30] Inserted by FBA; 'high Road' substituted for an unrecovered obliteration.

[31] Presumably Betty and John Hutton (above, p. 65).

⌐proceed—or indeed do any thing but indulge them tomorrow morning—perhaps I make a bold effort, by rising early & writing before Breakfast.

Wednesday Sept. [13]

According to promise, here I am but intolerably Hungry, & therefore not very entertaining—it must⌐ |

[top of following page cut away]

Friday I pass unnoticed—for so the world did by me!—⌐On Thursday we received charming pacquets from Lynn, by the means of Stephen Allen, who came with a fellow swain [xxxxx 2 lines] Every Body well—to say aught more would be *superfluous*—my observations & anecdotes *never* are!

The two youths supped with Hetty & me, for Papa was with Mr. Greville, & horridly stupid we all were. This Mr. John[32] is a *gentle swain* indeed—he cannot say more than yes or No for the world—nor even so much without stammering & colouring:—Niether is Stephen very bright, but much on an equality with the other.⌐ |

[top of page cut away]

it was my turn to sit up—[xxxxx ½ *line*] for papa made a late visit to Mr. Greville. When the Door opened I heard him & some other talking very earnestly & loud, & into the Room together they both *bolted*—& then ⌐⟨I heard⟩⌐ Dr. Hawkesworth.—He was engaged so deeply in Conversation, with papa, that niether seemed to know what they were about—However, on coming into the parlour the Doctor made his Compliments to me, & out of it they stalked again, & ran up into the study where they stayed some time, & then, flying down, the Dr. wished me good night, & got into the Coach again, & papa talked with him at the Door of it some Time: There is an earnestness, a spirit, in the Conversation of very superior men which | makes them absolutely forget every thing about them, & which, when one knows not the subject which engages them, ⌐makes them each⌐ appear ridiculous to *spectators*; to *hearers* the appearance

---

[32] Presumably his Christian name; perhaps a Lynn friend of Stephen's who was also a fellow student at Harrow. Not identified.

is very different.—I was only a *spectator*, & could not help laughing to see them *Capering* about all the Time they talked as if they were bewildered. [I believe it was only to look for Books, & authors, & authorities for what they said.][33] [xxxxx *1 line*] |

[*bottom of page cut away*]

⌐with the hopes of seeing him [Alexander Seton?] as soon as we came to London, Hetty & myself went to his lodging—but they had no expectations at all of seeing him. Papa has wrote an invitation to Kitty Cooke to come to our House for some time, as she is to be Commissioned by our *Daddy* to see the new Lodging for him near our House,[34]—for he declares he will no longer live so far from us as West⟨minster⟩—⌐ |

[*The bottom of the page has been cut away. On the next page FB describes another visit of Christopher Smart, the poet.*]

[? Mr. Smart said that he knew not if the] ⌐⟨horr⟩id *old Cat*—as he once politely called his wife,[35] ⟨be⟩ dead yet or not. [xxxxx *2 lines*] she had really used him uncommonly ill, even ⟨cruel⟩ly— nevertheless, it is extreamly shocking to hear him mention a Wife in so unfeeling a manner. & yet, the genius, talents & great merit as is rather so generally allowed to Mr. Smart, incline me very much to believe his provocation authorises his hatred—if, after all, any thing can.⌐

⌐He⌐ presented me with a Rose, ⌐which is uncommon in London at this time of the year—⌐'It was given me, said he, by a fair lady—though not so fair as *you*!'—

I always admired *poetical licence*! [xxxxx *3 lines*]

This, however, is nothing to what he afterwards amused himself with saying.

---

[33] Added by FBA.

[34] Presumably where SC would stay during his visits to town.

[35] Anna Maria Carnan (1732–1809), m. (1752) Christopher Smart. Smart's religious mania had led him to turn on his wife, a Roman Catholic, and they had been estranged for years. Mrs Smart had visited him just once during his confinements for madness, and Smart's hostility had no doubt been compounded by her sending their two daughters to a French convent (in late 1767 or early 1768). By all impartial accounts, though, Mrs Smart was a highly admirable person, and rather than being the guilty party, she probably separated from her husband only after extreme provocation. See F. E. Anderson, *Christopher Smart* (New York, 1974), pp. 32–4, 49; A. Sherbo, *Christopher Smart: Scholar of the University*, pp. 86, 125–8, and *passim*.

The Critical Reviewers, ever eager to ⌐ catch at every opportunity of lessening & deg[rad]ing the merit of this unfortunate
man, (who has be[en] twice confined in a mad House,)³⁶ would
think all th[e] most rancourous observations on his declining
pow[ers] fully justified, & perhaps even pronounce him to be in
a state of mind that rendered him a proper object to return a
third Time to Bedla[m]—if they heard that he had descended
to flatter & praise *me*! even me, *FB* or Q in a corner—³⁷

⌐Sunday Septʳ 17

Miss Cooke has accepted our invitation, and ⟨expects⟩ to be
in Town soon—Poor Mʳ Crisp continues ill at Chesington—
My dear Hetty makes herself very unhappy about this vile
man's [Seton's] behaviour—she met him to Day in the park—
he did indeed condescend to walk with her, but his manner
was cold, Indifferent & totally altered—he took every opportunity of saying sarcastick & even ill natured things to her—
how little does he merit the tenderness she cherishes for him &
how unworthy an obj[ect]⌐ ⌐

[*The top of the following page has been cut away. The fragment seems to be
about attempts by Charles Rousseau Burney to find the errant sailor JB.*]

[?Charles has] ⌐wrote my Brother an Invitation in his own
Name—[xxxxx 3½ *lines*] & if he ever receives the Letter, I can
not doubt his hastening to them [Charles Rousseau Burney
and EBB], but it seems he has never been to this Mr. Gibson's
since he saw Tom Burney,³⁸ except for a few minutes meerly to

───────

³⁶ See above, p. 36 n. 1. A typical critical reaction to Christopher Smart's productions after his second confinement is contained in the *Critical Review*, xvi (1763), 395.
Commenting on *Poems on Several Occasions* (1763), the reviewer observes: 'We wish,
from a regard to the reputation of Mr. Smart, who formerly made a considerable figure
in the world of literature, that they had been suppressed, as they can do him no
honour.' As for his latest work, the versified *Parables of Our Lord and Saviour Jesus Christ*
(1768), the *Monthly Review*, xxxviii (1768), 409, commented sarcastically that its dedication to the 3-year-old George Thornton was particularly appropriate. It should be
observed that not all of Smart's reviews since 1763 were unqualifiedly bad, and that
Smart himself was partly to blame for the rancour of the critics because of counter-
attacks he had made against them in print. See Sherbo, pp. 186–8, 246–8 and *passim*.

³⁷ *OED*, which cites only FB herself for this term (in *Cecilia*, Bk. I, chap. 3), surmises
that it is another name for the children's game 'puss in the corner' (see *OED* s.v. Q I. 3,
Puss 5). Perhaps the 'Q' stands for 'quiet', which would fit the '*silent, observant Miss
Fanny*'.

³⁸ Presumably Thomas Burney (b. 1738), who afterwards took the name of Holt (see

take away his money & some other things: his Chest & a Fiddle still remain there. All the People who Charles saw, (& they *all* ⟨saw⟩ him) declare that far from intending⌐ |

[*top of the page cut away*]

⌐good God!⌐ Poor Mʳ Hayes,[39] an Old, & intimate friend of Papa's is below—he has lost his wife while we were in Lynn, & I dread meeting him.

I live in perpetual alarm—every Rap at the Door I think will bring me News—my rest is ver[y] much disturbed—I Dream confused things of my Brot[her] for ever. But all that relates to *me* is nothing. My Papa observes my low spirits, & asks the cause: 'tis impossible for me to answer.—He is more k[ind,] more Affectionate to me than ever. Dearest best of ⌐men, I am convinced that a proper application would soften his rancour,[40] could we ⟨but⟩⌐ |

[*Some pages have been discarded here. At the top of the next page FBA has inserted:* Decʳ 20. My dear Brother has now been home these three weeks! *Some isolated words and phrases recovered from* 5½ *obliterated lines suggest that one evening the Burney sisters encouraged JB to intrude into his father's study and make up with him, which he apparently did.*]

my beloved Father Daily appears more & more kind & affectionate to the dear Brother: & we are now all happily settled. This affair never cost us more uneasiness, than thank God it does ⌐now⌐ happiness.

below, p. 110). Son of CB's older half-brother Thomas Burney (b. 1707), a dancing master who absconded to America about 1745, he 'was of so unimprovable a disposition, that he became a trouble & a clog upon the family, all the early part of his life' ('Worcester Mem.'; J. L. Chester, ed., *The Reister Booke of Saynte De'nis Backchurch* (1878), p. 168; IGI). Mr Gibson, with whom JB apparently stayed, has not been traced.

[39] John Hayes (*c.*1708–92). According to FBA, Hayes was reputed to be the natural son of Sir Robert Walpole (1676–1745), cr. (1742) E. of Orford (*Mem.* i. 102–3). Hayes's mother may have been the mysterious 'Mrs. Hayes' whom Horace Walpole visited at Paris in 1741 and again in 1765–6 and who at the earlier date was intimate with the entire Walpole family.

John Hayes was very close to Sir Robert's grandson George, 3rd E. of Orford (1730–91), and CB first met Hayes at Houghton, seat of the Orfords, in the early 1750s. The friendship of CB and Hayes continued unabated until Hayes's death in 1792. In his will (PCC, prob. 13 Nov. 1792) Hayes mentions a picture by 'Samuel Coates' (presumably the miniaturist Samuel Cotes) of his 1st wife; she has not been further identified. In 1771 Hayes remarried; for his 2nd wife see below, p. 156. See also *Mem.* iii. 150; *JL* i. 82 n. 10; iii. 5 n. 2; *YW* vii. 311, xxx. 21 and n. 10, xxxi. 65, xxxvii. 293 and n. 5.

[40] Against JB, presumably; see above, p. 83 n. 10, and immediately below.

James's character appears the same as ever—honest, generous, sensible, unpolished; always unwilling to take offence; yet
always eager to resent it: very careless, but possessed of an
uncommon share of good nature; full of humour, mirth & Jollity; ever delighted at mirth in others, & happy in a peculiar
talent of propagating it himself.

His Heart is full of love & affection for us,—I sincerely
believe he would perform the most difficult Task which could
possibly be imposed on him, to do us service. |

In short, he is a most worthy, deserving creature, & we are
extremely happy in his Company—tho' he complains that we
use him very ill, in making Engagements in which he cannot
join from ignorance of the partys—but ' *'twas unavoidable, Fate
& necessity,*' as Lord Ogleby says—[41]

⌐Sunday [24 Dec.]¬

[*There follow 7 obliterated lines, partially recovered, in which FB mentions
that* Hetty has received a lengthy letter, expressing the most vulgar,
low, unmeaning preference I ever saw, *and apparently describing EB as*
extremely tender, *and* a fit object for loving & kissing.]

⌐It was impossible to imagion for a minute that Mʳ Seton would
have wrote it, tho' it was evidently designed by the writer to be
charged to him, as his name is Alexander, & the direction is
apparently an imitation of his Hand.

⟨Andrew⟩ Pringle was the only person to whom¬ | [?I could
ascribe such an imposture][42]

[*The following 2 fragments are the bottom remnant of a leaf, recto and verso,
originally pasted to fo. 46ᵛ. Another fragment pasted there is printed in its
proper chronological position, i.e., in Feb. 1770 (below, p. 113).*]

[41] In David Garrick and George Colman's comedy *The Clandestine Marriage* (1766),
Act IV, scene iii.

[42] Conjecturally supplied for the beginning of the next page, which is missing. This
episode, suppressed by FBA, seems the inspiration for the improperly passionate letter
forged to Evelina in Lord Orville's name by Sir Clement Willoughby (*Evelina*, vol. ii,
letter 27). If FB in fact suspected Andrew Pringle initially of thus trying to discredit
Alexander Seton, she evidently dismissed the thought later, as she calls him a very
'worthy young man' (below, p. 117). In view of Seton's often peculiar behaviour before
(see especially above, p. 62), it is not impossible that he indeed sent the letter himself,
despite FB's refusal to believe it. If this is so, then one may suppose EB's silence on the
matter persuaded him that the gambit had failed.

Decr 26th

I have spent this Day alone, nevertheless very comfortably—I have at present so many persuits that my whole Time
can be very well employed at Home, & could if every Hour |

"I am very sorry that Hetty will renew her acquaintance with
Mrs. Debieg, where she must unavoidably meet again the
destroyer of her peace, who I hoped she had forgot, till her
eagerness for this" |

[?h]as doubled in length. I am now aiming at some [k]now-
ledge of the Grecian History; I began Stan[y]an some Time
since,[43] but never finished it,—[I] am just beginning to Read
Smith's translation of Thucydides history of the Peloponnesian
War—I mention the *translator*, lest I should be suspected of
Reading the original Greek! ... *I think the precaution
necessary!*—

"My Father, who Daily recovers in Health & spirits,[44] is gone
to spend a Week at Lynn—to return Mama's visit here[45]—
Charles is gone [?back to the Charterhouse and][46] will be" |

[*The bottom of the page has been cut away. The following passage, on the
verso, seems to contain FB's year's-end resolution henceforth to use her journals
more for serious self-examination and correction. If she did this, no doubt such
passages were destroyed by FBA as too personal and revealing.*]

"been conscious of, & that in indulging myself freely in an
impertinant knack at raillery would be some merit were I
owning [?it to] *somebody*, but at present I am meerly t[aking]
myself to task, which, for the future, I intend more ⟨suffi-
ciently⟩ to do than I hithe[rto] have, & that may make this

---

[43] See above, p. 58. William Smith (1711–87), DD (Oxon.), 1758, Dean of Chester,
1758, classical scholar, published in 1753 his trans. of *The History of the Peloponnesian
War ... from the Greek of Thucydides*. CB's copy of the 1st edn. is listed in *Lib.*, p. 54.
[44] CB was presumably still feeling the effects of an acute attack of rheumatism which
had 'confined him to his bed, or his chamber, during twenty days' (*Mem.* i. 218). In a
letter to FB probably written the previous month, SC chides CB for the overwork which
brought on the attack and impeded his recovery: 'When I come to Town. ... I shall
without Ceremony ... have a straight waistcoat immediately put on him, debar him
the use of Pen, Ink, paper & Books, to which (if he is mutinous) shall be added a dark
Room—what does he mean? ... the Booby has nothing to do but to allow some repose
to his thin Carcass to get well again ...' (SC to FB 13 Nov. [1769], Barrett).
[45] Presumably for Christmas.
[46] Conjecturally supplied for a portion of the last line cut away.

Journal sin[gular]ly useful to me. & this will be anoth[er] & very strong reason why I shall gaurd [*sic*] [?it] from all human Eyes—for it would not [be] very flattering or agreeable to sit down [to] write my ⟨past⟩ [?follies for all to see.]ⁿ |

AJ (Early Diary, iii, paginated 115–[78], foliated 1–73, refoliated 1–55, Berg), Journal for 1770.

Originally a cahier made of interfolded double sheets, from which sewn leaves have been cut away and the remains resewn with heavy black thread. Now 30 single sheets and 8 double sheets 4to, 92 pp., with 2 paste-overs.

Entitled (*by FBA*): Juvenile Journal. | N° 3. | 1770

Annotated: 17—to 18   only—To be sewen [*sic*] ✣⊕

Frances Burney
Memoirs
Addressed to a certain Miss Nobody.

January 10th

How very differently do I begin this Year to what I did the Last! O how unhappy I then was. My poor Susan on the Brink of the Grave! — — But I will not waste Time in recollecting past misfortunes, when present happiness opens so fair a prospect to make me forget them. In truth, I have a most delightful subject to commence the present Year with—such a one, as I fear I may never chance to meet with again—Yet why should I look into futurity with a gloomy Eye?—But let me Wave all this Nonsense, & tell you, my dear, faithful, ever attentive Nobody,—that I was last Monday [8 Jan.], at a masquerade!

Has Nobody any curiosity to Read an Account of this Frolick? I am sure Nobody has, and Nobody will I satisfy by Writing one. I am so good natured as to prevent Nobody's wishes.

This masquerade—how does that word grace my Journal!— was, however, a very private one & at the House of Mr Laluze,[1]

---

[1] Charles Lalauze (d. 1775), French dancer and actor. Lalauze made his London dancing début at the Haymarket in 1726. In 1734 he first appeared at Drury Lane, and from 1735 he danced principally at Covent Garden under the management of John Rich (d. 1761). His last appearance as a dancer was on 24 Apr. 1771 in a benefit for him at the Haymarket, and he died near Paris in Mar. 1775.

Lalauze's house was in Leicester Square. A news clipping of 1757 (in the Burney Collection of English Newspapers, BL) notes that 'Mr. Lalauze, Dancing-Master, of the

a French Dancing master. ⌜He at first intended it only as an
Amusement for his own scholars, but afterwards enlarged his
plans to inviting almost All his Acquaintance. *We* have meerly
a personal knowledge of him, & were invited on account of
Miss Strange, who was his scholar[2]—He has a Daughter[3]
whom we have often met at Mr. Strange's, & who is extremely
fond of my sister, & appears to be almost equally so of me, &
she was very desirous of our being masquerades. It is easy to
believe that we were niether of us averse to it, though it was
some time ere we had my Father's consent, not from his being
unwilling to give it, but from our being half afraid to ask it—
though we afterwards found that he had thought there would
be only Children there, on account of Mr. Laluze's profession,—& to that idea, I fancy we owed our Frolick.⌝

Hetty had for 3 months thought of nothing but the masquerade—no more had I.—She had long fixed ⌐ upon her Dress; my
stupid Head only set about one on Friday Evening. I could
think of no Character which I liked much, and could obtain; as
to Nuns, Quakers, &c, (which I was much advised to) I cannot
help thinking there is a gravity & extreme reserve required to
support them, which would have made me necessarily so dull
& stupid that I could not have met with much entertainment,
& being unable to fix on a *Character*, I resolved at length to go

Theatre Royal in Covent-Garden, is removed from Great Suffolk-street to Leicester-
square, where he has a large convenient Room separate from the House, and proposes
to teach young Gentlemen and Ladies, from six or seven years of Age to twelve, twice a
week, at Two Guineas a Quarter, and private Scholars as usual.'

FB mentions Lalauze's masquerade again in her Journal for 1779 (*DL* i. 250). It
probably suggested the masquerade scene in *Cecilia* (1782), Bk. II, chap. 3. See Highfill; below, pages following and p. 118.

[2] Mary Bruce Strange, her sister Isabella, and her brothers James, Thomas, and
Robert were all taught dancing by Lalauze. Her mother Mrs Strange wrote in 1763 that
'Bruce [Mary Bruce] dances very gently' (see Dennistoun, i. 303–12 *passim*).

[3] Miss Lalauze was about 16 years old at this time. She made her début as a dancer
in 1759 when, 'a Child between 5 and 6 years of age', she danced a minuet with her
father and a Miss Toogood in a benefit for her father at Covent Garden. She continued
to dance in benefits for him until 1771. By 1775 she appears to have become the
mistress of a Mr Masters. That year (as 'Mrs Masters') she made her acting and singing
débuts at Covent Garden.

After 1776 Miss Lalauze disappears from the lists of the *London Stage*, but she is probably identical with the Mrs Masters who played soubrettes and was a Columbine at
Bristol in 1778–9. She may also be the Mrs Masters who reappears at Covent Garden in
1788 and who acted and sang there until 1809. See Highfill; *LS*, *passim*; below, *passim*,
and vol. ii (where FB reports s.v. 10 June 1775, that 'Miss Strange has heard the story of
[Miss Lalauze's] *marriage* all contradicted').

in a meer *fancy Dress*. ⌜In truth, I was so long wavering & ir-
resolute, that I had done for no other, & at a masquerade every
thing is allowable.⌝

One Day—and who could do it less in?
The masqueraders spent in Dressing.—[4]

It is really true that all Monday we ⌐passed in *preparationing*[5]
for the Evening, ⌜for my own part, I was really working to the
last moment, & my Aunt Anne was assisting me.⌝

Oh, I must tell you, that speaking of my distress in regard to
a Dress one Day to Mrs Mancer,[6] a very notable, talkative good
sort of old Gentlewoman, & who is a half Aunt to us, she said—
'Why I'll te[ll] ⌜you who to⌝ Go; As Flora, the *Goddess of
Wisdom*!'

We had a *concourse* of People to see ⌜our Dresses here, for we
had mentioned our masquerade one Time before to our
acquaintances.⌝ Hetty, who was dressed Early, went down to
receive them: they sent me up repeated messages to hasten;
⌜but it was hardly in my power—& Captain Pringle[7] actually
came up to my Chamber Door, & beg'd that if I would not
come down to him, I would ⌐let him come up to me. I gave him
little answer besides Barring the Door⌝ & when I *was* ready,

---

[4] FB's adaptation of the opening lines of Swift's *The Lady's Dressing Room* (1730):
'Five Hours, (and who can do it less in?) / By haughty *Celia* spent in Dressing' (*Poems*,
ed. H. Williams (Oxford, 1958), ii. 525). She may have read this infamously scatological
poem in her father's copy of the collected *Works* (Dublin, 1735). See *Lib.*, p. 52.

[5] Presumably FB's humorous coinage, or perhaps she is echoing an illiterate servant
or a child. *OED* cites this passage, calling the term an obsolete nonce-word.

[6] Martha Burney (*c*.1706–80), who m. (25 Nov. 1739, in Rochester Cathedral)
William Manser. Born in Ireland, daughter of CB's father James MacBurney by his
first wife Rebecca née Ellis (1681–*pre* 1720), Mrs Manser died at Rochester in 1780
('Worcester Mem.'; IGI). Flora is of course the Roman goddess of flowers and Minerva
of wisdom.

[7] Robert Pringle (d. 1793), the eldest son of Mrs Pringle, the Burneys' neighbour in
Poland St. A career officer in the Royal Engineers, Pringle was promoted to Lt. in 1766
when he was recommended by Governor Melville of Grenada as Governor-Depute.
Despite FB's calling him 'Captain' here, he did not attain the regimental rank of Capt.-
Lt. until 1775, and Capt. in 1783. (Cf. 'Captain' Blomefield, below, p. 109.) After serving in America (see below, p. 199) he was appointed Engineer Commandant of
Gibralter (in 1785). He became a Lt.-Col. (army) in 1790 and a Lt.-Col. of Engineers in
1792. Pringle died while on a government mission to Grenada, on 17 June 1793. See
T. W. J. Conolly and R. F. Edwards, *Roll of Officers of the Corps of Royal Engineers, from
1760 to 1898* (Chatham, 1898), p. 8; A. Pringle, *The Record of the Pringles or Hoppringills of
the Scottish Border* (Edinburgh, 1933), pp. 177, 320; *Scots Magazine*, l (1788), 206; *AR*
xxix (1787), 27; Pringle's will, PCC, prob. 30 Nov. 1793; below, *passim*.

they had made so much *fuss*, that I was really ashamed to go down, and but for my mask which I put on, I could scarse have had courage to appear.

⌐I will now tell you our Dresses.¬

Hetty went as a Savoyard, with a ⌐Pompadour Jacket trimed with Blue, and a Blue Coat trimed with pompadour, a plain Gause Handkerchief tied under her Chin, white shoes & *Blue Roses*, a short Gause Apron very prettily trimed, white mittens, & to complete her a Vielle or¬ *Hurdy Gurdy* round her waist. Nothing could look more simple, innocent or pretty.

My Dress was, a close pink persian | *Vest*, ⌐with long close sleeves, to my Wrists, it was¬ covered with Gause, in loose pleats ⌐behind, & drawn half tight & half loose at the sleeve, puckered before, with very small pink Flowers fastened on to look like buttons; it came up high in the Neck, & had a Gause frill round the Waist. My Coat was white silk trimed also with small artificial flowers before, & a Gause train looped up behind, & pink ribband round the Bottom. I had pink silk shoes & Roses, a very small black color [collar] about my Neck,¬ a little Garland or Wreath of Flow[e]rs on the left side of my Head, ⌐& looped Pearl Earings.

Thus my Dress, being a regular one, has taken twice the Time to describe as Hetty's did.¬

When I came down, I found Assembled Captain Pringle, Mr Andrew, | the three Miss Pascalls, Mr Lambe their Father in Law,[8] ⌐Miss Barsanti,¬ my Aunt, James, Charles [Rousseau] & Hetty—⌐so that our Parlour was tolerably filled.¬

Both our Dresses met with approbation. Not one of the Company could forbear repeatedly wishing themselves of our party; nothing appears so gay, flattering and charming as a masquerade; & the sight of 2 who were going, & in very high spirits, was absolutely tantalising.

The Captain had a fine opportunity for gallantry—to say the truth, those whimsical dresses are not unbecoming. He made a story for me 'That I had been *incarcerated* by the Grand Seignor as a]^9 | part of the seraglio prisoner by the Russians in the present War;[10] & that the generosity of the commanding

---

[8] See above, p. 82 n. 5.

[9] Inserted by FBA for 4 lines cut away at the bottom of the page.

[10] The Russo-Turkish War, 1768–74. The Grand Signior or Sultan of the Turks was

Officer had prevailed with him to grant me my Liberty, & that I had consequently thrown myself into the protection of the bravest and noblest People of Europe, & sought shelter from oppression in this Land of Freedom.'

We stayed with this Company about half an Hour, & then ⌐as Papa came Home,⌐ the Captain Handed us into the Coach, & away we drove. |

[bottom of page cut away]

[xxxxx *1–2 words*] We called for Miss Strange, & then went to Mr Lalause, who lives in Leicester Square. Miss Strange had a White sattin Domino ⌐trimed with Blue.⌐ M^r & Mrs Lalause[11] were niether in masquerade, ⌐but received us in *propria Persona*.⌐ The Room was large, & very well lighted, *but*, when we first went in, not half filled, so that every Eye was turned on each new Comer—I felt extremely awkward & abashed, notwithstanding my mask, ⌐the more so as we were all seperated in a moment.⌐ Hetty went in, playing on her *Hurdy Gurdy*, & the Company flocked about her with much pleasure. I was soon found out by Miss Lalause who is a fine Girl, about 16, ⌐& appears to be very fond of Hetty & me:⌐ she had on a | *fancy* Dress, ⌐& except that she had a great deal of silver Braid on it, it was⌐ much in the style of mine. The first mask who accosted me was an Old Witch, Tall, shrivell'd, leaning on a Broom stick, &, in short a fear inspiring figure, apparently, by his Walk, a man. ⌐You must know that my mask had been made by my Cousin who was also one of the spectators of our curious Dresses & not quite so well as I expected, but it was finished too late for me to get another. The Witch began⌐ 'Thou thinkest, then, that that little bit of Black silk is a mask?—'

I was absolutely confounded, for I thought directly that he meant to laugh at my mask, but on rec[o]llection I believe he was going on with some ⌐thing else,⌐ but I was so unable to rally, that with a silly half Laugh, I turned | on my Heel & Walked away.

Mustafa III (1717–73). The capture of the Sultan's seraglio is the Captain's fiction, though it may have been suggested by the fall of the important fortress of Choczim (Khotin) the previous Sept. when, according to reports, the Russian soldiers found inside only a few women and children left behind by the fleeing Turkish army. See *AR* xii (1769), 27; *YW* xxiii. 70 n. 3, 81 n. 2; xxiv. 33 n. 7.

[11] Mrs Lalauze has not been further identified.

⌐O clever, thought I, this is a dismal beginning. However, I grew more courageous after being there some Time.⌐

I observed a Nun, Dressed in Black, who was speaking with great earnestness, & who discovered by her Voice to be a Miss Milne,[12] a pretty Scotch Nymph I have met at Mrs Stranges. I ⌐addressed myself⌐ to her. She turn'd about & took my Hand & led me into a Corner of the Room—'Beautiful Creature! cried she, in a plaintive Voice, 'with what pain do I see you here, beset by this Crowd of folly & deceit! O could I prevail on you to quit this wicked world, & all it's vices, & to follow my footsteps!'

'But how am I to account, said I, for the reason that one who so much despises the world, should chuse to mix with the gayest part of it?' |

'I come but, said she, to see & to save such innocent, beautiful, young Creatures as you from the snares of the Wicked. Listen to me, I was once such as you are, I mixed with the World; I was caressed by it, I loved it—I was deceived!— surrounded by an artful set of flattering, designing men, I fell but too easily into the net they spread for me; I am now convinced of the vanity of Life, & in this peaceful, tranquil state shall I pass the remainder of my Days.'

'It is so impossible, said I, to listen to you without being benefitted by your Conversation, that I shall to the utmost of my power *imitate you*, & always chuse to despise the World, & hold it in contempt.—at a *masquerade*!—.' |

'Alas, said she, I am here meerly to contemplate on the strange follys & vices of mankind—this scene affords me only a subject of joy to think I have quitted it.'

We were here interrupted, & parted. After that I had several short conversations with different masks—I will tell you the principal Dresses as well as I can recollect them. ⌐They were⌐

A Punch, who was indeed very completely Dressed, & who very well supported his Character. The Witch whom I mentioned before was a very capital Figure, & told many Fortunes with great humour. A shepherd, of all Characters the last, were

---

[12] Probably a relation of Robert Mylne (1734–1811), the architect and engineer, who was a long-time friend of the Stranges. Perhaps his sister Anne Mylne (d. 1822), who married (1775) Sir John Gordon (1720–95), 4th Bt. See Dennistoun, i. 307 and n.; R. S. Mylne, *The Master Masons to the Crown of Scotland and their Works* (Edinburgh, 1893), 'Pedigree of John Mylne of Dundee' following p. 304.

I a man, I should have wished to have assumed; A Harliquin, who hop'd & skip'd about very ⌐ lightly & gayly; A Huntsman, who indeed seemed suited for nothing but the Company of Dogs, A Garden[er,] A Persian, 2 or 3 Turks, & 2 Friars—A Merlin,[13] who spoke of spells, magick & charms with all the *mock heroick* and bombast manner which his Character could require. There were also two most jolly looking sailors, & many Dominos, besides some Dresses which I have forgot. Among the Females, two sweet little Nuns in white pleased me most; there was a very complete shepherdess, with the gayest Crook, the smartest little Hat, & most trifling Conversation one might desire; nevertheless full as clever as her choice of so hackneyed & insipid a Dress led one to expect—You may imagion that she was immediately & unavoidably paired with the amiable shepherd I mentioned before. There were 2 or 3 young pastoral Nymphs to keep her in Countenance; &, I can recollect no other Dresses, save an Indian Queen; & Dominos. ⌐

I siezed the first opportunity that offered of again joining my sage monitor the fair Nun—who did not seem averse to honouring me with her Conversation. She renewed her former subject, expatiated on the wicked⌐ness of mankind⌐ & degeneracy of the World, dwelt with great energy and warmth on the deceit & craft of man, & pressed me to join her holy Order with the zeal of an Enthusiast ⌐in religion. She⌐ [xxxxx *3 lines*] a pink Domino advanced, & charged her not to instill her preposterous sentiments into my mind; she answered him with so much contempt that he immediately quitted us.—We were then accosted by the shepherd, who would fain have appeared of some consequence, & aimed at being gallant & agreeable— Poor man! wofully was he the contrary. The Nun did not spare him. 'Hence,' cried she, 'thou gaudy Animal, with thy trifling & ridiculous trappings ⌐ away—Let not this fair Creature be corrupted by this Company. O fly the pernicious impertinance of these shadows which surround thee!—' 'The—the Lady— stammered the poor swain—'the Lady will be—will be more likely—to be hurt—by — — by you than—than—' 'Yes, yes,' cried she, 'she would be safe enough were she followed only by such as thee!' Hetty just then bid me observe a very droll old

---

[13] Henry Phipps, afterwards E. of Mulgrave, who later secured EB as his dancing partner.

Dutch man, who soon after joined us[14]—He accosted us in
High Dutch — — not that I would Quarrel with any one who
told me it was *Low* Dutch!—⌐Heaven knows⌐ it might be
Arabick for ought I could tell! He was very completely Dressed,
& had on an exceeding droll old man's mask, & was smoaking
a Pipe—He presented me with a Quid of Tobaco, I accepted it
very cordially:—the Nun was not disposed to be pleased—she
attacked poor Mynheer with much haughtiness—'Thou
savage!—hence to thy native Land of Brutes & Barbarians,
smoak thy Pipe there, but pollute not us with thy ⌐bestial⌐
coarse attempts at Wit & pleasantry—⌐Man, ⟨go to⟩ the Witch,
quit this civilised people & seek company suited to thy own
jovially vulgar manners, *this* set, believe me, is too polished, too
refined to be adapted to your taste!'⌐

The Dutch man however heeded her not, he amused himself
with talking & making signs to me, while the Nun ⌐abused⌐, &
I Laughed.—At last she took my Hand, & led me to another
part of the Room, where we renewed our former Conversation.
'You see,' she cried, 'what a Herd of Danglers flutter around
you; thus it once was with me; your form is elegant; your Face I
doubt not is beautiful; your sentiments are superior to both:
regard these Vipers then with a proper disdain; they will follow
you, will admire, Court, caress & flatter you—they will engage
your affections — — & then they will quit you! it is not that
you are less amiable, or that they cease to esteem you; but they
are weary of you; novelty must attone in another for every loss
they may regret in you:—it is not merit they seek, but variety. *I*
speak from experience!'

I could almost have taken my Nun for Mr Crisp in disguise.
''Tis rather surprising, said I, 'that one who speaks with such
vigour of the World,—& ⌐appears⌐ having quitted it from
knowing it's degeneracy, & who talks of experience in the style
of Age; should have a Voice which is a perpetual reminder of
her own Youth; & should in all visible respects, be so formed to
grace & adorn the World she holds in such contempt.'

'Hold,' cried she, 'remember my sacred order, & remember

---

[14] Actually a young man who 'scarce looked three & Twenty', and who afterwards
attempted unsuccessfully to court FB (see below, *passim*). A letter of MAR to FB,
17 Feb. 1774 (Berg), suggests that his name may have been 'Tomkin'; if so, perhaps a
son of the 'Edw. Tomkins, Esq' who died in Poland St. in 1767 (*GM* xxxvii (1767), 525).

that we Nuns can never admit to our Conferences that baleful
Enemy of innocence, Flattery! Alas, you learn this from men!
Would you but renounce them! what happiness would such a
Convert give me!' ⌐

⌐'Never yet did I see an example before me, said I, which
could possibly be so striking, & never did I feel *more* inclination
to quit this seducing World which has incurred your resentment & hatred. The example you just have set is peculiarly
engaging & in coming, like you, to masquerades, & entering
into the spirit of them to the utmost of my power, depend upon
my remembering your precepts, & following your example!'

The Nun had recourse to her former justification.⌐ The
Dutchman & the shepherd soon joined us again—the former
was very liberal of his tobaco, & supported his Character with
much drollery, speaking no English, but a few Dutch words, &
making signs. The shepherd seemed formed for all the stupidity of a Dutch man more than the man who assumed that
Dress; but *he* aimed at something superior.—⌐My mask gave
me a courage I never before had in the ⌐ presence of strangers, &
I did not spare either of them, though I cannot say I ventured so
far as⌐ the Nun, ⌐who⌐ looking on her Veil and Habit as a sanction to the utmost liberty of speech ⌐she desired,⌐ spoke to
them both without the lest ceremony. ⌐Niether did I *wish* to
use ⟨them as she had⟩ done⌐—All she said to *me* did honour to
the Name she assumed—it was sensible & delicate, it was *probably* very true; it was *certainly* very well adapted to her apparent
character: but when we were joined by men, her exhortation
degenerated into ⌐ranting⌐; which though she might intend the
better to support her part, by displaying her indignation
against the sex, nevertheless seemed suited to the virulency &
bitterness of a revengeful woman of the World, than the gentleness & dignity which were expected from the piety, patience &
forbearance of a Cloister. 'And what,' said she to the ⌐ Dutch
man, what can have induced such a savage to venture himself
here? Go, seek thy fellow Brutes! the vulgar, bestial society
thou art used too, [*sic*] is such alone as thou ought to mix with.'

He *jabbered* something in his defence, & seemed inclined to
make his Court to me. 'Perhaps, said she, 'it may be in the
power of this fair Creature to reform thee; she may civilise thy
gross & barbarous manners.' The Dutch man bowed, said

yaw, & put his Hand on his Heart in token of approbation. 'Ay, [said the poor shepherd, whose Eyes had the]¹⁵ ˥ most marked expression of stupidity (if stupidity can be said to have *any* expression) that I ever saw, & his words & manner so exactly coincided with his appearance, that he was meerly an object for Laughter—he served only for such to *me* at least; for indeed my spirits were not very low. ⌐*He* affected to Laugh at the Dutch man, who soon after left us. The Nun attacked him openly on his stupidity & advised him to be silent. I trust, said he, always stammering, I think [xxxxx *1½ lines*]˥ ˥

[*The bottom of the page has been cut away, and 6 more pages have been dis-carded, of which only the stubs remain. As transition FBA has inserted:* Refreshments were then brought, & every body was engaged with a Partner; Merlin, a delightful mask, secured Hetty, & the Dutchman my Ladyship. Everybody was then unmasked.]

[I] turned hastily round, & saw a ⌐young man˥ so very like Mr Young that at the first glance I thought it was him, but what was my surprise at seeing the Dutch man! I had no idea that he was under 50, when behold he scarse looked three & Twenty. I believe my surprise was very manifest, for Mynheer could not forbear Laughing. On his part he paid me many Compliments, repeatedly & with much civility congratulating himself on his ⌐Choice. Whether pleased or not he could not well help appearing, & he did not spare himself in Words to ⟨Paint⟩ himself so. But though few things are more agreeable at the moment than Compliments spoke with an air of sincerity, yet [½ *line cut away*] [?wi]sh to be repeated. I˥ ˥

[*bottom of page cut away*]

Nothing could be more droll than the first Dance we had after unmasking; to see the pleasure which appeared in some Countenances, & the disappointment pictured in others made the most singular contrast imaginable, & to see the Old turned Young, & the Young Old,—in short every Face appeared difer-ent from what we expected. The old Witch in particular we found was a young Officer; the Punch who had made himself as Broad as long, was a very young and handsome man; but what most surprised me, was ⌐that˥ the shepherd (whose own

---

¹⁵ Inserted by FBA; the bottom of the page has been cut away.

Face was so stupid that we could scarsely tell whether he had taken off his mask or not,) |

[*The bottom of the page has been cut away, and 24 more pages discarded. For the following obliterated passage (on the next extant page) FBA has substituted:* We have been engaged some time to a private dance at Reverend Mr. Pugh's . . .]

Tuesday [?23 Jan.]—

"engaged some time to my Cousin [Charles Rousseau Burney] who is spoke [?for.] Firstly, for my part, I am very ⟨Indisposed⟩—I have not been well some Time, & was so indifferent [in] the morning, that I did not rise till near Two, & that" with a resolution of sending an excuse;—but was prevented by Mʳ Pugh's[16] calling. He earnestly beg'd me not to disappoint him, & promised me I should rest as often as I pleased.—He protested he would not upon any account have me fail coming, as he has settled all the partners, & I should break his schemes—. 'I should be more particularly sorry at your absence, ma'am, said he, as I have engaged you to the most agreeable man of my whole Company—who would be extremely disappointed; & who, I flatter myself, would make the Evening very happy to you.'

I am never fond of being engaged unseen, as in those cases two People are frequently | disappointed. Mʳ Pugh was too urgent to be refused.—"my own inclination led me to hope I should be better—I have promised—unless too sick—to go.

I have been very poorly all Day—I am now however better—such as I am, I have been debating with myself whether it will be a greater mortification to the *gentleman* Mr. Pugh has done me the honour to engage me to, to find *no* Partner, or so woful a one as I shall be—Hetty says she fears I shall be obliged to leave the Room if I do go—however, I am now better.—"

How I have got this violent Cold I cannot tell—it affects me in a Cough—sore Throat, & most dreadful Head ach, attended with a slight Fever. I shall really be an amiable object, for I am

---

[16] Matthew Pugh (*c.*1739–1810); BA, 1758, MA, 1761 (Cantab.); Curate of St James's Westminster. An old friend of CB, he had married him to EAB at St James's on 2 Oct. 1767. FB describes him later as 'that smirking, insignificant, prating but good natured man'. See below, p. 269 and *passim*; *DL* i. 340; *JL* iv. 175 n. 4; *Mem.* i. 195.

pale as possible, & my Eyes heavy as lead. How would a Philosopher or moralist hold me [|] in contempt! to have so many complaints—yet go to a Ball! it appears ridiculous to me—⌐if I had not been so strongly pressed by Mr. Pugh, I should certainly have excused myself—he promised me I shall be as much ⟨rest⟩ed, & just as often as I can desire, but repeatedly & earnestly beg'd me not to disappoint him, because he has promised me to the most elegant Captain somebody. Hetty is engaged to Mr. Burney [Charles Rousseau].

Feby 7th
11 at Night

It is my turn to sit up with Papa to Night, &, being disposed for nothing better, I shall write a few words to Nobody—that good old friend of mine, who never refuses me her attention.⌐

Near a Fortnight has elapsed since our Dance at M^r ⌐Pugh's—nevertheless, as I past there perhaps a pleasanter evening than I ever again will on a similar occasion, I will at least give myself the satisfaction of keeping it in remembrance. [xxxxx ½ *line*]⌐

I was infinitely better that Evening than I had been, & when we set off for South Street, I was in much higher spirits than any of the party, though all very chearful. My Aunt Rebecca ⌐& her nephew [Charles Rousseau Burney] went with us.⌐ Mr Pugh welcomed us very joyfully—& introduced us to the Company [|] who were seated formally at Tea. Hetty told me she had fixed her Eye on my Partner.—⌐I was ashamed to look at any—⌐ 'The ⌐White Coat⌐ is ⌐he,⌐ said she, & I can Read in his Face every thing that is clever & agreeable. I hope *I* shall Dance a minuet with him.—' ⌐She was right in her conjectures, the White Coat was the man.⌐17

Tea being over we marched into a Larger Room, and minuets were began—'Come Gentleman, said Mr Pugh— 'chuse Hats—I won't let you chuse Partners!' Hetty, ⌐according to her wish, *did* Dance a minuet with the White Coat— I believe she would not have been sorry to have remained here, but for her first engagement, niether do I believe that *He* would have been sorry either. After all,⌐ I cannot

---

17 Capt. Blomefield; see below.

approve this plan of settling Partners unseen—the usual privilege the men have of pleasing themselves I think far preferable, as only one *can* be dissatisfied then, "but otherwise *two* may. The minuet over," Mr Pugh presented the Ladies to the Gentlemen—'This Lady, when he came to me, is your Partner, Captain Bloomfield.'[18] "I was ready to say God help" him! "he deserves a better!" Indeed he was very unfortunate—for he did not himself tire the whole Evening, & poor little I was fatigued to Death [a]fter the second Dance "& here in was I also unfor⟨tunate | so⟩ diferent was my lot."

I very much admired the Lady who Danced with Mr Pugh, who was very "pleasing & seemed to be very pretty at a little distance, though, when I was very near her afterwards, I did not think her so." I had said many things in her praise occasionally to Captain Bloomfield, & I asked if he knew her?—'I have the honour, Ma'am,' said he, 'to be her Brother!—don't you think,' added he Laughing, 'we are very like?'[19]

There was another young lady there who addressed herself so frequently to the Captain, & *smiled* so *tenderly* at him, that I could not forbear observing to Hetty that Mr Pugh was cruel to have given her any other Partner:—but when the Night was half over, I found this was another sister.

At Two o'clock we returned to the Parlour to sup. And here Mr Pugh & Captain Bloomfield seemed to vie with each other

---

[18] Thomas Blomefield (1744–1822), son of the Revd Thomas Blomefield (1691–1771), Rector of Hartley and Chalk, Kent, and Chaplain to the Duke of Dorset. A career officer in the Royal Artillery, he was promoted First Lt. in 1766, Capt.-Lt. in 1773, and Capt. in 1780. (His being called 'Captain' in 1770 is either loose usage or denoted a brevet or temporary rank.) Severely wounded in the head at the battle of Saratoga (1777), Blomefield survived to become Inspector of Artillery (1780). He commanded the artillery at the capture of Copenhagen in 1807, for which service he was created a Bt. He was promoted to Gen. in 1821, the year before his death.

MAR, in a letter to FB 17 Feb. 1774 (Berg), refers to Blomefield as one of FB's suitors, and FB in 1775 describes him as a rival of Sir Martin Folkes for the affections of Frances Turner (vol. ii). He finally married (1788) Elizabeth Wilmot (c.1745–1826), the 2nd daughter of Sir John Eardley Wilmot, Chief Justice of the Common Pleas. See A. Campling, *East Anglian Pedigrees Part II* (1945), p. 7; W. H. Askwith, *List of Officers of the Royal Regiment of Artillery* (4th edn., 1900), pp. 10, 170, 197, 198, 231.

[19] The printed sources and the Revd Thomas Blomefield's will (PCC, prob. 26 Jan. 1771) mention 1 sister, Ann, who was born c.1751 and who died unmarried in 1833. The other sister (below) may have been a half-sister, daughter of Mrs Mary (née Matthews) Blomefield (c.1711–84) by her 1st husband, William Branch. Such a sister, not further traced, would have been at least 30 years old at this time (Campling, loc. cit.; Hartley, Kent, parish registers).

which should have least ease & rest himself, or give most to ⌐
others: ⌐though both repetaedly said, when we apologised,
⟨that we gave⟩ to them pleasure at least equal to what they gave
to the Company.

About 3 o'clock we went again to the Ball Room. Captain
Bloomfield put a Handkerchief about my Head when we
Crossed the Garden, saying 'It is my *duty*, & much more—my
inclination, to take care of *you*'—But⌐ I was now scarse able to
move; I did however *force* my ⌐Feet⌐ to ⌐hop⌐ 2 or 3 Dances,
but with great pain ⌐to myself, being more fit for Bed,⌐ for
indeed I was very indifferent, ⌐& fatigued to Death;⌐ yet the
spirit which every Body supported, as well as the extreme
alacrity of Captain Bloomfield, made me ashamed to sit still—I
spoke of my distress to Hetty. — — There was a lady who
Danced with a Relation of our's, Mr Thomas Burney Holt,[20]
(which last name he has adopted ⌐ at the request of an Uncle) &
this Lady was as alert & lively as at the beginning of the Eveg:
while Mr Burney Holt was absolutely wearied,—I asked Hetty
if she thought I might ⌐without offence⌐ propose a change of
Partners?—she said certainly.—I was pretty well satisfied that
Miss Kirk[21] could have no objection, for this poor Cousin of
Our's is very deficient both in good Temper & good breeding,
which he manifested to all the Company by his behaviour to
this lady; for between any Dance when we were all seated, he
constantly marched to a distant part of the Room, & leaning
his Forehead on his arms, appeared to be sleeping ⌐& did not
take the least notice of his Partner: & when we went to supper
he was not to be found—I thought he had decamped in the
dumps; Captain Bloomfield said he expected he had fallen
asleep in Crossing the Garden! in short he was ridiculed by
every Body present—⌐ ⌐

As to Captain Bloomfield, he would assuredly be no sufferer
by an exchange, for Miss Kirk was very pretty & agreeable—
but ⌐to say the truth I felt a little for myself—for I found I really
could not Dance, and ⟨hat⟩ed to prevent *him*—& after having
gone down one,⌐ which compleatly finished me, Captain

---

[20] See above, p. 92 n. 38. The uncle was presumably the 'Walter Holt, Esq.' who
subscribed to *Hist. Mus.* Presumably he made Thomas Burney his heir on condition he
adopt his name. He was brother of Thomas's mother Frances née Holt. See D. Dawe,
Organists of the City of London, 1666–1850 (1983), p. 110.

[21] Not identified.

Bloomfield seeing me fatigued lead [*sic*] me to a seat.—Fast by me sat poor Miss Kirk,—'How perverse this is, said I, to him; here's a lady who is not at all tired, & there ⟨is⟩ a Gentleman who is—& here am *I* knocked up;—& you not at all!—'Well? said he, and what do you imply by that? I proposed an *exchange*.—'Do you want to get rid of me?—cried he.—I did not know what to say to this;—ᴿI certainly did *ask*—ᴺ nevertheless, I was convinced that only his delicacy prevented his being in *raptures* at the proposal;—therefore, after a short paus[e,] I pressed him much to ¹ Dance,—declaring myself very sorry to deprive him of that pleasure,—'But I would rather, said he, *sit* with *you*, than *Dance* with any Lady.' I cannot say I believed him:—on my further urging him, he told me he was too sensible of his happiness to fling it away;—As to Miss Kirk, I had made my proposal to *her* first, never imagining that Captain Bloom-field would object ᴿto it,ᴺ & she frankly & honestly agreed to it:—but nothing I could say would induce him:—he certainly thought I should regard it as a reproach on my inactivity; & he chose rather to suffer himself, than make another ashamed.

'And how do you know, said he, that the *Gentleman* would agree to quit his Partner? 'O—if that is any objection, cried I, *I* will undertake to speak to *him*!—you see he is tired to Death already—'O, that will pass off,' answ[ered] he—he might be as unwilling to relinquish ¹ his Partner, as I am m[ine,] for why should not he be contented & happy?—She is very pretty & agreeable; &, as you observed, looks all good humour.—'O leave him to me, said I, I will readily manage him.—

'Nothing, returned he, shall prevail on me to Dance without *you*, but your *really* desiring it, & unless it would do *you* a favour.—'

I regarded this as a delicate *assent*—therefore I answered—'It *will* do me a favour;—a great one!—'But *how*? said he; because you think it will oblige *me*? or because you wish to get rid of me? There was no answering this—& so I made no farther attempt: At 5 o'clock, or rather more, every one gave up. Late as it was, we could not go Home, as the Cariage was not to be found. We therefore returned again to the Parlour, where we were ¹ entertained with Catches by part of the Company, Namely Mʳ Pugh, Captain Bloomfield, Mʳ Porter,²² ᴿmy

²² William Porter (*c.*1736–93), BA, 1758, MA, 1761 (Cantab.); Curate of Woolwich,

Cousin [Charles Rousseau Burney]⌝ & my sister. Mr Porter is a Clergyman of Woolwich, whose Lady I must menti[on] ⌜not meerly on her own account, but as proof of that delicacy I have observed in the Captain—I com⌝mitted a fault from inattention, (chiefly owing to my extreme fatigue) which was ⌜sitting down⌝ after having gone down a Dance, without Walking it up again:—Captain Bloomfield either forgot this punctilio also or did not chuse to remind me of it: however, this lady took great offence at it—for while we were seated, she came & addressed herself to Captain Bloomfield keeping her back towards me, & affecting not to see me; &, not in the gentlest manner, she cried—'And so *you* are sit down!—*you*, who are such a *young* man give out first:—& that after going *down* a Dance, tho' you could not walk it up again—' This reproof I was conscious was meant for *me*;—the Captain, I believe was rather distressed:— the gentle Lady's volubility ⌜gave him some Time to consider⌝—for | —'Had you been really fatigued, continued she, you might have shewn it by sitting before you had gone down the Dance—I must say it w[a]s very ill bred—& I did not expect it from *you*, Captain Bloomfield! *you*, who are so *polite* [a]^{23} man!—' I was sensible the reproof was, to *me*, just; but nevertheless, it was exceeding gross & ill natured to address this discourse to *us*.—Captain Bloomfield did not once look towards me; he did not even plead my indisposition ⌜in my excuse,⌝ but, taking the whole affair to himself, with the utmost good humour, he said—'But I am sure you are too compassionate not to pity me, when you hear my disaster—for I was unable to Dance longer, as I sprain'd my Ancle,—& what could a poor man do?'

I believe she was somewhat calmed by his tranquility; for she softened her voice, but said, as she left us, 'Well, to be sure it might not be *your* fault— | but it was very rude, & I am very sorry *you* had any share in it!'

I was quite shocked & disconcerted at this unexpected lecture—The Captain very delicately still looked another way,

---

Kent; Vicar of Cobham, Kent, 1766–93; Reader of Highgate Chapel, and school-master. He m. (1761) Mary Horner of Tothill St., Westminster. Mrs Porter presumably predeceased her husband, as she is not named in his will, PCC, dated 9, prob. 15 June 1793.

^{23} Inserted by FBA.

& did not turn towards me ⌐as ⟨it⟩ was with an air that said—
well, madam, have I not defended you nobly?—¬ However, I
spoke to *him*—'you were in the right, said I, not to be angry, for
not one word of this was meant for *you*! ⌐⟨'And you, cried he,
have⟩ too much sweetness, I am sure, to think of it any more¬ |

[*bottom of page cut away*]

[?Mr. Pugh asked Hetty if he might] ⌐take the liberty to bring
Captain Bloomfield some morning to our House to hear some
musick, of which he is extremely fond. She said she should be
very happy to see him.

It was 7 o'clock & no Coach came for us—we feared papa
would be alarmed should we stay longer & therefore preparing
at last to Walk—Captain Bloomfield insisted on my putting his
Handkerchief about my Head, my own was tied round [?my
neck]¬ |

[*The bottom of the page is cut away. FBA has noted:* From 20 Burnt to 30
i.e. 10 leaves. She has inserted the following passage:

Soon after we came Home.

Mr. Pugh has since proposed bringing Captain Bloomfield
to a music party at our house & also has earnestly invited us to
another dance, at Woolwich, with Aunt Rebecca, where
Captain Bloomfield, he said, would be very happy to dance
again with Miss Fanny. But we did not go.

*The following fragment of a leaf, recto and verso, was originally pasted to fo.
46ᵛ in the Journal for 1769. The first side refers to JB's new voyage to India
in Feb. 1770 (see below, p. 115). The second seems to concern a peace offering
from Alexander Seton to EB, whom he had apparently been neglecting for
several months (see below, p. 115).*]

[James] has applied himself to the study of mathematics lately
& will take a very good collection of Books with him in his
Voyage |

⌐[xxxxx *2–3 words*] ⟨Hetty was⟩ not very disposed to accept of
them, but at last he [Seton] sent her a Note, begging to see
her¬ |

[About this time we received the following note from the Masquerade Dutchman:][24]

The Dutchman presents his Compliments to the Miss Burneys, & takes the liberty to enclose three tickets for the Chelsea Assembly hoping the Miss Burneys will have the goodness to find a Chapron. The Dutchman will do himself the honour to wait upon the Miss Burneys this evening, with the Doctor's permission, to know whether he may Exist again or not.

I never coloured so in my life, for papa was in the room, & Hetty read the Note out aloud, & then, laughing, flung it to me to answer, saying she knew she had nothing to do with it; & wishing me joy of my first serious Conquest.

I was so very much surprised I could not speak. Papa said it was coming to the point very quick indeed, & he must either be a very bold man, or a young man who knew nothing of the world: but he said I must return the Tickets, but might let him come to Tea, as he deserved civility, by naming him, (papa); & then we might see more how to judge him.

I was quite frightened at this—but very glad Papa & Hetty both left me to answer the note for myself, for as they thought him serious I determined to be so too.

"I am sure Captain Bloomfield would not have" been so abrupt—

I wrote the following answer, & sent it off without shewing it to papa, to put an end to the whole at once.

Miss Burney's present their Compliments to the Dutchman, &, as they cannot go to the Chelsea assembly, they beg leave to return the three Tickets, with many Thanks. They are Very sorry it will not be in their power to have the pleasure [of] seeing him this Evening, having [been] some Time pre-engaged.

February [21][25]—Wed. morn^g:

This Note will, I doubt not, be the [last] I shall have to answer from this [Ge]ntleman[26]—indeed it is the *first* also [th]at I have

24 Inserted by FBA.

25 Wrongly dated '19th' by FB.

26 FB wrote to SC in 1775 (vol. ii) that after her dancing with the Dutchman at Lalauze's masquerade, he had 'called two or 3 Times afterwards, & wrote 2 notes . . . however, after the answer he received to the 2d note, I heard of him no more'. It appears

Answered: nevertheless, I [fa]ncy he will Condescend to exist *still*. ⁿ⟨To be sure, a⟩ man of more consequence would not have been so forward. It was necessary to cut him short at once. ⁿ |

My dear James has been gone [some] Time—he went on board the Green[wich] East India Man,[27] he was in very [good] spirits, & we have all great hop[es] that he will have a happy & pro[spe]rous Voyage.

The same Evening that I sent th[e] Dutchman's Note, we spent at [Mrs.] Pringle's. Mʳ Seton, Mʳ Crawford, [Mrs.] Mackintosh[28] & her two sons made her pa[rty.] Mʳ Seton was all assiduity & attent[ion] to my sister.—Mʳ Crawford willingly would have been the same, bu[t] | ⁿHetty quite forgot her resolution [?of not shewing] any difference, & gave such partial preference to Mr. Seton, thatⁿ [no] one else could engage her for three [mi]nutes. As to the Captain [Pringle], it would [be] difficult to decide to whom he [add]ressed his conversation most—we [were] rival Queen's with him, but which [was t]he Statira is doubtful.[29]

Mʳ Mackintosh is a very stupid [youn]g man, who is unhappily possessed [of a] very great fortune, which could [hardly] be worse bestowed. He has per[sua]ded himself that he has a great [gen]ius for poetry, & has made [an] Acrostick on my Name which is very well worth pres[erving.] | ['Tis] the most laughable stuff I ever saw:

> Fancy ne'er painted a more beauteous mi[nd,]
> And a more pleasing Face You'll seldom find,
> None with her in wit can vie,
> No, not even Pallas, may I die!
> You'll all know this to be Fann[y!]

from an obliterated passage below (p. 118) that the Dutchman had already offered tickets (also refused) to Lalauze's benefit the week before. FBA's editing here makes his overture seem more abrupt than it really was.

[27] On 12 Feb. 1770 JB was entered as an ordinary seaman on the ship's books of the *Greenwich*, East Indiaman, Capt. Robert Carr. On 20 Feb. the *Greenwich* sailed from Gravesend, and 5 months later arrived at Bombay (on 21 July) (Manwaring, pp. 9–10). For JB's return, see below, p. 152.

[28] Perhaps widow of the 'John MacIntosh Esq.', who lived in Great Marlborough St. until 1761 (Rate Books). One of the sons was perhaps the 'Alexander Mackintosh' who subscribed to *Hist. Mus.* Not further traced.

[29] The allusion is to *The Rival Queens, or the Death of Alexander the Great* (1677), a tragedy by Nathaniel Lee (?1649–92). The central theme is the jealousy of Alexander's 1st wife, Roxana, for his 2nd wife, Statira.

Beautiful, witty and young,
Unskilled in all deceits of Ton[gue,]
Reflecting glory on her sex,
None can her in Compliments perple[x;]
Easy in her manners as in her Dr[ess—]
You'll that this is Fanny all must gu[ess.]

To complete the elegance & bri[lliancy] of this Acrostick, the
paper on which [it] is Wrote is cut out in the shape of a [Fan.]
ᵀ[?This] young Genius at present [Boards at Mr.] Porter's at
Woolwich.ᵀ30 |

After supper, Captain Pringle amused [h]imself with writing
Ladies names on [the] Glasses, beginning with our's, and
[th]en wrote Gentlemen's under them. [A]ndrew wrote *his*
under mine, Hetty [c]hose Lord Pigot for one; & I Crisp [for]
another. They had given up the Dance which Mʳ Seton hinted
of to us, but [pro]posed having a Farce, in which we [wer]e all to
perform, & after some Time [we] fixed on Miss in her Teens.³¹
Mʳ [Cr]awford undertook Rodolpho, Andrew [F]ribble (which
parts had been much [be]tter reversed) the Captain, Capt.
Flash, [M]ʳ Seton the man, Mʳˢ Pringle the [Au]nt, Hetty Miss
Biddy, & for me Tag. They were all very eager about it, & fixed
a Day for the Rehearsal,—but when I came Home and Read ᴵ
the Farce,³² I found the part of Tag w[as] quite shocking—
indeed I would not have done it for the universe, & I we[nt] &
told Mʳˢ Pringle so directly, who s[aid] she could not accuse me
of affectation, for the moment she Read it attentive[ly] she said

---

³⁰ See above, p. 111 n. 22.

³¹ .*Miss in her Teens, or the Medley of Lovers*, a farce by David Garrick, 1st performed in
1747. A year or so later (*c.*1748) CB played the role of Fribble to Fulke Greville's Flash
and Mrs Fanny Greville's Biddy Bellair, in an amateur performance at Wilbury House
(*Mem.* i. 60).

Capt. Bob Loveit, an honourable young soldier, under the alias of Rhodophil (not
'Rodolpho') has won the heart of the romantic Miss Biddy Bellair, 16 years old and
heiress to a fortune. Returning from the wars in Flanders, he claims her from his 'rivals'
Fribble (a fop) and Capt. Flash (a braggart soldier), whom Biddy has been trifling with
in his absence. The 'man' played by Mr Seton would probably be Puff, Capt. Loveit's
servant, or perhaps Jasper, servant to Sir Simon Loveit, father of Capt. Loveit. (Possibly
Seton was to play both roles.) The aunt (Mrs Pringle), a non-speaking role, is guardian
of Miss Biddy. Tag, whose part FB found 'shocking', is Puff's wife, abandoned by him,
who threatens to throttle him when they meet again by accident. She has been having
an affair with Jasper during her husband's desertion.

³² Edns. of the play had been published at London in 1747, 1748, 1749, and 1759.

to her sons she was sure [I] should not ⌐do⌐ it; which was very kind of [her.]

⌐At parting, Mr. Seton, with a ⟨look⟩ of tender respect as Hetty told [me] preferred her Hand to his Life.⌐

Not long after this visit we re[ceiv]ed ⌐this⌐ Note of invitation from Mrs. Debbieg. ⌐Mrs. Pr[ingle] ⟨and⟩ Mr. and Mrs. Debieg present their C[ompliments] to Miss Burney & Miss Fanny Bu[rney] and beg the favour of their Company to spend the Evening.

Hetty with the utmost rapture accepted the invitation—Mrs. Pringle⌐ | [and] the Captain went with us. Poor An[dre]w was gone. ⌐He is a very worthy [yo]ung man, & I have really great esteem [for] him. I should have much rather his [br]other had gone—he is to settle in [the East In]dies for at least seven years. I wish⌐ [he] may meet with my dear James.[33]

M^r & Mrs Debbieg are a charming [coup]le; & never was there more conjugal [ha]ppiness visible than in them. They [ha]ve 3 Children,[34] whom they doat on—[M^r]^s Debieg is gentle, polite, sensible [en]gaging—Mr Debieg is every thing [th]at can render him deserving of such [a]n amiable wife. Mr Seton lives chiefly with them, & there appears the most [a]ffectionate and [true][35] ⌐happiness in⌐ them all. M^r Se[ton] [again][35] [appe]ared to | me in a more favourable light; his ch[arm]ing sister ⌐would⌐ reflect honour on all [her] Relations. If the sincerity of this ma[n] equal'd his sense, wit, polite and ins[i]nuating address, I would not wish Hett[y] a happier lot than to be his. ⌐We ha[ve] never seen him since, though I beli[eve] the visit was made two months si[nce.][36]

---

[33] Virtually impossible, since JB sailed to Bombay, whereas Andrew Pringle went to Calcutta to join the Bengal Army. He may not have returned to England until 1803, the year of his death.

[34] A daughter (mentioned above, p. 59) and 2 sons. Clement Debbieg (d. 1819), the elder, was commissioned a Lt. in the 13th (or 1st Somersetshire) Foot, Ireland, 1783 (half-pay, 1789). He m. (1806) Lady Charlotte Butler (d. 1808), sister to the E. of Lanesborough (*AL* 1785, p. 75; 1789, p. 337; *AR* xlviii (1806), 474; *GM* lxxvi^1 (1806), 179; lxxxix^1 (1819), 487). Henry Debbieg (d. 1828/9) was commissioned an ensign in the 102nd Foot, East Indies, also in 1783. As a Captain in the 44th Foot (with army rank of Lt.-Col.), he was wounded at the Battle of New Orleans on 8 Jan. 1815. His last promotion was to Fort-Major of Dartmouth Garrison in 1827 (*AL* 1785, p. 140; 1828, pp. 30, 298, 604; 1829, s.v. 'Casualties since last Publication'; *GM* lxxxv^1 (1815), 356).

[35] Inserted by FBA for 1 or 2 words torn away.

[36] Probably more like 6 weeks, since the present entry dates no later than the 1st week of Apr. (see below, p. 119).

Though we refused the Dutchman's Tickets for⌐ M⌐ Lalause'
Benefit,[37] ⌐[?we found] it necessary to go to it, as we were [at]
his masquerade,⌐ though without the le[ast] expectation of
receiving pleasure, a[s the] play was an old revived one, & per-
for[med] by a *set of Ladies & gentlemen who ne[ver] appeared on any
stage before*.[38]

We went [with] M⌐ M⌐ˢ & Miss Stra[nge] ¦ [& so]me more
Company of their party, into the same Boxes.

It was most wretchedly performed, [it] is called Themistocles
& Aristides—[nev]er were Heroes more barbarously mur-
[de]red. Miss Lalause & her Father Danced [a] minuet ⌐&
Laure⌐ between an Act,[39] after which she came into our Box.
When the play was over, ⌐Mrs. Strange & ⟨her⟩ party, except
her Daughter & a French Gentleman, went away. M⌐ Henry⌐
Phips,[40] Hetty's masquerade Partner, came to speak to her—
⌐& after the play was quite over, the Dutchman came to us as
we waited for the carriage. He was grave & earnest, but very
civilly went himself to see after our Coach: I was ⟨vex⟩ed at his
finding us with only Gentlemen as we had ¦ talked so much
about Chaperons [xxxxx *1 line*] handed Miss Strange, Hetty &

[37] See above, p. 114 n. 26. The mainpiece of Lalauze's benefit, held at the Haymarket, 14 Feb. 1770, was *The Lovers of their Country, or Themistocles and Aristides*, a 5-act
tragedy by Samuel Madden (1686–1765). The play was 1st performed at Lincoln's Inn
Fields in 1729, closing that year after 9 evenings. This performance was its only revival
in the 18th c. The afterpiece was the pantomime of *The Country Farmer Deceived, or
Harlequin Statue*, by Joseph Yarrow, 1st performed at Covent Garden in 1739; Lalauze
danced the role of Pierrot (*LS 4* iii. 1455).
[38] 'A Set of Gentlemen and Ladies who never appeared on any stage' (playbill
reprinted, ibid.).
[39] A '*Louvre* and *Minuet*—Lalauze, Miss Lalauze', danced 'after the Play', according
to the playbill reprinted, ibid. The first dance is properly *loure* (*New Grove*).
The *Town and Country Magazine* reviewed the performance of *Themistocles* thus: 'The
house was as full as if Mr. Garrick was to have appeared in one of his first characters.
The person who spoke, or rather attempted to speak the prologue, was so intenacious
in his memory, that before he had repeated four lines he hitched; and, notwithstanding
the utmost assiduity of the prompter, joined to every effort of the speaker's recollection,
he could not get a single line farther: the audience seeing his distress, very good
naturedly remitted this part of the entertainment, not to delay the succeeding piece,
which was presented with *equal accuracy and propriety*' (cited Highfill; see also *LS*,
passim).
[40] Hon. Henry Phipps (1755–1831), 3rd son of Constantine Phipps (1722–75), cr.
(1767) B. Mulgrave. Currently a student at Eton, he later became a distinguished
soldier and statesman. He succeeded his brother as 3rd B. Mulgrave (Ireland), in 1792,
and was cr. B. Mulgrave (Great Britain), 1794, and E. of Mulgrave (United Kingdom),
1812. In 1795 he m. Martha Sophia Maling (d. 1849), 3rd daughter of Christopher and
Martha Maling and granddaughter of Mrs Sheeles.

I followed & Miss Lalause & this Mynhere were left last, but he prudently quitted [?her] & coming to Mrs. Pringle, said 'Will you give me leave Madam'? & Handed her to the Coach—very respectfully & quite solemn[ly.]⟧ And the next morning Mr. Phips called. He is more properly Mr Henry Phips, being the second son[41] of Lord Mulgrave. He is really one of the most amiable, sensible & well bred youths I ever saw. It is impossible not to forget while he is talking that he is so young a man[42] for he is so very clever & sensible, that not a word escapes him which wd not do credit to double his years. ⟦Hetty was⟧ |

[*At least one leaf has been discarded here.*]

Lynn Regis
April 20th

Is Nobody surprised at the Date of this?—ah, my good & excellent friend, when I last addressed myself to you from fair London Town,—I very little imagioned that my *next* address would be from Lynn!—I have now been here near a Fortnight, but have not had ⟦spirit or inclination⟧ to write to my Journal ⟦nor should I now, but from the pleasure I had taken in recollecting⟧ and relating what passed during the space of Time between my last writing & my Journey hither, ⟦though I know not where to begin, as I have forgot where I left off—I believe it was just as I had sent a Note to Miss Strange & her mother | to invite them to accompany us to Mrs. Cornelys'[43]—Miss Strange was ill & excused herself—at length Papa determined to go himself & take with us one of our nieghbour Pascalls. This Evening, it was Sunday [25 March], our two Cousins[44] &⟧ Sir Lionel Pilkington[45] spent with us. Sir Lionel is an old &

---

[41] Actually the 3rd (above, n. 40).

[42] He had just turned 15. In later years the painter Benjamin Haydon described him as 'a fine character, manly, perfectly bred, a high tory, and complete John Bull' (cited *DNB* s.v. Phipps, Henry).

[43] Teresa (née Imer) Cornelys (1723–97), singer and entrepreneur. Her public assemblies in Carlisle House, Soho Square, begun in 1760, were at the height of their popularity at this time, though by the end of 1772 she was forced into bankruptcy by her extravagant expenditures and by the success of the newly opened Pantheon. See Highfill.

[44] Presumably Charles Rousseau Burney and his brother James Adolphus Burney (see below, p. 130).

[45] Sir Lionel Pilkington (1707–78), 5th Bt., of Stanley, Yorks.; Sheriff, Yorks., 1740–1;

intimate Acquaintance of Papa's, a man famous for wit & *dry* humour: he is also, which is rare with men of that sort, very well bred ⌐& polite,¬ for in general they affect a bluntness & conciseness which quite excludes the attention & respect necessary for a *polite* man. ⌐He was extremely delighted with my Cousin Charles' performance on the Harpsichord—who indeed is not?¬

On Wednesday ⌐Evening [28 March], for the Annual Night was defer'd till then,¬ we went to Mrs Cornelys's[46] with Papa & Miss Nancy Pascall. The magnificence of the Room[s,] splendour of the illuminations & embillishments [*sic*], & the brilliant appearance of Company exceeded any thing I ever before saw. The Apartments were so crowded we had scarse Room to move, which was quite disagreeable; nevertheless, the flight of Apartments both up stairs & on the Ground Floor seemed endless. ⌐It was between 12 & 1 before we saw Lord Pigot, who was in deep mourning;¬[47] he spoke to Papa with his accustomed ease & ⌐politeness¬ & called Hetty his *little Friend*: niether did he forget little *me*.—He appeared to be of no particular Party, and frequently joined us: he asked Papa—'Dr Burney but when will you come[48] & Dine with me, & the young Ladies?' Papa did not fix any Time, & to my great concern, I have quitted Town before he did, for I had great pleasure in the thought of being of the Party.

The Rooms were so full & so hot that Nobody attempted to Dance, ⌐though at about 3 o'clock just 12 Couples stood up. It was past 4 ere we came Home.¬

MP, Horsham, 1748–68. This is the only mention of Sir Lionel that has been found in the Burney papers.

[46] 'SOHO-SQUARE. The Nobility and Gentry are respectfully informed, that the ANNUAL SUBSCRIPTION NIGHT will be this Day the 28th instant, instead of Tuesday, the 27th, (it being obliged to be postponed for one Day, on account of the Disappointment of some Workmen engaged in very material Preparations) when the whole House will be illuminated with some thousand additional Lights.

The ILLUMINATIONS, the DESERT [dessert], the EMBELLISHMENTS, on this Occasion, will be, in Part, like those of the Grand Gala, in Part like those of the late Masked Ball, and in Part wholly new; particularly the Great Tea Room, which will be transformed throughout.

The Doors will be opened just after Nine' (*Daily Adv.* 28 Mar. 1770).

[47] FB is probably joking, as attendance at Mrs Cornelys' assembly hardly seems appropriate behaviour for someone 'in deep mourning'.

[48] FBA has interpolated 'to one of my Concerts'. Ld. Pigot evidently gave regular musical parties in his home.

˛I must own this Evening's Entertainment more disappointed my expectations than Any I ever spent: for I had imagioned it would have been the most charming in the World—but Papa was but half recovered, ˥fearful of encreasing his Cold, and not at all entertained with any thing; he had gone much against his inclination, in low spirits, & merely to oblige us, &˥ because we should not be disappointed of seeing the Apartments: What other Father ˥in the whole World˥ would have been so very indulgent? ˥He prefer'd our wishes to his own, & though from his indifferent state of Health, & his lowness of spirits˥ he could not enjoy at all the Evening's ˥ *Entertainment*, yet was he all kindness & affection to us—he is one of the few who can be dejected without losing his sweetness of Temper:—nevertheless our knowledge of his indisposition prevented our being comfortable. ˥Besides these Publick places are never agreeable without a large & spirited Party. My dear Father, however, did not suffer afterwards from his goodness.˥

The next Evening [29 March] rather late Mrs Pringle sent an invitation to my sister & self, to Drink Tea, sending word she was quite alone. Hetty was out, but I went, & found ˥her˥ & Mr Seton sitting together, with little Clement Debieg, the latter's Nephew. ˥Mrs. Pringle apologised for sending so late, but said that Mr. Seton told her he was ⟨sure⟩ I at least was at Home, having seen me in the Parlour.˥ Soon aft[er Cap]tain & Mrs Debieg came, full [Dre]ssed [& in] *high* ˥ spirits; I was obliged to make excuses for *my* ⟨appeara⟩nce, which their chearfulness & good humour soon made me forget. M^r and Mrs Debieg & Mrs Pringle went to Cards, Mr Seton & myself declined Playing—I never do but at *Pope Joan*, ˥my lady's hole˥[49] or *my sow's Pig'd*!—We therefore entered into a very comfortable Conversation; he enquired much after my sister & regretted her absence. So did every Body. Captain Pringle did not come Home Till supper. I spent a very agreeable Evening, the Party though small were *select*, & each in [hi]gh good humour & spirits. Mr Debieg appears at every meeting to more & more advantage; he is really a charming man, ⟨sensible,⟩ well bred,

[49] Changed by FBA to 'commerce'. Mrs Delany mentions playing 'at my lady's hole' in a letter to her sister, Mrs Granville, in 1732 (Delany, *Corr.* i. 385). The game of 'My sow's Pigged' is mentioned in John Taylor's ('The Water Poet's') verses entitlèd *Taylors Motto: Et Habeo, et Careo, et Curo*, publ. 1621 (cited *OED* s.v. My 5).

unaffected, & very droll & [xxxxx *1 word*]—[M^rs] Debieg is happy, very happy I am sure [in the] possession of the Heart of ^| such a man; & his affectionate, ⟨very k⟩ind & obliging behaviour to her, evidently declare her to have retained, *though a Wife*, all the influence & power of a mistress. And this might perhaps be more universally the Case, were Women more universally such as Mrs Debieg;—she is indeed truly worthy her happy lot—with great *dis*advantage of Person, for she is actually ugly, her many amiable qualities, the goodness & excellence of her mind, are so marked in her Countenance, that she claims a place in the very Heart immediately.

I quite forgot whether I mentioned that at the visit we made to this charming Pair there were of their Company two Gentlemen of the Name [of] Dundas? Major Dundas,[50] the young[er,] was much *smitten* with Hetty; Mr Dundas[51] was at that Time [xxxxx *1 word*] engaged ^| in contesting an Election—Mr Debieg told me that he had gained his Cause; & I found that, by way of rejoicing, they intended having a Dance at their House, which they fixed to be the next Tuesday [3 April], because that was the aniversary of their mariage Day,[52] & they invited M^rs & Capt. Pringle, & my sister & self to it. I answered for *one*—I knew I *might* for the other, tho' I did not chuse it.

^┌At Twelve we all parted, Captain Pringle & Mr. Seton accompanying me Home, being but 3 yards—

Hetty was vexed when she heard who the Party were, that she was away, but consoled her self with the happy prospect of [Tues]day.

⟨Before⟩ going to Bed, I shall proceed with my *narrative* at leisure—also at Pleasure^┐ ^|

[*2 leaves cut away*]

[50] Robert Dundas (b. 1722), 2nd surviving son of George Dundas (1690–1762), 22nd laird of Dundas. A retired army officer and 'impertinent Coxcomb' (below, p. 129), he 'died unmarried' (R. Douglas, *The Baronage of Scotland* (Edinburgh, 1798), p. 175; T. L. Ormiston, *The Ormistons of Teviotdale* (Exeter, 1951), p. 257).

[51] James Dundas (1721–80), 1st surviving son of George Dundas of Dundas. The Dundases, the Cunynghames of Livingstone, and the Hopes, Earls of Hopetoun, were the principal families in Linlithgowshire. In the 1768 elections for Parliament James Dundas contested the county against John Hope. Defeated 20–15, he petitioned Parliament because of alleged irregularities in the voting and was seated in the place of Hope, 27 Mar. 1770. See Namier.

[52] Actually the Debbiegs' anniversary (their 17th) was 27 Mar., the day of Dundas's victory (Edinburgh parish registers).

[A formal Note followed next day, to Miss Burney & Miss Fanny Burney, with the invitation for Tuesday. Mrs Pringle *chaperoned* us, and we were]^53 almost the first in the Room; but I will mention the whole party by Name, for indeed they well deserve it: to begin, *as I ought*, with the women.

Mrs Seton, a very engaging woman, about 23 widow of Major Seton,^54 an Elder Brother of our Acquaintance.—She is rather handsome, extremely ˹well bred, even˺ elegant in her manners, & mild & sensible in her Conversation.

Mrs Pringle, who was as gay, chatty and clever as usual.

Mrs Debieg herself, who is always charming.

Miss Peggy Adams,^55 *an old flame of Mr Seton's* she is called: she is about 26 or 7, ugly in Person, & too reserved in manners to permit me to judge of her, but I will imagion she has some remarkable qualities to have engaged Mr Seton's attention, though I ˹do˺ not wonder he has transfered it to another Object, when I see how striking is the difference between them: nevertheless, I am | concerned to find this additional proof of the fickleness of his disposition.

Miss Stuart,^56 she is about 19 or 20, has a fine Face in spight of the small Pocks, is modest, well bred, & very silent.

Miss Dalrymple^57 who we have frequently seen at M^rs

---

^53 Inserted by FBA.

^54 Probably George Seton (b. 1734), 2nd son of Sir Henry Seton, 3rd Bt. In the East India Company naval service, he died in 1766 while serving as first mate of the *Britannia*, Capt. Thomas Bates Rous. (FB presumably confused 'mate' with 'major'.) He married Barbara Seton, of the family of Seton of Parbroath (R. Seton, *An Old Family: The Setons of Scotland and America* (New York, 1899), p. 166; B. G. Seton, *The House of Seton: A Study of Lost Causes* (Edinburgh, 1939), ii. 521–2; *Scots Magazine*, xxxii (1770), 630; C. Hardy and H. C. Hardy, *A Register of Ships . . . East India Company . . . 1760 to 1812* (1813), p. 22; Edinburgh parish registers).

^55 Margaret ('Peggy') Adam (*c.*1736–1820), youngest daughter of William Adam (1689–1748) of Maryburgh, architect, by (m. 1716) Mary Robertson (1699–1761); sister of the architects John, Robert, James, and William Adam (see H. Colvin, *Biographical Dictionary of British Architects 1600–1840* (1978), s.v. Adam; *GM* xc^2 (1820), 638; Margaret Adam's will, PCC, prob. 29 Dec. 1820; below, pp. 124, 242). John Fleming, *Robert Adam and His Circle in Edinburgh and Rome* (Cambridge, Mass., 1962), pp. 323, 381, assumes that she was the Margaret born to the Adams at Edinburgh on 15 Apr. 1731 (Baptismal Registers). However, R. Douglas, *Baronage of Scotland*, pp. 253–7, records 3 Margarets, 2 of whom died in infancy. *GM*, loc. cit., says that Margaret Adam died 'aged 84', which would place her birth about 1736.

^56 Not identified.

^57 Perhaps a relation of Sir William Dalrymple (1704–71), 3rd Bt., who in 1755 was an admirer of Peggy Adam's sister Helen (Nelly) Adam (Fleming, p. 187). Not further identified.

Pringle's. She too, is reported to be an old flame of Mr Seton's—she is about 28 or 9, rather handsome, lisps affectedly, simpers designedly, & lookes conceitedly. She is famed for never speaking ill to any ones Face, or well behind their Backs: an amiable Character.

Miss Burney & Miss Fanny Burney—sweet charming young Creatures!—I need not describe.

Now to the men; I must begin with

Mr Debieg, for whom I have conceived a great regard: he was all spirits & sweetness, & made, with his other half's assistance, all his Company happy.—

Sir Harry Seton,[58] the Eldest Brother of ⌐ Mr Seton—& Mrs Debieg; he is very unlike either; grave, reserved, silent; yet perfectly well bred, & very attentive; & there is something in his manners *prévenante*.

Mr Dundas, to whose successful Election we owe this meeting, almost the same words I have used for Sir Harry Seton would suit him, save only he was less reserved,—rather.[59]

Major Dundas, his younger Brother, very unlike him;— conceited, talkative, coxcombical.

Mr John Dundas,[60] a Cousin to these Gentlemen, a well behaved man, nothing extraordinary.

Mr Adams,[61] very sensible, very polite, & very agreeable,— the most so, Mr Debieg excepted, of the whole party.

M^r — Adams, his younger Brother, a well behaved good sort of young man.

Mr Farquar,[62] he is ⌐one who has been particularly suspected of having composed ⌐ the elegant Acrostick which was sent in

---

[58] Sir Henry Seton (1729–88), 4th Bt., of Abercorn. A career army officer who had served in North America, he retired this year and married Margaret Hay (d. 1809), daughter of Alexander Hay of Drumelzier.

[59] See below, p. 127.

[60] Probably John Dundas (d. 1778) of Duddingston. He m. (1745) Margaret Hope (1708–78), daughter of Charles Hope (1681–1742), cr. (1703) E. of Hopetoun (*Scots Peerage*, iv. 496–7; see also above, p. 122, n. 51).

[61] Robert Adam (1728–92), the noted architect. Adam, his brother James Adam (1732–94) (probably the other brother at the Debbies' party), and a 3rd brother, William Adam (1738–1822) were engaged at this time in the construction of the Adelphi, which FB mentions below (p. 243). See Fleming, pp. 323, 380–3.

[62] Walter Farquhar (1738–1819), apothecary and physician; cr. (1796) Bt. At this time Farquhar may have been apothecary to the Pringles and Debbiegs. Later he became physician to the Burney family, 'our wise and good Æsculapius' (*Mem.* iii. 380; *JL* i. 179).

my sister's name to Mr. Seton ⌐63—he is very droll, & a favourite rather of Hetty's.

Mr Robinson,[64] a very handsome Young man,—⌐I remember that about a year since I Danced with him at Mrs. Pringle's—he is⌐ agreeable;—tolerably, at least.

Captain Pringle, who has lately rather risen in my opinion, as he has forbore giving himself the Airs he formerly did: he seems less conceited, & speaks less in a Rhodomantide manner, & is also less liberal of flattery & Compliments.

Mr Alexander Seton, I need not give his Character—indeed I could not—I once thought I knew it—I now am sure I am ignorant of it.

I believe I have mentioned the whole Party; & though my account of them ˡ may be very faulty, it is such as I think.

We ⌐did not begin⌐ Dancing ⌐until about⌐ 9 O'clock:—then, when the Company stood up, Mr Seton took my Hand ⌐to my inexpressible surprise & to Hetty's great mortification, for though she was engag'd to Captain Pringle, Mr. Seton did not then know it.⌐ He was as entertaining & agreeable as ever: seemed in high spirits, & Danced extremely well, though he was ⌐not⌐ a moment silent. I told him of my *frolick* for Friday,[65]—he seemed sorry; he very gravely, with an '*upon my honour*,' assured me that nobody through out the Town would more sincerely regret my absence than himself. I thanked him kindly for his opinion of my friend's [Miss Nobody's] affection!

He is perpetually accusing me of *mauvaise honte*, tho' in civiller terms he exaggerated Compliments such as never were put together before. He ˡ often protested that he knows not any Living Creature who possesses so much ⌐modesty⌐ *with my parts & talents*!! which, *for my years, exceed all his acquaintance's*!! he says that till that morning he had that long conversation with me at our House, ⌐when he called after having Danced with Hetty,⌐66 he had no conception of my Character, & that but for that circumstance, he might never have known *my Abilities*!!! He very frequently & earnestly advises & presses me, *as a friend*, to join more generally in Conversation, &c &c &c—Ha! Ha! Ha!

⌐63 The acrostic is missing.
⌐64 Not identified. FB mentions him again in 1773 (p. 243) as one of the 'Scotch party'.   ⌐65 i.e., her journey to Lynn.   ⌐66 Above, pp. 44–9.

Mr Seton is artful: I have seen that he courts my good opinion, & I know why.—he flatters me in a peculiar style, always affecting a serious air, & assuring me he speaks his real sentiments:—I some times think he does not know *how* to do that;—though there ^| is an insinuating air of sincerity in his manner when ever he is serious, which often staggers me, in spight of the prejudice I have conceived against him for his unworthy trifling with so sweet, so amiable a Girl as Hetty:—in short, I have no fixed opinion of him. I know he is agreeable to a superior degree; & I believe he is as artful as agreeable.

'But for how long are you going?' said he: I told him for the whole summer.—'Just now, said he, that I have *begun* to be acquainted with you!—I never knew [your powers]^67 till the last Time I saw you at Mrs Pringle's when you ventured to open your mouth, & was really entertaining—I would not hear him on this subject, conscious as I am of my deficiency that way:— He admired the philosophy with which I bore this stroke [of leaving Town.]^67—I affected to need ^| none for it—'What would your sister say in a similar situation?' 'O there's very little to be said,—she would go as I do.' 'I believe she would have Hanged herself first.' Presently we sat down & joined her, when he said to her—'What do you think Miss Fanny says?—She tells me that if it had been your lot to be carried into the Country, you would have just taken your Garters & Hanged yourself—!'

I railed at him—to no purpose, he absolutely insisted *I* had told him so!—Hetty did not know which to believe: he ran on with more stuff to the same purpose, Hetty looked at me;—I cleared myself, & insisted on his clearing me:—'Well,' said he, Laughing, 'I ⌐only¬ added the Garters!' 'Why did I say any thing at all about *Hanging*?' cried I. 'Nay, returned he, when I had given the ^| Garters, I was obliged to give a use for them!'

At the end of two Dances, M^r ⌐Seton's behaviour was justified & explained—for Mr.¬ Debieg told us we were to change Partners every two Dances. ⌐I was extremely pleased with this scheme, for though I knew not how to account for it, I was well convinced that I was not Mr. Seton's choice, & there-fore should not have admired Dancing with him long: as this was the case, I would not blame his policy in chusing not to lead out Hetty first, for his attachment to her he has made suf-

---

^67 Inserted by FBA.

ficiently known already—who, else, would have thought of inventing those Acrosticks in his name?"[68]

M[r] John Dundas made his Bow to me. I "own I now still more admired this changing scheme, for I should not have wished to have retained him all the Evening!—Mr. Seton led out Hetty now—"|

Two Dances over, Captain Pringle marched to me.—M[r] Farquar to Hetty. The Captain professed much concern at my Journey:—though he seldom saw me, he said it was a pleasure to him to know he lived in the same Neighbourhood—rejoiced, however, that we did not both go,—then he should have put his whole House in mourning,—now only half of it.—&c &c

After that, I went down two Dances with M[r] Robinson. "I have nothing more to say of him than I already have said.

We had so much ⟨walking⟩ between Dances that it was now near one o'clock—we therefore went down stairs to" supper. During the Time of rest, I was happier than in Dancing, for I was "horridly fatigued with my walk and" more pleased with the Conversation I then had with M[r] Dundas, M[r] Adams, & others, than with my Partners, & they all |

[*top of page cut away*]

"[?Mr. Dundas][69] really was so free as to put his Arm round my Waist, & [xxxxx ½ *line*] we sat so near one another that Nobody could observe it—but I was quite disquieted, & fairly turned my back to him, though there by I was not much better pleased in facing the major [Dundas]. He then took hold of a Curl of my Hair, saying he carried scissors in his Pocket, & would have used them,[70] had I not honoured him with a significant frown, & again turned from him, which had the desired effect, for he was so much affronted, he spoke not to me again the whole Evening. Hetty afterwards smoked the [?quarrel]"|

[68] Missing.
[69] This identification is suggested by FB's remark above (p. 124) that James Dundas was like Sir Harry Seton, 'save only he was less reserved,—rather'. Dundas, 48 years old with a wife and married daughter (below, p. 131), was probably being merely playful, which would explain his being so affronted by FB's reaction. FB probably reacted so strongly because Dundas looked much younger than his years, and because she did not yet know that he was married. She writes below (p. 131) that she and EB both 'think very well of him'.
[70] Obviously inspired by the bold Baron in *The Rape of the Lock*.

[top of page cut away]

When supper was over, all who had Voices worth hearing were made [to][71] sing—none shone more than Mr Adams; tho' in truth he has little or no voice ⸢to boast of,⸣ yet he sung with so much taste & feeling, that few very *fine* Voices could give equal pleasure:[72] I cannot but much regret the probability there is of my never seeing him again. I may see many fools, ere I see such a sensible man ⸢again.⸣ | Mr Robinson also sung, & showed to advantage his fine Teeth & face:—Miss Dalrymple also showed to *dis*advantage her conceit & self approbation;—Hetty with *one* song only gave more pleasure than any other.

Poor Mrs Pringle, who hates musick, unless it be Maggy Lauder,[73] was on the Rack of impatience | & vexation all the Time.—She is seldom silent for 3 minutes, yet seldom speaks without applause; therefore this *musical* entertainment was absolute torture to her—For the life of me I could not forbear laughing—She gave as many hints as she possibly could, but nobody would take them—between every song, she cried,— 'pray Gentlemen & Ladies take Breath—upon my word you ought not to suffer for your complaisance—' Still they were not tired:—more eagerly than before, she cried out—'why, ⸢Lord⸣ bless me! you'll kill yourselves!—pray Mr Debieg speak!—Mr Adams & Miss Dalrymple are so very polite, that they won't consider themselves;—but *we* ought!—'

Finding this also fail, quite out of patience she exclaimed— 'Why ⸢Lord!⸣ good folks this is all very fine, but you should not give us too much of it! let us have a little Conversation.—Mr Debieg why won't you talk?—Come, Sir Harry, I am sure, is of my side;—⸢Lord⸣ bless us, what's to become of our tongues?'

Mr Seton did not let *his* be idle; his whole attention was confined to Hetty, & his | Conversation more *flattering* than ever;— equally so, at least.—Well might he be proud of engaging her as he did, for she met with the most flattering & apparent approbation of every one present.—⸢*How* can any man trifle with such a sweet Girl!⸣

[71] Inserted by FBA.

[72] Robert Adam's brother-in-law, John Clerk of Eldin, notes in biographical sketch that he sang 'delightfully well' with an excellent voice (cited Fleming, p. 80).

[73] *Maggie Lawder*, a popular song published at this time. It begins: 'O wha wad na be in love' (*BUCEM* ii. 642, 1144; see also *The Scots Musical Museum*, ed. J. Johnson and W. Stenhouse (Edinburgh, 1853), i. 99).

We took our leaves at about 3 in the morn, I mine with much concern, assured as I was of not seeing them again so long, if ever: for mama's not being acquainted with this family, may probably put an End to our intimacy when we are all in Town again.[74] Mr Seton Handed Hetty to the Cariage,—Mr John Dundas very civilly *beg'd the favour of my Hand*, which just as I had held towards him, Major Dundas, impertinent Coxcomb, pushed himself between us, & very cavalierly took it. I can't say it made any difference to me, but I cannot bear the airs of that major. Mr John Laughed it off very well, threatning to send him a Challenge next Day; bidding him remember Montague House;[75] & not imagion he would Pocket such an affront. |

Captain & Mrs Pringle came Home with us—the former intimated his intention of calling to pay me a farewell visit ere I went:—fearing the consequences of his despair, I would not prohibit him. Poor Hetty passed an uneasy Night, racked with uncertainty about this Seton, this eternal destroyer of her peace!— *Were* he sincere, she owned she could be happier in a union with him, than with any man breathing:—indeed he deserves her not;—but the next morning, when she had considered well of every thing, she declared were he to make her the most solemn offer of his Hand, she would refuse him;—& half added *accept of Charles*!—

Wednesday [4 April], at Breakfast entered Captain Pringle;—pitied Hetty, pitied himself for my intended absence—nor did he exclude *me* from his pity,—in truth it was I most mer⟨i⟩ted it.—He hoped however that I did not carry my *Heart* down with me? Assured me I should find it very troublesome in the Country, & vastly more entertaining to go without that, though not without a successor to it[76]— | he told me I was now at the most *susceptible Age*, & hoped I made not a bad use of my time:—said the Country was intolerably insipid without ^⌐*Love* &c—¬

Having stayed about two Hours, he made his Compliments,

[74] In fact the Burneys did drop Mrs Pringle and her circle in the autumn, mainly in order to get rid of Alexander Seton, whom they probably feared might have designs on FB after EB's marriage to Charles Rousseau Burney in Sept. See below, p. 140.

[75] From 1680 to 1750 the fields behind Montague House in Great Russell St. were the most frequented place for duels in London. In 1753 the British Museum was established in the House (Wheatley, ii. 555–7).

[76] Presumably he meant a coquette's heart.

& departed. Soon after Mʳ Seton called, on pretence of bringing Hetty a Poem which she had expressed a wish to Read, ⌐called the⌐ *Deserter*.⁷⁷—I wonder *he* chose to bring it! how blind to our *own* failings are we!—⌐In a few moments Mr. Charles Burney came, & we all four set off for Mr. Strange's Exhibition.⁷⁸ Mr. Seton & Hetty walked *so* slow! my Cousin & self not fast, yet ever & insensibly always before them—in our way who should we meet but Mr. Crawford! he will certainly conclude that Mr. Seton & my sister are ⟨really⟩ engaged—no great matter—my Cousin however, I am sure was piqued. He has been for some months past more than ever fond of Hetty, nor has she discouraged him at all. I know he has less of Jealousy or ⟨vanity⟩ than any [?man I know, but]⌐ |

[1 line cut away]

I now come to Thursday [5 April], my last Day ⌐in dear London!⌐

In the morning, Harry Phips called—& stayed some Time. Hetty & I wished to form a friendship [with]⁷⁹ him nor has he shewn Any Aversion to such a scheme;—there is something very engaging in him. Soon after, ⌐*Mr. Charles*—made *me* a visit—Hetty was not at home—& after an Hours Conversation, he took his *parting leave*—He was succeeded by his Brother, James, who stayed with me all day. [xxxxx ½ *line*] Though he was obliged to go by 6 o'clock, as he had promised to officiate some where for Charles, who was engaged at Ranelagh.⁸⁰ We *mutually* regretted our *mutual* disappointment the preceding Day, & *mutually* rejoiced at our *mutual* happiness in meeting them.

---

⁷⁷ By Edward Jerningham (1727–1812), poet and dramatist. Two edns. were published at London in 1770. The hero of the poem is a soldier who deserts *for* love (not *from* love), and suffers the death penalty. A summary of the poem is in *GM* xl (1770), 83. FB was to meet Jerningham at Bath in 1780 (*DL* i. 350).

⁷⁸ Opened formally the next day (5 Apr.), 'in the Great Room at the upper End of St. Martin's Lane, *An* EXHIBITION *of* PICTURES, Selected from the Roman, Florentine, Lombard, Venetian, Neapolitan, Flemish, French, and Spanish Schools. The whole collected abroad by ROBERT STRANGE' (*Daily Adv.* 5 Apr. 1770). The exhibition was first held in 1769 and originally included 87 pictures, besides 32 drawings which Strange had sold to Sir Lawrence Dundas. It closed 12 May, and the whole was sold by auction in Feb. 1771 (see Dennistoun, ii. 65–8; Frits Lugt, *Répertoire des catalogues de ventes publiques . . . 1600–1825* (The Hague, 1938), No. 1888).

⁷⁹ Inserted by FBA or 2 or 3 words obliterated.

⁸⁰ To perform a concerto on the organ (see *Daily Adv.* 2 Apr. 1770).

The Miss Pascalls honoured me with a visit also—they are very deserving young women, & | I could wish they were my Neighbours *here* [Lynn].

James & I were chatting very comfortably together, half merry, half sad, when tat tat⁷ at the Door—& enter Mʳ Seton!—I was quite amazed—he marched up to me, & presented me with a little Parcel, which on opening I found to contain a dozen Franks directed to Hetty, *Free Dundas*!—He had mentioned this to her before, tho' as she rather declined it from our little acquaintance with Mʳ Dundas, we did not expect them. Mʳ Seton said that my sister should have a dozen directed to me, if I would tell him my Direction.

Imagion my blushes, &c

He stayed near two Hours. I don't admire being obliged to him.—he says that *Mʳˢ Debieg* mentioned it to Mʳ Dundas—but it's much the same. Really Mʳ Dundas must ⁷think us mad to⁷ permit such a request after seeing him twice! I should not like he should think ill of us, for we think very well of him. Mʳ Seton told me that he has a wife[81] & Daughter in Scotland, the latter maried. ⁷I was much surprised, for he does not look to be much above thirty.[82] |

James stayed to the last moment—longer indeed than I fear he ought. I was obliged to hurry him away—he went with much reluctance—our parting was *almost* pathetic—seriously I have a very great regard for him—he is all good humour, he is never ⟨happ⟩y but when he is engaged in some obliging office, his heart is open, frank, ingenuous almost to a fault—I sincerely wished he would have accompanied me hither, & made a flying visit.

He was just gone, & had left me something in the dumps, when my Hetty came Home to console me. While we were standing at the window & talking over our affairs, 'Lord, cried she, there's Mr. Young! & presently tat tat tat announced his intention of entering. He was most⁷ absurdly Dressed for a common visit, being in light Blue, embroidered with silver, a

---

[81] Jean Maria Forbes (d. 1774), daughter of William Forbes (d. 1730), 14th Lord Forbes; m. (1748) James Dundas. Their daughter Dorothea Dundas (d. 1810) m. (1769) George Brown (*c.*1722–1806) of Ellison, a Commissioner of Excise for Scotland (*Scots Magazine*, lxviii (1806), 239; lxxii (1810), 879; T. L. Ormiston, *The Ormistons of Teviotdale*, p. 257; *Scots Peerage*, iv. 64; John Kay, *Original Portraits* (1877), i. 75).

[82] He was actually 48.

Bag & sword—and Walking in the Rain! he looked extremely
well, & looked tolerably *conscious* of it—upon my word he is
quite altered from what I thought him on our first Acquaintance—he ⌜was⌝ all airs & affectation;—assumed a ⎪ coxcombical assurance & indolence joined—yet I believe this was *put
on*—for what purpose I cannot tell, unless it were to let us see
what a power of transformation he possessed.

He Bowed to the Ground at entering, then, swinging his Hat
the full extent of his arm,—'This is the most unfortunate
shower! cried he or rather, I most unfortunate in being caught
in it.—pray how does Dr Burney do?—where is he?'—We, in
return enquired after Mrs Young—'She's very well, in the
Environs of Soho, I believe'—'At Mrs Cornely's, I presume?'
said Hetty. 'Ay, sure; returned he, 'just going to open a Ball
with Lord Carlisle[83]—But where is Dr Burney?' Once again we
answered, out, on business; & retorted a second enquiry after
Mrs Young.—'We just now parted in a pet!' said he; 'but I
think, we were to meet here.' — — Soon after she came, in a
Chair. After common salutations, 'Pray how came you to leave
me so? Mr Young?' cried she—'Only think,' turning to us, 'the
fellow of a Coachman drove the Horse's Heads towards a Court
in Soho Square, ⎪ pretended he could not move them; & M^r
Young was fool enough to get out—& let the man have his
way,—when he deserved to be Horse whipped.' '—Instead of
which,' returned he, 'I gave him a shilling! where's the difference?' 'Who but you,' cried she, 'would not have made the
man come on with us? or else not have paid him?—and so I
was forced to run into a Toy shop, where he politely left me to
my fate—& where I chanced to meet with a Chair.'

O rare matrimony! thought I.[84]

Mr Young turned to Hetty—'where is Dr Burney? 'Why,
⌜Lord!⌝—cried she, I told you twenty times, out, on business.'
'O! ay, I believe you did—'

'When will Miss Allen leave Bath,' said Mrs Young.

---

[83] A joke. Carlisle House in Soho Square, purchased by Mrs Cornelys in 1760 to
house her public assemblies, was built for the E. of Carlisle during the reign of
James II.

[84] By this time Arthur Young and his wife were entering a state of hostility which
lasted the rest of their lives. Young's biographer blames Mrs Young's shrewish temper
and Young's numerous (if innocent) flirtations as the joint cause of this enmity. See
Gazley, pp. 200, 635, and *passim*.

'Why, is Miss Allen at Bath?' cried he.

'⌐Lord⌐ Mʳ Young,' exclaimed she, 'how can you be so affected! why you knew she was there a month ago.'[85] 'Not I faith! never heard a syllable of the matter: ⌐upon my soul⌐— not a single syllable!' 'I have no patience with such affectation—you knew it as well as I did.' [cried she.][86] |

'Miss Burney,' cried Mʳ Young, fixing his Eyes ⟨earne⟩stly on her Face, 'how does Mʳ—whats his ⟨name⟩—Charles, I believe—Ay, how does Mʳ Charles Burney do?' 'Very well, I believe,' said she, half *smiling* in spight of a studied composure.

'When does my sister come to Town,' asked Mʳˢ Young— 'Next Tuesday [10 April],' said I, '& I go to Lynn to-morrow!' 'To morrow! is this magick? and why do you go?' 'To take mama's place & be very notable.' 'And for that do you go?— No reason besides?—' —'Not one!'—'I'll go too!—when is it?' — — 'Next Tuesday—' 'I'll go too, I protest!—' cried Mʳ Young—'Pray do;' said I, 'it will be very well worth while!' 'I will, upon my honour!'—

He then insisted on Hetty's singing—which she did, & most sweetly. They went away about 9. My dear papa soon after came Home.—I told him of my Franks, though in some fear that he should think me wrong in consenting to ⌐have them— but he has no idea of being⌐ |

[*The first foliation indicates that 6 leaves have been discarded here. The next leaf, cut away at the top, begins with FB's thoughts on the moral superiority of women, who are more* 'amiable' *than men.*]

⌐them frequently, nay generally amiable—I think *that* word expresses the best qualities both of Head *and* Heart. A man might think this partial at first, but on consideration, I dare believe a *candid* man would assent to the truth. If he would not, I would be judged by this expedient. I would challenge him to name as many valuable men as I can women.

This subject leads me to the Novel[87] I was reading to Susan

---

[85] She stayed there at least till May (SEB's Journal for 1770, McGill University Library).

[86] Inserted by FBA.

[87] Perhaps *The Mistakes of the Heart: or, Memoirs of Lady Carolina Pelham and Lady Victoria Nevil, in a Series of Letters* (3 vols., 1769; vol. iv, 1771), by Pierre Henri Treyssac de Vergy (*c*.1738–74), adventurer and novelist. It is mentioned in Sheridan's *The Rivals* (1775), Act I, sc. ii. In his preface ('The Editor to the Public') Treyssac de Vergy notes:

when I wrote last—the first Volume is charming, very entertaining, sentimental, & interesting: many of the reflections also are very *deep thought*, & elegantly expressed, but it is wrote by a Foreigner, who wanted some friend to correct it, as in some places it is absolute nonsense: but good God what a Picture of man does the *chief* Heroine draw—I am now well inclined to believe it just, However severe.⌐—ˡ

[*The following fragment, recto and verso, was originally pasted to fo. 52ᵛ.*]

⌐change my sentiments with every new whim that enters my Head, so I will even quit my own observations on it, & see what my Novelist says, for Susanna waits.⌐

May 3ᵈ

⌐I shall amuse myself with my Pen to keep off my—appetite I believe I may say, while I wait Breakfast, for Susan is not yet awoken.⌐ ˡ

My Susette & I are very comfortable here [Lynn]—⌐I was a great while reconciling myself to this place, but am now very well satisfied—to work,⌐ Read, Walk & play on the Harpsichord—these are our employments, & we find them sufficient to fill up all our Time without ever being tired.

I am reading again, the History of England,[88] ˡ

[*top of page cut away*]

to Read them. In the History of England I have read to the ˙riegn of George the Second, &, in spight of the dislike I have to Smollett's Language & style of writing, I am much entertained,

---

'If faults against language occur—wonder there are so few—the author is a foreigner' (see also *The Monthly Review*, xl (1769), 511). Lady Carolina Pelham's letters are full of sententiae and unflattering portraits of her admirers. See B. Sutherland, 'Pierre Henri Treyssac de Vergy', in *Modern Language Quarterly*, iv (1943), 293–307 *passim*.

[88] *A Complete History of England, Deduced from the Descent of Julius Caesar to the Treaty of Aix la Chapelle 1748* (4 vols., 1757–8), by Tobias Smollett (1721–71). A 2nd edn. appeared in 1758–9, followed by Smollett's *Continuation of the Complete History of England* (5 vols., 1760–5), which brought the history down to 1765. The work was later modified and frequently reprinted as a continuation of Hume's *History of England*, and FB probably read Smollett's work from the Revolution of 1688, where Hume's history ends. See L. M. Knapp, 'The Publication of Smollett's *Complete History* . . . and Continuation', *The Library*, ser. iv, xvi (1935–6), 295–308.

for scarse a name is now mentioned that is not familiar to my Ear, & I delight in thus *tracing* the *rise & progress* of the great Characters of the Age. ⌐If Mr. Smollett could write History as well as Novels I should be charmed with his Book—but this is far from being the case, therefore he had better not have attempted it—he wants both dignity & elegance &, however he shines in Ferdinand Fathom and Roderick Random,[89] he is quite lost in the History of England. The first made his Fame, the last has destroyed it with *me*—Is he not to be pitied for this?⌐

We meet with great civility & kindncss in this Town—&—

Friday

I was interrupted—I am just returned from | making a visit to 5 sisters, 2 maried & 3 single, who all Live together[90]—& rejoiced am I that I *am* returned. There is with them a child, not ⌐3⌐ years old, Grandson to one of them, who is the Idol of them All: the poor Boy, by their ill judged & ruinous indulgence, is rendered an object of dislike to all others: they have taught [h]im to speak, like a Parrot, only such words as they [d]ictate; they make him affect the Language of a [m]an, & then boast that *no child ever talked like* [*h*]*im*, & what is the effect of this singularity, but making him appear affected, troublesome [&] unnatural? How infinitely more amiable is [th]e native simplicity & artlessness with which [ch]ildren are ⟨born⟩! Then they permit him to [a]muse himself at pleasure with all Insects—[F]lys, Butterflys—poor little Animals—the torture [he] gav[e] to one of the last really turned me so [sic]k ⟨that⟩ I could not recover myself the whole [?eve]ning—⟨Is not⟩ humanity disgraced by this [bar]barity to the dumb creation? —the poor child [bel]ongs to a sex sufficiently prone to cruelty: [is i]t for *women* thus early to encourage it? [Ano]ther, to my thoughts, worse than absurd way [they] have chose to make him *shine*,—which is, [to] bid him say the Lords Prayer & Belief in | order to display his fine memory—why won't they

[89] *The Adventures of Roderick Random* (2 vols., 1748), and *The Adventures of Ferdinand Count Fathom* (1753). CB condemned Smollett's novels as 'so d——d gross that they are not fit reading for women with all their wit' (*ED* ii. 230).

[90] These sisters and the grandson have not been identified.

make him get Ballads by Heart? To sport thus with our religious duties is to me exceedingly shocking, & had I been old enough to dare speak my sentiment[s] unasked, I would have told them so.

[*rest of page blank*]

6   [Lynn Regis, July 1770]

To Esther Burney

The MS is now missing. Reprinted from *ED* i. 101–2. Mrs Ellis noted: 'On the back of this letter there is a date in pencil of "July, 1770," which may be in Fanny's writing' (*ED* i. 102 n. 1). The letter was addressed to EB at Chessington, where she was visiting SC.

EB has accepted Charles Rousseau Burney as her husband-to-be. They have informed FB and EAB, who have sent the news to CB, who on 6 June had left England on a six-month tour of France and Italy (to gather materials for *Hist. Mus.*). Because of his banker's 'neglect', however, 'a large packet of Letters from England written in June & July last had . . . lain at Paris & Lyon several Months' (CB to SC 19–24 Dec. 1770, Osborn), and CB heard nothing until 27 Oct., more than a month after the wedding (20 Sept.), when he wrote in his journal: 'A letter had arrived from Capt. Forbes from his mother at Rome, and he told me there was something in it which concerned me, and at the same time gave me joy. I could not conceive for what, when he read as follows. "The English papers say that Dr. Burney's daughter is married to one of his own name; I hope happily, and with his consent."—Had it been otherwise, the Captain's manner of breaking it to me, would not have been the most gentle in the world' (*Tours*, i. 263).

My dearest sister,

With a very short time to write, and a very great deal to say, I take up my pen to thank you most heartily for your comfortable letter.[91] I had thought it very long on the road. We are now in daily expectation of the important letter from papa—and let me say one thing—it seems to me not unlikely that immediately that papa receives the last pacquet, he will write to my uncle.[92] I hope therefore that you have ere now acquainted him

[91] Missing.
[92] Richard Burney of Barborne Lodge, Worcester, Charles Rousseau Burney's father.

Dr Burney at Calis in the year 1770

3. Dr Charles Burney. From a drawing by Joseph Nollekens, 1770.

with your affairs, or else that you directly will, as it would be shocking for him to hear of it first from abroad, and as he would then perhaps always believe that you intended to secret it from him.

How can it have got about, God knows, but every body here speaks of your marriage as a certain and speedy affair. So you will have it in town. I fear mama cannot go;—as for me, I am ready to break my heart when I think of being absent from you. O that it were in my power to quit this place directly! But I hope all for the best; indeed I cannot bear to *suppose* that I shall be away from you. Miss Allen goes to Snettisham[93] to-morrow—is too busy to write, but will from thence. Susette's best love attends you. I have had a sensible and affectionate letter[94] from my cousin [Charles Rousseau Burney], which I beg you to thank him for in my name.

Sweet Chesington!—abominable Lynn!

My dear Hetty, I shall write myself into the vapours and then give them to you—so I will have done. But I must say how much I admire your plan of life. Certainly it would seem very strange for you to have gone to the Coffee House,[95] for all his and your own acquaintance will be visiting you on the occasion. I will write to you the very instant we hear from Venice.[96] My kindest and best love to my ever dear Mr. Crisp[97] and to dear Kitty. Let us know about the Barbornes when you can. Adieu, my dearest, dear sister. I am in much haste. My first wish is to be with you. God forbid I should not! Believe me ever with the utmost affection

Your

FRANCES BURNEY

[93] 12 miles N. of Lynn: MA presumably went to visit the Stylemans, viz., Nicolas Styleman (1721–88) of Snettisham Hall, a Justice of the Peace and (1776) High Sheriff of Norfolk, who m. (1752) Catherine née Henley (*c.*1724–93). She later numbered the Styleman family among her 'Old Friends and Neighbours' in Norfolk (MAR to FB 28 June 1798, Barrett; *JL* iii. 8 n. 10). CB had received a rare collection of musical manuscripts from Styleman in 1760 (*Hist. Mus.* iii. 356).

[94] Missing.

[95] To be introduced to Charles Rousseau's friends. Which coffee-house is not known.

[96] CB was at Venice 3–18 August (*Tours*, i. 108–40).

[97] In his letter to SC of 19–24 Dec. 1770 (above, head-note), CB acknowledges a 'Friendly Letter', from SC 'in behalf of the young Folks', presumably containing SC's approval of the impending marriage. The letter was part of the large packet held up at Paris and Lyon.

[The Journal for 1770 continues. The following passage in brackets was substituted by FBA for 22 obliterated lines, a partial reading of which is given after.]

[Poland Street—

I have not wrote this age—& the reason is my thoughts have been all drawn away from myself & given up to my dear Hetty—& to her I have been writing without end[98]—so that all my time besides was due to my dearest Susette with whom I have been reading French, having taught myself that charming Language for the sake of its bewitching authors—for I shall never want to speak it. With this dear Susette and my sweet little Charlotte it is well I can be so happy—for Hetty, my dear Hetty, has given herself away from us—She has married at last her faithful Charles[99]—God send her happy! He is one of the worthiest young men living—I am come up to Town to spend a little time with them. They are now in our House till they can find a dwelling to their taste.[1]

Papa has bought a house in Queen Square.[2] It is settled by

[98] Only the letter above survives.

[99] EB and Charles Rousseau Burney were married in St Paul's Church, Covent Garden, on 20 Sept. 1770. The wedding was performed by Paul Elers Scott, curate *pro tempore*, and the witnesses were Robert Strange, Mary Bruce Strange, Ann Burney (Aunt Nanny), and Catherine ('Kitty') Cooke (*Registers of St. Paul's Church, Covent Garden*, ed. W. H. Hunt (1906–9), iii. 250). FB later remembered Charles Rousseau at his wedding as 'a shy, modest, embarrassed, half-formed youth' (FBA to Charlotte Broome 5–15 Oct. 1819, *JL* xi. 140), and notes below (p. 243) that everyone 'thought much higher for her [EB] than Mr. Burney, who has nothing to offer but the fruits of his profession'. As feared, the marriage, though loving, was impoverished, but FB was always to esteem Charles Rousseau for his probity and goodness of heart.

[1] After 5 weeks they moved from Poland St. (below, p. 141), probably to Charles St., Covent Garden, where MA reports them as living the following Sept. (MA to FB 7 Sept. 1771, Berg).

[2] 'A new house, purchased in his absence by Mrs. Burney, at the upper end of Queen-square; which was then beautifully open to a picturesque view of Hampstead and Highgate' (*Mem.* i. 223). The house, No. 42, Queen Square (S. side), Bloomsbury, had formerly been owned by Alderman John Barber (d. 1741), the friend of Swift (Wheatley, iii. 132; St Andrew Holborn and St George the Martyr Rate Books, Metropolitan Borough of Holborn Reference Library). Larger than the Poland St. dwelling, it was purchased with a view to accommodating both the Burney and Allen households, which till then had lived apart; at this time Mrs Burney gave up her house in Lynn (Lynn Rate Books, Norfolk Record Office). Another motive for the move was to get away from Mrs Pringle and her circle. An added attraction of Queen Square was that a number of the Burney's Norfolk acquaintance lived there, viz., William Folkes, Sir William Browne, and Sir Richard Betenson, uncle of Martin Folkes Rishton, MA's future husband (see below, *passim*).

Mr Crisp—to my very great grief, that we are quite to drop Mrs. Pringle—that we may see no more of Mr. Seton—]

[*The 22 obliterated lines for which the passage above was substituted have been only partially recovered.* not with standing appearances speak so much against her *may refer to Mrs Pringle's encouragement of Alexander Seton's pursuit of EB. Seton himself seems to be referred to in the following:* for I think he stands so little chance of ever contributing to the happiness of others that he can never know how to be happy himself *and* when he found she was lost to him for ever, he became more than sensible of it, *i.e. EB's worth (see below, p. 243). In the next line we have* Poor Mr. Seton. *Earlier there is* Mr. Robinson's *perhaps Walter Robertson (c.1703–72) of Lynn, but the phrases following* he is one of the most respectable & amiable of men and Picture of benevolence *seem rather to fit Robertson's son-in-law Henry Partridge (1711–93) with whom he is mentioned above (p. 85).*]

For this reason I shall be glad to quit Poland Street,—that I may no more see Mrs Pringle, since I dare not visit, or even speak to her, when it is not unavoidable, as it was a few Days since, when Miss Allen & I were standing at the Parlour Window, & Mrs Pringle passed, but seeing me, turned back & made a motion for me [to] open the window, which I did, though I was ter[ri]bly confused what to say to her, for it was not in my power to explain the reasons of my absence from her; yet, after so much kindness & civility as we have met with from her, I am sure excuses were very necessary. She asked me how I did, and [i]mmediately added—'Pray what ⌐is the meaning⌐ that you never come near me?—' I was much at a loss [w]hat to say, but stammered some thing about the hurry [o]f moving, want of Time, &c—She shook her Head—'Want of Time!—what only next Door? I'll assure you, I think it very ungrateful in you.—' Her bluntness confounded me, which I believe she saw, for she said in a softer manner 'well, my dear, I I am glad to see you so well—I wish you good morning.—' and walked away.

I am truly sorry to say, I believe this is the last Time I shall speak to Mrs Pringle. I have a very strong sense of the favours we have received from her, & were it in my power, would convince her that I have—but it is not. Just before her Eldest son, the Captain, went Abroad last spring,[3] he gave to my sister a Copy of Verses on her & me, which I will write out.

[3] Perhaps to Grenada, where he was Governor-Depute.

Belle Venus[4] et madame Minerve[5]
Du Ciel firent le Voyage un jour,
Et des Figures humains elles s'en serven[t]
Que les Graces, et les Pla[i]sirs entourent.

Ces deux jolies Filles, comme on dit,
Dans la Terre firent terrible ravage,
Et des milles Coeurs enchainés, les cris
Dans la Cour d' Olympe firent ta [*sic*] page.

Jupiter, supreme dans les Cieux,
Fut faché de voir ces Belles
S'egarer, et quitter les Dieux
Pour badiner chez les mortells. |

'Va, Déesses, indigne de ce Nom,
Soit a jamais eloignée d'ici,
'Va, demeure dans la Rue de Pologne,
Soit Femmes pour le reste de la vie

Can anything be more galant?[6] my sister & [my]self propose in future signing no other names than [t]hose of Venus & Minerva.

Queen's Square, Novr 16—

I have now changed my abode, & quitted dear Poland Street for ever. How well satisfied shall I be if after having Lived as long in Queen's Square I can look back to equally happy Days!

We have a charming House here. It is situated at the upper End of the square,[7] & has a delightful [pr]ospect of Hamstead & Hygate, we have more than [roo]m for our Family, large as it is, & all the [ro]oms are well fitted up, Convenient, ⌜large,⌝ & handsome.

I left M[r] Burney & my sister with regret—I had | passed 5 happy Weeks with them, ⌜& should have remained longer but that as Mama wanted all the Furniture from Poland Street they were in haste to quit it.—⌝ [xxxxx *3 lines*]

---

[4] 'Miss Hester' (FB's note).
[5] 'Miss Fanny Burney' (FB's note).
[6] FBA comments: 'The lines are out of all metre, and are not French.'
[7] The S. side. The open view to the N. is shown in a 1787 engraving by R. Pollard, after a drawing by E. Dayes, reproduced in G. H. Hamilton, *Queen Square: Its Neighbourhood and Its Institutions* (1926), facing p. 23.

10 December

To Wonder ⌜at any action of ⟨Ba⟩seness & perfidy in man, will, I believe, soon be over with me. Yet so flagrant an instance of ingratitude & cruelty as I ha[ve] lately seen, I should think would surprise Experience itself.

Mr. Rishton,[8] whom we all thought a young man of ⟨most⟩ meritorious constancy, after absolutely engaging himself to Miss Allen, whose Heart is devoted to him,—[has] for ever abandoned her though he was bound to her, [by] ⟨the ur⟩gent ties of Honour, Gratitude,—I was going [to] say Love—but that would be folly. He has wrote to her from Dover, a letter the most cruel & ungrateful I ever Read, in which he tells her it will be impossible for him *ever* to ask for her Hand—talks of h[is] own dependent situation, and of the power of love [xxxxx *1–2 words*] & wishes her happy with a more worthy man.

Hardened must be the Heart that could so dreadfully⌝ ⌐

[*end of Journal for 1770*]

---

[8] Martin Folkes William Rishton (*c.*1747–1820). He was a grandson of Martin Folkes (1690–1754), sometime President of the Royal Society, and nephew (by marriage) and heir presumptive of Sir Richard Betenson, Bt. (below, p. 231). Neither Sir Richard nor EAB approved of the romance between Rishton and MA. Sir Richard was perhaps wary of MA's capricious temperament, while EAB seems to have heard tales of Rishton's extravagance at Oxford (he matriculated at Oriel College in 1764 but did not graduate) and of his having done something not worthy of a gentleman (*ED* i. 115). In a letter to FB and SEB, Apr. 1771 (Berg), MA reveals that Sir Richard had sent Martin on the Grand Tour and 'made him promise he would stay two years abroad'. The jilting letter from Dover was no doubt sent partly under pressure from Sir Richard, but Martin seems to have had second thoughts himself about marrying MA. In any event, by the end of Mar. following, he had already returned to England, evidently without his uncle's approval, and seems to have resumed covertly his courtship of MA.

It was perhaps at this time that FB wrote 'Female Caution. Addressed to Miss Allen'. See below, Appendix 2; p. 146 and *passim*.

AJ (Early Diary, iv, paginated 199–[238] followed by 179–[202], re-paginated 179–[242], foliated [1]–33, Berg), Journal for 1771.
Originally several cahiers made of sewn double sheets. Now 19 single sheets and 7 double sheets 4to, 66 pp., with 1 paste-over. A later folder has been added.
Entitled (by FBA, on fo. 1ʳ): Nº 4. | April | Early Journal. | 1771
Annotated: ✳· ✳
In FBA's 'List of Persons' for 1771 are a number of names not in the extant journal. 'Leoni' was perhaps the 'Signor Leoni', 'principal performer on the harpsichord' at Lyons, whom CB had met there in June 1770; possibly identical with the Benedetto Leoni who published harpsichord lessons in London c.1768 (Tours, i. 37; New Grove, s.v. Leoni, Michael). 'Miss Mainstone' was perhaps a connection of the 'James Mainstone, Esq.', who subscribed to Hist. Mus. (probably James Mainstone of Essex St., Strand, a prominent solicitor who died in 1799; see GM lxix² (1799), 909). 'Miss Const' and 'Mrs. Const' were possibly relations of the 'Fr[anci]s Const' whose signature and bookplate (mostly torn away) are in a copy (in the possession of Dr Alvaro Ribeiro) of the first edition of CB's The Present State of Music in France and Italy, published later this year; this was probably the 'Fra. Const, esq.' who died in Villiers St., aged 72, in 1793 (GM lxiii² (1793), 1156). 'Miss Riddle' was perhaps related to John Riddell, surgeon in Great Marlborough St. (Thomas Mortimer, Universal Director (1763), p. 54). Also listed is 'Mrs. Burney Senʳ', i.e., Mrs Ann (Cooper) Burney. For 'Molly Stancliffe', see below, p. 222, and for 'Mrs. Sansom' and 'Miss Molly Sansom', below, p. 171.

April 11ᵗʰ

Wonder, they say, is the attribute of Fools.[1] I cannot think it. Is it possible to live without it? Does a Day pass that we meet not with something strange, unexpected, unaccountable? The guilty only—or those who have very severely suffered by Other's Guilt,—such alone can Live in the World without Wonder.

Surely this maxim should be confined to intellectual ignorance.—ˮto those who stare with stupid and uninformed astonishment at the Works of Art—who exclaim at the sight of any thing unusual—Lord! how is this done? Lord! I wonder how that is done?ˮ But it seems to me to be very unjust to impute to |

[1] Cf. 'Wonder is the effect of ignorance' (Samuel Johnson, The Rambler, No. 137). The concept goes back at least to Horace's nil admirari.

folly the wonder of inexperience at the Works of man. It should rather be called Innocence.

What can one think of the natural Disposition of a young Person who, with an Eye of suspicion, looks around for secret Designs in the appearance of kindness, & evil intentions in the profession of friendship?

I could not think well of such apprehensions & expectations in youth. A bad opinion of the World should be dearly bought to be excusable. Why then is Wonder the attribute of Fools? Who without it, however sensible, if not Hackneyed in the ways of Vice, can behold Ingratitude in the Obliged? Indifference in the beloved? discontent ׀ in the Prosperous? Deceit in the Trusted? & gaiety in the depth of mourning ⌐and not Wonder?⌐

I *do*, I *will* hope that Instances of these kinds are uncommon enough to authorise & create Wonder in All; except indeed, those very miserable Beings, who having met with perfidy & deceit in every Individual they have unhappily relied upon, regard the whole World as being depraved, treacherous, selfish & ⌐infamous.⌐

I have, of late, been led into many reflections of this nature from the strange & unexpected behaviour I have seen on several occasions.—One happened this morning.

Mrs Colman, Wife of the famous Author Mr Colman, a sweet, amiable ׀ Woman, was taken ill & Died suddenly rather more than a Fortnight since.[2] We were intimately acquainted with, & very sincerely regretted her. In point of understanding she was infinitely inferiour to Mr Colman, but she possessed an uncommon sweetness of Temper, much sensibility, & a generous & restless desire of obliging, & of making her friends happy.

So amiable a Character must, I am sure, endear her infinitely to Mr Colman, of whom she, with the greatest reason, was beyond expression attached to. He is one of the best Tempered, (though I believe very passionate) of men, lively, agreeable, open Hearted, & clever.

Her Daughter, Miss Ford,[3] is about 16, very genteel in

---

[2] She died on 29 Mar. 1771 after accidentally taking a dose of the wrong medicine for a minor illness (George Colman the younger, *Random Records of My Life* (1830), i. 44–5).

[3] Harriet Ann Ford (b. *c.*1754), Mrs Colman's illegitimate daughter by Henry

Person, well bred, & very well Educated. Her son, George Colman[4] is still younger. Poor Mrs Colman was doatingly fond of both her Children—"Her Daughter has been Papa's scholar some years—"[5] I have heartily pitied them for the loss of such a mother ever since I heard of it.

This morning it happen'd that only I was at Home "—Mama is gone to Chesington, her Health very indifferent, but I hope Change of air & Mr. Crisp's Care & attention will recover her—Miss Allen is returned from Lynn—but was Out—"

I heard a violent Rap at the Door, & John came in with Miss Ford's Name.—I felt myself almost shudder with the idea of what she must suffer from entering a House in which her mother had been so intimate & while her Death was so recent; & when she came in, I knew not what to do with my Eyes, to prevent their meeting her's. I was equally distressed for Words, not knowing how to address her on this melancholy occasion. — — But I soon found my apprehensions were needless, for she received my salute, & seated herself with great composure, & without manifesting any concern. I talked, as well as I was able, of indifferent matters, & she followed as I led, with the utmost ease & serenity; offered to call upon me any morning that would be agreeable to me, to go on an airing, spoke just as usual of Mr. Colman & her Brother, who I enquired much after; & with the ready politeness of a mistress of a Family, hoped soon to have the pleasure of seeing me in Queen Street!—Then said she was going to St. James', & so many places that she could not possibly stay longer.

I held up my Hands & Eyes with astonishment when she left me. "Good God," thought I, is all the tenderness of the fondest of mothers so soon forgot? or is it that, becoming the mistress of the House, for such Mr Colman has made her, having his

Mossop, the Irish actor, who kept her as his mistress before Colman. An actress and dancer at Drury Lane (1762–7) and Covent Garden (1767–9), she later married a 'John Wilkinson Gentleman' and was perhaps the 'Harriett, wife of J. J. Wilkinson, esq. of Seymour-place, Euston-square, and of the Temple' who died in 1825 (*GM* xcv[1] (1825), 188; Highfill s.v. Ford, Harriet Ann; *DL* ii. 155; Garrick, *Letters*, iii. 1053).

[4] George Colman the younger (1762–1836) was 8 years old at this time. Like his father he was to become a noted dramatist and in 1789 succeeded him as manager of the Haymarket, which the elder Colman had taken over in 1777.

[5] She is listed as having a lesson on 2 Jan. 1768 on a leaf remaining from CB's pocket memoranda book for that year (Berg).

servants & Equipage at her command—is it such things that
compensate for the best of Parents?[6]

April 20.

I was last Night, with mama & Miss Allen, at Ranelagh.
⌜Mr. Rishton was there, he either did not, or, which is much
more probable, *would not*, see us. The Room was extremely
Crowded & very brilliant. I wish that man was at Jerusalem, or
any where rather than in London.⌝[7] I saw few People ⌜there⌝
that I knew, & none that I cared for. ⌐

May 8th

My Father's Book, on *The Present State of Music*,[8] made it's
appearance in the World the 5th of this month, & we flatter ourselves it will be favourably received.

Last Sunday [5 May] was the first Day for some Time past,
that my Father has favoured us with his company, in the ⌜par-
lour⌝ stile, having been so exceedingly occupied by Writing in
those few Hours he spends at Home, that he really seemed lost
to his Family; & the comfort of his society & Conversation are
almost as new as grateful to us.

He Prints this Book for himself.[9] He has sent a multitude of
them to his particular friends as presents. Among others, to the

---

[6] Several possible reasons suggest themselves for Miss Ford's behaviour. She may
have had a naturally cold personality; her doting mother may have spoiled her so much
that she had lost all feeling except for herself; she may have looked down on her mother
because of her 'inferiour' understanding and lack of education; or she may have always
resented her mother for bringing her into the world a bastard. (Did Mrs Colman's
doting fondness for her children reflect a guilt complex?) On the other hand, Miss Ford
may simply have been a better actress than FB realized.

[7] MA wrote to FB and SEB from Lynn, *pre* 11 Apr. 1771 (Berg), that she had just
learned of Rishton's sudden and unexpected return to England, after only 'five months'
abroad—'I neither Eat drink nor Sleep for thinking of it'. He seems to have resumed
covertly his courtship of MA, though with such vacillation that MA half welcomed her
mother's decision to send her to Geneva in the autumn, ostensibly to finish her education but probably to remove her from Rishton's influence. See below, p. 169.

[8] *The Present State of Music in France and Italy: or, The Journal of a Tour through those
Countries, undertaken to collect Materials for a General History of Music: By Charles Burney,
Mus. D.*, was published in 1 vol. 8vo, by Thomas Becket, bookseller in the Strand. The
'5th' is presumably a slip, as 5 May 1771 fell on a Sunday. A 2nd edn., corrected, was
published in 1773 by Becket, James Robson in New Bond Street, and George Robinson in Paternoster Row.

[9] That is, at his own risk, without subscribers.

famous Dr. Hawkesworth, to that charming Poet M[r] Mason,[10] to M[r] Garrick[11] & M[r] Crisp—who all four were consulted about it when a manuscript & interested themselves much with it.[12] Dr. Shepherd, M[r] Colman, Dr. Armstrong, M[r] Strange, Dr. Bever,[13] Giardini,[14] & many others, had likewise Books ⌜sent them⌝ before the Publication. ⌜My Father even sent one to Mr. Hawkins,[15] who is writing also a History of music, & with whom Mr. Daines Barrington[16] made him acquainted.⌝

We had a great deal of Company last Sunday. M[rs] Sheeles[17]

---

[10] William Mason (1724–97); Horace Walpole's correspondent and a close friend and editor of Thomas Gray. CB first met Mason *c.*1748 at the house of Ld. Holdernesse, to whom Mason became chaplain in 1754 (Lonsdale, p. 16).

[11] David Garrick (1717–79). CB probably first met him in 1745 at the home of the famous actress Mrs Susannah Maria Cibber, sister of CB's music master Dr Thomas Arne (Lonsdale, p. 11). The two, except for a few temporary fallings out, remained close friends to the end of Garrick's life. See below, *passim*.

[12] According to CB's introduction to the unpublished portions of his travel diary, his chief advisors were Mason, Garrick, and Ld. Holdernesse, who all counselled him to exclude from publication the non-musical parts. This advice he followed, over the protests of Crisp, who 'assured me that my miscellaneous observations had entertained him far more than the musical' (*Tours*, i, pp. xxix–xxx).

[13] Thomas Bever (1725–91), DCL (Oxon.), 1758; admitted to Doctors' Commons, 1758; judge of the Cinque Ports and chancellor of Lincoln and Bangor. A writer on civil law, he took a special interest in music and the fine arts, and gave CB a letter or letters of introduction for his Italian tour (Lonsdale, p. 86).

[14] Felice de Giardini (1716–96), Italian violinist and composer. CB met him when he first came to England in 1750. Widely regarded as the greatest violinist of his time, he was evidently a splenetic and difficult person (though he could be very witty and entertaining). See 'Mem.' App. B. 8 and nn.; also Highfill; *New Grove*; Mercer, ii. 895—6; Lonsdale, p. 78 and *passim*; Scholes, i. 120 and *passim*.

[15] John Hawkins (1719–89), cr. (1772) Kt. Hawkins had for many years been engaged in writing a history of music, and the first vol. was already in print by summer 1771. The entire work was published in 5 vols. 4to, in 1776, entitled *A General History of the Science and Practice of Music*. CB first met Hawkins some time before his trip to Italy. For a detailed account of their subsequent rivalry, see Lonsdale, pp. 189–225. See also B. H. Davis, *A Proof of Eminence: The Life of Sir John Hawkins* (Bloomington, 1973), p. 121.

[16] The Hon. Daines Barrington (1727–1800), judge, naturalist, and antiquary, successfully proposed CB as a candidate for the Royal Society in 1773 (A. F. V. Ribeiro, 'An Edition of the Letters of Dr. Charles Burney from 1751 to 1783' (Univ. of Oxford Ph.D. thesis 1980), ii. 130).

[17] Anne Elizabeth Irwin, m. (1735) John Sheeles *or* Shields. Her husband, who was apparently still living in 1765 but was presumably dead by now, had originally run two boarding-schools, one at or near Chessington, and the other in Queen Square. CB taught music in the Queen Square school from his return to London in 1760 until about 1775. His children FB, SEB, and CB Jr. had stayed there during the last week of his first wife's fatal illness, in Sept. 1762. Mrs Sheeles's name last appears in the Queen Square rate books in 1775, when she may have died and the school presumably closed.

The Sheeleses' only daughter, Martha Sophia Sheeles (1748–1832), m. (1769, as his

& M^r & Mrs Mailing, her son & Daughter, Dined & spent the Evening with us. Mrs Mailing is a sweet Woman, with whom we were intimate before her marriage, & who now, to our great regret, lives in the North of England. After Dinner, Sir Thomas Clarges,[18] a modest young Baronet, & Mr Price,[19] a young man of Fashion, called & sat about two Hours. The latter is lately returned from his Travels, & was eager to *compare Notes* with my Father. He is a very intelligent, sensible & clever young man. He is kinsman to Mr Greville.

˹Mr. Burney favoured us for some Time with his Company, but my sister not being well, we did not see her.

Dr. Bever, full of compliments & fine speeches — — as full, I own, as such a heavy[20] Creature can be—came to make his thanks for the Book &c.˹

But after Tea, we were *cheered* indeed,—for—Rap Tap, tap—& enter M^r & Mrs Garrick,[21] with their two Nieces.[22] Mr Garrick, who has lately been very ill, is delightfully recovered,[23] looks as handsome as ever ˹I saw him,˹ is in charming spirits—& was all animation & good humour.

2nd wife) Christopher Thompson Maling (1741–1810) of West Herrington, Co. Durham. The Malings' 3rd daughter, Martha Sophia Maling (d. 1849), m. (1795) Henry Phipps, Baron Mulgrave. See 'Mem.' No. 84 and n. 8; *HFB* p. 11; *JL* xi. 273 n. 6; *GM* cii² (1832), 285; subscription list in Christopher Smart, *A Translation of the Psalms of David* (1765).

[18] Sir Thomas Clarges (1751–82), 3rd Bt. See vol. ii for his infatuation with Elizabeth Linley, later wife of Richard Brinsley Sheridan. He m. (1777) Louisa Skrine (1760–1809), a musical lady who became a close friend of SEB (*JL* v. 387 n. 6). In his pocket memoranda book for 1768 (Berg) CB lists '2 Miss Clarges' as his scholars, one of whom was probably Sir Thomas's sister Mary Clarges (d. 1823), who m. (1777) N. Vincent.

[19] Probably Uvedale Price (1747–1829), cr. (1828) Bt., a first cousin of Clarges, who later became a noted writer on the picturesque. He had gone on the Grand Tour with Charles James Fox. The two visited Rome, Venice, Turin, and Geneva, and called on Voltaire at Ferney in the summer of 1768. Fox then returned to England, but Price continued his travels, crossing the finest parts of Switzerland and descending the Rhine to Spa. See C. J. Fox, *Memorials and Correspondence*, ed. J. Russell (1853–7), i. 27–9, 46–7.

[20] i.e., 'heavy-headed', as FBA inserts further on in the MS.

[21] Eva Maria Veigel (1724–1822), called 'Violette', dancer, m. (1749) David Garrick.

[22] Arabella ('Bell') Garrick (1753–1819) and Catherine ('Kitty') Garrick (1756–*post* 1822), daughters of Garrick's youngest brother George Garrick (1723–79) by his 1st wife (m. 1751/2) Catherine née Carrington (d. 1771). Arabella m. (1778) Capt. Frederick Bridges Schaw of the Surrey militia; Catherine m. (1781) John George Payne. See Stone, pp. 20, 654; Highfill; John Baker, *Diary*, ed. P. Yorke (1931), p. 254; *GM* xlviii (1778), 237.

[23] Garrick wrote to James Boswell, 18 Apr. 1771: 'I have been confin'd very near two Months with the Gout; Nothing till lately could subdue my Spirits, but I begin to discover that I am growing Old . . .' (*Letters*, ii. 733).

4. David Garrick. From a portrait by Benjamin Vandergucht, 1768.

Mrs Garrick is the most attentively polite & perfectly well bred Woman in the World—her speech is all softness, her manners all elegance, her smiles all sweetness. There is something so ⏐ peculiarly graceful in her motion, and pleasing in her address, that the most trifling Words have weight & power when spoken by her to oblige & even delight.

The Miss Garricks resemble, the Eldest her Aunt, the youngest her Uncle in a striking manner. Softness, modesty, reserve & silence characterise Miss Garrick, while Kitty is all animation, spirit & openness. They are both very fine Girls, but the youngest is most handsome—her Face is the most expressive I almost ever saw of liveliness & sweetness.

⌐I had not seen any of these Ladies for a very long time [xxxxx *2–3 words*] for, as I have before mentioned, our acquaintance with the Family was dropt. I am infinitely rejoiced at this renewal.⌐[24]

Dr. King,[25] who has just taken ⏐ that Degree, came in, & figured away to his own satisfaction before Mr Garrick, who he so engrossed, that I thought it quite effrontery ⌐in him.⌐ I wonder he had the courage to open his mouth but men of half Understandings have generally, I believe, too little feeling to be over powered with diffidence: ⌐besides, the man is used to preach, & that has taught him to *prose*, which he does unmercifully.⌐ Dr. Bever, who had listened with attentive admiration to every Word Mr Garrick spoke, upon something being advanced relative to ⌐Law,⌐ ventured to ⌐open his mouth to⌐ reply—I really pitied the poor man, for when Mr Garrick turned round to him, & every Body was silent ⌐to hear him,⌐ his Voice failed him, he hesitated, confounded his own meaning, & was in so ⏐ much confusion that he could not make himself understood.

I sat by the youngest Miss Garrick, ⟨&⟩ had ⟨some⟩ com-

[24] The reason for this temporary breach is not known. Lonsdale, pp. 73—4, notes a misunderstanding between CB and Garrick in 1767 over a musical setting of the burlesque 'Orpheus', and FB mentions another quarrel below, p. 322 and vol. ii.

[25] John Glen King (1731–87); MA (Cantab.), 1763; Vicar of Little Barwick, Norfolk, 1760–4; chaplain to the English factory at St Petersburg, 1764. King was responsible for the loss of EAB's entire dowry of £5,000, which he had persuaded her to lend to an English merchant in Russia who went bankrupt about 1767. Despite this calamity, however, he remained a friend of the Burneys. He had taken the degree of DD at Oxford on 23 Mar. 1771; earlier in the year he was elected FSA (10 Jan.) and FRS (21 Feb.). See 'Mem.' No. 113.

fortab⟨le Conversation⟩ with her. M⟨rs⟩ Garrick with much kindness took my Hand when she spoke to me, & Mr Garrick enquired most particularly after ⟨every⟩ one of the Family. I never saw in my life such brilliant, piercing Eyes as his are—in looking at him, when I have chanced to meet them, I have really not been able to bear their lustre. I remember three lines which I once heard Mrs Playdell repeat, (they were her own) upon Mr Garrick speaking of his Face:

> That mouth, that might Envy with Passion inspire,
> Those Eyes!—fraught with Genius, with sweetness,
>   with Fire,
> And every thing else that the Heart can desire — —

This sweet Poetess, on the very Sunday I am writing of, set out for the East Indies[26] ⌐with her Husband & Children[27]—I am ⌐ very sorry that I did not first see her, but my sister, with whom I intended calling upon her, has constantly met with some Engagement that has prevented us.⌐

June 3^d

Alas! my poor forsaken Journal! how long have I neglected thee! faithful friend that thou hast been to me, I blush at my inconstancy but, I know not how it is, I have lost my *Goût* for Writing,—I have known the Time, when I could enjoy Nothing, without relating it—but now, how many subjects of joy, how very many of sorrow, have I met with of late, without

---

[26] The next ship to leave for India was the *Hampshire*, Capt. Thomas Taylor, which left the Downs on 13 May (C. and H. C. A. Hardy, *A Register of Ships . . . in the . . . East India Company* (1835), p. 50). As a parting gift Mrs Playdell gave CB 'a Chinese painting on ivory, which she had inherited from her father; and which he, Governor Holwell, estimated as a sort of treasure' (*Mem.* i. 204; see also Scholes, i. 271; *Mus. Lib.*, p. 41).

[27] The Playdells' eldest son, John Martin Playdell (b. 1761), came back to Europe several years later to complete 'his Education in the Mercantile line' in England and Holland, and then returned in 1777 to Bengal, where he became a career civil servant, dying at Behar in 1803 (MS memorial of John Zephaniah Holwell, Martin Yorke, and William Birch to the Directors of the East India Company, 27 Jan. 1780, IOR J/1/10, fos. 35–36, India Office Library; E. Dodwell and J. S. Miles, *Alphabetical List of the . . . Bengal Civil Servants* (1839), pp. 392–3). Another son, James William Playdell, was probably born in England in 1770; he became a career officer in the Bengal Army and died in 1821 (V. C. P. Hodson, *List of the Officers of the Bengal Army 1758–1834* (1927–47), iii. 536–7). A daughter, Elizabeth, is mentioned in Charles Stafford Playdell's will, dated 13 July 1776 and proved 2 June 1779 at Calcutta (Bengal Wills, India Office Library).

the least wish of applying to my old friend for participation or relief?

Perhaps I am myself the only one who would not rather be amazed that a humour so particular should have lasted so long.—Nevertheless, I shall not discourage the small remains of it which this Night prompt me to ⟨resume⟩ my Pen. |

My dear Brother James ⟨is⟩ returned Home[28]—in very good Health & spirits, to mine—& all his family's, sincere satisfaction. As to *merchandise*, the few Ventures he took out with him, he has brought back unchanged! poor soul, he was never designed for Trading.

My dear Father has gained more honour by his Book than I had dared flatter myself would have attended it. We hear Daily of new Readers & approvers. Mr Mason has wrote him a very polite Letter upon it desiring to introduce him to Sir James Gray,[29] one of the most accomplished men of the Age, who was so much pleased with my Father's Book, as to beg of Mr Mason to make them Acquainted.

Dr. Brookes[30]—Husband to the Mrs Brookes who wrote

---

[28] From Bombay. His ship, the *Greenwich* East Indiaman, stayed there from July to Nov. 1770 while the Company's trading was being conducted. It left on the homeward voyage 19 Nov., and reached Woolwich 31 May 1771. JB received his discharge at Woolwich on 27 June, being paid the sum of £18 8s. 5d. for a service of 16 months and 15 days. A voyage to the East Indies was a potentially lucrative adventure for those with any capital to invest in private trade, but JB was evidently unable to take advantage of the opportunity. See Manwaring, pp. 9–11.

[29] Sir James Gray (c.1708–73), 2nd Bt.; KB (1761); diplomatist and antiquary. Mason wrote to CB 9 May 1771 (Osborn): 'I am going out of Town for a few days, & therefore have not time to thank you in person for the present of your Journal, w[hi]ch I have read thro with much pleasure. . . . I met the other day with S[i]r James Gray, who admires it greatly, & wishes to be made acquainted with you. . . . as S[i]r James has lived much in Italy, & is acquainted with many of the Persons you mention in your book, I imagine you will find him both an agreeable & useful acquaintance.' Sir James was the British Resident at Venice, 1746–53, Envoy to Naples 1753–65, and Ambassador to Spain, 1767–9. When CB undertook his German tour in 1772, Sir James provided him with letters of introduction to the composer Johann Adolf Hasse and to the British Minister at Berlin, James Harris. See Lonsdale, pp. 104, 114; D. B. Horn, ed., *British Diplomatic Representatives 1689–1789* (1932), pp. 76, 85, 136.

[30] The Revd John Brooke (1709–89), DD; Vicar of St Augustine's, Norwich, 1733; Rector of Colney, Norfolk, 1744; Minor Canon of Norwich. His letter is missing. He m. (c.1756) Frances Moore (1723/4–89), authoress. Her novel *The History of Lady Julia Mandeville* was pub. in 1763. By 1771 she had also published a periodical, *The Old Maid* (1755–6; repub. 1764); a tragedy in verse, *Virginia* (1756), and a 2nd novel, *The History of Emily Montague* (4 vols., 1769), besides 3 translations from the French. In 1773 she and her husband became joint managers of the Opera with the Yateses. FB was to meet Mrs Brooke for the first time in 1774 (vol. ii). See

Lady Julia Mandeville, & many other Books,—has also wrote to praise it. |

Mrs Young has been on a Visit to us for some Days. She & her Caro Sposo ⌜were of our party to see Mr. Garrick act for the decayed Actors, when he did the part of Benedick, last Week.[31] They have been here very frequently of late. They⌝ are a very strange Couple—She is grown so immoderately fat, that ⟨I⟩ believe she would at least weigh ⟨two times⟩ more than her Husband. ⟨I⟩ wonder he could every marry her! They have, however, given over those violent disputes & quarrels with which they used to entertain their friends; not that Mrs Young has any reason to congratulate herself upon it—quite the con-⟨trary,⟩ for the extreme violence of her ⟨ov⟩erbearing Temper has at length so entirely wearried [*sic*] Mr Young that he disdains any controversy with her, scarse ever contradic⟨ting her,⟩ & Lives a Life of calm, easy contempt.

I had the favour of a short Tête a Tête with him t'other Day, Mama, &c, being ⟨out,⟩ or engaged. | He had taken up Mr Greville's *Characters, Maxims & Reflections*, & asked if it was written by *our* Mr Greville.[32] He opened it, & Read aloud:[33]

'There, cried he, Laughing, that's his opinion of the sex! what do you think of that, Miss Fanny?'

'O, he gave the Reins to his *wit* there—I am sure he has nevertheless a very *high* opinion of Women—'

'Well but, ⌜God⌝—what is there against a Woman that she yields to temptation? why a Woman who could resist all possible temptations must be an Animal out of Nature! Such a one never could Exist—'

⌜'O, but you did not mean to infer any good from that sentiment,—or to imagine Mr. Greville meant any.'

L. McMullen, *An Odd Attempt in a Woman: The Literary Life of Frances Brooke* (Vancouver, 1983), *passim*.

[31] Garrick played the role of Benedick in *Much Ado about Nothing*, a 'Benefit for Theatrical Fund', at Drury Lane, Friday, 24 May 1771. He also provided an occasional epilogue (*LS 4* iii. 1552).

[32] See above, p. 33 n. 91.

[33] Here FB left an empty space of 2 or 3 lines. She obviously meant to copy in what Young had read, but, as in a few other cases, did not do so. Perhaps the passage read was the following: 'It is a mistake to imagine, that libertinism in women must proceed from too much sensibility; it proceeds very often, I believe, from too little' (*Maxims, Characters, and Reflections* (1757 edn.), p. 181).

'Why not? where's the harm?'

'Did not you Laugh at his opinion of our sex?' |

He shook his Head at me, & Laugh'd &ⁿ asked me what made me say Mʳ Greville had so high an opinion of Women?

'His Conversation—& his Connections.—ʳit would be very extraordinary if he had not.'

'Why so, Why so?'ⁿ

'His Wife is so very superiour & amiable a Woman, that—'

'O ʳGodⁿ! that's Nothing! that does not value a straw. ʳA sex is not to be judged of by an Individual.'

'But we are very apt to judge of others from those we are nearest connected with.'

'Butⁿ Man & Wife can never judge fairly of each other;— from the moment they are married, they are too prejudiced to know each other.—The last Character a man is acquainted with is his Wife's; because he is in extremes; he either Loves, or Hates her.—

'O! I don't think that. I believe there are many more who niether Love or Hate, than there are who do either.'

'It's no such thing! cried the| impetuous Creature, 'You will find no such thing in Life as a medium,—*all* is *Love* or *Hatred* —! —

I *could* have said, it is much oftener *Indifference* than either, but I thought it would be too pointed, & dropt the Argument. I recommended to him to Read the Characters of Mʳˢ Greville & Mʳˢ Garrick, which are written under the Names of Camilla & Flora. He Read the former in silence; when he came to the latter, he gave the involuntary preference of immediately Reading Loud.—Camilla he said was too celestial—He was perfectly enraptured with the description of Flora.³⁴

ʳThey have given us such a hearty & earnest invitation to Bradmore Farm, that I believe they will be quite angry if it is not accepted.ⁿ

The famous Philidor,³⁵ so much celebrated for his surprising

---

³⁴ 'How different from lovely Camilla is the beloved Flora! in Camilla, nature has displayed the beauty of exact regularity, and the elegant softness of female propriety: In Flora, she charms with a certain artless poignancy, a graceful negligence, and an uncontroulled yet blameless freedom. . . . Camilla puts you in mind of the most perfect music that can be composed; Flora, of the wild sweetness which is sometimes produced by the irregular play of the breeze upon the Æolian harp' (ibid., pp. 45–6). The character of Camilla immediately precedes that of Flora (pp. 43–5).

[*See opposite page for n. 35*]

skill at the Game of Chess, is just come to England | ʳfrom Paris, where he now Lives, after an absence of near 20 years. Heᵑ brought my Father a Letter of recommendation from the very justly celebrated M. Diderot.[36] He is going to have a new Edition, with considerable amendments & additions, of a Book upon Chess he wrote, when formerly in England. A plan of his Work M. Diderot has drawn up for him, & he had got it ʳmostᵑ vilely translated. ʳHe speaks tolerable English, & understands the Language very well. He has been often here, & being much distressed upon account of the bad manner his plan was translated in,ᵑ my Father had the patience, from the good natured benevolence of his Heart, to Translate it for him himself. M. Philidor is a well bred, obliging, & very sociable man; he is also a very good musician.

My Father has been honoured with Letters from the great Rousseau,[37] M. Diderot,[38] & Padre Martini,[39] three as eminent

[35] François-André Danican Philidor (1726–95), French composer and chess player. A talented composer of comic operas, he was better known to his contemporaries as a chess master, and was perhaps the greatest player and theoretician of the 18th c. He was in England, supporting himself by chess, from the late 1740s until 1754 when he returned to Paris, resolved to devote himself to musical composition. In his letter of introduction to CB, 15 May 1771, Diderot calls Philidor 'un nom qui ne peut être omis dans l'histoire de la musique. C'est le fondateur de la musique italienne en France' (Osborn; in Diderot, *Correspondance*, ed. G. Roth (1955–70), xi. 37–8).

Philidor's book on chess, *L'analyze des échecs*, was written at Aachen in 1748 and, with the help of the D. of Cumberland, pub. in London in 1749. An English trans., *Chess Analyzed*, was first published in 1750, by John Nourse and Paul Vaillant, followed by a 2nd edn. in 1762. The prospectus for an enlarged edn. evidently did not impress Nourse and Vaillant, who simply reprinted the work in 1773. Philidor then found a new publisher, Peter Elmsley, who published *Analysis of the Game of Chess; a new edition, greatly enlarged*, in 1777. The original prospectus and CB's trans. of it are missing. See *New Grove*.

[36] Denis Diderot (1713–84). CB had met him at Paris in Dec. 1770, at a dinner party at Baron d'Holbach's. Diderot greeted CB 'as cordially as if we had been acquaintances of long standing', for CB had been one of the earliest subscribers to the *Encyclopédie*. Several days later Diderot presented CB with 'a great heap of MSS. [on music] in his own hand writing, sufficient for a folio upon the same subject which he gave me to make just what use I pleased of' (*Tours*, i. 312, 316). For about a year afterwards they carried on a correspondence about musical matters. See also Lonsdale, pp. 95–6, 103–4.

[37] Jean-Jacques Rousseau (1712–78). Rousseau's letter to CB, 8 Apr. 1771, thanks him, not for the *Italian Tour*, but for copies of Jomelli's *Passione* and of *The Cunning Man*, CB's own adaptation of Rousseau's operetta *Le Devin du village* (1752), first presented at Drury Lane in 1766 and pub. that year. He sent Rousseau a copy of the *Italian Tour* in May, but apparently got no acknowledgement. Rousseau had cordially received CB in his Paris apartment in Dec. 1770, when they conversed at length on musical matters. See Lonsdale, pp. 70–3, 94–5, 100–3; *Mem.* i. 257–8; Rousseau,

[*See p. 156 for n. 37 cont. and nn. 38–9*]

as the Age has produced, I believe, upon [|] his Book. I have lately spent several Evenings in paying visits with Mama & Miss Allen, & have been tolerably tired of it. I was at Ranelagh with them last Week, but I had not the good fortune to see any Body I wished. I went there again last Friday, with my sister, ⟨my two⟩ Aunts, & Mr Burney—& fortune was equally kind. However, we were very well pleased—the sense of my Aunt Anne, the good nature of her sister Rebecca, the obliging disposition of Mr Burney, & the lively, engaging sweetness of my beloved Hetty, formed a party I could not but be happy with.

July 3^d

We have had a visit from a Bridegroom this Afternoon — — it would not be very easy to guess him—Mr Hayes!—

That poor old man has suffered the severest grief from the great loss he sustained by the Death of his first Wife;[40] he has never ceased to regret her;— [|] nor ever will he!—contracted is that mind which immediately doubts his sincerity, from his second marriage: but how could a man at his Time of Life,

---

Correspondance complète, ed. R. A. Leigh (Geneva and Oxford, 1965–), xxxviii. 214–15, 224–5; *Tours*, i. 313–15.

[38] CB did not send Diderot the *Italian Tour* until late May, and Diderot thanked him in a long letter of 18 Aug. 1771: 'Je vous dois des remerciements pour l'ouvrage que vous avez eu la bonté de m'envoyer. Je l'ai lu avec toute la satisfaction possible' (Diderot, *Correspondance*, xi. 95–9).

[39] Giovanni Battista Martini (1706–84), Italian writer on music, teacher, and composer. An ordained priest in the Franciscan order, Martini was himself engaged on a huge *Storia della musica* in 5 vols., the 2nd vol. of which appeared in late 1770. CB had met him in the convent in Bologna in Aug. 1770, and the two men liked and respected each other immediately. Martini generously placed at CB's disposal all the MSS and printed resources of his great library (amounting to 17,000 vols.), and CB read, transcribed, and took copious notes in the days following. After CB left Bologna the two historians did not meet again, but corresponded until Martini's death in 1784.

In a letter to SC, 31 May 1771, CB mentions receiving 'last week' a letter from Martini, brought to him by Baretti. Again, this letter, dated 7 Apr. 1771 (Osborn), is not on CB's book but there is a brief note of greeting in which Martini expresses his hope that CB has by now received a copy of the 2nd vol. of his *Storia della musica*. (CB had not.) CB no doubt sent Martini a copy of the *Italian Tour*, but his covering letter and Martini's acknowledgement are missing. See Lonsdale, pp. 89–90; *Tours*, i. 145–7; *New Grove*; H. Brofsky, 'Doctor Burney and Padre Martini: Writing a General History of Music', *The Musical Quarterly*, lxv (1979), 313–45.

[40] See above, p. 93. Hayes married secondly (20 June 1771) Mary Nicolson, who died *pre* 24 Oct. 1791 (*JL* i. 82 and n. 10). FB's observations here are of course as much about her own father as about Mr Hayes.

having no Children or near Relations, support himself Alone, with the most sociable disposition in the Universe? his beloved Wife never could be restored to him, & he has therefore sought a Companion whose esteem & society may tranquilize the remainder of his Days. For my own part, I applaud & honóur every Body, who, having that lively & agonising sensibility which is *tremblingly Alive* to each emotion of sorrow, can so far subdue the too exquisite refinement of their feelings as to permit themselves to be consoled in affliction. Why should Despair find entrance into the short Life of man?—it is praiseworthy to fly from it—it is *true Philosophy*, ⌐says⌐ ⌐ my dear Father, to *accomodate* ourselves without murmuring to our Fortune.

⌐No wonder I should moralize, for Oh! my dear Nobody, I am turned of 19!—[41] 'tis shocking—but I must endeavour to *accomodate* myself. This is a trial! does Nobody think so?⌐

I am just returned from Chesington, to which dear place Miss Allen took me.—⌐I am even now ashamed to think what I owe to her too great kindness—I even feel ashamed to mention it—not I trust from ingratitude, but from a real consciousness of so very little meriting the trouble I have ⟨caused⟩ her—Mrs. Hamilton, at whose House Mr.⌐ Crisp, &c., Boards, is the—in short, & to cut the matter so, their generous Gusto, determined to oblige me even in my own despight at having been ⌐

[*top of page cut away*]

of an ⌐obligation was not very desir[?ous] but Miss Allen payed no regard to my declarations—& finding I persisted in this without saying a word to me, came into the study where my Father & self were, & after a long preamble, & inter⟨ruption⟩ [xxxxx *1 word*] begged as the greatest favour [xxxxx *1 word*] that he would permit one of *his daughters* to accompany her to Chesington. As Susan had been there since me,[42] I knew that this one must be myself⌐ ⌐

[*top of page cut away*]

Our party was large & comfortable. I had not been at Chesington for almost 5 Years. The Country is extremely

[41] On 13 June.
[42] SEB had visited Chessington in Apr. 1767 (fragment of her Journal for 1767, McGill University Library).

pleasant—the House is situated on very high Ground, & has only Cottages about it for some miles.

A sketch of our Party

Mrs Hamilton is the mistress of the House, which was her Brother's,[43] who having Lived too much at his ease, left her in such circumstances as obliged her to take Boarders | for her maintainance. She is a very good little old Woman, hospitable & even Tempered.

Mademoiselle Rosat,[44] who Boards with her. She is about ⌐or near¬ 40, Tall & elegant in Person & Dress, very sensible, extremely well-bred, &, when in spirits, droll & humourous but she has been very unhappy, & her misfortunes have left indelible traces on her mind, which subjects her to extreme low spirits. I think her a great acquisition to Chesington.

Miss Cooke,—who I believe is 40 too, but has so much good Nature & love of mirth in her, that she still appears a Girl. ⌐She is a good Creature, though, poor soul, it must be owned, very uncultivated, yet with good natural sense.¬

My sister Burney [EBB], ⌐whose Health still keeps her at Chesington. She is, however, much recovered, though very thin.¬

Miss Barsanti, who is a great favourite of my sisters, & was by her & Miss Allen invited to Chesington. She is extremely clever & entertaining, possesses amazing powers of mimickry, & an uncommon share of humour.

Miss Allen & myself end the females. |

Mr Crisp, whose Health is happily restored—I think I need not give his Character.

Mr Featherstone.[45] Brother of Sir Mathew, ⌐a weak-Hearted,

---

[43] Chrysostome or Christopher Hamilton (1698–1758/9). A ruined spendthrift, Hamilton before his death had already turned Chessington Hall into a boarding-home. SC was a friend of Hamilton, and in the 1750s, when his own fortune was lost, he moved to Chessington from his expensive house at Hampton (*HFB* pp. 16–18; *JL* i. 144 n. 4; 'Mem.' No. 105).

[44] Mademoiselle Rosat, whom FB last mentions in 1774, has not been further traced.

[45] Probably Robert Fetherstonhaugh, brother of Sir Matthew Fetherstonhaugh (?1714–74) of Uppark, Sussex, cr. (1747) Bt. He was presumably a bachelor or widower who was also a boarder in Chessington Hall (see vol. ii). He is named in his brother's will (PCC, dated 19 Mar., prob. 28 Mar. 1774), by which he received an annuity of £100. Another brother, the Revd Ulrick Fetherstonhaugh (*c*.1718–88), was Rector of Oxted, Surrey, about 15 miles from Chessington. See M. Meade-Fetherstonhaugh and O. Warner, *Uppark and its People* (1964), pp. 37, 46–7.

dirty, pettish, absurd Creature,⌐ middle Aged ⌐but having broken his leg walks upon Crutches. He is equally ugly & cross.⌐

M⌐ Charles Burney brings up the Rear. I Would ⌐to Heaven⌐ my Father did!

⌐However great my inducements, I know not that I ever acted against my judgement without expecting [?trouble.][46]

Poor Mr. Burney was ill almost the whole Fortnight of my stay—my dear sister terrified to Death, always with him, & but very indifferent herself. Mr. Crisp perpetually employed in making some alterations in his Closet, which kept him almost constantly from us—Miss Allen the first Week sprained her Ancle, which is not yet quite well—I too had continually the Tooth ach [*sic*]—& the Weather in general was cold & Rainy. The most agreeable party in the World must be dampt by such *dis*agreeable circumstances. However, we were not without ⟨mirth,⟩ though disappointed of much we expected.⌐

Miss Barsanti has great Theatrical talents; her Voice is entirely lost,[47] but ⌐still⌐ her mother designs her for the stage, ⌐& as she was his pupil⌐ my Father ⌐consulted them about it, & he went to⌐ beg M⌐ Crisp would hear her *spout*, while she was at Chesington.[48] To make her acting less formidable to her, Miss Allen & myself proposed to perform with her; & accordingly we got by heart some scenes from the Careless Husband,[49] in which she chose to be Edging—myself Lady Easy—& Miss Allen Sir Charles!—that ⌐good⌐ Girl has so very great a love of sport & mirth, that there is nothing upon Earth she will not do to contribute to it.

We had no sooner fixed upon this scheme, than we were perplexed about the Dressing of Sir Charles.—We all agreed that it would be ridiculous for that gallant man to appear in Petticoats, & ⌐Allen⌐ had no idea of *spoiling sport*,—she only determined not to exhibit before M⌐ Featherstone; as to M⌐

[46] The rest of the line is blank, but the sentence calls for completion. Possibly a word or phrase has worn away.

[47] CB, in his article on her father in Rees, notes that 'she totally lost her singing voice, on going to Oxford to perform at a choral meeting, by sickness in a stage coach'. For Jane Barsanti's stage début, see below, pp. 177, 197.

[48] SC was author of a tragedy, *Virginia*, produced at Drury Lane in 1754.

[49] By Colley Cibber (1671–1757), dramatist and poet laureate. The comedy was first performed in 1704.

Crisp, as he was half author of the project, we knew it would be in vain to attempt excluding him,—& Mʳ Burney could not be avoided.—besides, ⌜a Brother!—⌝his Cloaths she intended to borrow; but unluckily, we found upon enquiry, he had no Wardrobe with him, ⌜& the Cloaths he wore were all his stock.⌝ This quite disconcerted us. Mʳ Crisp was so tall & large, it was impossible ⌜Allen⌝ could wear any thing of his.—We were long in great perplexity upon this account; but, being unwilling to give the frolic up, Allen at length, though very mad at it, resolved upon the only expedient left—to borrow Cloaths of Mʳ Featherstone. I never met a character so little damped by difficulties as hers—indeed she seldom sees any,—& when she cannot help it, always surmounts them, ⌜& never submits to be conquered by any, however formidable they may appear.⌝

To ask this of him, made his being one of the Audience inevitable;—but it was the last resource. Accordingly, ⌜Allen⌝ & Barsanti watched one morning for his coming into the Gallery up stairs, from which all the Bed chambers lead, & addressed themselves to him very gravely, to ⌜beg⌝ the favour of him to lend them a suit of Cloaths. ⌜The man⌝ laughed monstrously, & assumed no small consequence, on their begging him to keep the affair secret, as they intended to surprise the company, for they were obliged to explain the motives of the request. This seemed something like confidence, & flattered him into better temper than we ever saw him in. He led them to his Wardrobe, & ⌜begged⌝ Allen to chuse to her fancy. She fixed upon a suit of dark blue uncut Velvet.—I was in a Closet at the End of the Gallery, not able to compose my countenance sufficiently to join them, till a loud Laugh raised my curiosity.—I found she had just been begging the favour of a Wig; & he produced a most beautiful tye, which he told her his man should dress for her. She then asked for stock, shoes, Buckles, Ruffles, ⌜stockings,⌝ & all with great gravity, assisted by Barsanti, who reminded her of so many things, I thought she could never have been satisfied. Mʳ Featherstone enjoyed it prodigiously, sniggering & joking, & resting upon his Crutches to Laugh: for my own part, the torrent [of][50] their ridiculous requests, made me every minute march out of the Room [to laugh more freely.][50] ⌜When every thing was adjusted & we were all retiring, Barsanti, as if suddenly recollecting herself,

[50] Inserted by FBA.

returned, & with great gravity, told Mr. Featherstone that Miss Allen was ashamed to tell him that he had forgot a shirt. I now ran away with all speed, not able any longer to keep with them, both from laughter, & really from shame.

As my departing for Town was fixed for the Monday [1 July] following this curious scene,⌐ we settled ⌐Sunday⌐ Evening for our performance. Meanwhile, Mʳ Featherstone was observed, as he hobbled up & down the Garden, to continually burst into Horse Laughs, from the diversion of his own thoughts ⌐upon the occasion.⌐

On ⌐Sunday⌐ morning, rehearsing ¦ our parts, we found them so short that we wished to add another scene, & as there is a good deal of drollery in the quarel⌐ling scene⌐ between Sir Charles Easy & Lady Graveairs,[51] we fixed upon that, Miss Allen to continue as Sir Charles, & Barsanti to change her Cap, or so, & appear as Lady Graveairs. ⌐It was with great difficulty I prevailed upon them to give up the 1ˢᵗ scene of the 5ᵗʰ Act, but I had an insuperable aversion to doing any part, even that of Lady Easy, in such a scene.⌐[52]

While they studied their parts, Kitty Cooke & myself, as we frequently did, walked out, visiting all the Cottages within a mile of Chesington. Upon our return to Dinner, Barsanti told us she found the *new scene* too long to get in Time, ⌐& said she had given ¦ it up.⌐ Miss Allen & I, ⌐being⌐ both sorry, after some deliberation, agreed to perform it ourselves, &, accordingly, ⌐after Dinner,⌐ we hurried up stairs, & made all possible Expedition in getting our parts, resolving not to Act till after supper, [xxxxx *2 words*] ⌐not being ready then.⌐ While we were studdying with great diligence, Miss Barsanti ran up ⌐stairs,⌐ & told us that Mʳ Crisp had informed all the Company of our intention, & that they were ⌐now⌐ very eager for our performance, & declared they would never forgive us if we disappointed them. This flurried me violently, insomuch, that my memory failed me, & I forgot my old part, without seeming to harm my new one. I can, in general, get by Heart with the *utmost facility*, but I really was so much ⌐agitated⌐ that my Head seemed to turn round, & I scarce knew what I was about.

---

⁵¹ Act III, sc. i.
⁵² FB probably objected mainly to Sir Charles and Lady Graveairs making another assignation in this scene.

They, too, were flurried, but my ⏐ excessive ⌈emotion⌉ seemed to lessen their's. I must own it was quite ridiculous: but I could not command myself.

⌈We were monstrously provoked at Tea Time, by the appearance of Visitors from Epsom.[53] Allen & Barsanti were both in *disabille*, [*sic*] they sat together, laughing & whispering all the time we were in the Parlour, till Mademoiselle Rosat was quite angry with them. We Practised all the Evening, as much as my *tremors* would allow me. Mrs. Hamilton was so provoking as to hasten supper—I could hardly swallow, & would have given the World to have been disengaged from the affair but⌉ my repentance came too late.

We ⌈all⌉ retired after supper, & could not forbear being highly diverted at seeing ⌈Allen⌉ Dress herself. Mr Featherstone's cloaths fitted her horribly—the back preposterously broad—the sleeves too ⏐ wide,—the Cuffs hiding her Hand—yet the Coat hardly long enough—niether was the Wig large enough to hide her Hair; &, in short, she appeared the most dapper, ill shaped, ridiculous figure I ever saw. Yet her Face looked remarkably well.

⌈Hetty, who was not well, & refused to join us, nevertheless was eager to make us begin⌉—my ⌈ *Terour* ⌉ [*sic*] every moment encreased—but in vain—they insisted upon no further delay—& accordingly we descended.—⌈Hetty first joined our audience, having prepared us a stage.⌉ As we came down, the servants were all in the Hall, & the first object that struck us, was Mr Featherstone's man, staring in speechless astonishment at the Figure in his master's Cloaths.

Unfortunately for me, I was to appear first, & alone.[54]—I was pushed on,—they clapped violently—I was fool enough ⏐ to run off, quite overset, & unable to speak. I was really in an agony of fear & shame!—& when, at last, ⌈Allen⌉ & Barsanti persuaded me to go on again,—the former, ⌈having,⌉ in the lively warmth of her Temper, called to ⌈them⌉ not to *Clap again, for it was very impertinant*;—I had lost all power of speaking steadily, & almost of being understood; & as to action, I had not the presence of mind to attempt it: ⌈surely,⌉ only Mr Crisp could excite such extreme terror ⌈in me!⌉ My soliloquy at length

---

[53] Epsom is about 2 miles from Chessington.
[54] Lady Easy's soliloquy opens the play.

over, *Edging* entered, with great spirit, & spoke very well. I was almost breathless the whole scene—& O how glad when it was over!—Sir Charles's appearance raised outrageous mirth,— ⌐*Horse*⌐ *laughs* were ecchoed from side to side, & nothing else could be heard. She required all her resolution to ¦ stand it— Hetty was almost in convulsions—Mr Crisp hollowed—Mr Featherstone absolutely *wept* with excessive laughing—& even Mamselle Rosat lent her Elbows on her lap, & could not support herself upright. What rendered her appearance more ridiculous, was that, being wholly unused to Acting, she forgot her Audience, & acted as often with her back to them as her Face—& her back was really quite too absurd[—the full breadth of her height.]^55

I had soon after to make my appearance as Lady Graveairs.^56 To be sure I was in proper spirits for the part—however, a few exceptionable speeches, I had insisted upon omitting,^57 & I was greatly recovered compared to my former appearance. Barsanti, at a sudden thought, went on & made an apology, 'that the *gentlewoman* who was to have performed ¦ Lady Graveairs, being taken ill, her place was to be supplied by the performer of Lady Easy.' To be sure it was rather in the Barn style.

I acquitted myself with rather a better grace now, & we were *much applauded*. Not having Performers sufficient for a regular plan, we finished with [such]^58 a short, unsatisfactory scene, that they all called out for *more*.—Allen, intending to carry the affair off with *a joke*, took Barsanti & me each by the Hand, & led us on—but, whether from shame, or what I know not, when *she* had Bowed, & *we* had curtsied, she was wholly at a loss, & could not think of a Word to say—so after keeping the Company in a minutes suspence, 'In short, cried she, 'You know the rest;—' & ran off.

It is easy to suppose laughs were not spared for this ridiculous attempt. [xxxxx *1 line*] ¦

---

⁵⁵ Inserted by FBA.

⁵⁶ In the 'quarrel scene', Act III.

⁵⁷ Undoubtedly FB omitted Lady Graveairs's suggestion to Sir Charles that, in his desire for an 'obedient' lover, he should turn to prostitutes: 'You had better take [a lover] that's broken to your Hand,—There are such Souls to be hir'd, I believe; Things that will rub your Temples in an Evening 'till you fall fast asleep in their Laps. Creatures too that think their Wages their Reward . . .' (1735 edn., p. 48).

⁵⁸ Inserted by FBA.

[*The top of the next leaf has been cut away. The first obliterated part remaining (on the recto) is presumably about Miss Barsanti: FB notes her greater gift for comedy. The second part (verso) also seems to be about her, i.e., about the social ostracism her new profession will cause. Barsanti did, however, visit the Burneys at home later (e.g., see below, p. 172). Perhaps FB's ideas on the social punctilios involved were excessively severe at this point. She does mention further on giving up her 'former delicacy' of not visiting Barsanti privately (vol. ii).*]

[?In Tragedy she wants a] ⌐certain elegance of pronounciation, which it requires, though her figure is noble, & her attitudes striking. I was too sincere with her to recommend this style to her thoughts, as in Comedy, she will, I doubt not, make a very superiour Actress. Her desire of improve[ment]⌐ |

[?She cannot] ⌐possibly visit at our House, & we can only see her by accident.⌐

We all left Chesington with regret. It is a place of peace, ease, freedom & chearfulness, & all its inhabitants are good humoured & obliging—& my dear Mr Crisp alone would make it, to us, a Paradise. |

[*post* 12] August

Dr. Hawkesworth has this moment left us;—he called on my Father, who, with Mama, is at present at Mrs Allen's in Lynn; but he did me the favour to sit here some minutes nevertheless, only Susan & myself at home. ⌐He has been extremely obliging to my Father in relation to his Book & during the Time of it's publication, very frequently favoured us with his company.⌐ The admiration I have of his Works has [c]reated great esteem for their Author,[59] ⌐who I fear is now very idle, for I hear of nothing new from his Pen.[60] His last publication was a translation of Telemachus, a most complete & *elaborate* Work, to use his favourite Word.

My Father's Book still continues to give him much honour, it seems to be universally Read, & universally approved—if *I*

---

[59] FBA has substituted for the obliterated passage: 'though he is too precise to be really agreeable—that is to be natural—like Mr. Crisp & my dear Father.—'

[60] In fact, Hawkesworth was author of the first review of the *Italian Tour,* which appeared in the May number of *GM* xli (1771), 222–4 (see Lonsdale, p. 105). He had been official literary editor of *GM* since 1756 (Abbott, pp. 93, 108). For his next (and last) book, see below, p. 173 and *passim*.

may say so.—He has lately received, through Mr. Garrick's hands, an exceeding polite offer of ⌐ ⟨assistance to⟩ his Work from Dr. Warton,[61] an eminent literary man, Editor of Pitt's Æneid, & translator of Virgil's Eclogues & Georgics, as well as author of the Essay on Pope, & many other critical Works. He had also a share in the Adventurer which made me mention his Civility to Dr. Hawkesworth, who spoke highly of him, giving him, on account, I suspect, of his love of criticism & antiquity, the appelation of a *very curious* man.⌐

But now I speak of Authors, let me pay the small tribute of regret & concern, due to the memory of poor Mʳ Smart, who Died lately, in the King's Bench Prison.[62] A man by Nature endowed with talents, wit & vivacity in an eminent degree, & whose unhappy loss of his senses was a Public as well as Private misfortune. I never knew him in his glory, but ever respected him in his ⌐ *decline*, from the fine proofs he had left of his better Day, & from the account I have heard ⌐from my Father⌐ of his Youth, who was then his intimate companion; as, of late years,

---

[61] Joseph Warton (1722–1800), DD (Oxon.), 1768, poet and literary critic; head-master of Winchester, 1766–93. Warton wrote to Garrick, 30 July 1771, praising CB's book and asking him to convey to CB the enclosed 'Title & Contents of an old Treatise of Music which I have accidentally found in Our [Winchester] College Library' (Osborn). Garrick duly transmitted Warton's letter and enclosure to CB with a cover-ing letter on 9 Aug., and CB wrote Warton a long letter of thanks on 12 Aug. The work in question was the 3rd edn. of *Practica Musicae utriusque cantus* (Brescia, 1502), by Franchinus Gaffurius (1451–1522), priest, musical theorist, and composer. CB had not known of this edition, and he mentions it along with three others (in Padre Martini's library) in *Hist. Mus.* iii. 153 (Mercer, ii. 130).

Warton's edition of the works of Virgil, in both Latin and English, was published in 4 vols. in 1753; it included his own translations of the *Ecologues* and *Georgics*, and the rendering of the *Aeneid* by Christopher Pitt (1699–1748), first pub. in full in 1740. The 1st vol. of his influential *Essay on the Genius and Writings of Pope* appeared in 1756; the 2nd vol. was not pub. until 1782. From 1753 to 1754 Warton contributed 24 numbers to *The Adventurer*, which Hawkesworth edited. CB's copies of Warton's edn. of Virgil and his *Essay on . . . Pope* are listed in *Lib.*, pp. 58–9. See also Garrick, *Letters*, ii. 753–4; J. Wool, *Biographical Memoirs of the Late Revᵈ Joseph Warton, D.D.* (1806), pp. 382–5; *New Grove*.

[62] Smart was imprisoned for debt in Apr. 1770. He died 20 May 1771, 'of a disorder in his liver', and was buried in the since destroyed Church of St Gregory by St Paul on 26 May (A. Sherbo, *Christopher Smart: Scholar of the University* (East Lansing, 1967), pp. 255, 265). On 26 Apr. 1770 Smart had written to CB from the King's Bench, commending himself to 'a benevolent and thriving Friend' (MS in the possession of Mr James Gilvarry, pub. *RES* n.s. xxxv (1984), 511). FB mentions in *Mem.* i. 280 'a small subscription, of which Dr. Burney was at the head', which gave Smart 'a miserable little pittance beyond the prison allowance'. The letter from Smart which FB quotes here is missing.

he has been his most active & generous friend, having raised a kind of fund for his relief, though he was ever in distress. His intellects so cruelly impaired, I doubt not, affected his whole conduct. In a Letter he sent my Father, not long before his Death to ask his assistance for a fellow sufferer, & good offices for him 'in that Charity over which he presides,' he made use of an Expression which pleased me much—'that he had himself assisted[63] him, *according to his willing poverty*.' |

Mr Gray[64] too, the justly and greatly celebrated Gray is Dead! How many Centuries had he been spared, if Death had been as kind to him, as Fame will be to his Works!

August

Dr. King has been with me this afternoon—amusing himself with spouting Shakespeare, Pope, & others; though I say amusing *himself*, I must however own, that it was the only way he had any chance of amusing *me*; but his Visit was unconscionably long, & as I happened to be alone, I had the whole weight of it. I did not ⌐however, for the first time,¬ regret Miss Allen's absence;[65] for she sees the ridiculous part of this man's character in so strong a light, that she cannot forbear shewing that she despises him every moment. The strongest *trait* of her own Character is sincerity,—one of the most ^|^ noble of virtues, &, perhaps, without any exception, *the most* uncommon;—but, if it is possible, she is *too* sincere; she pays too little regard to the World, & indulges herself with too much .freedom of raillery & pride of disdain, towards those whose vices or follies offend her. Were this a *general* rule of conduct, what real benefit might it bring to society! but being *particular*, it only hurts & provokes Individuals: but yet, I am unjust to my own opinion in censuring the first who shall venture, in a good cause, to break through the confinement of custom, & at least shew the way to a new & Open path;—I mean but to blame severity to *harmless* folly, which claims pity, & not scorn: though I cannot but acknowledge it to be infinitely tiresome, &, for any length of Time, even—or almost—disgustful.— |

---

63 Altered from 'given' by FB.
64 Thomas Gray (b. 1716), the poet, died 30 July 1771 in Cambridge.
65 She was on a visit to Norfolk (see below, p. 169 n. 74).

Dr. King fancies himself a Genius for the Theatre—he had the weakness to pretend to shew me how Garrick performed a scene of Macbeth—! 'I generally, said he, say to myself how *I* should perform such & such a part, before I see it; & when Garrick is on the stage, how *I* should speak such or such a speech; & I am generally so happy as to find we agree: but the scene where he fancies he sees the Dagger in Macbeth, he surprised me in—he has a stroke in that quite new; *I* had never thought of it.[66]—if you will stand here, I will shew you—' Stand I did, as well as I could, for laughter.—

Could any thing be more absurd? *He*, with his clumsy arms, & vacant Eyes, imitate Mʳ Garrick!

We Live very peacably & quietly—I rise very early, 5—6—or 7 my latest Hour. I have just finished Middleton's History of Cicero,[67] which I read immediately after Hooke's Roman History:[68] it is a delightful Book: the style is manly & elegant, & though he may be too partial to Cicero, the fine writings he occasionally translates of that great man, Authorise & excuse his partiality. |

Many of my Father's Italian Friends, and of the English ones he made in ⌐his Italian journey have been & are in England this summer. I neglected at the time to mention the arrival of Signora Biccheli,[69] the *Mignatrice*, Paintress, of whose singing

[66] What this 'stroke' might have been is not clear. In this scene (Act II, sc. i) Garrick would 'rivet his Eyes to the *imaginary* Object, as if it *really* was there', his hands and fingers would be '*immoveable*', and he would clutch at the dagger 'with *one* motion only'. By contrast his predecessor James Quin (1693–1766) showed 'an *unsettled Motion* in his Eye', his hands were 'restless', and he made 'several *successive* catches' at the dagger (Garrick's *Essay on Acting* (1744), cited in Stone, pp. 551–2). Garrick had last played Macbeth in 1768 (*LS 4* iii. 1352), and was not to play the role again.

[67] *The History of the Life of Marcus Tullius Cicero*, by Conyers Middleton (1683–1750). CB owned 2 copies of the 1st edn., 1741 (*Lib.*, p. 40). In 1742 Middleton pub. *The Epistles of M. T. Cicero to M. Brutus and of Brutus to Cicero*, the Latin with English trans. Middleton had used these epistles in the *Life*, and translated extensively from Cicero's other writings as well. See *YW* xv. 10 n. 1.

[68] *The Roman History, from the Building of Rome to the Ruin of the Commonwealth* (4 vols., 1738–71), by Nathaniel Hooke (d. 1763). CB's copy is listed *Lib.*, p. 32, and also a set described as '3 vol. ——1757.'

[69] Signorina Baccheli (*fl.* 1771–1810), a singer and paintress whom CB had met at Rome the previous year; called 'the Mignatrice' in reference to her painting miniatures. While there CB also met Domenico Corri (1746–1825), whom Signorina Baccheli afterwards married. CB describes Corri as 'an ingenious composer, and sings in a very good taste'; the Baccheli he praises 'for brilliancy and variety of stile' (*Tours*, i. 202, 235; see also i. 224). The Corris were on their way to Edinburgh, where Corri had been invited

my Father ⟨speaks so⟩ highly in his journal, & of her Husband
Signor Corri, who is also mentioned with praise. They only
passed through London in their way to Scotland where Signora
Biccheli is engaged as a singer—they spent a Day with us. She
sings finely, with an Execution that is astonishingly neat & brilliant, her voice is powerful & strong, her taste refined, & her
Expression delicate. She is extremely pretty, her Eyes the most
lovely in the World, & a continual smile of complacency and a
desire of obliging is on her Face. I would have given the World
to have spoke Italian, for she could not say a Word of English.
Niether could her husband, but happily for my Father ⌐ [Signor
Martinelli[70] was of our party,]⌐[71] for he would not otherwise have
had them both attended to as he wished, himself being the only
one of our Family able to speak Italian.⌐ Signor Martinelli That
original Genius has been intimate in our Family from my
Infancy. He is Author of the *Lettere familiare e critiche*: & is now
writing a History of our Country in Italian, ⌐of which he has
finished one Volume. He is truly an original, he⌐ has a most
uncommon flow of wit, & with it, the utmost bitterness of
satire, & raillery of ill-nature. His vanity & self conceit exceed
every person's I ever saw; & far from endeavouring to conceal
this weakness, he glories in it, & thinks he but does himself
justice in esteeming himself the Head of whatever company he
is in, & [openly][72] manifesting that he does. He is not satisfied
with priding himself that he speaks to the Great with *sincerity*;
he piques himself upon treating them with ⌐ *rudeness*. He was

by the Musical Society of Edinburgh to come and conduct their concerts; they arrived
there in Aug. 1771. See *New Grove*; Highfill; vol. ii.

[70] Vincenzio Martinelli (1702–85), Italian writer and adventurer. Martinelli settled
in England in 1748, and CB had met him frequently through Ld. Orford at Houghton
during his years in Lynn. Martinelli, whom CB described as 'a man of strong parts,
with much wit & Italian humour', had encouraged him then in his Italian studies and
more recently supplied him with letters of introduction for his Italian tour. Martinelli
was author, among other works, of *Lettere familiari e critiche* (1758), and of the first
history of England in Italian, *Istoria d'Inghilterra* (3 vols., 1770–3). This work extends
from the Roman occupation to the death of Queen Anne. By 1776 Martinelli had
returned to Italy, where he was granted a pension by the Grand Duke Leopold of
Tuscany, and he died at Florence in 1785. See Lonsdale, pp. 43, 86; *Enciclopedia italiana*
(Milan and Rome, 1929–39), xxii. 440; *Life*, ii. 220–2, 504.

[71] The phrase in brackets appears to have been cut off at the top of the page. FB
repeated it below ('Signor Martinelli was of our party. That original Genius . . .'), then
deleted 'was of our party'.

[72] Inserted by FBA for an obliterated word, not recovered.

boasting to this effect in his broken English, & said—'I hear the nobleman talk—I give him great attention—I make him low Bow—& I say my Lord! you are a very great man—but, for all that—a Blockhead!—'

⌈Yet this man actually subsists by the munificence of our Great People, who for the sake of his talents, caress & support him.⌉[73] He is an admirable *story teller*, if he could forbear making himself the Hero of all his Tales; but the every purport of his speaking is to acquaint the company of his consequence.

Septr 13th

⌈My dear Allen is returned to us.[74] I cannot forbear incessantly regretting her resolution of going abroad. She is the life of our House & family, her good humour, generosity, spirit & drollery, & above all, her unabating, or rather increasing affection render her daily more dear to us. She has wrote us | a minute & faithful Journal of all her transactions & sentiments during her absence, in which she as ingenuously displays her foibles as her excellences, nay, far more obviously, because designedly. To my infinite satisfaction, the time of her stay with us is unexpectedly prolonged, for every Day now is precious. In regard to the state of her affairs her unreserved confidence calls for my utmost discretion, & in future, I am determined never, even in this repository of all *my* affairs, to mention any of hers, but what are *public* or *indifferent*. Mama is gone to Lynn, Bessy

[73] Besides Ld. Orford, Martinelli's English patrons included Charles Townshend (1725–67), Chanceller of the Exchequer, 1766–7, and Thomas Walpole (1727–1803), MP, a cousin of Ld. Orford, who paid for the cost of publishing his *Istoria d'Inghilterra* (see *Life*, ii. 222, 504). The list of subscribers to his *Istoria critica della vita civile* (London, 1752), pp. 5–10, includes the names of many noble and influential Englishmen and women.

[74] MA had been visiting in Norfolk. On 7 Sept. she wrote to FB and SEB from Warham, the seat of Sir John Turner, heralding her imminent return to 'the Two divinities of Queen Square' (Berg). She mentions 'an exact Journal' she has kept 'ever since I have been out—. . . [I] propose myself the pleasure of reading it with a proper emphasis & delivery When we meet.' She also mentions her uncertainty about 'the Heart of [Rishton] . . . to raise your Curiosity more I will Just inform you I have seen him—& danced next Couple to him a whole Eve—but where or when I shall have time to unravel. . . .' She is still determined 'to spend the winter Abroad', though she has encountered difficulties about her lodgings in Geneva and her grandmother Mrs Allen 'has absolutely forbid' her mother from accompanying her there. She may have to 'set out at an uncertainty' which 'tho' it will be very disagreeable is better than what my future prospects are in England'. See below, pp. 176, 215, 222.

with her & Charlotte is put to school in the neighbourhood. I always miss her.

Sept. 15th

Poor M^{rs} N⟨ew⟩bury[75] is yet living & her son is returned, having left her & the whole family much delighted with his dutiful & consolatory visit, & the sweet sufferer even somewhat better. ⌐ |

[*Some 6 leaves have been cut away here.* 'The Deuce is in him' *may be a reference to the two-act farce of that title by George Colman the elder, first performed in 1763 and most recently at the Haymarket, 8 July 1771; or perhaps it refers to Martin Rishton's vagaries as a suitor of MA.*]

⌐the Deuce is in him. Perhaps I ought to be ashamed as it is, but this is a kind of discussion I am too particularly fond of, to resist any opportunity of being engaged in. ⌐

I had the pleasure to meet Dr. Armstrong yesterday. He is an amazing old man—I believe he is 70[76]—& he yet retains spirits & wit to a great degree; ⌐his memory is rather impaired, but⌐ his Health seems perfect & he says, ⌐though⌐ by *starts*, most excellent things. The generality of People at his time of life, are confined by infirmities; but he Walks out perpetually, & always unattended. His conversation is, indeed, very unequal, but he has sallies of humour that are delightful. He has lately made a short tour of Italy, but was past the Age of enjoying foreign [C]ountries or manners.[77] |

[75] The reading is uncertain. If correct, probably Mary née Hounshill (*c.*1707–80), who m. 1 William Carnan (d. 1737), proprietor and editor of the *Reading Mercury*; m. 2 (*c.*1739) John Newbery (1713–67), publisher of children's books and friend of CB; mother-in-law of Christopher Smart. As her sons Thomas Carnan (d. 1788) and Francis Newbery (1743–1818), publishers, both lived in London, the son mentioned here, who evidently lived out of town, was probably John Carnan, who had taken over the *Reading Mercury* and died there in 1785. See Maxted; Mary Newbery's will, PCC, prob. 19 Feb. 1780; *GM* 1 (1780), 102; 1v^1 (1785), 324; A. Sherbo, *Christopher Smart: Scholar of the University*, pp. 122, 243.

[76] He was actually about 62.

[77] Bothered by a wracking cough, Armstrong had sailed for Italy in Nov. 1769. One of his companions was the painter Henry Fuseli, who was on his way to study at Rome. They parted at Genoa, and Armstrong thereafter moved from place to place, making notes by the way, and paying a short visit to the dying Smollett at Leghorn. He returned to England in Sept. 1770: on the 22nd of that month Andrew Lumisden wrote from Paris that 'my cousin Dr. Armstrong is now with me. . . . He is now tolerably well, and intends to set out for London in a few days' (Dennistoun, ii. 137). Earlier in 1771 Armstrong published *A Short Ramble through Some Parts of France and Italy*. The *Monthly*

ᴴWednesday, Octʳ 1[st][78]

Now, in due order, to our Play, which I shall presently Copy a Bill of.

There was just a Week's interval from our proposing & performing it.

But I will begin with a *Play Bill* which I had the honour to draw up.

This Day, Monday the 29ᵗʰ [September]
Will be presented,
By a Company of Comedians in Queen Square
The Drummer[79]
Sir George Truman, Miss Allen
Drummer, Miss Sukey Burney
Vellum, by a Gentleman[80]
Butler, Mr. James Burney
Coachman Mr. Sansom,[81] Gardener, Mr. Sleepe[82]

Review for Aug. (xlv (1771), 130–3) condemns the book for its 'spleen', while the *Critical Review* for June (xxxi (1771), 478) dismisses it as 'the last effort of expiring genius'. See W. J. Maloney, *George and John Armstrong of Castleton* . . . (Edinburgh, 1954), p. 62.

[78] So in MS. Here as occasionally elsewhere FB appears to be a day off in her date. 1 Oct. 1771 occurred on a Tuesday, and 29 Sept. 1771 on a Sunday; probably the dates should be 2 Oct. and 30 Sept.

[79] *The Drummer, or the Haunted House* (1716), a comedy by Joseph Addison (1672–1719). After an absence of almost 8 years it was revived at Drury Lane on 6 Nov. 1771, and repeated by royal command on 20 Nov. (*LS 4* iii. 1582, 1586). More than 20 years later MAR recalled this amateur performance in a letter to SBP 12 Aug. 1793 (Berg): 'Do you remember when we Acted the Drummer the prudish Lady Truman [FB]—on rehearsing the first time insisted upon it at our Tender Meeting in the fifth Act, that I [Sir George Truman] should only kiss her hand—after an absence of three or 4 years and beleiving me dead in the field of honour—and till I was quite Angry and said I would give up the part of Sir George, if she made the Scene so unnatural—she at last Allowd a Chaste Embrace.' For FB's prudishness in theatricals, see also the Introduction and vol. ii.

[80] Perhaps CB.

[81] Presumably FB's 1st cousin James Sansom or his brother Francis Sansom, named in FBA's 'List of Persons' for 1771. James Sansom (1751–1822) was son of John Sansom (d. *c.*1769) who m. (1743) Mary Sleepe (1715–?78), sister of FB's mother. James Sansom may have helped CB Jr. in 1777 when the latter was sent down from Cambridge and for a time barred from his father's house (see vol. ii). In 1802 he was in the employ of CB Jr. at Greenwich as a man of all work, and after CB Jr.'s death he became a pensioner of both JB and FBA. He m. (1790) Elizabeth Margaret Wood (living 1822).

His brother Francis Sansom (b. 1756) was living in Brompton in 1808 when he is listed as a subscriber to James Sansom's *Greenwich, A Poem, Descriptive and Historical* (1808), 2 copies of which are in the London Guildhall Library. Mrs Mary Sansom, the mother, is also in FBA's 'List of Persons' for 1771, as is 'Miss Molly Sansom', presumably her daughter Mary Sansom (b. 1745). It was probably the elder Mary Sansom who

[*See p. 172 for n. 81 cont. and n. 82*]

And
Tinsel by Miss Barsanti
Lady Truman Miss Burney
And
Abigail by Mr. Charles Burney.[83]
Prologue written & spoken by Mr. James Burney
The House to be lighted with six Candles.
By Command of the Performers, no Company to be admitted between the scenes. N.B: the Fire to be stir'd between the acts.⸣ |

[*a leaf (or leaves) cut away*]

⸢'The West Indian! exclaimed I, why Good God, does not Mr. Garrick play Kitely[84] to night?—She then gave me a Bill, importing that dear Creature's being taken suddenly ill, & being unable to Act. Sorry, disappointed & provoked we tore out of the House[85] faster than we had into it. We have, however, heard that he is much recovered.⸣

My Father spent a few Days lately at Hinchinbroke at Lord Sandwich's,[86] to meet Mr Banks, Captain Cooke & Dr. Sol-

was buried in the church vault of St Michael le Quern on 18 Jan. 1778. See *JL* iv. 175, v. 155, ix. 205, x. 925, xi. 43 n. 16; W. A. Littledale, ed., *The Registers of St. Vedast, Foster Lane, and of St. Michael Le Quern* (1902–3), i. 172, 177, ii. 356; CB Jr. to FB [late 1769 or 1770] (Osborn); IGI.

[82] Presumably FB's uncle James Sleepe (1716–94). A handyman or messenger and sometime parish clerk, he was semi-literate and poor, but a great favourite of all the Burneys because of his kindnesses and amiable nature (*JL* i. 68 n. 7). Despite Charlotte Burney Francis's statement, in a letter to FB 5 July 1791 (Barrett), that Mr Sleepe 'says he is within 3 years of 80', which would place his birth *c.*1714, he appears to be the James, son of Richard and Frances Sleepe, who was baptized 13 May 1716 in Christ Church Greyfriars, Newgate St. (IGI).

[83] Presumably CB Jr., aged 13, whose voice may not yet have changed.

[84] The jealous merchant in *Every Man in his Humour* by Ben Jonson, as altered by Garrick (1751). Garrick was scheduled to play the role, one of his most popular, the evening of 1 Nov.: 'Bills for *Every Man in his Humour* were posted to day—but Mr G. being taken very ill the Play was oblig'd to be chang'd & fresh Bills put up about Twelve o'clock' (William Hopkin's MS Diary, 1769–76, cited *LS 4* iii. 1580). In its place was performed *The West Indian*, by Richard Cumberland (1732–1811), a new play, which had opened at Drury Lane the preceding Jan. Garrick soon recovered and played Kitely on 8 Nov. (*LS 4* iii. 1583; see also Stone, pp. 278–82, 509–11).

[85] The Drury Lane playhouse.

[86] John Montagu (1718–92), 4th E. of Sandwich; First Lord of the Admiralty; the notorious 'Jemmy Twitcher' (see vol. ii). CB had probably met Sandwich before 1771 since Sandwich was a prominent figure in London musical life, but this encounter and the earlier one mentioned below are the earliest recorded. In a mutilated fragment of his Memoirs for 1771 he notes that he was invited in October to spend '4 [or] 5 days' at

ander, who have just made the Voyage round the World, & are going speedily to make another. My Father, through his lordship's means, made interest for James to go with them, & we have reason to hope he will have a prosperous & agreeable Voyage.

My Father has had a happy opportunity of extremely obliging Dr. Hawkesworth. During his stay in Norfolk, he waited upon ∣ Lord Orford,[87] who has always been particularly friendly to him: he there, among others, met with Lord Sandwich. His Lordship was speaking of the late Voyage round the World, & mentioned his having the papers of it in his possession—for he is first Lord of the Admiralty—& said that they were not arranged, but meer rough Draughts, & that he should be much obliged to any one who could recommend a proper Person to *Write the Voyage*. My Father directly named Dr. Hawkesworth, & his Lordship did him the honour to accept his recommendation; the Doctor waited upon Lord Sandwich, & they both ⌜sent⌝ my Father particular thanks for their meeting.[88]

Hinchingbrooke, Sandwich's seat in Huntingdonshire (Osborn). There he met Capt. James Cook (1728–79), who had returned in July from his first circumnavigation of the globe (1768–71); Joseph Banks (1744–1820), cr. (1781) Bt., PRS, 1778–1820, who at his own expense had accompanied Cook as the expedition's naturalist; and Dr Daniel Carl Solander (1736–82), a Swedish botanist and student of Linnaeus who went as Banks's companion.

CB notes also that 'my eldest Son the Seaman was there presented by Ld Sandwich to Capt. Cook, begging him, if in the Course of his 2d Voyage of discovery he had any occasion to make a midshipman he wd prefer my Son'. JB embarked on the second expedition as an able seaman, being promoted to second lieutenant after several months (see below, p. 251). A further benefit of CB's meeting with Sandwich was that Sandwich provided him the next year with letters of introduction to British ministers for use on his German tour.

[87] George Walpole (1730–91), 3rd E. of Orford; eccentric grandson of Sir Robert Walpole and nephew of Horace Walpole. Orford had befriended CB during his Lynn years and frequently invited him to his seat at Houghton. During his visit to Lynn in Sept. CB was invited to Houghton by William Bewley 'in my Lord Orford's name'. 'Lord Sandwich is here, together with a female friend of his, Miss [Martha] Ray, with whose sweet pipe I have been entranced all this afternoon. . . . She is accompanied [musically] by a Mr Bates, a Mr Warren, & two more'; Bewley requests that CB 'join this harmonical groupe' (letter from Houghton dated 'Tuesday Night', Osborn; see also Lonsdale, p. 41; 'Mem.' No. 67).

[88] On 14 Sept. CB wrote to Hawkesworth about this lucrative offer by Sandwich to revise and edit Cook's account of his voyage. Hawkesworth answered CB's (missing) letter on 18 Sept.: 'Many, many thanks . . . there is nothing about which I would so willingly be employed as the work you mention. . . . I am very unwilling to wait for Lord S's application without doing something to anticipate or quicken it. Will you tell him by a line that I most heartily concur in the proposal?' On 6 Oct. Hawkesworth

Yet I cannot but be amazed that a man of Lord Sandwich's power, &c, should be so ignorant of men of ⌐ learning & merit, as to apply to an almost stranger for recommendation. Pity! pity! that those ⌐only⌐ should be sensible of who cannot reward worth!

⌐Dr. Shepherd & Dr. Hawkesworth were of the Hinchin-broke party—the latter ingenuously said he should not have been there, but for my Father.

The *Musical Tour* has not·yet received all its homage. Letters from every Day are only yet sunk to every week. The last was from Germany, from a *Dilletante*[89] of Hambrugh [*sic*], who writes tolerably good English, & is extremely polite & flatter-ing.⌐ My Father is at present most diligently studying German. He has an unquenchable thirst of knowledge—⌐& would in⌐ time, I believe, be the first Linguist in England.[90] ⌐

⌐Nov[r] 4th

Returning this morning from Madame Grifardiere's,[91] I went through Poland Street—a place I cannot but love, from

wrote again to CB: 'I am now happy in telling you that "your Labour of Love was not in vain". . . . Accept my best Thanks, dear Sir, for the Advantage which this work must necessarily secure me, which will be very considerable.' In a letter dated 'Wednesday morning' in Oct., Sandwich offered CB 'some flutes from the island of Otahee [Tahiti]' and returned him 'his particular thanks, for having made him acquainted with Dr Hawksworth' (all 3 letters in National Library of Australia, Canberra).

Hawkesworth's work appeared in 1773 and contained not only Cook's voyage (supplemented by the papers of Joseph Banks) but also the voyages of Byron, Wallis, and Carteret. The severe criticisms heaped upon it for inaccuracies, impieties, and indecencies probably hastened Hawkesworth's death. See below, pp. 313, 325–7.

[89] Christoph Daniel Ebeling (1741–1817), German writer on music; currently Vice-Director of the Hamburg Academy of Commerce. He had written CB from 'Ham-bourgh the 20 August' praising CB's book and offering him assistance on German music for *Hist. Mus.* (Staats-und-Universitäts Bibliothek, Hamburg; pub. in Scholes, i. 199–200). He also suggested that CB make a musical tour of Germany. CB entered into a correspondence with him and met him the following year at Hamburg. Ebeling trans-lated CB's *Italian Tour* into German (Hamburg, 1772). Ebeling was displeased by CB's claim in the *German Tour* that the Germans lacked innate genius, but none the less helped to translate that book also. See Lonsdale, pp. 112, 118, 124–7, 498–9; *New Grove*.

[90] CB, however, never fully mastered the German language. See CB to C. I. Latrobe, [1788] (Osborn).

[91] Jeanne-Adrienne Peschier (1734–1806), who m. the Revd Charles de Guiffardière (*c.*1740–1810), a French protestant minister who later appears in FB's Court Journals as Mr Turbulent, an obstreperous teaser and joker. Mme Guiffardière's widowed mother, Jeanne (Roux) Peschier, kept a lodging-house in Geneva where MA had hoped to stay during her European trip, but she wrote FB, 7 Sept. 1771 (Berg), that 'my

remembering the happiness I have known there. I passed with
great regret by Mrs. Pringle's Windows, but looking at the
Door, I saw the name of Rishman[92] on it. I have too much
regard for Mrs. Pringle, to be indifferent to what is become of
her—a Woman was at the Door—I asked if she knew where
Mrs. Pringle was gone? She did not; but my curiosity was
excited, & I waited till a servant came to open the Door. I made
the same question—without answering, the servant went &
rapt at the Parlour Door—I was in some confusion, lest Mrs.
Pringle might be there, & pondered upon what possible excuse
I could make for my long absence, I even felt a sort of *guilt*, in
having [to] all appearance, made a stolen visit—but [after] a
minute or two, a Gentleman, made his [appearance—I] asked
him where Mrs. Pringle was?—'Ma'am, said he, ⌐ gone to the
East Indies.'

O that I had ⌐sooner⌐ known her intention! nothing should
have prevented my [s]eeing her, if I had had the least idea [o]f
her quitting England. I imagine she [is] gone to her son
Andrew.[93] ⌐I am quite grieved at the sentiments she must
undoubtedly entertain of us.⌐—I would [of]ten have given the
World to have met [he]r *by chance*, though I have not dared
[*se*]*ek* her. ⌐Certain I am, she deserves a more grateful return
than she met with, for her kindness & friendship to us.⌐

And thus, I suppose, will close for [eve]r all acquaintance
with [*sic*] this agreeable [wo]man and our Family. On my side,
how unwillingly! for I cannot join in the ba[d] opinion Mama
& M[r] Crisp have so strangely, so causelessly conceived of her.[94]
⌐Her kindness to *us*, as she could have no interest in, it would
be ingratitude not to regard her for.⌐

Mother received a letter from Madame Griffodière who informed her that she had
received a letter from her Mother at Geneva who had not room for any more in her
Family nor coud not procure me lodgings near her . . .' MA nevertheless had written to
Mme Guiffardière, asking her if she or her mother 'could recommend any other place',
and asked FB to visit her to be sure she had received the letter. After reaching Geneva
MA wrote FB (21 Nov. 1771, Berg) begging 'you will go to Mc Griffodière and present
my best compliments & wear them both out to look for some conveyance for my instru-
ment ['my tiny forte'] and music. . . .' At this time the Guiffardières lived in Wells St.
See *JL* i. 11 n. 4, 126 n. 18.

[92] A John Rishman lived at Mrs Pringle's old address in Poland St. until 1784 or
1785 (rate books).

[93] She had actually gone to the Isle of Wight (below, p. 198).

[94] They perhaps suspected her of scheming to match Mr Seton and EB.

Independant of these more serious re[a]sons for regret at her departure, I must also own, that since we have droped her Acquaintance, we have never made any half so lively & agreeable. But what principally concerns me, is that she left the kingdom with an idea of our ingrat[i]tude. Dear, wise, & good Mr. Crisp has surely been too severe in his judgment. What a misfortune I should deem it to think so ill of mankind as He, the wisest of its race, trie[s] to make me think!

My dear Susette has been very ill, but thank G[od] is recovered. She is the most engaging Creature livin[g,] & has a fund of sense & feeling almost incomparab[le.] |

⌜My poor sister [EBB] has been extremely ill, & attended by Dr. Armstrong.[95] She is now, thank God, enough recovered to go to Chesington, which she did yesterday, with Mama, who [xxxxx *1 word*] accompanied her there, & will almost immediately return.⌝

We have had a charming Pacquet from Miss Allen, from Paris, ⌜containing an ample Journal of her affairs, &c, ever since she left us. We have since heard she is arrived at Geneva.[96]

I have just heard that my sister is better.⌝

⌜Sukey⌝ & myself are extremely engaged at present, in studying a Book lately Published, under M. Diderot's direction, & which he sent to Papa, upon music.[97] It promises to

---

[95] This was perhaps a recurrence of the complaint which had sent EBB to Chessington earlier in the year.

[96] MA had set out for Geneva sometime after 29 Sept. (see above, p. 169). In a letter to FB from Geneva, 21 Nov. 1771 (Berg), received in Dec., she mentions having already written to her mother 'from Brighthelmstone Dieppe Rouenne Lyons and since I came here', and that she also sent all 'a large pacquet of my Journal from Paris which you must have received before now'. She frets over having received no letters from England and having already spent all her money on clothes at Paris and Lyons, which has forced her to borrow from a Madame Porte. She also alludes to her uncles (Edmund and Maxey Allen's) displeasure at her quitting England, and asks FB to commission EBB 'to buy me any trifles I want in England that I ca[nt] ge[t] here'. Years later she recalls CB's kindness in sending her money at Geneva when her own family did not (MAR to CB, 1 Nov. [1796], Barrett). She stayed at Geneva till the following spring. See below, pp. 215, 222.

[97] *Leçons de clavecin, et principles d'harmonie* (Paris, 1771), by Anton Bemetzrieder (1743 or 1748–*c.*1817), revised by Diderot, a copy of which he sent to CB in exchange for CB's present of his *Italian Tour*. Diderot took a keen interest in the musical education of his daughter, Marie-Angélique (1753–1824), whom CB called 'one of the finest harpsichord-players in Paris and who was taught by Bemetzrieder' (*Tours*, i. 317; *New Grove*, s.v. Bemetzrieder). In Sept. 1772 she was to marry Abel-François-Nicolas Caroillon, marquis de Vandeul; to Diderot's great regret, she failed to progress further in music (R. A. Leigh, 'Les Amitiés françaises du Dr. Burney', *Revue de littérature comparée*,

teach us Harmony ⌐ & the Theory of music. ⌐M. Diderot's Daughter was taught by the method made use of in it. However, I have no expectation of going very deep in the science myself.⌐

I am Reading—I blush to say for the first Time, Pope's works.[98] He is a darling Poet of our Family: it is with exquisite delight I make myself acquainted with him.

⌐I have before mentioned, that Miss Barsanti had intentions to go on the stage. According to them, she applied to my Father to speak to Mr Colman concerning her. My Father, to oblige her, consented, though unwillingly, having a superiour regard for Mr Garrick; but Drury Lane Theatre has 2 actresses already in Barsanti's style.[99] Mr Colman professed great regard for my Father's recommendation, but deferred till another time, settling when to see her.⌐ ⌐

Decr 8th

⌐I am quite afflicted.⌐

M^r and Mrs Young have been in Town a few Days. They are in a situation that quite afflicts me: how brought on, I know not, but I fear by extravagance. Be that as it may, they are at present reduced to a most distressful state: they seem to have almost ruined themselves, & to be quite ignorant in what manner to retrieve their affairs.[1]

xxv (1951), 175–6). In a letter to Diderot of 10 Oct. 1771 (pub. ibid. 183–5), CB mentions his intention of trying out Bemetzrieder's method on SEB, 'one of my own daughters who also plays pretty well on the Harpsichord; but who has not learned as yet, either accompaniment or Modulation'.

[98] i.e., Pope's own works. She had presumably already read his translations of the *Iliad* and *Odyssey*. She probably read the works in the 1751 edn. of Warburton (see above, p. 37 and n. 40).

[99] FB perhaps means Mrs Frances Abington (1737–1815) and Miss Jane Pope (1742–1818), Garrick's leading comic actresses. Jane Barsanti was to perform many of the same roles as Mrs Abington, e.g., Estifania in *Rule a Wife and Have a Wife*, Lydia Languish in *The Rivals* (a role which Barsanti created), Charlotte Rusport in *The West Indian*, and Mrs Oakly in *The Jealous Wife*. On 26 Nov. 1771 Miss Pope played Edging in *The Careless Husband*, the part which Miss Barsanti had chosen earlier in the year for the amateur performance at Chessington (see above, p. 159; *LS 4* iii. 1587), and on 4 Dec. she performed the title role of the afterpiece *The Musical Lady*, which Barsanti was to play in 1773 (ibid. 1590; see also Highfill; below, p. 261). Colman apparently deferred an audition until the following summer. Barsanti so impressed him then that he wrote a dramatic 'Occasional Prelude' for her to perform as her début, opening the new season at Covent Garden on 21 Sept. See below, p. 197.

[1] The details of their financial difficulties at this time are not known. As usual Young was publishing works on agriculture at a prolific rate. His writings provoked some

Mr Young, whose study & dependance is Agriculture, has half undone himself by *experiments*: his writings upon this subject have been amazingly well received by the Public, & in his Tours through England, he has been caressed & assisted almost universally. Indeed his Conversation & Appearance must ever secure him Welcome & admiration.—But of late, some of his *facts* have been disputed, & though I believe it to be only by envious & malignant People, yet reports of $^|$ that kind are fatal to an Author whose whole credit must subsist upon his veracity:—in short, by slow, but sure degrees, his fame has been sported with, & his fortune destroyed. I grieve for him inexpressibly: he truly merits a better fate. Too successful in his early life, he expected a constancy in Fortune that has cruelly disappointed him. His Children,^{2} happily, have their mother's jointure settled upon them—He has some thoughts of going Abroad;^{3} but his Wife is averse to it: he is an enterprising Genius, &, I sincerely hope, will be able to struggle effectually with his bad fortune: but *how*, I know not.

They went with us one Day to Mr Colman's Box: but poor Mr Young has only *forced* spirits: *those* he does indeed exert in an uncommon manner. She, too, bears herself with more resolution & better Temper than I thought her equal to. $^|$

[*a leaf or leaves cut away*]

adhere to, than this.

^{r}Harry Partridge^4 called here last Week. I am sorry to see how much he alters. He was ever too anxiously careful of pecuniary affairs, but they now seem wholly to engross him.$^¬$

severe criticisms, especially from the Revd Thomas Comber (d. 1778), in the influential *Monthly Review*. In the preface to his *Farmer's Tour through the East of England*, pub. this year in 4 vols., Young summarized these criticisms: that he was only a pretended farmer without land; that he had elaborated his works into many vols. when all he had to say might have been easily compressed into one; that he had written only to make money, and had rushed into print too rapidly. In spite of the reviewers, Young in 1771 also received flattering letters from many prominent men, including Edmund Burke. See Gazley, pp. 18, 58–75, 705.

   ^{2} Young's children at this time, aged 2 to 5, were Mary Young (1766–1851); Elizabeth ('Bessy') Young (1768–94), m. (1791) the Revd Samuel Hoole; and Arthur Young (1769–1827), later a clergyman, who m. (1799) Jane Berry. See Gazley, pp. 726–7 and *passim*.

   ^{3} To America (Gazley, p. 75).

   ^{4} Henry Partridge the younger, MA's former suitor.

But now that I am in a scribbling vein, I cannot forbear mentioning that the Reading of Pope's Letters[5] has made me quite melancholy. He laments with such generous sorrow the misfortunes of his friends, that every Line I read, raises his Character higher in [m]y estimation. But it is not possible to find with unconcern, that all his best & dearest friends Die before him. [O] great misery of length of Days, | to preserve Life only to know its little value! Pope had but one great end in view, to render this World supportable to him—that was *Friendship — The peculiar gift of Heaven*.[6]—this did he nobly deserve—& obtain—but for how short a Time!—Jealousy deprived him of the affection he assiduously sought from M[r] Whycherly[7]—& many others—but Death, cruel Death was far *more* cruel—the dearest ties of his Heart all yielded to his stroke.—the modest Digby[8]—the gentle, virtuous Gay.[9] the worthy Arbuthnot[10]—the exiled Atterbu[ry][11]—but why should I enumerate these excellent men, when their very name[s] | deject me? But in nothing does Pope equally charm me, as in his conduct to his mother.[12] It is truly Noble. He gives up all his Time, thought & [a]ttention to her ease & comfort.— [I] dare not begin to mention his [lo]ng friendship with the admirable [S]wift,[13] because I shall not know where [to] stop; for the attachment of such [em]inent men to one another, has

---

[5] In Warburton, vols. vii–ix.

[6] FB is apparently quoting the opening line of Samuel Johnson's 'An Ode on Friendship' (*Poems*, ed. E. L. McAdam and G. Milne (New Haven, 1964), pp. 70–1); but see also Pope's 'January and May', l. 52, in Warburton, ii. 89.

[7] William Wycherley (?1640–1716), dramatist and poet. Wycherley befriended the precocious Pope in 1704, when Pope was 16. He subsequently permitted him to edit his poems before publication, but Pope confided to Joseph Spence that 'Mr. Wycherley was really angry with me for correcting his verses so much. I was extremely plagued up and down for almost two years with them.' Spence in turn observed to Pope that 'People have pitied you extremely on reading your letters to Wycherley; surely 'twas a very difficult thing for you to keep well with him?' (Spence, *Observations, Anecdotes, and Characters of Books and Men*, ed. J. M. Osborn (Oxford, 1966), i. 35, 38; see also Warburton, vii. 93 n. *a*).

[8] The Hon. Robert Digby (d. 1726), younger son of the 5th Ld. Digby; MP.

[9] John Gay (1685–1732), poet and dramatist.

[10] Dr John Arbuthnot (1667–1735), physician and author.

[11] Francis Atterbury (1662–1732), Bp. of Rochester. He was imprisoned in the Tower in 1722 for his involvement with the Jacobites. Exiled in 1723, he never returned to England.

[12] Edith Turner (1643–1733), m. Alexander Pope (1646–1717), father of the poet.

[13] Jonathan Swift (1667–1745).

[som]ething in it almost awes me—& [at] the same time, inexpressibly delights [me.]—I must tear myself from this. |

[*bottom of page cut away*]

[Yes, my dear Journal, yes! — —][14] with the more pleasure shall I regard Thee, thou faithful repository of my Thoughts & Actions.

Yet I cannot forbear thinking of some Lines of my dear Pope's upon a Birth Day[15]—applicable to my poor dear Journal—

> With added Years, if Life bring nothing [new,]
> But, like a sieve, let every pleasure th[ro',]
> [Some joy still lost, as each vain year runs o'er,]
> & all we gain, one sad reflection more[;]
> Is this a Birth Day?—'tis alas too cle[ar,]
> 'Tis but the Fun'ral of a former Yea[r.]

[*bottom of page cut away*]

---

[14] Inserted by FBA; possibly copied from the missing bottom of the preceding page.

[15] 'To Mrs. M[artha] B[lount] on her Birth-day.' The original version was composed in 1723. FB's quotation appears to be an amalgam of the 2 versions in Warburton (at vi. 79 and viii. 166–7). The 1st line follows Warburton vi, the 2nd and 5th lines Warburton viii. Lines 4 and 6 differ from both ('one' for 'some' in line 4 and 'a' for 'the' in line 6). The 3rd line, the same in both Warburton versions, is supplied by the present editor. FB omitted it in the MS, leaving a blank line with elision marks, either for conciseness or because memory failed her. See also Pope, *Minor Poems*, ed. N. Ault and J. Butt (1954), pp. 244–7 (Twickenham edn., vol. vi).

AJ (Early Diary, v, paginated 239–[86], foliated 1–[42], Berg), Journal for 1772.

Originally a cahier of sewn double sheets. Now 39 single sheets and 3 double sheets 4to, 90 pp. with a cover entitled (by FBA): Juvenile Journal | N° 5 | 1772.

The extant journal ends on 31 May. The extent of the missing portions is indicated by the absence of 45 persons named in FBA's 'List' for 1772. People mentioned in earlier journals are George Colman the elder, Robert Strange and his daughter Mary Bruce Strange, the Miss Pascals, Capt. Cook, Mrs Ann (Cooper) Burney, CB Jr., Ann and Rebecca Burney, the Revd Matthew Pugh, Mrs and Miss Lidderdale, Stephen Allen, Mrs Martha Young, John Parke, and John Hayes. Names identified in later years are Martin Folkes, Dr Hunter, Lady Anne Lindsay, Miss Ann Burney (after Mrs Hawkins), the Duke of Dorset, Mr Edwards, Mr and Mrs Barthélemon, Mr Brydone, Sir John Turner, Miss Fitzgerald, and Mr Nollekens. Mrs Stanley and Miss Arlond are identified with John Stanley, below, p. 192 n. 31. Susanna Sharpin and Hannah Maria Burney are dealt with in a bridge passage at the end of this year.

After these, there remain 11 names not mentioned elsewhere in FB's journals before 1778. 'Mr. Sloper' was probably William Sloper (1709–89) of West Woodhay, Berkshire, one of CB's 'early friends, made previous to my going into Norfolk'. The actress Mrs Susannah Cibber (1714–66), sister of CB's music master Dr Arne, was Sloper's mistress, and their natural daughter Maria Susannah Sloper had been CB's pupil ('Mem.' No. 94 and n. 1; No. 106 and n. 6). 'Mynhere Bohmen' was probably the 'Mr. Böhmen', a mutual friend of CB and C. D. Ebeling, who early in 1772 brought to Ebeling a copy of CB's edition of the Holy Week music performed in the Sistine Chapel (published Jan. 1772; see CB to Ebeling 30 Mar. 1772, Staats-und-Universitäts Bibliothek, Hamburg; Public Advertiser, 29 Jan. 1772). This was perhaps Johann Gottlob Böhme or Böhmen (1717–80), German writer and professor of history at Leipzig, who had provided an introduction and notes to a German translation of Walter Harte's History of the Life of Gustavus Adolphus (1759). CB may have known Harte (and hence Böhme) through the Allen family and Arthur Young (see Lib., p. 23; also Gazley, pp. 14, 19–20; Young, Autobiography, pp. 32–43, 49).

'Mr. Hanbury', who is preceded in FBA's 'List' by the Duke of Dorset, was probably William Hanbury (c.1748–1807) of Kelmarsh, Northamptonshire, amateur dramatist and later (1790–9) British agent and consul to the Circle of Lower Saxony, at whose house CB dined with the Duke in Apr. 1784 (CB to SBP [25]–6 Apr. 1784, Osborn; GM lx² (1790), 962; lxxvii² (1807), 1176; Garrick, Letters, iii. 951–3, 955–7; YW xxxii. 168–9). 'Mr. Bremner' was Robert Bremner (c.1713–89), CB's music publisher, who in Jan. 1772 published his edition of the Holy Week music (above) and also in Mar. his

Second Number of Two Sonatas for the Harpsichord and Forte Piano, with Accompany-
ments for a Violin and Violoncello (Scholes, ii. 347–8; *New Grove*).

'Mr. Parsons' was probably William Parsons (*c.*1746–1817), cr. (1795) Kt.,
a young musician whom CB had befriended at Rome in 1770. In 1786 he was
appointed Master of the King's Band in the place of John Stanley, a post
which CB had expected to receive (see Scholes, i. 179; Lonsdale, pp. 319–22).
'Mr. Mathias' was James Mathias (*c.*1710–82), a wealthy merchant and
King's Resident at Hamburg, whom CB met there through letters of introduction in Oct. 1772 (*Tours*, ii. 215; CB to Mrs Thrale 29 [Aug. 1779],
Rylands; *Life*, iv. 489).

'Mr. George Garrick' (1723–79) was David Garrick's youngest brother and
deputy in the Drury Lane Theatre. 'Mrs. Arne' was Cecilia née Young
(1711–89), singer, who m. (1737) Thomas Arne, CB's music master. Long
separated from her husband, she lived with the Barthélemons. (Mrs Barthélemon was her niece.)

'Mynhere Spandau' was a French horn player, musician to the Stadholder,
whom CB met at The Hague later this year, and who visited London in 1773.
In 1770 he had astounded listeners with his virtuosity in the Concerts Spirituels at Paris (*Tours*, ii. 234 and n. 2; Rees, s.v. Horn; C. Pierre, *Histoire du*
Concert Spirituel 1725–1790 (Paris, 1975), pp. 151, 299). 'Mlle Le Chantre' (b.
*c.*1752) was an organist and pianist, 'habile musicienne, fort applaudie' who
performed in the Concerts Spirituels from 1767 to 1770. EB and SEB had met
her during their stay in France in the mid 1760s, and she and EB corresponded for a time. (The letters are missing.) CB attended the last Concert
Spirituel in which Mlle Le Chantre played (on 8 Dec. 1770), though he does
not mention her in his account of it. In 1770 she published *Deux concertos pour*
le clavecin ou piano-forte avec accompagnement, Op. 1 (SEB's Journal for 1767,
written 1770, McGill University Library; C. Pierre, pp. 144, 152, 292–9;
M. Brenet, *Les Concerts en France sous l'ancien régime* (Paris, 1900), p. 292;
Tours, i. 310). 'Mad^e Le Chantre', presumably Mlle Le Chantre's mother,
was a harpsichordist. She and her daughter performed in a benefit concert for
the mother at Almack's on 24 Apr. 1773, advertised in the *Morning Chronicle*,
23 Apr. 1773.

[3^d Jan^y]^1

Mr Young called here lately. I ⌜saw⌝ him with sorrow. He is
not well, & appears almost overcome with the ⌜heaviness⌝ of
his situation. ⌜I fear he is almost destitute.⌝ I fancy he is himself
undetermined yet what Plan to persue. This is a dreadful Trial
for him; yet I am persuaded he will still find some means of
extricating himself from his distresses: At least if genius, spirit
& Enterprise can avail.

In defiance of the gloom his misfortunes have cast over him,

---

^{1} Inserted by FBA, but perhaps a slip for '23^d Jan^y'. The preface which FB cites
below is dated 'London, Jan. 7, 1772' (p. xix).

some starts of his former, his native vivacity, break out. Dr. King has lately Published a Book, entitled 'The Rites (&c) of the Greek Church'[2]—Mr Young took it up, & opening at the Preface—⌐*God*¬ so, what's here?' cried | he—& read aloud that 'he had undertaken this Work to relieve his mind from a most severe affliction, occasioned by the loss of a virtuous & affectionate'—'But it would be impertinent to obtrude my private misfortunes on the Public'—

'He means his Wife,'[3] said I.

'It would serve as well for his mistress,' answered he.

'For my own part,' added I, (*very good naturedly*) it appears ridiculous ostentation to me, as I am almost certain he had very little regard for her, & he was never in his Life more gay than since her Death.'

For I have heard well authenticated particulars of his marriage.—'& therefore it seems ⌐meer¬'—

'Well, ⌐God¬,' cried he, 'I honour a man who dares to be singular,—I like to | see a man's oddities in his Works;—'

'But I think,' said I, 'you are no friend to *Affectation*, which to us who know him, this appears.—'

'Affected!' exclaimed he, with all his wonted impetuousity,—'I had rather be a murderer!'—

Jany 26th

Mr Garrick is this moment gone. Unfortunately my Father was out, & Mama not come down stairs—Yet, to my great satisfaction, he came in.—Dick[4] ran to him as the Door was

---

[2] *The Rites and Ceremonies of the Greek Church, in Russia; Containing an Account of its Doctrine, Worship, and Discipline*, in 1 vol., royal 4to, by Dr John Glen King. The work, described by *DNB* as 'learned and exhaustive', was heralded in the *Daily Adv.* 21 Dec. 1771 but not pub. until 24 Jan. 1772 (*Daily Adv.* 24 Jan.). The copy FB refers to here was probably a pre-publication offering from King to CB; King was probably one of the 'many others' to whom CB had sent a copy of his *Italian Tour* (above, p. 147).

[3] Anne Magdalene née Combrune, daughter of Michael Combrune of Hampstead, author of *The Theory and Practice of Brewing* (1762). Dr King married secondly (1776, at Greenwich) a Jane Hyde, who d. in 1789 (*Miscellanea Genealogica et Heraldica*, 4th ser. i. 43). The quoted passage, slightly shortened here, concludes the Preface to King's work (p. xix).

[4] Richard Thomas Burney (1768–1808), FB's half-brother, 3 years old at this time. A beautiful child, he apparently grew up spoiled by his doting parents. When 18 or 19 he was exiled to India, probably because of libidinous conduct which may have led to resultant victimization by blackmailing and debts; the details have been largely suppressed. In India he married (1787, at Calcutta) Jane Ross (1772–1842) and had a

opened—we were all seated at Breakfast.—'What! my bright Eyed Beauty! cried he—& then flinging himself back in a Theatric posture—'& here ye all are—one—two—three—four—[5] Beauties all—' He then ⌐came in, &⌐ with a great deal of humour, played with Dick—How many pities that he has no Children, for he is ⌐extremely, nay⌐ passionately fond of them.[6]

'Well, but, Madam,—so your Father is out—*why* I can never see him!—he calls upon me—I call upon him—but we never meet.—Can he come & Dine with me to Day?—Can he?—

I could not possibly tell.

'Well don't let him send, or make any fuss—if he can come, he shall find Beef & Pudding—but I *must* have him on Tuesday—some of his friends are to be with me, & I *must* have him then'—

I could not venture to promise.

'I had not had a moment to myself till this morning, I can't tell when—I |

[*5 leaves cut away*]

February 3rd

It is amazing to me how such a man as Dr. King can have ingratiated himself into the good graces & Acquaintance of the first men of the Nation, which he really has. It would be curious to discover by what method he has so raised himself above his possible expectations—at least, above what his friends could conceive he formed! When he left Lynn about 9 Years since, he knew—Nobody, I was going to say—And now, he is acquainted with all the men of Letters in England! He is Chaplain to the British Factory at St. Petersburg, & perhaps he owes his happy connections to having been Abroad,—though, at least in my opinion, he has not much the appearance of a *Travelled Gentleman*.

large family of perhaps 16 children. Apparently repenting his earlier behaviour, he became a convert to Methodism and was from 1795 till his death headmaster of the Orphan School of Kiddepore. See *JL* i, pp. lxxiii, 203 n. 50; below, *passim*.

[5] Presumably Dick, FB, SEB, and Bessy Allen; Charlotte was at school in Norfolk.

[6] Garrick was rumoured to have had several natural children, including the actor Samuel Cautherley, whose career he assiduously promoted. He took a strong interest in the welfare of his brother George's 5 children, and in his will left his nieces Arabella and Catherine £6,000 apiece. See Highfill; Stone, pp. 20–1, 57.

He appointed to bring a Russian Gentleman, & an English Clergyman, both fond of music, to my Father Yesterday, for a ⌐ *Conversatione*. It ⌐was Sunday Evening⌐—but unfortunately my Father was obliged by a sudden summons to attend a Committee for the purpose of settling a Benefit for decayed musicians.[7] Mama was too indifferent to quit her Room[8]—& ⌐I had only Dick with me when these Gentlemen came. Susan made her appearance afterwards.⌐

Dr. King, with an attempted Politeness, introduced them— 'Mr Pogenpohl,[9] *justement arrivé de Russia*'[10]—& Mr Lattice[11] who I found was just returned from Denmark. *Never* was an introduction less requisite than to the first. With the ⌐best bred⌐ address ⌐I think I ever saw⌐ he made his own Compliments in French—I did not dare return mine in the same Language—but I found he extremely well understood English, & spoke it, for a Foreigner, amazingly though as he ⌐ found I perfectly understood him in French, he rather chose, the whole Evening, to speak it, while poor *Fanny Bull*, as my Father calls me, always answered in English.

I never saw a Russian before. Contrary to all my former ideas, I shall in future annex politeness & good breeding to the thought of one. This Gentleman appears about 22—⌐extremely⌐ genteel, in his Person, & agreeable in his Face. His manners ⌐were the most polished I hardly ever

---

[7] The Society of Musicians (now the Royal Society of Musicians of Great Britain) was established in 1738 for the maintenance of aged and infirm musicians, their widows and orphans. Founding members included the composers Handel, Arne, and Boyce; CB joined the Society in 1749. The annual benefit concert at the King's Theatre, Haymarket, was advertised for 14 Feb. but postponed to 21 Feb. because of the death of the Princess Dowager of Wales. See *New Grove*; *LS 4* iii. 1606–8; *Daily Adv.* 18 Jan., 21 Feb. 1772; Scholes, ii. 64; below, p. 194.

[8] EAB, aged 43, was pregnant with her last surviving child, Sarah Harriet Burney, born in Aug.

[9] William Henry Poggenpohl, whom FB describes below as an officer on his travels, was from 1771 an unsalaried member of the Imperial College of Foreign Affairs at St Petersburg. Detailed that year to the Russian Embassy in London, he was promoted to 'titular consul' in 1782. MAR later refers to him as one of FB's admirers (to FB, 17 Feb. 1774, Berg). He was dead by 1814. See V. N. Aleksandrenko, *Russkie diplomaticheskie agenty v Londonie v XVIII v* (Warsaw, 1897; repr. Cambridge, 1971), ii. 350, 396; E. Dodwell and J. S. Miles, *Alphabetical List of Officers of the Indian Army [1760–1834]* (London, 1838), pp. 140–1; IGI; *GM* lxxxiv² (1814), 82.

[10] FB is probably poking fun at Dr King's anglicized French.

[11] John Lettice (1737–1832), poet and divine, DD (Cantab.), 1797, was secretary and chaplain to the British Embassy at Copenhagen, 1768–71. In later years he was tutor to the Beckford family and chaplain to the D. of Hamilton.

observed⌐—his Conversation lively, entertaining & sensible—
⌐his Address truly elegant—& himself a very compleat *real* fine
Gentleman with⌐ out any mixture of foppery & pretension.

I made my Father's apologies as well as I could, &
acquainted them that I expected him Home ⌐again⌐ soon. Mʳ
Lattice looked a good sort of half stupid man enough—the
Russian ⌐seated himself next to me, &⌐ immediately entered
into Conversation. | It is amazing with what ease & facility
Foreigners in general converse with strangers. Poor Mʳ Lattice
was in the Room near half an Hour before he ventured a Word.

Dr. King, *by way of Joke*, said he was very sorry to hear
Mama was so *shabby*.—¹²

'So *shabby*! said the Russian with a smile, j'ai toujours—I
had always understood that Word in a ⌐different⌐ sense!—'

'Why,' cried the Dr., 'I don't know whether Mʳˢ Burney
taught *me* that word, or I, *her*.—'

Presently after, some other such Word being used, the
Russian drolly said '*Cela vaut autant que shabby*!—'

'⌐Upon my Word, this Gentleman, said I, has not only learnt
to speak our Language well, but to *discriminate* its criticisms.'⌐¹³

They extremely admired the beautiful Dick, when I called
⌐him⌐ *malcheek*—I suppose I spell the Word terribly,—it is
Russ for Boy, as Dr. | King had told me. M. Pogenpohl
Laughed heartily at my speaking it—I told him I was too proud
of knowing a Russ Word, not to publish it. 'But did Dr. King,
cried he, teach you *that* Word?—O fie!—that can give you no
idea of the softness of our Language.—'

'M. Pogenpohl,' said the Dr., 'will teach you much better
than ⌐me.⌐—but did not I tell you some other Word? ⌐did
not I?⌐

'No, indeed.'

The Russian then ran on most fluently, repeating Russ
expressions & Words of soft sounds,—&, if I may trust to his
manner, soft meaning!—I observed Dr. King Laughed, and [so
I]¹⁴ did not dare repeat them after him, though he stoped [*sic*]
for that purpose—& said *sallimani*¹⁵ or *some such word*, several

---

¹² In the sense of unwell or out of sorts (Scottish and Northumbrian dialect; see *SND* and *EDD*).

¹³ i.e., its distinctions or subtleties; an obsolete sense (*OED* s.v. Criticism 4).

¹⁴ Inserted by FBA.

¹⁵ Perhaps *tselui menia*, i.e., 'kiss me'.

times over.—& appealed seriously to me, to judge if it was not a more pleasing Word than malcheek?—

'O,' cried I, 'I shall never remember so much at once—⌐I have not a *Head* for so much.—'¬ |

'*Mais, si mademoiselle voulez bien me donnez*[16] *l'honneur de repeter mes Leçons*—'

Dr. King, by way of wit, I suppose, then amused himself with saying some Russ too;—What it meant, I know not; but M. Pogenpohl exclaimed—'O fie!—' which at the same Time raised my good opinion of *him*, & lessened it of the Doctor, who was inexcusablc if he said any thing reprehensible, even in an unknown Language. The Russian, ⌐I will venture to affirm, contented himself with *drollery*, without glancing towards indelicacy—¬ Though I must confess, there was so much archness in his look, that I did not chuse to ask the meaning of what he said.

He told me he had been 5 months in England. 'But when I first came,' said he, 'I learnt nothing:—I spoke only French with my sisters;[17]—Afterwards,—Lord—Morris[18] (I believe you would call him in |

[*top of next page cut away*]

though,' said I, 'they may talk so much as to save you the trouble of speaking? if you only desired ⟨to learn⟩ the Language, indeed, the Ladies may be very proper!'

⌐When I first mixed with them, I just essayed to say 10 words of French with 2 of English, with very bad pronunciation,—'

And now, said I, you just ⟨reverse⟩ it, & speak 10 Words English to 2 French—'

'*Du moins, je l'éspere avant de quitter l'angleterre*—

'He does not deserve praise, said the Dr., for his English, for he did not teach himself—the Ladies—'

'*C'est un[e] reconnaissance*, cried he, which advanced me—'¬ |

[*top of page cut away*]

---

[16] Changed by FBA to 'veut bien me donner'.
[17] Not further identified.
[18] There was currently no one of that title in England. Poggenpohl perhaps meant Ld. *Mount*morres, i.e., Hervey Redmond Morres (*c.*1743–97), 2nd Visc. Mountmorres.

When Tea was over, I began to be uneasy at my Father's not returning. Dr. King, I saw looked displeased;—but the politeness and liv[e]liness of the Russian, who was too ⌐well bred⌐ to appear dissatisfied, soon disipated my anxiety. He ⌐prevented the conversation's ever dropping, &⌐ never once seemed to have any thing wanting, or any End unanswered in his Visit: While Dr. King looked at his Watch;—listened attentively to every Rap ⌐at the Door—⌐started whenever the parlour Door opened, & was in visible concern the whole Evening.

Music was now proposed. M. Pogenpohl had often heard Bach of Berlin,[19] & by his conversation shewed so fine a taste & so good a judgment of the art, that ⌐ niether Susan nor I could be induced to touch a Note. Indeed we never do: though M. Pogenpohl's great love of music made me more than ever regret my deficiency. We however, ⟨pe⟩rsuaded Mʳ Lattice to Play, which he did, in a horrible old-fashioned style;[20] in so much, that I did not dare meet the Russian's Eyes, I was so sure it must be ridiculous to him.

After this, both Mʳ Lattice & the Russian most furiously attacked me to play ⌐—I really recollect with pain the earnest entreaties of the latter. Yet I could not—I did not dare comply.—He said every thing that the most earnest politeness could suggest, in the most beseeching manner to persuade me—I was really distressed—yet could not for my life prevail with my self to ⌐ make an attempt—though the almost irresistable Russian, by his rhetorick & entreaties did once so entirely overpower both my Judgment & inclination, as to make me move involuntarily towards the Harpsichord, for it seemed impossible to me to any longer refuse him—but Susan happened to stand before me & I absolutely was so struck with the ridiculous figure I should make in her Eye, that I recoiled—but really unable to stand his persuasions, I *made my Escape* to another End of the Room. From the moment I entertained the

[19] Carl Philipp Emanuel Bach (1714–88), 2nd surviving son of Johann Sebastian Bach, who was his teacher. Known as the 'Berlin Bach' or 'Hamburg Bach', he was Court harpsichordist to Frederick the Great at Berlin, 1740–68, and Kantor and music director of Hamburg, 1768–88 (*New Grove*). CB met him later this year at Hamburg; see *Tours*, ii. 211–21.

[20] FB probably means that his playing was stiff and inexpressive. Lettice presumably had not learned CB's method 'of adding neatness to brilliancy, by curving the fingers, and rounding the hand, in a manner that gave them a grace upon the Keys', a technique which FBA says CB 'invented' as a young man (*Mem.* i. 29).

slightest idea of playing, my very knees shook under me, so much that I could hardly support myself."

He then made a similar attack up[on] "Sukey"—who, after a long defence, sat dow[n] "as was most sensible for her to do, for such extreme *hipishness* [*sic*][21]—I can use no better word—as mine serves only to make myself troublesome to others & uneasy to myself—however, I take all the pains I can to overcome it."

"Sukey" had just finished her first movement—when Dr. King hastily & eagerly made his Bow.—He had sat upon Thorns some Time, & when I made all the speeches I could for my Father, he told me *he was a macaroni; invited Company to his House, & then went out*!—And, indeed, but for the Russian's peculiar address & politeness, I should have been in an exceeding disagreeable situation, for they came between 6 & 7—& it was $\frac{1}{2}$ past 9 before they offered to go—& yet, no Dr. Burney appeared!—

[*bottom of page cut away*]

"'It is so difficult a thing, said the Dr., with an air of importance, to find an Evening when these two Gentlemen [Poggenpohl and Lettice] can be together!'—Mr. Lattice accepted my apologies very easily. I could not forbear most particularly making them to the Russian, because he seemed least to require them by his ease & contentment, yet I was very sure he was far the best judge of politeness or its failure in the Room, & though he appeared most satisfied, I doubt not but he was most—*surprised*, shall I say?—

I was charmed to hear him say when I told him how sorry my Father would be at having missed them, that"

[*bottom of page cut away*]

"It was certainly a very singular visit. They must doubtless be very much surprised at spending the Evening with two Girls, when they came with such different expectations.

The Russian is one of the most accomplished & elegant young men I ever saw. And at the same Time, he is fond of drollery & humour that too seldom, I believe, is united to

[21] Low spirits or hypochondria; *OED* cites John Ash, *The New and Complete Dictionary of the English Language* (1775).

politeness. He is an Officer, & on his Travels. He has been in England 5 months. I am extremely surprised at the proficiency, in so short a Time, he has made in learning our Language. But he is not only uncommonly *agreeable*, he appears to me to be really *clever*.⌐ Dr. King & Mʳ Lattice entered into a Dispute with him concerning the *beaux Esprits* of his & of our ⌐Nation in which he shone amazingly.⌐ He seems to love his Country with a Patriot warmth, yet, with the best grace in the ˡWorld, he gave up to us Philosophy and Poetry.—the former with a smile, that drolly implied our too great tendency that way. Civil Law, &c—he strenuously supported his right to, & indeed, his Antagonists had not much to urge against him. ⌐But, with all the fire of Youth & vivacity, he constantly maintained as assertive, as elegant a politeness, as the Coolness of Age & deliberation could ever have arrived at.⌐ Dr. King, who is really ill bred in an Argument, & Mʳ Lattice, who is a plain common sort of man, both, like true John Bulls, fought with better will than justice for old England, giving every virtue & science under the sun ⌐preferably to her yet I could not but observe, that when they were most violent, the unassuming modesty and ⟨elegant politeness⟩ of the Russian insensibly ˡ silenced & conquered them.⌐

Dr. King was absolutely ridiculous. He ⌐gave England credit for *Every* thing, though he did not understand himself what he talked⌐ of. My Father has often observed of this man, that he has a knack of talking for 3 Hours, upon any given subject, without saying Any thing! For my own part, I very frequently, after a long Argument, have endeavoured to recollect what he aimed at; or even what he said,—in vain!—for he has *no meaning*, & therefore dives in the dark for one.

To regard it in no other light—would any man of common ⌐politeness,⌐ amuse a Foreigner with exaggerated praises of England, grossly given at the Expence of all other Nations?— ˡ

'Our Universities, Sir, said he, are the only schools for learning. They bring forth Geniuses superiour to all the World.—'

'Are they then,' said the Russian, archly, '*all* Geniuses, Sir?'

'They are the Noblest schools in the World,' said the Doctor,—

'You think them superiour to *all* others, Sir? cried Mʳ Pogenpohl, naming some one which I have forgot.

'Undoubtedly, Sir. What Nation has brought forth such men as ours?—have we not Lock?[22]—'

'Oh oui!—& you have Newton![23]—but then, have we not Volfe[24]—& Beraman[25]—was not he the Father of Civil Law?—Who have you, Sirs, in that Class?—'

'Why as to that—' said the Doctor—'As to that,' repeated Mr Lattice—'I can't say—' —'But, Sir,' continued the Doctor with vehemence, | which, rude as it was, was ⌐really⌐ *put on*, to give himself imaginary consequence;—'*but*, Sir, are we not superiour to all the World in Astronomy?—in Natural History?—in Poetry? Philosophy?—in musick?'—

'*La musique!*' repeated Mr Pogenpohl—'la musique!'—& flung back, as if he felt the utter impossibility of arguing with a man so imposing & so very ignorant.—For ⌐I could not help myself bursting into Laughter—⌐Give *England* music!—⌐Good Heaven!—But how absurd in Dr. King, to speak, & so decisively too, of a subject, he is totally unacquainted with! ridiculous pretention!⌐

Mr Lattice too, then took up the argument. He is however, really modest, & gave his opinions with diffidence. But his taste is terribly *fogrum*[26] & old fashioned. He ⌐therefore⌐ began an Eloge on our English music & | Performers. Dr. King, without knowing what he said, joined with him. For I am sure he does not know at all the music of one master, or even one Nation from Another.

'And pray, Sir?' cried the Russian, drily—'Who are they?—your English Composers?'—

---

[22] John Locke (1632–1704), English philosopher.

[23] Sir Isaac Newton (1642–1727), English mathematician and natural philosopher.

[24] Poggenpohl probably means Christian Wolff (1679–1754), German philosopher and mathematician. A systematizer and popularizer of the doctrines of Leibnitz, his philosophy held sway in Germany until the Kantian revolution. Another possibility is the German-born Russian academician Caspar Friedrich Wolff (1734–94), biologist, author of the theory of epigenesis (*DSB*).

[25] Perhaps Just-Henning Böhmer (1674–1749), a German legal writer who published in 1709 the highly regarded *Introductio in ius publicum universale*, which gives a definitive account of European civil law at the beginning of the 13th c. He later turned his attention to ecclesiastical law. Like Christian Wolff, he was a professor and sometime chancellor of the University of Halle (*NBG*).

[26] Yorkshire dialect for old-fashioned, out of date; cf. 'fogy'. CB acquired the term from Fulke Greville, who adopted it 'for whatever speech, action, or mode of conduct, he disdainfully believed to be beneath the high *ton* to which he considered himself to be born and bred' (*Mem.* i. 46). See *OED*; *EDD*.

'Who, Sir?', cried the Doctor—'why—why we have Smith![27] —There's a great man!—'

'But he, Sir,' answered M[r] Pogenpohl, 'wrote *on* music—I only speak of music for the Ear.—Only tell me *who* are your Composers.'

M[r] Lattice paused. Dr. King, too *bright* to consider, named Handel[28]—Ha! Ha! Ha!

'O—pardonnez moi, monsieur—Handel was not an *English* Composer!—But you all tell me of your excellent English music—& yet nobody will name any Composer to me!—'

'Why Sir,' after some hesitation said M[r] Lattice—'We have Avison[29]—& Worgan[30]—& Stanley[31]—' |

[*A leaf or leaves have been cut away. The* 'sweet Innocent' *Harriet whose death is reported in the following passage may have been an otherwise unrecorded child of CB and EAB, born the preceding year. The naming of their next child 'Sarah Harriet' lends some support to this conjecture. The letter from SC is missing, and the nurse has not been identified.*]

[r]may envy her innocent little life, & early End!—The melancholy Letter which brought the fatal tydings was from Mr. Crisp to me. Mama is gone to spend a month with her mother at Lynn, in hopes of entirely recovering her Health by change of Air. She was, however, prepared to hear of the poor Harriet's

---

[27] Dr Robert Smith (1689–1768), English mathematician; author of *Harmonics or the Philosophy of Musical Sounds* (1748; 2nd enlarged edn. 1759) and *Postscript upon the Changeable Harpsichord* (1762). CB's copy of *Harmonics*, 'Cambridge, 1749', is listed *Mus. Lib.*, p. 36. See *New Grove*; J. C. Kassler, *The Science of Music in Britain, 1714–1830* (New York, 1979), ii. 948–53.

[28] George Frideric Handel (1685–1759). Born in Germany, he settled permanently in England in 1712. CB was introduced to Handel by Dr Arne in 1745 and has left a number of valuable personal impressions and anecdotes of the composer, as well as general assessments of his work. See 'Mem.' No. 30 and n. 5.

[29] Charles Avison (1709–70), English composer, conductor, writer on music, and organist. He was the most important English concerto composer of the 18th c. (*New Grove*).

[30] John Worgan (1724–90), organist and composer. As a composer he was gifted but considered old-fashioned because of his adherence to the style of the late Baroque (ibid.).

[31] John Stanley (1712–86), the famous blind English composer and organist. The Burneys were friends of Stanley and his wife (m. 1738) Sarah née Arlond (d. by 1786), who is in FBA's 'List' for this year. Also listed is his sister-in-law and amanuensis, Ann Arlond (living 1786), who lived with the Stanleys. See *New Grove*; G. Finzi, 'John Stanley (1713–1786)', *Tempo*, xxvii (1953), 23.

Death, by ⟨a full⟩ account of her illness. She had all possible care, we have great reason to believe, taken of her, Mr. Crisp, Mrs. Hamilton & Miss Cooke seeing her Daily. The Nurse was fond of her to an uncommon degree, & tender to her as to her own. It would have been a dreadful consideration, that the sweet Innocent had been lost from neglect. |

I must now go a month back.

I finished my last account with relating the disappointing visit which Dr. King, Mr. Lattice, & Mr. Pogenpohl made. My Father returned⌐ soon after they went. He had been detained greatly against his Will ⌐& unavoidably⌐ at the Committee. He was extremely vexed, & much the more, on hearing from us what he had lost in missing the Russian, whose Taste in music alone, was enough to excite in my Father a good opinion of him. And we spoke so much in his praise, that he declared he *must* see him.

He called on Dr. King the next Day—& made his apologies & peace, & settled to have the same ⌐meeting,⌐ if the Dr's friends were disengaged, the following ⌐Sunday⌐ [9 Feb.]. Mr Burney & my sister came to meet them. ⌐Their curiosity was raised to see the Young Russian. My⌐ Father sent also ⌐in the morning to Mr. [Daines] Barrington to invite him to bring a friend of his, | Mr. Hudson,[32] who had long been desirous to hear Mr. Bur⟨ney,⟩ in the Evening.

My sister ⟨& myse⟩lf were up stairs when they came⌐ [xxxxx *8 lines*]

⟨Dr.⟩ King with his accustomed parade, ⟨introduced⟩ his ⟨frien⟩ds to Mama & my sister—⌐[xxxxx *1½ lines*] till Dr. King, seeing me, turned to Mr. Pogenpohl, & cried 'There's your old Acquaintance!' And then—[xxxxx *2–3 words*] | [xxxxx *2 words*] ⟨said⟩ Mr. Pogenpohl ashamed, bowing, to me—Ah! vous voila Mlle!—je suis bien aise de vous voir—mais je me res-souviens bien que vous n'avez pas voulu me toucher le Clavecin—et cela m'a donnè tant de chagrin!' 'Indeed 'twas impossible,' I answered—but he Continued his reproaches—&

talking to my Father, 'Monsieur, said he, cette Demoiselle—je l'ai *tant* demande de jouer!'

My Father laughed, & I took the opportunity to march off. When we were seated, I happened to sit between Hetty & Mr. Pogenpohl, who I had the pleasure of a great deal of Conversation with. He called Dick *un tres joli Malcheeke*, & told me again, that I ought to learn *salimani*—and⌐ speaking of the Death of the Princess Dowager of Wales, which happend 2 Days before[33]—'This is a very dull Week for strangers,—said he,—no Diversions!—no any thing!—all shut up!—¦

⌐The Town will be very dismal till she is buried.'⌐

'She is not, I think, ⌐returned he,⌐ *very* much regretted by the Nation?—but *I*—I regret her *very much*!—She is *great loss* to strangers!—'

⌐The Tea things were then brought to me—& my Father came & seated himself next to Mr. Pogenpohl with whom he entered into a very lively Conversation concerning music, musicians, &c,—& they were niether, I fancy, the less pleased to find their Tastes exactly the same for what [xxxxx *3 lines*] But their Conversation was soon interrupted, by the Entrance of Mr. Hudson. Mr. Barrington was engaged. As soon as he had paid ¦ his Compliments to my Father, he advanced to Mr. Pogenpohl, whom I found he had known at Bath—mutual congratulations & Enquiries over, we again, took our places.

Mr. Pogenpohl had paid his court to Bessy violently the last Sunday, & she, contrary to her usual custom, was extremely shy. The reason was, that Dr. King told him that Bessy spoke French very well, when in fact she has but lately begun to learn it. When she appeared again, Mr. Pogenpohl, with much drollery, renewed his sollicitations that she would speak to him. 'Est ce que vous ne voudrez jamais faire connoissance avec moi, Mlle?—pourquoi me fuyez vous?

Bessy, not understanding a Word, would have run away, but he caught hold of her Frock. 'Ah, Mlle, vous ne m'echappez pas—vous voila prisonniere!' ¦

---

[33] Actually the day before. Augusta, Princess Dowager of Wales (b. 1719), widow of Frederick Lewis, Prince of Wales (1707–51), mother of George III, died 8 Feb. and was buried 15 Feb. in Westminster Abbey. She had long been the object of scurrilous attacks because of her close relationship with George III's favourite, Ld. Bute. See *The Letters of Junius*, ed. J. Cannon (Oxford, 1978), p. 220 n. 1; Horace Walpole, *Last Journals*, ed. A. F. Steuart (1910), i. 17.

Finding it in vain to endeavour to make her speak French he began a Conversation with her in English, for Bessy, though half ashamed, was not a little pleased with the flirtation.⌐ I could gather by what he said—though all *in badinage*, with what ridicule—perhaps contempt—he had remarked the prejudiced opinions our Nation in general entertain of the Russians—the droll absurd account he gave her of his Country, could have no other meaning.

'Will you not go to Russia with me? said he—O—you will admire it beyond expression!—' 'No,' cried Bessy, 'I should not, I am sure I should not like your Country—'

'No!—why?'

'Oh—I don't know!—but I should not like it.'

'O yes, you would;—very much—if you will go with me— you will find it charming.—you should live in the Woods, with wild Beasts?' |

⌐'O, no I would not—'⌐

'O yes—you would like it vastly!—you should always be with a Tyger, or a Lyon, or a Wolfe—or some such fine Beast—'

'No, no—I won't go—'

'O yes—very agreeable!—& you should live on high mountains, covered with snow—& sit upon ice.—& you should Eat Trees—and sometimes Hay;—& you should have Grass & briers for sauce—'

'O no—I should not like it at all—'

'O yes!—very good!—very excellent!—& you should have the sea always before you; & the Waves should dash against you—& you should Dress in Tyger's skins—'

'O no, indeed Sir, I won't go!—'

'O very agreeable!—you will like my Country.

⌐'Aren't you a French man?—'⌐ |

'A French man?—for why do you think me a French man?'

'I don't know, Sir;—because you are one—'

'I a French man!—look at me another Time!—do I look like a French man?'

'Yes, Sir.'

'In what? tell me?—'

'Why I don't know, Sir. — — because you don't look like an English man—'

'No?—look at me another Time!—why don't I look like an English man?—'

'Why—because an English man don't wear such a thing as this.' taking hold of his shoulder knot—

'O yes, they do—the English Officer wear all the same—only they have silver, & mine are Gold.[34] And don't you like that?'

'Yes—I like it very well—but an English man does not wear such a Coat as this.' |

'O yes—it is only a Uniform—all Officer wear their Uniform.—And now what have I like a French man?'

'Why—this thing here—' taking hold of a Gold tassel hanging to his sword.

'O yes—very common. Nothing in that. & now—look at me another Time—'

'Why *this* is not like an English man—' pointing to the scarf round his Arm.

'O—every Officer wear it—it is only for mourning, for the Princess of Hesse[35]—& it will be soon for the Princess of Wales.—'

Bessy, quite at a loss, broke from him, & ran to Dr. King.

'Ah, Mlle, cried he, vous aimez le Docteur mieux que moi,—mais c'est faute de votre bon Gout!

⌐Hetty & I could not help observing to the Doctor Mr. Pogenpohl's complete knowledge of our Language, for his short⌐ |

[*Here some 12 leaves have been cut away. The* 'she' *following may be MA and the* 'affair' *her involvement with Martin Rishton. It is apparent from her letter to FB, 6 Apr. 1772 (Berg), that she had confessed to being infatuated with Rishton in a missing journal or letter to FB. See below, p. 222.*]

⌐-tion so she had not received it—I think with nothing but dread of that affair, in relation to her—or ourselves but

We hear often from Mama who is better.⌐

---

[34] In fact some English regiments wore gold shoulder knots, others, silver (*ED* i. 160 n. 1).

[35] Princess Mary (1723–72), 4th daughter of George II and Queen Caroline; aunt of George III; m. (1740) Friedrich II, Landgrave of Hesse-Cassel. She died 14 Jan. at Hanau; the news reached London 25 Jan. (*YW* xxiii. 375 and n. 11).

[April 1ˢᵗ—]³⁶

A new month, to my great regret, is begun—How fast, how imperceptibly, does Time fly, where the mind is at ease!—
⌐Barsanti ⟨has come⟩ here often lately. She improves upon me every time I see her. She is really excessively clever. She has talents that I am sure will in Time, in the style of life she is designed for,³⁷ raise her to the highest pitch of Fame & I have the greatest Hope that she will deserve the noblest of Commendation, namely that she will preserve an unsullied Reputation in the midst of Danger, for she is a very good Girl, she has formed herself the most amiable relations, & listens with a determination to profit, to what her friends form for her. I never met with a Character more happily attentive ╎ to advice, or more desirous of hearing it. Giddy & thoughtless as she is, if she had not these good qualities how dreadful a situation would her's be. She has spoken to me all her Parts, & insisted on my frankly telling her my opinion which I generally do, & never without finding her ready & willing to profit from the smallest hint— what she most fails in is the pronunciation of Words. She has the art of mimickry in the greatest perfection I ever saw. I doubt not that not a soul, even of our Family, has escaped it—it is a dangerous talent but in her profession, it will be a very shining one.⌐

I Drank Tea last Saturday [28 March] with Mʳˢ Strange. I am very glad to find her Journey to Paris defered till June.³⁸

---

³⁶ Inserted by FBA.

³⁷ As an actress. CB negotiated a 3-year contract for her with George Colman, beginning at 3 guineas a week the first season and increasing to 4 and 5 guineas. SC, in a letter to FB 11 Aug. 1772 (Essex), mentions having seen 'a faint Sketch of Mʳ Colman's Plan about [Barsanti's] first appearance . . .'. She made her début at Covent Garden 21 Sept., opening the season with a dramatic 'Occasional Prelude' which Colman had written especially for her. The 'Prelude' was designed to highlight her talent for mimicry, which FB mentions below; in it she imitated some of the leading Italian and English singers of the day. (She evidently had enough singing voice left to bring this off.) She succeeded well in the 'Prelude', which was repeated for 11 nights, and on 23 Oct. she was given her first big role, Estifania in *Rule a Wife and Have a Wife*. Letitia Hawkins reports in her *Anecdotes* that the very day of Barsanti's début her aged father Francesco suffered a stroke at the dinner table. This must have put a great additional strain upon Barsanti and makes her success all the more noteworthy. Her father survived another 3 years, dying in 1775. See Highfill; E. R. Page, *George Colman the Elder* (New York, 1935), pp. 199–200; vol. ii.

³⁸ She did not go go. About this time she was called to Scotland to the death-bed of her cousin, Henry Bruce of Clackmannan. She had hoped to visit again her brother

A Gentleman was sitting next to her when I went in, whom I
thought I had met before, but remember very imperfectly—&
as he did not speak to me, imagined myself mistaken. But at
Tea Time, Dr. Smyth[39] came in—he addressed me by my
Name, & asked | after my Father—'God bless me,—cried this
Gentleman—why is this a Daughter of Dr. Burney?—' 'Yes'—
cried Mrs Strange—'My dear Miss Burney—(cried he, rising &
embracing me with great cordiality) how glad I am to see you!—
but why do you wear this great thing over your Face?—(turning up my Hat) why it prevented my knowing you.'[40] Quite
unable to recollect who he was, I told him I fancied he was mistaken, & meant my sister—'Oh no'—cried he—'I know your
sister too—I know your married sister—& your sister Charlotte.'—Still I could not help doubting, though he assured me
he was my old Acquaintance—'I knew you, said he, in Poland
Street—but I wonder *you* should forget *me*,—I thought I was
too *big* to be forgotten!'—seeing me still perplexed, he asked
my Christian Name—when I told him—O aye, cried he—Miss
Fanny—why I knew Miss Fanny very well—I used to meet you
at Mrs Pringle's—

Then—in a moment—I recollected Mr Scot!—I was both
ashamed & surprised at having forgot him.—[But he is much
altered.][41] |

I was extremely glad of the opportunity of enquiring after my
old friends—he told me that Mrs Pringle was *not* gone to the
East Indies—but to the Isle of Wight, to try whether sea Bathing would be of any service to her youngest Boy,[42] who, poor

Andrew Lumsiden, whom she met at Paris the previous Aug. after a separation of
25 years. See Dennistoun, ii. 139, 143.

[39] James Carmichael Smyth (1741–1821), physician and medical writer; MD (Edinburgh), 1764; FRS, 1779; physician extraordinary to George III; FRCP, 1788
(W. Munk, *Roll of the Royal College of Physicians of London* (1878), ii. 383–5). Smyth was
friend and family physician to the Stranges. Mrs Strange had recommended him to FB
during one of CB's illnesses (undated letter to FB, Barrett). This probably occurred in
Feb. 1771 when CB collapsed and was confined to bed for several weeks; presumably
Smyth was called for during Dr Armstrong's absence (see Lonsdale, p. 100).

[40] The current fashion of wearing large hats turned down over the face is mentioned
by Horace Walpole in a letter to Lady Ossory, 14 Nov. 1774: 'The only time I saw Lady
Mary Somerset she had moulted her feathers [ostrich feathers for a head-dress] and
wore a hat over her nose, so I only fell in love with her chin' (*YW* xxxii. 216–17).

[41] Inserted by FBA.

[42] Mark Pringle, namesake of his father. He may have been dead by 1791 as he is not
mentioned in the will of his brother Robert, dated 1 Feb. 1791 (PCC, prob. 30 Nov.

thing, is an absolute Ideot. And that Captain Pringle was gone to Newfoundland, as Engineer, under Captain Debieg, who was gone as commanding Officer.—"That their stay must be 3 years at least.[43] That Mrs. Debieg remained in England with her Family." I then asked after M[r] Seton—he told me that he had been extremely ill—that he was not gone with his Brother in Law [Debbieg] but that *something*, he understood, *was in agitation for him.*[44]

This Mr. Scot was sub-preceptor to the king.

We are still without Mama.—We live in the most serene comfort possible[45]—we have hardly a wish. |

April 2[d]

Dr. Armstrong called here on Sunday morning [29 March] —my Father was Engaged.—He was in very good spirits, & very droll. He is a most amazing old man.

I told him that I had had the honour at the Haberdasher's Hall, of seeing the Lord Mayor[46]—for the first Time I "saw" One—

'And how did you like him?—'

'O—very well—'

'Why I think, (said he, very gravely) he is somewhat of the human species!—there is some resemblance to mankind in him'—

"We went on Monday to the finest Concert I ever was at, for the benefit of Fischer—[47] every great Performer in England,

---

1793; see also A. Pringle, *The Records of the Pringles or Hoppringills of the Scottish Border*, p. 177).

[43] Presumably in connection with this command Debbieg was promoted to the army rank of major on 23 July 1772. During this year Pringle's memoranda regarding the defence of Newfoundland and its fisheries were sent in, and in 1773 they were considered and approved by the Board of Ordnance in London (American MSS Royal Institution, cited Pringle, p. 320). Despite what FB says here, she saw Debbieg and Pringle back in London the following Feb.

[44] Seton returned to Edinburgh this year upon being given a sublease of the family brewery. The move seems to have been permanent.

[45] An inadvertent reference to the increasing friction between the Burney daughters and their stepmother. More explicit passages in these Early Journals, if such existed, were doubtless destroyed by FBA. See *HFB* pp. 35–40.

[46] The current Lord Mayor was William Nash, who died at the end of this year (on 31 Dec.). See A. B. Beaven, *The Aldermen of the City of London* (1908–13), ii. 133.

[47] Johann Christian Fischer (1733–1800), German oboist and composer. He played an oboe concerto (presumably one of his own) in his benefit concert, given at the Haymarket on Monday, 30 Mar. The other solo instrumentalists, all of whom are

almost, was there—Abel—Fischer—Duport—Ponta—Wendling—Linley—& two sweet singers, Savoi & Grassi.

—Our Cousin Eliza[48] was with us—we were beyond measure delighted.

We saw Mr. Pogenpohl in a side Box seated next to Lady Margaret Fordyce[49] — — | they conversed together the whole Evening—there seems quite a flirtation between them. She, as usual, looked all loveliness & He, all Grace. Had she been unmarried, they would have made the most amiable Couple in the World—though she must be some years the Eldest.⊓—[50]

But the Day after [31 March]—we were happy indeed—for we saw Garrick—the inimitable Garrick—in Bayes![51]—O he was great beyond measure!—Betsy & James[52]—Sue & I made up our Party—I was almost in convulsions with excessive laughter—which he kept me in from the moment he entered, to the End of the Play—never in my life did I see any thing so Entertaining, so ridiculous—so humourous,—so absurd—! Sue & I have talked of Nothing else—& we have laughed almost as much at the recollection, as at the representation.

mentioned by FB, were Carl Friedrich Abel (1723–87), German composer and viola da gamba player; Jean Pierre Duport (1741–1818), French composer and violoncellist; Johann Baptist Wendling (1723–97), German composer and flautist; Thomas Linley (1756–78), English composer and violinist; and 'Giovanni Punto' or 'Ponta' (stage name of Jan Václav Stich) (1746–1803), Bohemian horn player, perhaps the greatest of all time. The singers were Cecilia Grassi (1740–*post* May 1782), Italian soprano, later wife of J. C. Bach; and Gasparo Savoi, Italian castrato singer, active in the London Opera from 1765 to 1777. CB writes of Savoi that he 'had a very fine contralto voice, but was too idle to make the most of it by application and study. . . . His voice, however, was so rich, sweet, and powerful, that though he had no shake, and his execution was heavy and inarticulate, he was heard with pleasure' (Rees). See *New Grove*; Highfill; *LS 4* iii. 1621 and *passim*.

[48] Elizabeth Warren Burney (1755–1832), called 'Betsy' and later 'Blue', another of FB's Worcester cousins. FB mentions below (p. 220) her talent for drawing and 'excellent Heart', and her eulogy in the 'Worcester Mem.', p. 96, notes that 'she was a general favorite' with all her family.

[49] Lady Margaret Lindsay (1753–1814), 2nd daughter of the 5th E. of Balcarres, m. 1 (1770) Alexander Fordyce (d. 1789), banker; m. 2 (1812) Sir James Bland Burges; a noted beauty of the day.

[50] She was in fact only 19. FB estimates Poggenpohl's age above (p. 185) as 'about 22'.

[51] The hapless playwright in Buckingham's *The Rehearsal* (1671). Garrick played the part to 'Great Applause' (William Hopkins, MS Diary, 1769–76, cited *LS 4* iii. 1621). It was one of his most frequent and popular comic roles; during his career he performed Bayes a total of 91 times (Stone, pp. 476–80, 656).

[52] Presumably Elizabeth Warren Burney and JB.

Mr Young Dined with Sue & me to Day. Fortune, I hope, smiles on him again—for he again smiles on the World[53]—He has $^|$

[*A leaf or leaves have been cut away. For the following obliterated passage FBA substituted:*

We—Susan & I—had a long visit to-day [?4 April] from the Genius—as he is called—of the Elder Branch of the Burney race—Richard Burney of Worcester, Junior—a young man of very uncommon talents & parts, & of the utmost sweetness of Disposition. But unluckily for his Fortitude of mind, or modesty of Character, he is so handsome, so elegantly formed, & so lively & amusing from never-failing spirits, that he is quite adored by the whole county of Worcester, & so spoilt that he seems, at times, to be made up of self-admiration—yet, at others, he laughs at his own foppery as cordially as his most sarcastic censurers & then he will take himself off, in his high airs, as drolly & gaily as he takes off with incomparable mimicry, the airs of his neighbours.]

^{r}go out—For my own part, I believe with the most negligent ease—to the fine Gentleman & never once spared him whenever an opportunity offered of *complimenting* him. But he is changeable as the moon—whether he found that this ⟨*fadeur*⟩ would not do—or was himself tired of it—I know not—but by degrees, he quite flung it off—& though he *was* the Fop yet he [was] excessively entertaining. But far from disguising or blushing at his foppery, he seemed to glory in it & to desire nothing more than to be noticed for it. That Nature should have flung away the Talent & Parts she has endowed the young man with, but makes his absurdity more ⟨regrettable!⟩^{𐎠}

He gave us a very entertaining account of his life in the Country, & suffered us to laugh at his affectation with the utmost good-humour, & flung out occasions for it as frequent as possible, even joining in our mirth, & seeming happy to be *smoaked*.[54] What a strange Character! but I will recollect some of his Conversation. $^|$

I observed he frequently rapt his Hand, ⟨in lieu⟩ of a snuff

---

[53] But he was still having financial difficulties in 1773 (Gazley, pp. 82–3).
[54] Made fun of. FBA substituted the more modern 'quizzed'.

Box & He told me he had been *so unhappy* as ⟨to⟩ leave ⌐it¬ in the Country. 'I am amazed, said I, you did not send an express for it!—' 'Perhaps, said ⌐Sukey,¬ your Brother James may make use of it for you—'

⌐But I will follow the Grandison way of writing Dialogue, which is vastly preferable to [xxxxx *2–3 words*]¬

⌐Rich^d¬ O ⌐God¬—Aye—so he will—O, Jem's a fine Fellow,—the Country would be insupportable to me without ⟨him⟩—his coming to Town was the finest thing in the World—he improved more in those few weeks,[55] than he had done for years in Worcester.

⌐Fanny¬ Particularly, I suppose, in his Drawing!—

⌐Rich^d¬ not so—⌐Lord¬ no, no—no—as for Drawing, ⌐Dancing¬—music—all those things were quite out of the question—but then he understood the Cut of a Coat!—knew the size of a Bag[56]—could order his shoes. And then he got the finest easy Carriage—⌐God so¬—you can't conceive any thing like it!—his Arms would fall with such ease!—his bow was so extremely genteel!—& then—nothing disturbs him—if the whole House is in confusion, he is as calm & careless as ever & ⌐O! God¬ he's a fine fellow!—'

(Then he rose, & took him off with inimitable humour, still pretending to admire him—though, in fact, he must be a meer [co]py of himself.)

'Then his Tooth Picks, continued he, are in [the] most exact order—he has 3 different sizes, [fo]r different Times—and he amuses himself with [pi]cking his Teeth half the Day—'

⌐Fanny¬—'I should be afraid it would be Catching.

(By the way *he* does it almost continually.)

⌐Rich^d¬—'Then his Tradesmen!—such wretches!—O [ins]upportable!—here's a shoe!—& then what a [coa]t!—Why that man has not 3 ideas in a Week—[The]n—we do so loll in a chaise!—for when I go [my] rounds, I always take a Chaise & 4—and [we] are *so* much at our ease!—I go from Barborne [on] my own Horse—& so the good Folks there [thin]k I ride her all the way—Ha—Ha—Ha!—but [the] first Inn I come to—I leave the poor Jade behind me, order a Chaise & 4—& as I return stop at the same Inn—& go back to Barbor[ne] on my Horse!'

[55] In 1770.   [56] For a bag wig.

⌐Fanny⌐—This, I own, I much admire—it is so considerate for
the poor Horse—to let her rest;—th[at] is really humane!—'

⌐Rich^d⌐—'O—meerly for the Horse!—& I always feed it with
Corn.—The Creature grows so fat & plump! In truth, I believe
riding saves my life—otherwise my late Hours—Do you know,
[it] stands me in a hundred a year for Chaises—the Time I
spend at Inns—which is very little[—]and there—I can only get
Port & Madeira—for People—hang 'em—won't sell any thing
better—

⌐If he had not looked very archy, & *meant* to be a Coxcomb
himself I would have despised him but his own drollery carried
it off.

Fanny⌐—But I would advise you to set up a fe[w] Inns of your
own—that may accommodate you [bet]ter.

⌐Richd.⌐—Then again, I subscribe to every thing—t[hey]
always bring me all subscription Papers—'Come—[you] know
you'll give us your Name—I know you ar[e] a young man that
encourage these sort of things |

⌐Fanny⌐—O—I dare say—any arts & sciences.'—

⌐Richd.⌐—And then—Ha! ha!—God so—I often sign [th]em
without Reading!—& when I've wrote my [Na]me—I look
over what it's to!—'

Here he burst out a laughing as at his [ow]n absurdity—&
we cordially accompanied him.

⌐Richd⌐—Then they keep monstrous Tables in the
Coun[try]—not that I care for the victuals — — not in the
[leas]t—only the *shew*—nay I dislike their Dishes—[thoug]h I
always Eat them—but then—the Beef is al[wa]ys put on the
side Table!—So I swallow the [rago]ut that is before me—
though, faith, I love the [beef bes]t of all things—but it would
be impossible [to c]all for it, you know.'

⌐Fanny⌐—'O utterly—that would be having such a [*vulg*]*ar
appetite*!'

⌐Rich^d⌐ '—Ha—Ha—Ha—*a vulgar appetite*!—Then again, [I
am] master of the Ceremonies at all the Balls—[& Con]ductor
at all the Concerts—'

⌐'Upon my word! you are a little *improved* since we had
you—

He bit his lip—'I dare say—you think me | *altered*'—

I will not deny it.—

He stayed till near 8—I did not press him to Drink Tea with us—indeed from the moment he came, I determined never to *ask* him to our House—it is a pride, that towards those vain kind of Characters, I do not seek to repress.⌐

He wished us of his Party at the Opera⌐[57]—made his Bow—said it would go off with t[wice] the spirit if we were there—& decamped ⌐Leaving me not a little at a loss whether *most* to despise or admire him.⌐ His Foppery, Air[s &] Affectation are ⌐dreadful⌐—but he has, at ti[mes,] strong humour, great quickness, & in spight of all his follies, is sensible, clever & agreeable. And it is very obvious, that he takes much mo[re] trouble to be a Coxcomb, than he need to be a man of sense. ⌐When we knew him formerly ⟨he w⟩as quite a Boy, but so agreeable, sensible, so gay, so pleasing, & well *natured*, you would not think him the same person.⌐|

[*a leaf or leaves cut away*]

⌐[?wa]s out.⌐

Tuesday, April [?7]

⌐I have a monstrous deal to write—this [is] quite a lively Time to us, though we never [?go] out. But as I know too well that it will [be] dull again ere long,[58] I choose to be mischevous, [for] my future Entertainment.

I return then to Sunday.⌐

About ⌐12⌐ my uncle[59] came,—Mr Richard with [h]im. The former went with my Father into [the] study—& we had a *sequel* to the Saturdays [Con]versation—⌐part of which I cannot forbear [relati]ng.⌐ Speaking of the Clubs in & about Worces[ter,] he spoke with infinite pleasure of being [*Pres*]*ident*—I found they were chiefly musical ones,[60] [&] I

---

[57] See below, p. 207.

[58] Perhaps a reference to the forthcoming Easter holidays (12–19 Apr.).

[59] CB's brother Richard Burney of Barborne Lodge, Worcester.

[60] Richard Gustavus Burney's obituary in the *Shrewsbury Chronicle*, Nov. 1790, notes his memberships in the Worcester and Gloucester Musical Societies, 'to which he lent an essential aid' (cited 'Worcester Mem.' 31). D. Lysons *et al.*, *Origin and Progress of the Meeting of the Three Choirs of Gloucester, Worcester and Hereford* . . . (Gloucester, 1895), p. 8, mentions 'certain musical societies', in 'Gloucester, Worcester, and Hereford', consisting 'of members of the choirs of their respective Cathedrals, and other lovers of music in those cities and their neighbourhood'. The members of these local societies were members at large of the Society of the Three Choirs, which met annually at one of the

asked him how he came to be *always* [cha]irman, which he said
he was—ᴿ'O Ma'am—[Gad]'s so. I'm first Fiddle—so I have
the Chair [of Hon]our—O! it's the finest thing in the World!'—
[Fann]y.—And why?—
[Rich]ardᴿ.—O—Ma'am, why I have it all my own [?way] I
have all power—I direct & fix every ǀ thing—Nothing can be
done without my consen[t.] I have a casting Vote—I make all
the motions—i[n] short, my power [i]s unlimited—'
ᴿFannyᴿ—'And I don't doubt but you make a good use of
it—& keep them all in order—And what else do you do?—'
ᴿRichard.ᴿ—'Why—I put about the wine—take car[e] they all
give their Toasts—First we go rou[nd] with sentiments, & then
ladies—'
ᴿFannyᴿ—'And you take care they take but ha[lf] Glasses? I am
sure;—or at least that they dri[nk] half water?—'
ᴿRichard.ᴿ—O Lord no, Ma'am—that is always a[n] affront—
no, a full Bumper!—ᴿthoughᴿ'
ᴿFanny.ᴿ—'And do you all give Toasts?—'
ᴿRichard.ᴿ—'O yes, Ma'am, every body.'
ᴿFanny.ᴿ—'And how many have you?—Three or [Four?']
ᴿRichard.ᴿ—'Three or Four?—Lord bless me!—t[hree] or four
& twenty!—'
ᴿFanny.ᴿ—'And does every body Drink 3 or 4 [&] Twenty
toasts?—ᴿGood God!—what—ᴿ
ᴿRichardᴿ—'O—we never go beyond the [?twenty-third] ǀ but I
give permission, some times, to some of [th]em to mix a little
Water—we don't like it—[bu]t I connive at a few.
ᴿFannyᴿ—'O fie! that's terrible want of spirit!—
ᴿSusan—Now she's taking the other side!
Fanny. Ay, any for the sake of contradiction!ᴿ—[Bu]t I can't
imagine how you find Time for all [thi]s.'
ᴿRichard.ᴿ—O—with great difficulty—but there would [be] no
living in the Country without.—All Day I [a]m fagging at
business—then in the Evening [I b]egin to Live—We never
break up till morning—[Some] times, I go to Bed at 3—or
4—& am up [ag]ain at 6—& begin my rides—which keep me
[in] Health—But I am convinced that People may [liv]e upon a
third part of the sleep they give [the]mselves, if it is sound.—It is

above cities (in rotation) for several days of performances. The D. of Beaufort was
president of this last Society till his death in 1803.

all custom—[For] my part—I can't bear Bed—it is such [a] total loss of Time!

⌐Fanny.—But how does your Father like this [Wa]y of life?—⌐

Richard—God bless your soul, ma'am, he knows nothing of it. I am never at Hom[e] but on Sunday—My business lays all from Home, & I have not gone to Bed by 12 o'clock till I came now to London with him, not these [?3 months]

Fanny—O—There's nothing like London for sober Hours!—

Richard.—Why (shrugging) we must ⟨*conform*⟩!—[to] Hours— and humours too!—The Night be[fore] I came to Town—nay indeed—I had hardly on[ce] been in Bed, a month before I came—Ther[e] was a Concert at Bewdley which is miles fr[om] Barborne—the night before we set out I was obliged to attend—but that I should not have thought of—only there was a Ball after it—I was⌐ master of the Ceremonies, obliged to call all the minuets—lead out the ladies—fix on the Gentlemen— O! I have such a fuss to settle disputes!—every thing is ref[erred] to me—'Sir—was not this *my* Dance—' —'no, Sir, I am sure it was my turn—' 'now p[ray,]⌐ Sir, tell me, did not this Gentle⟨man⟩ do so—or so—' ⌐God,⌐ it's such fun!—& then put on such a [s]olemn Countenance—& decide with such importance—I am of such Consequence!—Then, I am obliged to study precendency—who is the [o]ldest Family?—Who is the first Title—

⌐Fanny.⌐—'But the worst of all this, is that it calls you into *notice*—it must ⟨be⟩ quite dreadful!—[xxxxx *1 line*]

⌐Richard.⌐ '⟨Why⟩ true—you know I am given to [b]e bashful;—always wanted Courage!—'

⌐Fanny.⌐—'that is what I pity you for!

⌐Richard.⌐—'O—dreadful indeed ⌐(& he spoke very drolly)⌐ to know one's self looked at by every body—that one is the object the most observed in the Room—O, it's horrible! Ha! Ha! Ha!'

⌐Fanny—if you could *but* get a little Courage, you only want that to complete you!

Richard.—True—if I had—you think I might get through the world?

Fanny. Tis a thousand pities that you do not ⌐ but you say so little to ⟨attract the notice⟩ of the world! — —

He then gave us an account of a riot that had happened the

preceding evening at the Opera House,[61] & which ended in 2
men *settling* to fight a Duel. I exclaimed [xxxxx *1 word*] against
the barbarous custom—which he most solemnly defended. For
we got into such a way of speaking ⟨sat⟩irically to one another
that we seldom spoke any otherwise."

About three O'clock, the rest of our company came. And
from that Time, was *my* comfort over—for my uncle is so—
"disagreeable, I must say—that I really do ⟨declare⟩ he set a
damper & restraint upon every thing—"but yet, I should not
have regarded *him*, if Mama had been at Home—but upon my
word, appearing as *mistress of the House*, distressed me beyond
imagination—& before so criticizing an Eye—& one who
makes no allowance—I would not go through such another
Day for the World.[62] |

[*a leaf or leaves cut away*]

"humourous, entertaining & charming.

Our Conversation [xxxxx *4 words*] turned up⟨on⟩ foppery.
Though nothing directly *to*, we said several things *at* him, & he
appeared to feel them all, [xxxxx *2 words*] &, contrary to his
custom, without laughing them off—I even thought, at last,
that he looked *humbled*—& therefore changed the subject." I
had heard his Brother Charles often mention a Mrs Soly,[63] a
woman of fortune & figure, who lives near Bewdley, & had
taken a most violent liking to Richard—in so much as to invite
him to Town with her"—& so, in short, I heard it all over again
from himself, & well recollect his own words. 1st prefacing, that

---

[61] He probably attended the performance, 4 Apr., of Piccinni's *La Schiava* (*LS 4* iii.
1623). No other account has been found of the disturbance he mentions. Such 'riots'
were of course common. *Lloyd's Evening Post*, 10–13 Apr. 1772, s.v. 'April 13' (xxx. 357–
8), reports that on 'Thursday evening [9 Apr.] three persons of rank caused a great riot
in Long Acre, and drawing their swords wounded several persons; they were at last dis-
armed, and carried to Covent Garden Round-house, and Saturday [11 Apr.], after an
examination before Justice Kynaston, were discharged, on paying five guineas each to
the injured parties, &c.'

[62] Later, however, FB notes her uncle's great kindness to her at Worcester (in 1777;
see vol. ii), and in *Mem.* i. 11 she describes him as 'a man of true worth and vigorous
understanding, enriched with a strong vein of native humour'.

[63] Probably the wife of John Soley, Esq. (d. 1775), of Sandbourne, Recorder of
Bewdley, 1745–75 (J. R. Burton, *A History of Bewdley* (1883), p. xli; *GM* xlv (1775), 103).
Richard describes her below (p. 209) as 'about 30, or rather more', with '[m]uch the
look of an Italian'. She and her husband were perhaps Catholics or nonconformists, as
no record has been found of them or their daughters in the local (Ribbesford) parish
registers.

all the things that seemed most ⟨improbable⟩, I had heard before from such good authority as Charles's, & therefore can not doubt. And really we both *drew* him out, whether he would or not. I introduced the subject, by asking him if⌐ he had visited M⌐ˢ Soly since he came to Town?[64]—

'No—he had not had Time to call.

⌐Yet he had found Time to be every Day at [xxxxx *3 words*] Square—*we* forgave him⌐ |

⌐Fanny.⌐—'I hear you go there [Bewdley] very often and are much in favour—'

⌐Richard.⌐—'O!—I am *such* a Favourite! ⟨She⟩ does nothing but flatter me—⌐& say *such* things to me!⌐—though I doubt not but she abuses me behind my back—O—I know she does, by what she says of others.—but, ⌐Lord,⌐ I seem to be every thing there—the moment I go in—she runs up to me—"*my dear Burney*"—& leaves whoever is there, to themselves—⌐& makes me sit by her—though perhaps there may be some body of consequence in the Room—but⌐ she flings herself on her settee— and calls me to her—& there we sit, and laugh at the old codgers—who stare so at us!—Ha, ha—ha!—then she'll begin to tell me the London News of the Winter—& private anecdotes of lady Sarah this, & my lord Duke—& the marquis—& does she run on!—and abuses every body—& I know the moment I am gone, 'tis the same | with me.'

⌐Fanny.⌐—'What a strange Character!—But how every body must wonder at her!—

⌐Richard.⌐—⌐Lord⌐—why they'll come in, & hardly get a word from her—but she lolls at one side & I at the other—& we have all our own talk—And we *so* enjoy their wonder!—and if any body comes in—she'll just turn her Head & say '*How do do?—how do do?*—well, & so Burney—' & then run on again to me, and take no more Notice of them ⌐than if—⌐

⌐Fanny.⌐—'Why I think she can't be much visited—

⌐Richard.⌐—'O—she *won't*—she won't let them come near her—& some times she'll be denied to people when she's at the Window—but she always lets me in — — & says such things to me before her Husband!—[65]

---

[64] The Soleys had a town residence in Holborn (*Alumni Oxon.*, s.v. Soley, John [the son]).

[65] See above, n. 63.

'Her Husband, we both exclaimed; what is He alive?
'O yes—'
❝Fanny❞—'And what sort of man is he? ǀ
❝Richard.❞ A very good natured man (archly) upon my word!—*very* good-natured!—
❝Fanny.❞ But how does he like this strange Conduct?
❝Richard.❞ Why I don't know,—she does not mind him—he's a spruce little Counsellor—but we seldom speak with him—the two Miss S❞olys,❞⁶⁶ the mother & I, get into a Party,—& we leave him as much to himself as if he was not in the Room!
❝Susan.❞ How old is Miss S❞oly❞?
❝Richard.❞ About 15 or 16.—a very fine Girl.—
❝Fanny.❞ What a strange Family it must seem in the Country!'
❝Richard.❞ O ❝God❞ yes!—She sees I *smoak* her, & that has kept me in favour.
❝Fanny. Yet You seem pretty well to enter into her humours—& to understand them.—
Richard. You'd be surprised to hear the things she says to me—such flattery—& insists upon it's all being true—& I laugh! I never laugh any where so much!❞—But she praises People in such a manner to their Faces!—& so many of them believe her—& then—they ǀ are done for!—she'll never see'em again—no,—it won't do!—she gets rid of them as fast as possible. & so she would of me, if I had been taken in. The People at Bewdley are all so *surprised*—'❝God,❞ they say, why how does Burney manage to keep well in that House so long?'
❝Fanny.❞ O—if she saw you believed her, she would soon discard you!—❝but your entering into her humour—But❞ pray what Age is she?
❝Richard.❞ About 30, or rather more. She has very much the look of an Italian—black Eyes, & Hair, & a sallow Complection.—❝O when she was young, what a Coquet she was! She entertains me with histories of her amours⁶⁷ before her marriage & tells me who she *really* liked, & who not—and all before her Husband!—
Fanny. O, I think the better of her for that.—

---

⁶⁶ Described below as aged about 15 or 16 and 13. The younger, 'Bet', was perhaps the Mrs Elizabeth Soley who died in 'John-street, Bedford-row, aged 58', in 1814 (*GM* lxxxiv¹ (1814), 629).

⁶⁷ FBA has noted at the page's bottom: ❝I am sure, by what he sd. of her afterwards that he did not mean what is generally meant by amours.❞

Richard. Why yes—perhaps—but its [*sic*] very—its odd!—
Fanny. It is indeed, that she should talk so at all⌐—but what
does the poor man do?
⌐Richard.⌐ Why he walks about the Room—as I[68] | have seen
other men, at a quick rate, up & down as if for exercise, thus—
⌐(mocking him)⌐ and this he will do for Hours. Then, he
whistles—And sometimes he'll stop & take up my Hat—& put
it on—'my dear—have you seen Burney's new Hat?—' Then
he['ll] walk to the Glass, & turn it about—'⌐Lord⌐, these young
Fellows!'—Then M^rs S^r oly⌐ calls out—'I wish you would let
the Hat alone—you know nothing at all of the matter—do pray
put it down—' —'Well, my dear—I only—' And then he walks
again!—Sometimes he examines my Cane—or any thing that
is new—'pray, my dear, have you seen Burney's Cane?—' &
then she scolds—'M^r S^r oly⌐—will you leave Mr Burney's
things alone?—'
⌐Fanny.⌐ But I can't help pitying the Daughters—
⌐Richard. O they like it of all things. We 4 are always of a
Party—
Fanny. But it's a strange Education for Girls—
Richard. O they have all the best masters, and Instructions that
can be procured—
Fanny. But still, she must be a very improper woman to bring
up young People—⌐
⌐Richard.⌐ Why, really, I believe she is in fact a woman of as
good principles as lives— | &, when she is serious, extremely
humane—
⌐Fanny.⌐ She is the oddest Character I ever heard of—how was
you first introduced to her?
⌐Richard.⌐ Why Milton[69] (n.b. Milton is a Relation of his, &
⌐was formerly assistant to his Father) went there to tune the
Harpsichord—& I believe taught there, some time before I saw
them—O God!⌐ how they do laugh at Milton!—well, one Day
when I was at Bewdley, ⌐⟨just⟩ after my first leaving London,⌐
near 5 years ago, it was settled that I should ride over there with
him. We were shewn into a parlour—Mrs Soly was with Company in Another—So I seated myself at the Harpsichord,

----

[68] The next 2 pages in the MS are blank. FB evidently turned over 2 leaves at once by
accident.
[69] Milton has not been further traced.

& began playing — — soon after, she came in—with such an Air!—& flung [he]rself on a Chair by the Harpsichord, lent on [bo]th her Elbows, & stared me full in the Face!—

⌐'How strange!¬—

⌐I¬ was a little upon the reserve at first, [bu]t I found it would not do—no.—I was [ob]liged to fling it off — — And the Bewdley [Peo]ple think me so different!—for one is ob[lig]ed to Adapt one's self a little to the ˡ Company one is with—so there, I appear so serious & sedate!—& then when they see me at Mrs Solys—I am all Airs & graces & affectation—& so fine!—so much the thing!—⌐You have heard of the Countess of Danorf?[70]—

'Every body has. She was brought up at Mrs. Sheeles's—& ever famous for the most mischievous Girl in the school.'

'Well—about the Time that affair happened between the Duke of Cumberland & lady Grosvenor[71]—'

'In which she got much disgrace—'

'About that time—Mrs Soly—who winks at those kind of things—brought her into the Country, where she thought the affair might not have reached—& while she was there we had such diversion!—'¬

'I am quite sorry for the Miss Solys!—it is terrible to have them brought up in such a manner.'

'O they enjoy it of all things.—⌐And we used to get into such romps—sometimes till morning— ˡ And I had them all to

[70] Lady Camilla Elizabeth Bennet (1747–1821), 1st daughter of Charles, 3rd E. of Tankerville, m. 1 (5 Sept. 1764) Ct. Dennoff or Dunhoff of Poland (d. 25 Sept. 1764); m. 2 (1778) Robert Robinson (*YW* xxxii. 120 n. 20).

[71] Henry Frederick (1745–90), cr. (1766) D. of Cumberland, brother of George III; and Henrietta Vernon (d. 1828), m. 1 (1764) Richard Grosvenor, cr. (1761) B. Grosvenor, and (1784) E. of Grosvenor; m. 2 (1802) Lt.-Gen. George Porter (after 1819, de Hochepied), B. de Hochepied in Hungary. On 1 Mar. 1770 Ld. Grosvenor exhibited a libel against Lady Grosvenor for adultery with the Duke (in Apr. or May 1769). Lady Grosvenor filed countercharges of Ld. Grosvenor's adultery with various women of the town, but Grosvenor was awarded £10,000 and a separation. Lady Dennoff's deposition was the first in the Grosvenor trial; she testified that she saw at her house in Cavendish Square the Duke and Lady Grosvenor in the act of committing adultery. In the *Public Advertiser* 13 May 1770, in a letter signed 'The Temple Rhapsody', she is referred to as 'a noted courtesan in Polish alliance'. 'She will part with her virtue, not for the pardonable enticement of an affection or a handsome figure, but for the mean, despicable consideration of a paltry bribe. Mind she has none.' The 'Tête-à-Tête' portrait in the *Town and Country Magazine* for Sept. 1769 links her and the Duke as lovers. See *YW* xxiii. 165 nn. 14–15; xxxii. 20 nn. 18, 20, and sources there cited; also Edward Gibbon, *Letters*, ed. J. E. Norton (1956), i. 307.

manage—they were all 4 against me at a time & 'twas the finest thing—She is amazingly handsome—'

'You seemed to grow soon acquainted—'

'O yes! the first time I went there after she came down—I went down the Avenue—on Horseback—& met her, walking quite alone—& I took her for one of the maids, as neither Mrs Soly or the Young ladies were with her—so when I came up to her, I stop'd, & said "Pray—is Mrs. Soly at Home"—yes—she said, & I rode on. When I went in—pray—said I—where did you pick up that Pretty maid?—for she likes to have me admire her maids—maid! cried they—oddso—it's the Countess of Danorf!—And she would take the hint from Mrs. Soly, & ⟨tease⟩ me in the same manner—"indeed, Mr. Burney, what Mrs. Soly says is very true"—

'What a strange way of living!'—

'O, she⌐ [Mrs. Soly] knows nothing at all of her Family— she leans both her Arms on the Table, when we go to Dinner, & looks ⌐ about her, as if to see what there is—but she makes her Husband Carve—then she'll peer about—"pray what's that?— in that corner?—what have you got behind that Dish?—it looks Nasty—Burney, you sha'n't Eat that."—Then she takes great pleasure in *pumping* me—& is for ev[er] telling me reports she says she hears—meerly to *pump* me—So I always *Assent*—I never contradict her—"do you really?—" "ay—I hear that such a One—" "do you indeed?—" —Then she'll run on to me about the people she wants me to see—"O Burney, you *must* see lady Betty! you will be quite in love with her—the sweetest Creature—you must see Lady Betty—" Then she used to form *such* schemes for my coming to Town!—& she charged me, if I did not, that I would write to her.

'Upon my word!—'

'O, you can conceive nothing like it—if I am not exact to my time—when I get to Bewdley, I am sure to find a Note waiting for me, ⌐ & such enquiries sent about Bewdley—& often I find 2 or 3 Notes—read this first, wrote upon ⌐one— And if Mrs Soly is not well, all the time I am teaching the Daughter, the youngest Soly comes in every other minute with messages from the mother—though all to the same purpose—such as to desire me to stay Dinner, or she would never forgive me—& so on—& when she *is* in the Room, she engages me in talk the whole time—& the Girl too joins perpetually in that.

'I dare say she improves greatly—

'Then she tells me such ridiculous storys & the Daughter is an excellent mimic—& the moment any body goes out of the Room, takes them off—& then, perhaps *I* think of something that has not struck them either in their manners, or speech, or figure—& then they laugh!—& pay them such compliments—"indeed, Burney you are a *so* & so—indeed you are!"—Then I rise—& Bow—& she ⟨cries⟩ "O God!—⟨"O⟩ⁿ | my dear Madam!—"'

Here he mimicked his own foppery to admiration.

'Then the moment I am gone—I dare say, she calls me Puppy, Coxcomb, Prig, & all the Names she can invent.—Not that I ever heard she did—but she serves every body so. Then she takes great pleasure in telling us of her old favourites—"That was such a sweet fellow!—O Bet!—if you had seen Vincent?—what a sweet fellow!—O God how I loved him!"—& her Husband in the Room all the while!—Ha! Ha! Ha!

'But what can the poor man say?—'

'Say!—why he talks about the Roads—& whistles—"Pray Burney, have you got that place mended in the Road yet?—" Then she'll pull me by the sleeve—"never mind *him*—So, what did he say next?"—"I say, Burney, that's a very bad Road that leads to your | House—when will it be mended?—" "Why, Sir, it's—" "Lord, don't mind *him*—well, who came"—"Pray, Burney, have you heard who was at the Turnpike meeting on Monday?"—Then she always pulls my sleeve, & won't let me answer him—I just turn round to him—"Sir, it's, I think—O God, Ma'am, there was such sport—O, Sir—it's next—so Mʳ such a one—it's next Tuesday, Sir, — — and afterwards, Mʳˢ—"'

He turned from side to side with such ʳdrolleryⁿ that I could almost fancy I saw them, & we laughed till we were tired—

'Then, she'll call the Youngest Girl to me & take off her Cap, to shew me her Hair, which is the finest in the World, and she even makes me feel it—'

'How old is she?'

'About 13—& quite beautiful:—& she says every thing she can in her praise, and | makes me say the same—& then she

tells me, that she is very like me!—& when I come in—
"Burney, I've thought of nothing but you since you were
here—& indeed, I never can look at that Girl without thinking
of you—" though, in truth, the Girl is no more like me than the
moon—nay, she even—you would be surprised—

He stop'd—but we beg'd him to go on—

'Why, she took great pains to *Pump* me, to know how my
affections stood — — &, in short—asked me how I should like
her Bet for a Wife?—Ha—Ha—Ha—but I took her to be in
jest—and I told her—that—I was *engaged*.—But a little while
after, I heard of it at Bewdley—that she had said—why Burney
must have very high views, for he refused my Bet—who can he
be possibly engaged to?—he is very young indeed for any
Engagement of that sort— |

'How provoking for Miss Soly—how dreadful to have such a
mother! to *offer* her—& what a dangerous life for young
people—'

'Why yes—if any body was to take *advantage* of their situation—

'But yet, I think it's ungrateful in *you* not to have visited them
yet—'

'Why, I have had no Time.' |

[bottom of page cut away]

ᴦ[?both] of us laughed till we were quite fatigued. Would to
Heaven, I was but oftener *so* fatigued!—

Well—I have no Time for Comments, so will proceed with
facts, which I am obliged to keep *minutes* of, they multiply so fast.

About 10, the same Evening, Dʳ King called. He goes to
Russia next Week.ᴦ[72] |

*[The bottom of the page has been cut away and, judging by the stubs left, so
have at least 20 leaves following.]*

April 30ᵗʰ

Now for a little Domestic business, after [s]o much *foreign*.

Mama came Home on Saturday Evening [25 April], [i]nᴦ per-
fectᴨ Health, spirits & embonpoint. ᴦShe is quite ⟨recovere⟩d &

---

[72] Dr King attended a Burney musical party in early May, but after that he disappears from FB's journals until 1775, when he reappears with Prince Orlov of Russia,
his 'Patron during his Chaplainship in Petersburg' (vol. ii).

looks very ⟨well⟩ & ⟨much fatter⟩[73] than when she left us. She is [xxxxx *1½ lines*] to make her preserve the ⟨health⟩ she has attained.⁷

We have not heard lately from Geneva, but expect Miss Allen Home next June.[74]

My Father continues in good Health, excellent spirits, and ever in good humour. His Book flourishes with praise, & we hear almost Daily of new Readers & admirers, & if he had Time & inclination for it, he might Daily encrease his Acquaintance among the learned & the Great.—but his Time is terribly occupied, and his inclinations lead to retirement and quiet. If his Business did not draw him into the World by necessity, I believe he would live almost wholly with his Family.

We went yesterday [29 April] to make *a round of visits*, & drank Tea at Lady Dalston's,[75] who is a very good sort of Woman, & a very old Acquaintance of both my Father & mother. I shall take notice of only two of the Houses we stopt at.—And first—we were so happy as to be let in at Mr Garrick's, And saw his new House, in the Adelphi Buildings,[76] a sweet situation.—The House is large, & most elegantly fitted up. Mrs Garrick received us with a politeness & sweetness of manners, inseperable from her.

I explained to Mr Garrick ⌐the affair of the Card [of invitation], which, I⌐ told him, my Father said *required no answer*, as he had given it one himself, by saying at the bottom that *no excuse would be taken*.—

'Why Ay—said he—I could not take an excuse—*but*—if he had niether come *or* sent me a Card!—

'O—he certainly would have done one or the other—'

---

[73] A guess, suggested by EAB's pregnancy.

[74] See below, p. 222. FB's last letter from MA has a London postmark of 6 April (Berg).

[75] Probably Anne Huxley (d. 1776), m. (1742) Sir George Dalston (1718–65), 4th Bt.; MP. No other mention has been found of her acquaintance with the Burneys (Namier; *AR* xix. 229).

[76] The Garricks in Mar. had completed their move from No. 27 Southampton St., to a grand new house in the Adam brothers' Adelphi Terrace. The house was large, in the classical style, with Adam-designed furniture. The magnificent drawing-room had an elaborate plaster ceiling with nine medallion paintings encircling the central circular panel by Antonio Zucchi. Visitors noticed, however, that the rest of the house was mostly gloomy and ill lit. See Highfill; below, p. 243.

'*If* he had not—why then we two must have fought!—I think you have pretty convenient Fields near your House?—'

⸢The other House I mean to mention is that of Mrs. Forbes,[77] a clever Scotch Woman, just returned from Italy, with her two Daughters, one of whom is a Paintress, & for whose improvement, the Family resided 3 years in Italy. Miss Forbes is soft & amiable, & very ingenious in her Profession. She appears to be about 23—Her sister is a large, handsome, maudlin woman. With the eldest, I hope to be better acquainted.⸥

My design upon [the correspondence of][78] Mr Crisp has succeeded to my wish. He has sent me the kindest & most flattering Answer—which encourages me to write again. He says more in three lines, than I shall in a hundred while I live. |

Dr. Hawkesworth called here lately. He has been, & still is, extremely engaged in writing this Voyage round the World, which I doubt not, will be a very charming Book.[79] He is very pressing in inviting my Father and Family to Bromley, where he Lives. I should extremely like such a Jaunt.

I have had the honour, also, of seeing Mr Baretti, Author of the Journey to Spain[80] & many other Books. He is a very good looking man, which is all I can say, as I have not exchanged more than half a dozen Words with him. But I have a most prodigious enthusiasm for Authors, & wish to see all of all sorts. And I believe they find it out, for they all look at me with

[77] Margaret née Aikman, daughter of William Aikman (1682–1731), the painter, and widow of Hugh Forbes (d. 1760), a principal clerk of the Court of Session, Edinburgh. CB had met Mrs Forbes and her family at Rome in 1770 (*Tours*, i. 223, 225). The paintress was Anne Forbes (1745–1834) who this year exhibited 4 portraits at the Royal Academy. A portrait of her by David Allan, 1781, is in the Scottish National Portrait Gallery. Her brother, John Forbes, an army officer, was CB's cicerone at Rome and accompanied him to Naples. Both John Forbes and his mother were still living in 1793. The other daughter has not been further traced. See *AL* 1769, p. 30; *Tours*, i. 203–302 *passim*; Thieme; J. L. Caw, *Scottish Painting Past and Present* (Edinburgh, 1908), pp. 23–5, 49–50; R. Douglas, *Baronage of Scotland* (Edinburgh, 1798), p. 442; *The Bee, or Literary Weekly Intelligencer*, 6 Nov. 1793, xviii. 8–9; *Scots Magazine* xxii (1760), 334.

[78] Inserted by FBA. The letters referred to here are missing. By the end of the following year FB had entered into a 'very particular Correspondance' with SC, entertaining and informative on her side, amusing and instructive on his (see below, p. 319).

[79] See below, pp. 313, 325–7. Hawkesworth was still inviting the Burneys to Bromley in Kent the following Feb., but they apparently never went.

[80] FB presumably means Baretti's *A Journey from London to Genoa, through England, Portugal, Spain, and France* (1770). CB's copy is listed *Lib.*, p. 3. *DNB* lists 22 other works by Baretti by 1772, including the well-known *Dictionary of the English and Italian Languages* (1760).

benevolence.—[though perhaps it is the Nature of literary pursuits & meditations to soften the manners & the Countenance. What would I not go through to see Dr Johnson! Mr. Bewley accepted as a present, or relic, a tuft of his hearth Broom, which my Father secretly cut off, & sent to him in a Frank. He thinks it more precious than pearls.][81] |

⌈Monday⌉ May [4][82]

If my Father was disposed to *cultivate* with the World, what a delightful Acquaintance he might have! We had Yesterday another Noble Concert, at which we had again Celestini[83]— who led *the Band*, & charmed [u]s all with a solo. We had Tacet,[84] also, who gave us a solo on the Flute.

Sir William Hamilton,[85] who my Father knew at Naples, where he was Ambassadour, honoured us *with his Assistance*. He

[81] Bracketed passage inserted by FBA. The incident she refers to occurred in 1760. CB did not confess his 'theft' to Johnson until 1780, when the flattered author sent Bewley a copy of the 1st vols. of his *Lives of the Poets*, addressed 'for the Broom Gentleman'. In 1783 Bewley had the pleasure of being introduced to Johnson by CB and 'conversing a considerable time, not a fortnight before his [Bewley's] death'. See 'Mem.' No. 85 and nn. 3–4, 6–8.

[82] Emended from '5' by the editor. Here, as occasionally elsewhere in the journals, FB is a day off in her date.

[83] Eligio Celistino (1739–1812), Italian violinist and composer. CB first heard him at Rome in Sept. 1770, at a concert in the D. of Dorset's house. He 'is a very neat, and expressive performer. . . . Signor Celestini played, among other things, one of his own solos, which was very pleasing, though extremely difficult, with great brilliancy, taste, and precision' (*Tours*, i. 202; *New Grove*).

[84] Joseph Tacet, 'an eminent performer and master on the German flute, born, we believe, in France; but who came to England so early, and continued here so long, that by forgetting his own language, he spoke English like a native of the island' (Rees). *LS* records performances by him from 1755 to 1775, and he is mentioned in the *A B C Dario Musico* (Bath, 1780), p. 45; he also performed in the *concerts spirituels* at Paris in 1751 (C. Pierre, *Histoire du Concert Spirituel 1725–1790* (Paris, 1975), p. 259).

[85] William Hamilton (1730–1803), cr. (15 Jan. 1772) KB; British envoy to Naples, 1764–1800; archeologist; m. 1 (1758) Catherine Barlow (d. 1782); m. 2 (1791) Emma Lyon (Nelson's Lady Hamilton). CB was cordially greeted by the Hamiltons at Naples on 26 Oct. 1770. Ten days later he took his leave of them 'with infinite regret, as the countenance and assistance with which I was honoured by them, during my residence at Naples, were not only of the utmost utility to me and my plan, but such as gratitude will never suffer me to forget' (*Tours*, i. 260, 281). CB notes, in his article on Giardini in Rees, that Hamilton was one of Giardini's first scholars on the violin in England. In *Tours*, i. 264 he praises Lady Hamilton's performance on the harpsichord: 'She has great neatness, and more expression and meaning in her playing, than is often found among lady-players; for ladies, it must be owned, though frequently neat in execution, seldom aim at expression.'

is mentioned with gratitude in my Father's Book, for his very
great attention to him when abroad; as is his Lady for her fine
Playing. They were then M^r and Mrs Hamilton—but he has
since been created Knight of the Bath. He Played out of
Celestini's Book, &, I believe, very well. [xxxxx *1 line*]

Mr Beckford[86] brought his Flute with him. & Played under
Tacet. He has won all our Hearts, by the extreme openness,
good-humour | & friendly fervency of his manners.

$^\ulcorner$My Father & Mr. Burney, in the full Pieces, played violins.
We had a violin cello player[87] who Sir William brought from
Italy with him.$^\urcorner$

M^r [Uvedale] Price, who I have mentioned formerly & who is
the macarony of the Age, came with Sir William.

Mr Fitzgerald,[88] a very sensible old Acquaintance of the
Family's, was another Hearer as was Mr Bagnall,[89] a yet *more*
sensible *new* Acquaintance.—He is, indeed, a sweet man—his
manners are all gentleness; his Countenance the Picture of
Benevolence,—I hear from my Father that he is learned, fond
of the polite Arts, & himself well versed in them. $^\ulcorner$He seems, in
short, to be all that is proper, & all that is amiable in man.$^\urcorner$

His son & Daughter came with him. The son has just
purchased a Commission in the Guards. He is too insignificant
to deserve further mention. |

Miss Bagnall, too, though modest and obliging, does not

[86] William Beckford (1744–99), illegitimate son of Richard Beckford (1712–56) and
heir to his Jamaican estates, was first cousin of the author of *Vathek*. CB met him at
Rome in Sept. 1770 and was to esteem him always for his 'most excellent taste and
goodness of heart' (CB to FB 4 Oct. 1791, Osborn). See *JL* i. 126–7 and n. 19; *Tours*, i.
201; F. Cundall, *Historic Jamaica* (1915), pp. 362–7.

[87] Sir William's page. 'Mr Hamilton has two pages of his household who are excellent performers, one on the violin, and the other on the violoncello' (*Tours*, i. 261). Not
further identified.

[88] Keane Fitzgerald (d. 1782), FRS; experimental scientist. Fitzgerald had been the
Burney's next-door neighbour and landlord in Poland St. (*JL* iii. 260 n. 3).

[89] John Bagnall (d. 1802) of Erleigh Court near Reading, Berkshire. Described as 'a
learned and rich philosopher', he was perhaps the John Bagnall who was elected FRS
in 1774 (*Record of the Royal Society of London* . . . (4th edn., 1940), p. 425; *Vict. Co. Hist.
Berkshire*, iii. 216). His eldest daughter, Anna Maria Bagnall (*c.*1755–1809), m. (1781)
William Scott (1745–1836), cr. (1821) B. Stowell of Stowell Park, an eminent judge and
friend of CB and Dr Johnson (see CB to SBP ?26 Dec. 1784, Comyn). The son, John
Bagnall, was commissioned an ensign in the 2nd (Coldstream) Regiment of Foot
Guards on 2 July 1771 (*AL* 1773, p. 51). Gone from *AL* by 1775, he was apparently
dead by 1803, when his father's estate passed down to his sisters (*Vict. Co. Hist. Berkshire*, iii. 217).

appear to ⌜merit⌝ a Father [o]f such shining, & winning merit, as M^r [B]agnall, ⌜who, added to his accomplishments, has a Face for a middle aged man, perfectly handsome. If I spoke of his *Countenance* added to his Features, I should say *beautiful*— for it is a Countenance expressive of all that can please & interest.⌝

Dr. King completes my list.

Mr Burney was again the king of the Evening. His Performance will never, I believe, cease to be wonderful, even to such frequent hearers.

When the Concert was over, my Father talked over with Sir William Hamilton, his Italian Expedition.—Sir William is a very curious[90] man.—a very great Naturalist, & Antiquary, he took a House[91]—or for ought I know, built it, within a short distance of Mount Vesuwius [*sic*], on purpose to observe its ⌜motions⌝—& ran ˡ Daily the utmost risque of his life, to satisfy his curiosity. He spoke with great pleasure of the *fine Eruptions* he had seen—& told us that Mount Ætna was now *Playing the Devil*.—He has wrote several accounts of both these mountains to the Royal Society, ⌜which have been printed, &⌝ which, he said, he was now correcting & collecting, to Print them all in one Volume.[92] He is to return in June to Naples, unless there is an Installation, which will detain him, as he has yet received no *star*, only the Gartar.[93] He said he should pass through Germany—'shall you—cried my Father—'why I believe *I* shall go to Germany this summer.—' 'Well—cried Sir William—if you'll go with me, I'll give you a Cook & a Bed.—'

I verily believe, though this was said *en passant*, that my Father will reflect upon it—for he has an insatiable rage of

---

[90] In the obsolete sense of 'skilled as a connoisseur or virtuoso' (*OED* s.v. Curious 6).

[91] The Villa Angelica, a 'small' house at the foot of Vesuvius which Hamilton 'fitted up himself' (*Tours*, i. 260). The Hamiltons' main residence was the Palazzo Sessa.

[92] *Observations on Mount Vesuvius, Mount Etna, and other Volcanos in a Series of Letters addressed to the Royal Society*, pub. 13 June (*Daily Adv.* 13 June 1772). The letters were first printed in the *Transactions* of the Royal Society.

[93] A slip for 'ribband'. Sir William was invested with the ribbon and badge of the Order on 15 Jan. (*London Gazette*, 14–18 Jan. 1772, s.v. 'St. James's, January 15'). On 15 June he and 14 other Knights of the Bath were installed in Westminster Abbey (ibid. 13–16 June); he there received the collar and star.

Sir William and his Lady did not begin their return journey until the autumn, finally arriving back in Naples in early Jan. 1773 after visits to Voltaire at Ferney, to the Court of Vienna, and to the Pope at Rome (B. Fothergill, *Sir William Hamilton: Envoy Extraordinary* (1969), pp. 119–26).

adding to the materials for his History.—and could not go in better Company.[94] |

Sir William has, in a striking degree, ⸢the air of a man of Fashion. He is Guardian to the Duke of Hamilton.[95] His⸣ look is sensible, penetrating & even piercing.—His singularly curious & enterprising turn, seems marked strongly in his Countenance.

To this select Party—had Mr Crisp and Miss Allen been added—we should scarse have wish'd another.

⸢But poor Hetty was not well, & could not come. She is now, thank Heaven, recovered.[96] Betsy, my Worcester cousin, who came to Town chiefly on a Plan of improvement, having some genius for Drawing,[97] is left behind, which I am glad of as she improves upon me. I find she has many good qualities, which her manner, either Cold or blunt, had prejudiced me against. She has an excellent Heart, & is very good tempered, notwithstanding her great foible of taking delight in what is mortifyingly ridiculous or distressing in others. I believe it is only want of reflexion, not of Heart⸣— |

Sunday, May 10th

⸢A Dreadful stupid Sunday after so many charming ones!

We have, however, brighter Prospects in view. My dear Allen is on the Road Home—we may hope to see her next week—I am inexpressibly eager for the Day. Her affairs are, as yet, perfectly safe. Perhaps—& I hope so—they may take a more happy turn than I have apprehended.⸣

My Brother took leave of us last Week In Health & spirits. I should prefer this Voyage to any in the World, if my ill stars had destined me a sailor. I had a Letter from him yesterday, in which he tells me they shall not sail till near July.[98] I have some Hope, therefore, that he will be with us again.

[94] See below, p. 224.

[95] Douglas Hamilton (1756–99), 8th D. of Hamilton, 1769. Sir William was the Duke's cousin.

[96] EBB's illness was perhaps connected with her pregnancy (see below, p. 227).

[97] Her brother Edward Francesco Burney, in a letter to CB Jr. 4 Mar. 1780 (Osborn), calls her 'the Enraged Drawing Mistress' who 'goes sometimes recruiting into Worcester' (quoted Scholes, ii. 35–6).

[98] The letter is missing. On 13 July JB sailed from Plymouth as able seaman on board the *Resolution*, commanded by Capt. Cook on his second voyage of discovery. In Nov. he was promoted to second lieutenant of the *Adventure*, the other ship on the

⌜Betsy has received a very kind Letter from her ⟨Bro⟩ther,[99] in which he very much urges us speeding our visit, & accompanying Betsy, in her return, which will be in June. I have pleasure in the Prospect of the Journey, which I have long wished to make.[1]⌝ |

[*top of page cut away*]

⌜We then heard Millico,[2] the new singer, who disappointed us while my Uncle was in Town. While He sang—I forgot every thing but himself—He is, indeed, a delightful Performer—he sings much in the style of La Bichieli, who we ⟨had⟩ here last summer. It renewed my regret for our disappointment, as the Worcester family may never have another opportunity of hearing this charming singer.[1]⌝ |

[*top of page cut away*]

Monsieur l'abbè Morellet[3] spent the Evening with my voyage. The *Adventure* was to explore the Antarctic, Tasmania, Tahiti, Tonga, and New Zealand before returning to England in July 1774, a year before the *Resolution*. JB's private journal of his voyage has been published as *With Captain James Cook in the Antarctic and Pacific*, ed. B. Hooper (Canberra, 1975). See also *The Voyage of the Resolution and Adventure 1772–1775*, ed. J. C. Beaglehole (Cambridge, 1961; vol. ii of *The Journals of Captain James Cook on his Voyages of Discovery*); Manwaring, pp. 13–47; below, pp. 251–2.

[99] Presumably Richard Gustavus Burney.

[1] FB did not visit Worcester until 1777 (vol. ii).

[2] Giuseppe Millico (1737–1802), Italian soprano castrato, composer, and singing teacher. He came to London from Vienna in the spring of 1772, first performing on 25 Apr. in Hasse's *Artaserse* at the Haymarket. Initially hissed because of a cabal against new singers, he won over his critics and was highly esteemed at the time of his departure from England two years later. CB calls him a 'judicious performer, and worthy man . . . whose voice had received its greatest beauties from art' (Mercer, ii. 877–8). See *New Grove*; Rees, s.v. Millico, Giuseppe; *LS 4* iii. 1629; below, *passim*.

[3] Abbé André Morellet (1727–1819), economist and writer. CB had met him at Paris in Dec. 1770 (*Tours*, i. 312). The Abbé came to England at the end of Apr., at the invitation of Ld. Shelburne. He was also a close friend of Garrick, and CB wrote to Baron d'Holbach, 2 June 1772 (Osborn), that 'I have had the pleasure of frequently seeing M. Morellet, & of dining with him twice at Garricks . . .'. Morellet returned to France toward the end of October. He describes his visit in his *Mémoires* . . ., ed. P.-É. Lémontey (Paris, 1821), i. 195–210. FB was to renew her acquaintance with Morellet in France in 1805 (*JL* vi. 514).

CB notes (in Rees, s.v. Morellet, Abbé) that Morellet 'had much taste and passion for all the fine arts, but chiefly for music, which he had studied. . . . In 1759, he published a small pamphlet, "On Musical Expression and Imitation," which is full of ingenious ideas, and well written.' This work, *De l'Expression en musique*, was actually written in Italy in 1759 and inserted in the *Mercure de France*, Nov. 1771, pp. 113–43. A copy of the work, published separately in 12mo and without a date, is in the BL.

Father. He is a French Writer of Fame, his subject *Commerce* & agriculture. He is a man of science & learning and has lately written a Book on music, which has been very much approved. He is come to England for a few months, & w[e] hope to have the favour of seeing him of[ten.] It was to meet this very Abbè that Mr Garrick sent the Card I have before mentioned.[4]

Thursday, May 21st

Miss Allen—for the last Time I shall so call her—came Home on Monday last [18 May]—Her *Novel* not yet over—Nevertheless—she—was married last Saturday![5]—

Good Heaven—what a romantic Life has this beloved friend Lived!—I dare not commit particulars to Paper—[r]but will briefly say that Mr. Rishton & she settled to meet in her Journey Home and that then they confer'd upon my mother's dislike to him—which they apprehended might fling difficulties in their way that, in the End, might frustrate all their intentions and Mr. Rishton much fear'd her influence over the dear Eloper—& at length [?sett]led with her to marry him[n]

[*bottom of page cut away*]

[r]in the French Language.

Mr. Rishton travelled with her to Calais [from Ypres]—where to prevent discovery ⟨she star⟩ted before—⟨she⟩ sent ⟨for⟩ her man servant[6] & there she parted from him [Rishton], Crossed the Water—& then sent back her man [to Rishton at Calais] lest he should betray her—He is now in Mr. Rishton's service.

Molly Stancliffe,[7] her maid, was the only Person at her Wedding except two Creature[s][6] who went as Witnesses.

[4] See above, p. 215.

[5] MA and Martin Folkes Rishton were secretly married at Ypres on Saturday, 16 May 1772, probably in the same Reformed Church where MA's sister Elizabeth ('Bessy') was to marry Samuel Meeke 5 years later (MS extract from the register of the Reformed Church, on a loose leaf in the baptismal registers, St Margaret's Church, King's Lynn). While at Geneva MA had carried on a number of half-hearted flirtations (SC to FB 11 Aug. 1772, Essex). Finally she sent Martin a passionate declaration of her love (MA to FB *pm* 6 April 1772, Berg), which apparently determined him at last to wed her. MA wrote to FB 8 June 1772 (Berg) that 'the Marriage was well witnessed and con-sum——d at S[t] [*sic*] Ypres', though further on in the same letter SB inserts that 'they were married in the *Morning*, & parted almost immediately'. See below.

[6] Not further identified.

[7] Mary ('Molly') Stancliffe, daughter of a fishing boat captain, became the Rishtons'

How strange—how wonderful an affair!—

But I ought to say that Mr. Rishton has wholly Cleared himself from Blame on account of his former Conduct, which was the result of the most real necessity.[8] All I know of it, I will bury in my own Breas[t] & not Commit to this memoir, *under* ⌐ |

[bottom of page cut away]

and till they have taken a House, & got their servants, Equipage, &c, ⌐in order, & ready for their being together.⌐ In the mean Time, from the moment he [Rishton] arrives, he is openly to appear as *her Lover*—and they intend being married again in England.[9]

What scenes we shall have!—⌐ *The Bride* is to write to Mr. Rishton by the Foreign Post tomorrow.[10]

Friday ⟨the 22ᵈ⟩

The Bride has spoken to my Father but has not revealed her marriage—which nothing but necessity will induce her to Publish. He has promised her his assistance, and is to speak to my mother the first favourable opportunity. I hear every Instant new Incidents, to the honour of this ⟨couple⟩, & I am fully persuaded they will be completely happy.⌐[11]

I have just left Sir William Browne,[12] a most extraordinary old man—who lives | in the Square, & is here on a Visit. He has been a very renowned phisician—whether for saving or for killing, I cannot say. He is near 80, & enjoys prodigious Health & spirits—& is galant to the Ladies to a most ridiculous degree—

head housekeeper. MAR's letters to FB repeatedly mention her good qualities and chronic ill health. In spite of the latter she outlived both her mistress and master, and in 1821 was left an annuity of £30 by Rishton (will PCC, prob. 17 Jan. 1821).

[8] Presumably an allusion to the opposition of Rishton's uncle, Sir Richard Betenson (see above, p. 142 n. 8; below, p. 231).

[9] This second wedding did not take place. See below, p. 226.

[10] Letters to the Continent were dispatched from London on Tuesdays and Fridays (*Royal Kalendar* (1772), p. 128).

[11] See below, p. 226.

[12] Sir William Browne (1692–1774), MD (1721), FRS (1739), cr. Kt. (1748), President of the Royal College of Physicians (1765–6). Sir William had practised medicine at King's Lynn from 1716 to 1749, when he moved to Queen Square, London, where he lived for the rest of his life. His daughter, Mary (d. 1773), was the second wife of William Folkes (1700–73) of Queen Square and Hillington Hall, Norfolk (see *GM* xliii (1773), 203), and mother of Sir Martin Browne Folkes (q.v.). For Sir William's published verses, see *DNB*.

He never comes without repeating some of his Verses—& I can now recollect a stanza he has just told us—occasioned by some little flirtation with a Lady's Fan—

> No Wonder that this Fan should prove
> A Vehicle to convey[13] Love:
> But to return it I desire,
> Lest it too much should Fan the Fire.

I think the Lines *worth preserving*, so flew out to write them ⌐down.⌐

I have had a very clever Letter[14] from my dear Daddy Crisp—I am charmed at entering into a Correspondence with him.

⌐From my dear Allen for, after all—I must call her so since Friends began so⌐ |

[*a leaf or leaves cut away*]

⌐Rishton's Picture, as she would a Cross, hung round her Neck. She also settled a time to go to him [SC?] [xxxxx *1 line*]⌐

My dear Father intends going to Germany this summer, to see if he can gather any materials there for his History of music. If the most indefatigable pains & industry, will render his Work worthy of approbation, it will meet with the greatest.[15]

May 30[th 16]

Maria, Susan & myself ⌐made a successful effort⌐ to see Garrick, last Night, in Richard the Third. We [had always

---

[13] Changed by FBA to 'carry'.

[14] Missing.

[15] CB left England the 1st week of July on a tour that would take him through the Netherlands, the United Provinces, Germany, Austria, and Bohemia. The high point of the journey was the 2 weeks he spent at Vienna (30 Aug.–13 Sept.), where he met the poet Metastasio and the composers Gluck and Hasse. He was back in London by early Nov. See *Tours*, ii; Lonsdale, pp. 113–18; Scholes, i. 198–242.

[16] So in the MS, but correctly 'May 31ˢᵗ', as the performance 'last Night' which FB describes took place at Drury Lane on Saturday, 30 May. Of this performance William Hopkins noted (in his MS Diary, 1769–76): 'Mr G very fine—Voice clear to the last great Applause' (cited *LS 4* iii. 1642). An anonymous commentator in the *Morning Chronicle* (1 June 1772) found it hard to determine 'whether that transcending actor excelled most in the deliberating subtle calm and protean variability of political ambition, or in the explosive impetuosity and fire-eyed execution of intrepid heroism' (cited Stone, pp. 522–3). Garrick played the role, in the version of Cibber, a total of 83 times in his career (ibid., p. 524).

longed to see him in all his great characters, though least in this which is *so* shocking][17] [xxxxx *1 word*], though not the least, of the praise of his acting. ⌐We rode in ⟨chairs, so⟩ that we got in the instant ⟨we arrived⟩, without the least difficulty. The ⟨chair⟩, however tiresome & fatiguing, is the only way for ⟨going to the theatre,⟩ & I never attempt to ⟨step out⟩, but in that manner.⌐ |

Garrick was sublimely horrible!—⌐Good Heaven⌐—how he made me shudder whenever he appeared! it is inconceivable, how terribly great he is in this Character. I will never see him so disfigured again—he seemed so truly the monster he performed, that I felt myself glow with indignation every time I saw him. The Applause he met with exceeds all belief of the Absent. I thought, at the End, they would have torn the House down: Our seats shook under us.

⌐My mother has, at length, spoke to Maria about Mr. Rishton, & I hope this affair will end amiably. Certain it is, that she will so soon be of age,[18] &, consequently, wholly independent, that opposition would be very fruitless even supposing she was unmarried, which Mama doubtless does suppose. And this, I imagine, has determined Mama to wave an Authority so short-Lived, & let her dislike to this Martin sleep in peace.⌐ |

[*The extant Journal for 1772 ends here. In the first week of June MAR and SEB went to Chessington to break the news of the marriage to SC. On 8 June they wrote FB a joint letter from there (Berg): '[MAR] My dear Fan—All's over—Crisp knows I am Maria Rishton that the marriage was well witness'd and consum——d at S[t] [sic] Ypres w[ch] he says is an important point.... He took me aside the first Night—after I had by hints hums and ha's told him Rishy and I were to be One—and shewd him the dogs picture—well the Old devil grew so scurrilous—he almost made me mad ... So I sent him a Message by Kate [Kitty Cooke]—who with her Thick Skull Guessed the whole affair from the beginning—that M[rs] Rishton sent comp[ts] and hoped to see him at Stanhoe this summer.' '[SEB] He came into the Room to us—Maria fell on her knees instantly & hid her face on the bed—why what is all this, s[d] he & Kate claw'd hold of her left hand, & shewed him the Ring ... he enquired particularly where she was married—by whom—who were the witnesses &c &c & lastly—what time they spent together—Maria upon this ... told a*

---

[17] The phrase in brackets has been retraced over the original, or may be FBA's alteration.

[18] MA was born on 20 July 1751 (*HFB* p. 25 n. 1).

hundred lyes in a moment — they were married in the Morning, & parted almost imediately . . .' SC took MAR aside into his own room, and after he received '[MAR] a minute Account of every thing that had passed—[he] changed his Tone immediately about my sposo—he said in the Room before Sue &c you may see he is a man of sence and a gentleman—and he had before call'd him all the designing worthless Dogs he could think of—he wont hear of our being married again as he says that would be putting odd thoughts into peoples heads—and nothing was wanting if he had the certificate and my Relations might write to Ypres . . . but he insisted on the affair being imme-diately Known and declared in a public way . . . he has wrote to Mama to tell her the whole affair and insists on my going back to Queens Square Mrs Rishton and writing immediately to Martin to come over . . .'

Though SC accepted the marriage as a fait accompli *and could even laugh about it in the scene above, his true feelings are revealed in his letter to FB of 11 Aug. 1772 (Essex), where he accuses MAR of wild, childish, trifling con-duct, cynically implying that she married Martin merely to satisfy her lust for him. The reactions of MAR's parents were mixed. CB, for his part, seems to have immediately accepted the marriage and his new son-in-law in a typically kind and generous fashion. EAB, on the other hand, despite FB's hopes to the contrary, appears never to have succeeded completely in suppressing her con-tinued aversion to Rishton or her resentment of MAR's flaunting her authority and embarrassing her by her elopement. In an undated letter of late 1772 or early 1773 (Berg), MAR complains to FB of her mother's 'resentment . . . [I] believe she must have been hurt as my Marriage destroyed all her favorite schemes—but sure if she reflects coolly she will not think she has acted quite right after I was married—to tell my Husband every vice fault or foible I had ever been guilty of since my Infancy . . .' And FB reports in Jan. 1773 (below, p. 234) that 'All Connections' have, 'in a manner', been 'formally broken between [the Rishtons] & my mother'.*

The first several years of the Rishtons' marriage seem to have been happy ones with MAR writing to FB of the love and admiration she felt for her husband. Rishton, as far as can be determined, also appears to have been rea-sonably contented and to have returned MAR's affection. Already present, how-ever, were signs of the jealousy and possessiveness that were increasingly to oppress MAR. In a short time she was relegated almost to the life of a country recluse, waiting upon her imperious husband while he indulged his favourite pursuits of gentleman farming and hunting at their seat in Norfolk. More and more their social life was limited to Rishton's family and friends, as MAR was gradually cut off from her own relations.

About 1778 Rishton began a liaison with his wife's erstwhile best friend, Mrs Dorothy ('Dolly') Hogg (see above, p. 9 n. 28). He may have been influ-enced to do this by the example of his cousin and friend, Edmund Rolfe (1738–1817), who had had an illegitimate son by a woman in Switzerland in 1760

(V. Berry, The Rolfe Papers: The Chronicle of a Norfolk Family 1559–1908 *(Norwich, 1979), p. x); MAR later accused Rolfe of being in collusion with her husband (MAR to FB 5 July 1798, Barrett). Rishton may have been frustrated by MAR's failure to provide him with an heir. Dolly Hogg did give him a son, Edward Hogg (b. 1784), whom he made his residuary legatee after MAR's death. Incredibly, MAR seems not to have known of the affair until 1798, when she accidentally came across some letters from her husband to Mrs Hogg. She then left Rishton but returned to him after several years, remaining with him till her death.*

The Burneys were to receive another blow in October of this year when the 17-year-old Stephen Allen, no doubt emboldened by the example of his elder sister, eloped to Gretna Green with Susanna ('Sukey') Sharpin, also 17, daughter of a Norfolk physician. EAB was in a particularly bad state to receive this shock since she had recently been very ill following the birth (on 29 Aug.) of her last surviving child, the future novelist Sarah Harriet Burney (1772–1844) (see HFB *p. 46; Dorothy Young to FB 2 Sept. 1772, Barrett). Another child born this year was Hannah Maria (or 'Marianne') Burney (1772–1856), the eldest offspring of EBB and Charles Rousseau Burney, who was baptized 16 July in St Paul's Church, Covent Garden* (Register of St. Paul's Church, Covent Garden, *ii. 65). A preponderance of such personal (and, in the case of Stephen Allen, embarrassing) matters may be the reason for FBA's destruction of her journals for the latter half of 1772.]*

JOURNAL 1773

AJ (Early Diary, vi, paginated 287–360, 387–[406], foliated 1–[50], Berg), Journal for 1773. Following FBA's instructions, her 'Tingmouth Journal' is inserted between fos. 41 and 42 (see below).

Originally perhaps a cahier or cahiers of double sheets which were dismembered and then the gatherings repinned or resewn. Now 37 single sheets and 8 double sheets 4to, 106 pp., with a paste-over (by Charlotte Barrett).

Entitled (*by FBA, on fo. 1'*): Juvenile Diary | N° 6 | 1773

Annotated: NB. *Tingmouth* This Year. to be inserted Between page [*sic*] 41. and 42.

Names in FBA's 'List of Persons' for 1773 which are not in the extant journal include CB Jr., Mrs Strange, Major Stanton, Mr Ormsby, M. Saccherets, Mrs Barwell, Miss Rochford, Mrs Browne, Mr Palmer, Sir James and Lady Lake and the Misses Lake (see vol. ii), Miss Milner, and Miss Mary Milner. 'Major' Stanton was perhaps John Stanton, Capt. in the 14th Ft., 1772, and Major, 1778, who disappears from *AL* after 1780. Mrs Barwell was an acquaintance of the Hawkesworths whom FB mentions meeting again in 1782; she had been Christopher Smart's landlady (see Abbott p. 123; FB's Journal for Dec. 1782 (Berg), p. 1684). Mrs Browne was possibly Mary Browne (d. 1777), wife of Scarlet Browne (d. 1786), town clerk of Lynn (burial registers, St Nicholas, Lynn; Hamon Le Strange, *Norfolk Official Lists* (Norwich, 1890), p. 203).

Mr Palmer was probably the Revd Joseph Palmer (1749–1829), author, nephew of Sir Joshua Reynolds, whom CB met this year (see Lonsdale, pp. 128–9). Miss Milner and Miss Mary Milner were probably Elizabeth and Anastasia-Maria Milner (*c.*1753–1838), the first and second daughters of Sir William Milner (1719–74), 2nd Bt. They may have been CB's students (see *GM* cviii[1] (1838), 329). Mr Ormsby, M. Saccherets, and Miss Rochford have not been traced.

January N° 6[1]

January 16th
Queen's Square
London

I shall begin this year without any preamble, having nothing new to say. I am in the situation of the Poet Laureat[2]—& with him, may exclaim

[1] Emended by FB from '7'.

[2] William Whitehead (1715–85) succeeded Colley Cibber as poet laureate upon the latter's death in 1757. The lines below, however, have not been found in Whitehead, and are probably FB's own. Laurence Eusden, the laureate from 1718 to 1730, began the custom of producing two annual odes, on the New Year and the King's Birthday.

For on a subject so to Tatters tore
What can be said—that ha'n't been said before?

This is my 5th or 6th Journal Book—yet will not, I am persuaded, be my last. But it would require very superiour talents to write an Annual Exordium. I must therefore content myself with plainly & concisely proceeding with my Life and Opinions, addressed to [|] myself.

And first—it is my opinion that this World is very ill used in being called a bad One; if People did but know how to enjoy the Blessings they meet, they would learn that, very often, our share of misfortunes serve but to enhance their Value. But grief makes a much deeper impression on the mind, & leaves far more lasting traces than joy. We relate all our Afflications more frequently than we do our pleasures. Every Individual's chagrins, are mentioned as proofs of his ill fate, while their more fortunate Circumstances are suffered to pass unnoticed by themselves, as the meer effect of their own Wisdom. Could every man consider his own intrinsic Worth—perhaps he would find that the *still, small Voice*[3] of Conscience, Accords better with his Fortune, than the loud [|] & declamatory flow of Eloquence. What I mean, is that our Happiness is generally equal to our Deserts.

Exceptions, Fordyce[4] says, do only *confirm* a General Rule. For my own part, how well should I think of myself, if my Deserts equalled my Happiness!—My Father has ever been more Deserving than fortunate—This saying *could* not be reversed in him. The longer I Live, & the more I see of the World, the more am I both Astonished & delighted at the Goodness, the merit, & the sweetness of that best of men.—All that is *Amiable*, added to all that is *Agreeable*,—every thing that is *striking*, joined to every thing that is *pleasing*;—Learning, Taste, Judgement, Wit & Humour—Candour, Temperance, Patience, Benevolence—every Virtue under the sun—is His!— [|]

[3] Cf. 1 Kings 19: 12.

[4] James Fordyce (1720–96), DD, Presbyterian divine and writer. FB is echoing a sentiment in his *Sermons to Young Women* (2 vols., 1765; 7th edn., 1771): 'Have you not heard, that a rule is not overthrown, but rather confirmed, by exceptions?' (Sermon VIII, 'On Female Virtue, with Intellectual Accomplishments', 1766 edn., i. 127). MA, writing from Geneva in 1771, had asked FB to send her a copy of these sermons, which were a staple for young ladies (MA to FB 21 Nov. 1771, Berg; see also *HFB* pp. 19–21).

But now to Events, which will otherwise Crowd so fast upon me—, that I shall not be able to recollect them. What a loss would that be!—to (my dear) Nobody!—

ᴦWe were last Sunday Evening [10 Jan.] again at a Concert at Mr. Barthelemon's,[5] at which he performed his part very delightfully. His pretty wife sang. Mr. Burney played the Harpsichord. Hetty, too, was persuaded to play one Lesson of Mr. Barthelemon's; for, since her marriage, she has almost entirely given up Practising; however, we have, at present, concerts so frequently that she has been prevailed upon to recover her fingers a little. Mr. Burney's *overpowering* Execution had, joined to her repeated illnesses, wholly discouraged her. Cirri,[6] a violoncello player, gave us a solo, Mr. Tacet another on the Flute. They played several new & very ingenious Compositions of Mr. Barthelemon's Trios, Quartettos & fullᴨ |

[*Two leaves have been cut away. In the next scene FB is at the lodgings of the Rishtons, who have come to town. She angers Martin Rishton by refusing to accept a free ticket to the theatre, for fear of displeasing EAB.*]

ᴦas I really could not, I told her to intreat that he would not even mention it to me, as I could not possibly help it.

She took him into another Room & told him. They were some time together. When they came back, as I had requested it, he was too delicate to say a word to me, but I heard that he was very much provoked.

[He did not pay for *his own* place, he said, nor for his wife's: the Box was all taken by Sir Richard Bettenson, his uncle, who ˙invited *them*, & through them, *me* to take *one* [xxxxx *1–2 words*]—but he was forced to keep the ⟨ticket,⟩ and][7] at Dinner, we were extremely comfortable. Mr. Rishton then, with great cordiality, invited me to Bath. She joined in the most affection-

---

[5] François-Hippolyte Barthélemon (1741–1808), French violinist and composer. He moved to London in 1764 and for the next 4 decades was a leading figure in the city's musical life. CB refers to his 'powerful hand and truly vocal adagio' (Mercer, ii. 1021), and FB, in *Evelina*, calls him 'a player of exquisite fancy, feeling and variety' (cited Scholes, i. 358). He married (1766) Mary (Polly) Young (*c.*1749–99), soprano singer, who was a niece of Mrs Arne. See Highfill; *New Grove*.

[6] Giovanni Battista Cirri (1724–1808), Italian cellist and composer who lived in London from 1764 to 1780. CB calls him 'a more useful than shining performer' who 'wrote correctly for several instruments besides his own' (Rees). *New Grove* praises his music for its 'harmonic and formal control' and 'melodic freshness'.

[7] Inserted by FBA.

ate & pressing manner. That I could but accept it! She told me that she has a little Room fitted up for me—and wishes me to stay all the Time that she remains there. She proposed writing to my Father—coming and speaking to him—or doing any thing ¹ if there was but a probability of success—but I am too well convinced, that in the present situation of affairs, I should be refused, & I know that the indulgent Heart of my dear Father, suffers as much to deny, as I to be denied. But it is very unfortunate. Would to Heaven, that all Parties were but satisfied as I am of the merits of each other! But what is so blind as Anger! or so Deaf as Prejudice?ᵀ⁸

Mrs Bettenson, & Sir Richard Bettenson,⁹ Uncle & Aunt of Mr Rishton, were to ⌐be of⌐ our party at the Play. The Baronet has a Fortune of 5000 per. annum—& Mr Rishton is his *presumptive Heir*; though not a *declared* one, yet he is the nearest Relation. They Live in our square, & we went to take them up Early, as the *Prelude*¹⁰ was to be done. ¹The servant beg'd us to ⌐come in,⌐ as his mistress was not ready—the moment the Coach stop'd, Mr Rishton said to me, 'Now take no Notice, but you will see presently one of the *oddest* Women you ever yet have seen—off the stage!—' Mrs Rishton, who was extremely eager to see Barsanti, having never yet, on the stage, was very much vexed at this delay — — her Husband, more impetuous, exclaimed against ⌐her⌐ [Mrs Betenson's] ill-breeding—'How truly vulgar! to make People wait!—' But he would not get out:—'Let's sit still, cried he, it will save both Time & Compliments.' In about 5 minutes, Mrs Bettenson appeared in the Passage. She is a fat, squab, ugly, vulgar Woman, yet, I am told, extremely proud, of her Family!—however, she was this Evening all Condescendsion [*sic*].

⁸ A reference to the lingering hostility of EAB to the Rishtons. FB was permitted, however, to visit them at Teignmouth in the summer (below, pp. 274–311).

⁹ Sir Richard Betenson (d. 1786), 4th Bt., and his unmarried sister Helen Betenson (d. 1788). Sir Richard's wife Lucretia née Folkes (*c.*1722–58) was Martin Rishton's aunt. Betenson is described by William Stukeley (in *The Family Memoirs*, ed. W. C. Lukis (1853), i. 100) as 'indigent' on his marriage in 1756 to Lucretia Folkes, who brought him a fortune of £30,000. He was further enriched by the sale that year of the library and collections of Martin Folkes, Lucretia's father (Martin Rishton's grandfather), and by the bequest by Henry Bosville in 1761 of extensive estates in Kent near Sevenoaks including Brabourne, which became his principal residence (*GM* xxvi (1756), 314, xxviii (1758), 292, lviii² (1788), 1032; Nichols, *Lit. Anec.* ii. 589, 592; E. Hasted, *History and . . . Survey . . . of Kent* (1778), i. 350, ii. 68, 236, 368).

¹⁰ George Colman's 'Occasional Prelude', written for Jenny Barsanti.

Won't you come in, Mrs Rishton?—why ¦ Lord, I have been ready this good while;—we only wait for my Brother. But he says he can't ⌐with⌐ 5 in a Coach.'

This was a delicate speech for me! I began to say I was sorry, &c—but Mrs Rishton whispered me 'Remember *they* are the intruders, *we* made our Party first.' Mr Rishton was now obliged to get out. & after a decent quantity of speaches & Compliments, the Baronet & his amiable sister came in.

We had ⌐two Rows of⌐ an upper Box.

Barsanti acted extremely well, & was much admired. 'And how do *you* like this Prelude, ma'am? asked Sir Richard, little thinking that I have seen it near a Dozen Times. I am glad to find it so long Lived.[11] The Play was again Elfrida,[12] with a new Entertainment called Cross Purposes in which is introduced a macaroni Footman, who had on exactly the Undress Livery of Mr Rishton's servants! Mrs Rishton ¦ could not forbear Laughing as well as myself—*she* looked up to Mr Rishton—*I* did not venture. After all, his foible is certainly Dress & love of being *distinguished* from the vulgar Crew.[13]

In going back to the Coach, Sir Richard & his sister gave a polite invitation to supper. I desired to be set down at Home, but they all joined in asking me, & I was too happy to be any where with the Rishtons to refuse.

Mr Rishton was in high spirits, & prodigiously agreeable. Mrs Bettenson, among her other amiable Qualities, has to an uncommon degree, that of Thriftiness, of which her Brother, though not so apparently, participates. I had been told before

---

[11] This was its 18th performance (*LS 4* iii. 1657–86 *passim*).

[12] *Elfrida, a Dramatic Poem, Written on the Model of the Ancient Greek Tragedy* (1752; 9th edn., 1773), by William Mason, was adapted for the stage by George Colman, with music provided by Dr Arne. It was first performed at Covent Garden in Nov. 1772 (see *YW* xxviii. 53–6). The afterpiece was *Cross Purposes*, a 2-act farce by William O'Brien (d. 1815), actor and dramatist, first staged in Dec. 1772 (*LS 4* iii. 1677 and *passim*). The performances of the 'Prelude', *Elfrida*, and *Cross Purposes* together date the present theatre excursion as taking place on Wednesday, 13 Jan. 1773, the only time that this combination occurred.

[13] FBA has inserted: 'I had the pleasure to see Prior's celebrated Fair "Kitty beautiful & young," now called Kitty *beautiful & old*, in the stage Box; i.e. the Duchess of Queensbury.' This was Catherine Hyde (*c.*1701–77), m. (1720) Charles Douglas (1698–1778), 3rd D. of Queensberry, who is celebrated in verses 'Upon Lady Katherine H——de's first appearing at the Play-House in Drury Lane' (1718), also entitled 'The Female Phaeton' and attributed dubiously to Matthew Prior. The poem begins: 'Thus *Kitty*, beautiful and young . . .'. See *YW* xxxii. 132–3; Matthew Prior, *Literary Works*, ed. H. B. Wright and M. K. Spears (2nd edn., Oxford, 1971), ii. 787–8, 1073–5.

by Mr Rishton, that whenever she had Company, she was always so unlucky as to have *just parted with her Cook*.—so that I had the utmost difficulty ˡ to keep my Countenance, when, upon my apologising for my Visit, she said 'O dear Ma'am, you do me a great deal of Honour,—I am only sorry you will not have better fare—but indeed my Cook—& an excellent one she was,—went away yesterday.'

In considering the partial dispensation of Riches, I think the Poor should ever have in remembrance this Querry [*sic*]

—which is worse
Want—with a full—or with an empty Purse?[14]

The Table was covered with half, or less than half, filled Dishes—I should not, however, have mentioned this, but to speak of Mr Rishton, whose behaviour was unmerciful; it is a general custom with him to Eat little or no supper—but he affected a voracious appetite, & Eat as if he had fasted 3 Days. I own I had malice enough to enjoy this, ˡ as I have no pity for *Grand Penury*. Riches & Pride—without Liberality—how odious![15]

Mr Rishton raised my Admiration by his behaviour to this Pair, from whom he has reason to expect so much: far from flattering, he even *trims* them for their foibles, & whenever they seem to exact any deference, he treats them most cavalierly. He declares to his Wife, that he would not descend to cringe & Court them, for the surety of all his Uncle's Estate. If he Humbled himself to them, he is convinced they would trample on him. Such is the insolence of Wealth.[16]

At Twelve O'clock Mr Rishton ordered his Carriage—And turning to me, with a very wicked smile, said 'The *Play* will be over *late* to Night, Miss Burney!—'

---

[14] Pope, *Epistle to Bathurst* (*Moral Essays* III), ll. 319–20: 'Resolve me, Reason, which of these is worse, / Want with a full, or with an empty purse?' (Pope, *Epistles to Several Persons*, ed. F. W. Bateson (1951), p. 116).

[15] *GM* lviii² (1788), 1123, notes that at her death Mrs Betenson (to whom the estate of Sir Richard passed) 'left a vast sum of money, which in her life-time she had not the spirit to make use of, hardly allowing herself and servants common necessities'. She did, however, bequeath £30,760 to various charities and institutions (*GM* lix¹ (1789), 119).

[16] Rishton's independence may have cost him a great deal. Mrs Betenson did leave him the moiety of the dividends on £30,000 and a house in Queen Square, but she passed him over for the executorship, naming instead Ld. Stanhope, Ld. Amherst, and Multon Lambarde, who shared the residue of her vast estate, including the principal seat at Brabourne (ibid.).

However, I knew my offence was given in *going*,—my *staying* did not much signify.[17] |

⌐They set me down at our Door when the coach stop'd—& I was going, he stayed me, & drew up the Glass, to say—'You may tell your mother, with a safe Conscience, that *I* did not pay for you—as to the rest, you will settle it with Mrs. Rishton—I beg your pardon—I am sorry to mention it at all'—

I promised Mrs. Rishton to see her some Time the next Day [14 Jan.], as they had resolved to leave Town on Friday [15 Jan.] she wished me to Breakfast with her. However, I had no opportunity to go. All Connections being, in a manner, formally broken between them & my mother, it is inconceivable how difficult & how disagreeable a task it is, to mention the name of Rishton!

In the Evening, Susan & I, niether of us in Rapture, accompanied Mama in making a *Round of Visits*. We were only let in at Miss Forbes, the young Paintress,[18] and at¬ |

[*a leaf or leaves cut away*]

⌐Town. The music[19] is divine—& Millico, the first singer, is truly great, pathetic, & delightful.

Monday,¬ Jan. 25th

We had, Yesterday, the most ⌐heavenly¬ Evening!—Millico, the ⌐divine¬ Millico, was here—& with him, Sigr Sacchini,[20] and Sigr Celestini, that sweet Violinist who I have often mentioned.

We had no further Party; which I greatly rejoice at, as we were at full liberty to devote every instant to these 3. Sigr Sacchini is a very elegant man, & extremely handsome. ⌐He &

---

[17] A reference to FB's difficulty in obtaining permission from EAB to see the Rishtons; FBA has interpolated above (on fo. 3r, obliterated), 'Leave, however, I obtained, though a dry one.' Rishton evidently anticipated a 'scene' when FB got home.

[18] Miss Forbes lived in St Martin's Lane (A. Graves, *The Royal Academy . . . 1769 to 1904* (1905–6), iii. 134).

[19] Of *Il Cid*. See below.

[20] Antonio (Maria Gasparo Gioacchino) Sacchini (1730–86), Italian composer, a leading figure in serious opera of the late 18th c. CB met him at Venice in 1770, and he moved to London in 1772, remaining there until 1781. After his death CB eulogized him as 'this graceful, elegant, and judicious composer' (Mercer, ii. 895; see also Rees; *New Grove*; below, *passim*).

Celestini came very early. We were all in terror lest Millico should fail us, because he had promised my Father to come with them,—however, just as we were assembled to Tea, he made his appearance. ⌐

⌐He is⌐ an immense Figure, and | not handsome *at all*, *at all*,—but his Countenance is strongly expressive of sweetness of Disposition, & his Conversation is exceedingly sensible.

He was very much surprised at the size of our Family. My Father has so young a look, that all strangers are astonished to find him such a *Patriarch*. ⌐He enquired with great curiosity, who we all were, & if the *signorine* (Hetty, Sue & me) were all my Father's. Sacchini declared he had taken us for his sisters!

His [Millico's] next enquiry was 'if we did not Play? My Father came up to us, & told us—I went back with Answer, that *one* (Hetty) would play, on *Conditione* that *he* would sing. He said he was *pas trop bien*, but would do what he could. ⌐

His Conversation was partly Italian, and partly French—& Sacchini's almost all Italian, | but they niether of them speak 3 Words of English, ⌐which I very much regretted.⌐

Hetty being called upon, ⌐we all went into the study. She played a Trio of my Father's, accompanied by himself [on violin], & Celestini. They were greatly pleased both with the music & performance. Millico turned over the leaves for her, & Sacchini stood on the other side of the Harpsichord. Two of the first men of their Profession in the World, Sacchini as Composer, Millico as singer.

Hetty, on first sitting Down, while Celestini tuned his Violin, ⌐ began a Rondeau in the Overture to Sacchini's new Opera,[21] which has been performed but twice; but she had been to 3 Rehearsals, & has gotten almost half the Opera by Ear.

Sacchini almost started—he looked at first in the utmost perplexity, as if doubting | his own Ears, as the music of *il Cid* has never been published.[22] Millico clapt his Hands, &

[21] *Il Cid*, the libretto by G. Bottarelli, was first performed at the Haymarket on 19 and 23 Jan. 1773. It was Sacchini's revision of his own *Il gran Cidde* (Rome, 1764), the 'music entirely new'. Millico was the first man, and his airs were written expressly for him, 'in the delicate and pathetic style of that singer' (Mercer, ii. 894). Sacchini's opera was performed a total of 22 times this season but was not revived. See *LS 4* iii. 1688–9 and *passim*.

[22] A full score of *The Favourite Songs in the Opera Il Cid* was published by Robert Bremner in 3 numbers, from 8 Feb. to 10 Apr. 1773 (*Daily Adv.* 8 Feb., 10 Apr. 1773).

laughed,—'ah! Brava, Brava!—' Sacchini then Bowed—and my Father explained the manner of her having got this Rondeau! at which he seemed much pleased.

When she had finished her Lesson, "she claimed her *Conditione* of my Father—who" applied to Millico. "Millico declared himself not well, for the Opera House the night before [23 Jan.] was so violently crowded, & the stage so filled with Gentlemen, that the excessive heat, added to 3 encores, had fatigued him almost to illness—nevertheless, he" readily complied, and, with the utmost good Nature, sang his most favourite Air in the new Opera, only accompanied by Sacchini on the Harpsichord.

I have no Words to express the delight which his singing gave me. More, far away, | than I have ever received—even at the opera—for his Voice is so sweet, that it wants no Instruments to cover it.—He was not, however, satisfied with himself — — he complained "again" of his Cold,—but seeing us all charmed,— with a sweetness that enchanted me in so great a Performer, he said 'Eh bien, Encore une fois;—la Voix commence a venir.—' & sung it again—& O! how divinely!—I am sure he must then satisfy *himself*—& he will never find any other Person equally difficult.—For my own part, the mere recollection fills me with *rapture*—my terms are strong, & yet they but weakly express my "meaning."

After this, he made Sacchini himself sing—(though not without difficulty) saying, 'il a une petite Voix,—mais il chante trés bien—' Sacchini, with the utmost merit, has the truest modesty;—when he found he could not excuse himself, he complied with the most | gracefull diffidence imaginable.

He has very little Voice, but great taste. Millico led the applause that was given him. This Composer & singer appear to be most Affectionate friends. They do indeed seem born to make each others merit conspicuous.

Millico has Read in my Father's Countenance, I suppose, the excellence of his Heart; for though their acquaintance is of short Date, he reposes great confidence in him: in as much, as that he has given him some manuscript music of his own Composition, which he intends for his Benefit;[23] "but which has never yet been Published. However, Millico has heard much of

[23] 25 Feb.; see below, p. 244.

my Father by Letters from abroad & had Dined with him at
Mr. Garrick's & at Lord March's.[24]⌐

This M.S. is for an Ode which he has had Written,[25] expressing his gratitude for ⌐his Reception in England. The Verses are
pretty, & he has set them with great propriety. He sat down
himself to the Harpsichord, & played & sung his part
through,—as the Words are English, ⌐which he knows so little
of,⌐ he desired, ⌐in Italian,⌐ that we would all try whether we
could understand them ⌐from him,⌐ which, to say the truth,
was not very easy. ⌐And⌐ he made my Father correct his
prononciation.

⌐He could not but observe, how much every note from his
Voice enchanted us—& he said to my Father, that his *Figliuole*
had *musical souls*, in Italian which I can somewhat understand,
though not much.

Sacchini, after this, at Millico's motion, sung another, &, a
very fine song⌐—when they moved from the Harpsichord, to
draw them back, Hetty began another ⌐ Air of Millico's, in 'Il
Cid.'—This had the desired effect—Millico, all good Nature,
was prevailed upon to sing it. which he did

— — 'in Notes so sweet & clear
'The sound still vibrates on my ravish'd Ear.[26]

Admiration can certainly be no new tribute to the merit of
this ⌐divine⌐ singer—yet, he two or 3 Times observed our
delight, to my Father, & repeated that we had *l'alma Har-
monica*[27]—& on Sacchini's singing an air which was quite new
to us, but which we were highly pleased with, he said

---

[24] William Douglas (1725–1810), 3rd E. of March, succeeded (1778) as 4th D. of
Queensberry ('Old Q.'). A notorious gambler and debauchee, March was also a gener-
ous patron of the Italian opera and was said to have 'displayed great taste in a song'
(*DNB*). CB writes that he 'renewed' his acquaintance with March in 1763 ('Mem.'
No. 95); he had probably met him through Fulke Greville in the late 1740s (see Scholes,
i. 102; also H. Blyth, *Old Q: The Rake of Piccadilly* (1967)).

[25] By Garrick; see below, p. 244.

[26] CB's own translation of the motto on the title-page of his *Italian Tour*, 'Ei
cantarono allor si dolcemente, / Che la dolcezza ancor dentro mi suona', from the
second canto of Dante's *Purgatorio*. 'The motto was thus translated, though not printed,
by Dr. Burney. "They sung their strains in notes so sweet and clear / The sound still
vibrates on my ravished ear"' (*Mem.* i. 225–6).

[27] Properly *l'alma armonica*, 'the harmonious soul'.

╖'Comme elles aiment la╖ musique![28]—cela les touche *à l'instant.*'

╖They all went together, soon after the last air.╖ I again repeat, the Evening was *heavenly*!—if any thing on *Earth* can be so, 'tis surely, perfection of Vocal music. |

My Father Dined with this Orfeo ╖last week,╖ who has invited himself to favour us again soon, & promised to bring his Harp, on which he sometimes accompanies himself.

But our affection to Millico has occasioned our meeting with a very disagreeable accident, ╖which had any other cause occasioned it, might have been terribly regretted.╖ Last Saturday Evening [6 Feb.], Mama suddenly proposed going to the Opera, Il Cid, the fame of which had excited her curiosity. Susy & myself joyfully skipt at the proposal, & the Coach was instantly ordered. ╖It was very late, & the Overture & 5 songs were over when we got there.╖ The Opera is the sweetest I ever heard, & Millico sung like an Angel. ╖The House was amazingly crowded & we had very back seats, but were glad of any, &, indeed, to hear such music & such singing, I would be content to sit in a Barn.╖ |

╖I imagine that Millico was pleased to find my Father with only his own Family—which his [CB's] own delicacy had made him determine on, for though he might have greatly obliged some of his friends, yet it would have been, perhaps, indelicate to Millico, to have appeared to have invited him to *shew him off*. Singers require more *mènagement* than any set of People.╖

Nothing is more charming, than to see great talents without Affectation. My Father says, that there are hardly in all Italy, 3 such modest men as Millico, Sacchini, & Celestini. They did whatever was asked of them, with the most unaffected good humour. They are wholly free from vanity—yet seemed as much to enjoy giving Pleasure, as we did receiving it.

In taking leave, Millico turned to | Hetty, Susan & me, & Bowing, said—'Je veindrai [*sic*] un autre fois, et nous passerons la soirèe *comme il faut*.'

Feby 13th

On the above assurance have I lived ever since. The Voice of Millico seems continually sounding in my Ear, & harmonizing

[28] Emended by FBA to 'Elles connoissent la bonne musique!'

my soul. Never have I known pleasure so exquisite, so Heart felt, so *divinely penetrating*, as this sweet singer has given me. He is ever present to my imagination, his singing & his songs, are the constant Companions of my recollection. ⌐Whatever else occurs to me, seems obtrusive & impertinant. I express myself in very strong terms, but all terms, all words, are unequal and inadequate to speak of the extreme Delight which Millico's singing affords me. If this Journal was not *sacred* to myself, I am not ignorant that *any* other Reader would ⎮ immediately give me credit either for affectation or some degree of Craziness: but I am too much my own friend, ever to expose my *Raptures* to those who cannot simpathize in them, though I have never written my feelings with more honesty.⌐

We stayed very late, to avoid the Crowd, ⌐but the House emptied very slowly, the Pit & Boxes being quite full.⌐ When we went down, we got with difficulty to our Coach; but, after the usual perils & dangers,[29] we were drove out of the Hay-market, & into Suffolk Street. Here we concluded we were safe,—but, as we afterwards found, there had been left a load of Gravel in the street, which the shade (of a moonlight) hid from the Coach man. We found ourselves suddenly mounting on one side—Mama, who is soon alarmed, cried out 'We are going! we are going!' I sat quite quiet, thinking it a false alarm: but presently the Coach was entirely overturned, & we came side ways on the Ground. Stupified between surprise & fright, I fell without moving a finger, & laid quite silent—the Glass at my side was fortunately down, & the Blind up, which saved my Temples from the Pavement, but the Glass above me broke, & the Pieces fell on ⌐me⌐—Mama & Susan both imagined me to be most in danger—⌐& Susan⌐ ⎮ called out to me, repeatedly, 'Fanny, are you hurt? are you *very* much hurt, Fanny? my dear Fanny?—'

It was some time, from an unaccountable effect of fear, before I could answer;—but the falling of the Glass roused me. ⌐I had a Bever Hat on, which ⟨cover⟩ed my Face & saved me

---

[29] Of traffic congestion. By Nov. 1774 this problem had become acute enough to occasion the insertion in playbills of notices like the following: 'In order to prevent Inconveniences to the Ladies in getting to and from their Carriages, they are requested to order their coachmen to set down with their horses heads toward Pall Mall, and to take up with their heads toward Picadilly. The door in Market Lane and the King's door for Chairs only' (playbill for the King's Opera House, 8 Nov. 1774, cited *LS 4* i, p. xlii).

very much."—some People immediately gathered about the Cariage, &, I believe, opened the Door, which was now at the Top of the Coach. Mama called out 'Here's Nobody hurt!—' but desired them to assist me,—with some difficulty, I made shift to stand up—& a Gentleman lifted me out. He had no Hat on, being come out of a Neighbouring House. He beg'd me to go with him, & promised to take care of me:—but I was now terified [*sic*] for Mama & Susan, & could not leave the Place, for I heard the former call out that her arm was broken! I quite wrung my Hands with horror—This Gentleman took hold of me, & almost used violence to make me go away—I remember I called out to him, "as I broke from him," that he would drive me distracted!—he assured me that "Mama" would be safe;—"& because" he had not had trouble enough with me, I answered all his civilities to me, with 'But why can't you go & help Them?' However he would not leave me, for which I believe I am very much obliged to him, as I was surrounded by a mob, & as there were Assistants enough about the Coach. When Mama & Susan were taken out, we accepted this Gentleman's offer, & went into his House, where we were very hospitably received, by some ladies—my poor mother had her Arm dreadfully hurt. Susan had only sprained two Fingers in supporting herself from falling on us.—my Face was very bloody, from two small Cuts I had received on my Nose. We stayed here near a q'r of an Hour, & met with the utmost kindness & civility. "We were dreadfully frightened but yet happy to have Escaped without Broken Bones."

Mama declared she would walk Home. My *Deliverer* insisted on accompanying us—but John[30] "came to us, &" assured us that the Coach was not further injured than by the Glasses being broke, and that we might very safely go Home in it, which we accordingly did: though in much terror.

Mama has been confined ever since.—M'r Bromfield[31] has examined it [her arm] but it is so much swelled, that it can only be Polticed at present, & he has not said whether it has received

[30] Presumably the Burneys' servant John Hutton.

[31] Presumably William Bromfield (1712–92), surgeon of St George's Hospital and surgeon to Her Majesty's household; probably the 'William Bromfield, Esq.' who subscribed to *Hist. Mus.*

any further injury than a most violent sprain. I fear it will be a very tedious affair. Susan, thank God, is very well, & so am I.

The next Day, which was Sunday [7 Feb.], Dr. Hawkesworth & his lady,[32] by Appointment, Dined & spent the Evening here. I like the Doctor more & more every Time I have the pleasure of seeing him; that stiffness, & something resembling Pedantry, which formerly struck me in him, upon further Acquaintance & more intimacy, either wear off, or disappear. He was extremely natural & agreeable. His Wife is a very well bred, obliging, & sweet tempered Woman. ⌐He invites us very much to Bromley, where he lives, but my Father's Time grows Daily more precious.⌐

We were all of opinion that it was necessary to wait on the family in Suffolk Street, to return them thanks for their Assistance: but Mama was obliged to keep her Room,—Susan was engaged— | & therefore on Monday [8 Feb.] I went, John knowing the ⌐directions⌐ to the House. They appear to be an agreeable family, consisting of a Brother & 3 sisters. I felt very awkward when I got into the street, lest I should ⌐mistake the House, or⌐ be forgot. However, I determined to venture, rather than omit paying thanks so well deserved. However, they all immediately recollected me, & seemed very glad to hear of our safety. Their Names are Miland.[33]

Feby 19th

⌐My Father's German Tour is now in the Press,[34] & he is hurried & fatigued beyond expression, for this is a Time of Year when his Business is at its height.

Mrs. Rishton has been ill of a sore throat but I thank God is recovered. She is going with her Husband to Spa this spring.[35]

[32] Mary Brown (*c.*1722–96), daughter of John Brown, a butcher of Bromley, Kent; m. (1744) John Hawkesworth. Mrs Hawkesworth kept a girls' school at Bromley. She is described by Joseph Cradock (1742–1826), who met her about this time, as 'excellent and intelligent', 'an unassuming woman of very superior talent' (*Literary and Miscellaneous Memoirs* (1828), iv. 185; Abbott, pp. 12–13 and *passim*; additional information kindly supplied by Prof. Abbott; see also Samuel Johnson, *Letters*, ed. R. W. Chapman (Oxford, 1952), i. 89, iii. 383; *GM* lxvi² (1796), 798; Bromley parish registers).

[33] This name does not appear in the rate books for Suffolk Street, and the Milands have not been further traced.

[34] See below, p. 252.

[35] This trip did not take place. The Rishtons were currently at Bath, whence MAR wrote FB on 22 Feb. (Berg).

She very earnestly wishes me to go with her but I am certain such a proposal would, at present, *raise a storm*.⁷

We had yesterday the—I know not whether to say *pain* or *pleasure*,—of seeing Mʳ Garrick in the part of Lear.³⁶ He was exquisitely Great—every idea which I had formed of his talents, although I have ever idolized him, was exceeded— ¹ I am sorry that this play is Acted with Cibbers Alterations, as every Line of his, is immediately to be distinguished from Shakespeare,—who, with all his imperfections, is too superiour to any other Dramatic Writer, for them to bear so near a comparison: &, to my Ears, every Line of Cibber's, is feeble & paltry.³⁷

Thursday February 25ᵗʰ

Mʳ Adams & his Brother, two Gentlemen who my sister [EB] & self formerly met with at Captain Debieg's, had this Day exposed to public sale, a large & valuable collection of Busts, statues, Bas Reliefs, Pictures, &c, which they purchased many years since in Italy.³⁸

These Gentlemen, with another of their Brothers,³⁹ ˙have,

³⁶ This may have been written on 20 Feb., as Garrick performed Lear at Drury Lane on 17 and 19 Feb. Of the 1st performance William Hopkins comments (MS Diary, 1769–76), 'Mr G. very happy in Lear. great Applause', and of the second, 'Mr G. never better. monstrous Applause' (*LS 4* iii. 1695–6). Garrick played the role 85 times in his career (Stone, pp. 532–40, 656).

³⁷ FB is confusing Colly Cibber's alteration of *Richard III* (1700) with Nahum Tate's of *King Lear* (1681). Tate's version of *Lear* held the stage into the 19th c. though Garrick cut out many of the Tate scenes and phrases and restored many of the original lines (ibid. 532–3).

³⁸ Robert Adam had made the Grand Tour in 1754–8, and his brother James in 1760–3. The sale, in 'the Great Room belonging to the Society of Artists of Great Britain, between Exeter-Change and the Bottom of Catherine-Street in the Strand', 25–7 Feb., 1–2 Mar. 1773, was of 'a most superb unique Collection of ancient Statues, Bustos, Basreliefs, Urns, and other Antiquities, chiefly the Workmanship of Grecian Artists . . . purchased by the Mess. Adams, during their stay in Italy, from . . . the Vatican, Barbarini, Mattie, &c . . .' and 'Pictures, by the greatest Masters of the Italian and Flemish Schools'. The collection had gone on view 23 Feb. (*Daily Adv.* 23 Feb.– 2 Mar. 1773).

³⁹ Presumably FB means the youngest brother, William Adam (*c.*1738–1822), business partner of Robert and James. However, the 4th and eldest brother, John Adam (1721–92), who had inherited the family patrimony, was also a party to the Adelphi venture. The Adelphi (from the Greek for 'brothers'), largely destroyed in 1937, was built from 1768 to 1774 on the site of Durham Yard on the N. bank of the Thames. Stately buildings and streets were constructed on vaulted arches, under which was a warehouse area, fronting on the river. In 1772 the government had decided not to hire the warehouses, and the Adam brothers were already in debt to the sum of

since our acquaintance with Mrs Debieg has dropt, Built the Adelphi, so called from the 3 Brothers being concerned in it. The Undertaking was, I believe, too great for them—& they have suffered much in their ⌐ Fortunes. I cannot but wonder that so Noble & elegant a Plan should fail of encouragement.

I went, yesterday morning, with my sister, to the View of these things. I could not but greatly pity the *Collector* who, I fear, is obliged to part with them. As I have niether knowledge or Judgment in these matters, I venture at no farther opinion than that to me the sight was a great ⌐Treat.⌐

We saw many of our old friends of the Scotch Party, but were not known ⌐to any. Whether we were retired, or they did not see us, I presume not to determine. I looked very hard for Mr. Seton, but am pretty sure he was not there. Those whom I saw were Mr. Robinson, Capt. Debieg, Mr. Craufurd, Cousin of Hetty's old Admirer & Mr. Pringle.[40]

To Day, we went again to the first [s]ale. They will not be over till next Tuesday. Besides again seeing Capt. Debieg & Mr. [Ro]binson, we saw one of the Mr. Adams, and Mrs. Pringle, though far distant from us.

I suspect—notwithstanding his savageness, [Mr.] Seton really meant seriously by my sister [and] therefore⌐ that his friends, & his party, knowing disappointment, & not knowing how his behaviour incurred it, all ⌐resent⌐ her [mar]riage as if it was jilting him. I know, [that] they all thought much higher for her [tha]n Mr. Burney, who has nothing to offer but the fruits of his profession; & she is [so] pretty, & so accomplished, so agreeable & so active, that both in & out of her family [it w]as imagined she would connect herself to far [mor]e worldly advantage. The extreme worth, however, [&] excellent though unpretending understanding [of] Mr. Burney, & his goodness of Heart, & regard from Childhood [will,] I trust & hope, make her happy, & make ⌐him deserve her.

£140,000. Later in 1773 and 1774 they disposed of their assets, except the estate, by lottery, mortgaged their estate, and dismissed hundreds of workers, thus recouping their losses (D. Yarwood, *Robert Adam* (New York, 1970), pp. 40, 143–7, 182).

[40] Presumably Robert Pringle. Evidently he and Debbieg were temporarily back from their assignment in Newfoundland (see above, p. 199). FB reports Pringle to be back in Newfoundland in 1775 (vol. ii).

Saturday Feb[y] 27

The morning is lovely, & I shall again go to the Adams' sale for I am going to that part of the Town, to make a *Bride Visit*.

Miss Molly Turner is, at length, married to her constant Lover, John Allen,[41] & they are come to Town, with Mr. & Mrs. Turner, for [a] few Days, in their way to Bath, where t[hey] are going to make a Visit to Mrs. Ri[shton.] They all supped here last Tuesday [23 Feb.], in ex[cellent] spirits, & good humour.

Thursday Evening [25 Feb.], we went to Mr. [xxxxx *2 lines*] The Opera was Artaxerxes[42] [xxxxx *1 line*] after that, a Cantata, written in English by Mr. Garrick, & set to music by himse[lf] [Millico] expressing his gratitude for his Reception in England, was performed. The music was ex[tr]emely pretty, the Words very well adapted [to] the occasion [xxxxx *2 words*] he was accompanied⌐ |

[*A leaf or leaves have been cut away. It is not clear what* 'disagreement' *is referred to in the next paragraph.*]

⌐final End will be put to all Coldness as well as disagreement. Yet I shall somewhat dread the first Personal Interview.⌐

My Father's German Tour will be Published next Week;[43] Heaven grant it as favourable a reception as the Italian one ⌐met with!⌐ He is extremely anxious; & diffident beyond any Author that ever, I believe, existed.

---

[41] The Revd John Towers Allen (*c.*1744–87), m. (Feb. 1773, at King's Lynn) Mary ('Pow') Turner. Allen was a native of Terrington St Clement, Norfolk, 4 miles W. of Lynn, and he and his wife were to reside at Wiggenhall St German, 4½ miles SW. of Lynn. He later became rector of Barwick, Norfolk (1783–7). MAR mentions the Allens' and Turners' forthcoming visit in her letter to FB 22 Feb. (Berg).

[42] By Thomas Arne. This work, first performed at Covent Garden in 1762, was the first and only English opera 'after the Italian manner' to hold the stage until the 19th c. (*New Grove*). The advertisement for this performance, which was a benefit for Millico, announced that 'Millico will sing two Cantatas in English (Music composed by himself) in which he will sing several songs accompanied by Fisher [Johann Christian Fischer] on *Hautboy*, and some by himself on the *Harp*' (*LS 4* iii. 1697). The text of Garrick's 'English Cantata' was printed in *Lloyd's Evening Post*, 26 Feb.–1 Mar. 1773, xxxii. 204; the music was apparently never published (see above, p. 236). Horace Walpole did not share FB's good opinion of the work; he wrote to William Mason, 2 Mar. 1773: 'Garrick has written a cantata for Millico's benefit: a lyre tumbled out of heaven to play to it; but it was so bad, the audience wished themselves at the devil' (*YW* xxviii. 65–6 and nn. 4–5).

[43] It was not published until 23 Apr. See below, p. 252.

He has shut himelf up entirely from all who know him, but his own family; Dr. Armstrong, among others, has called 50 Times unsuccessfully, though he has always the galantry to say, *that he wants Nobody when he sees us*. I had the pleasure of a long Tête à Tête with him last Monday.

He asked me what I conjectured to be the *Prime Cost*[44] of the most Capital Picture in Mr Strange's last sale?[45]— ⎸it is a Landscape by Nicolas Poussine[46]—& was purchased by Sir Watkins Wynn, at the sum of 600 & 50 pounds. I told him that I could not possibly guess, but I supposed it to be much less than was then given for it. 'But I can tell you exactly, said he, for I have it from a Gentleman who was well acquainted with the transaction: the *Prime Cost* was 7 pounds, odd shillings! & for that sum, Poussine sold it![47] What Mr Strange might purchase it for at Paris, I cannot say.'

How very hard that the man by whose labour & talents this fine Landscape was produced, should have Worked so much for the Advantage of others, & so little for his own!

Dr. Armstrong told me of some particulars in the Will of the famous Lord Chesterfield,[48] who is just Dead; ⎸'he has given, said he, some very excellent advice to Mr Stanhope,[49] his Heir,

[44] i.e., the original price.

[45] 'A Capital and Elegant Collection of Pictures, selected from the Roman, Florentine, Lombard, and other Schools, collected abroad by Robert Strange', was sold at Christie's Great Room in Pall Mall, 5 and 6 Mar. 1773 (*Daily Adv.* 5, 6 Mar. 1773).

[46] Nicolas Poussin (1594–1665), painter. His 'Landscape with a Man killed by a Snake', lot 113 at the Christie sale and now in the National Portrait Gallery in London, was purchased by Sir Watkin Williams Wynn (1748–89), 4th Bt., a collector and member of the Dilettanti Society. Horace Walpole, in a letter to Horace Mann 12 Mar. 1773, comments on the extravagance of this purchase, which undoubtedly contributed to the reputation for gullibility which Wynn was gaining (*YW* xxiii. 466 and nn. 11–12; see also *GM* lix² (1789), 765).

[47] Poussin painted the landscape for a M. Pointel, probably in 1648 (A. Blunt, *The Paintings of Nicolas Poussin: A Critical Catalogue* (1966), p. 143). The identity of the 'Gentleman' who gave Armstrong this figure (suspiciously in English currency) is not known. Strange bought the painting from the Nyert family, to whom it had passed by descent (ibid.; see also A. Blunt, *Nicolas Poussin* (New York, 1967), i. 286–91, ii, plates 182–3).

[48] Philip Dormer Stanhope (1694–1773), 4th E. of Chesterfield, had died on 24 Mar.

[49] Philip Stanhope (1755–1815), 5th E. of Chesterfield, Ld. Chesterfield's cousin and godson, was a student in Leipzig when he succeeded to the peerage. Chesterfield's will, dated 4 June 1772, with a codicil 11 Feb. 1773, stipulated that 'the several devises and bequests ... [to] Philip Stanhope shall be subject to the condition and restriction ... that in case ... [he] shall at any time hereafter keep, or be concerned in the keeping of any racehorse or racehorses, or pack or packs of hounds, or reside one night at Newmarket, that infamous seminary of iniquity and ill manners, during the course of the

admonishing him never to indulge himself in the pernicious practice of Gaming; & he has taken some pretty effectual measures towards securing his Advice from being forgot; as he has added a Clause to it, that if ever he loses 100. £ by Gaming, he is to forfeit 5,000.! In another Article, he has represented the ill consequences of Horse-Racing, earnestly begging him not to give into that Diversion; & to this salutary Counsel, he has annexed a small Clause, that if ever Mr Stanhope is seen upon New Market Heath, he is immediately to forfeit 5.000 pounds.! & these forfeited sums are all to be given in Charity, by the Dean & Chapter of Canterbury.'

I fancy it would be of great service if this Will should prove a model for | future one's. It was but last Week that this Nobleman purchased two of the Capital Pictures of Mr Strange's Collection, though he was then so much confined, that he was obliged to have them carried to his own Room, to examine:[50] An evident Proof that he retained not only his senses, but his love of the Arts, to his last moments.

I have likewise had the honour of two (short) Conversations with Mr Baretti. He called with a Letter from Dr. Marsili,[51] a phisician of Padua, who desired him to send my Father's Italian Tour to him, which he was very impatient to see, as he was my Father's *Ciceroni* at Padua. Mr Baretti appears to be very *facetious*; he amused himself very much with Charlotte,[52]

races there, or shall resort to the said races, or shall lose in any one day at any game or bet whatsoever the sum of £500, then, and in any of the cases aforesaid, it is my express will that he . . . shall forfeit and pay . . . the sum of £5000 to and for the use of the Dean and Chapter of Westminster' (*GM* xliii (1773), 318). Dr Armstrong may have seen a newspaper account such as the paragraph in the *London Chronicle*, 27–30 Mar., xxxiii. 298, which incorrectly cites the Dean and Chapter of Canterbury as recipient of the forfeited sums. See *YW* xxxii. 112–13 and nn. 40–2.

[50] Chesterfield bought 4 pictures at the sale, 6 Mar.: 'The Departure of Jacob' by Claude Lorrain (painted for the Abbé Chevalier at Rome in 1677; purchased in 1952 by the Clark Art Institute, Williamstown, Massachusetts), 400 guineas; a Primaticio for 35 guineas; a portrait of Madame de la Vallière by Hyacinthe Rigaud, for 4 guineas; and a Van Goyen landscape, for 1½ guineas. Presumably he had first noted these pictures in the sale catalogue and had them brought to him for examination; he then sent his valet Thomas Walsh to bid on them (ibid. xxxii. 102–3 and nn. 20–3).

[51] Giovanni Marsili (1727–95), MD, Professor of Botany and Prefect of the botanical garden in the University of Padua. Baretti had given CB a letter of introduction to Marsili, whom CB met at Padua in July 1770. See P. A. Saccardo, *La Botanica in Italia* (Venice, 1895–1901), i. 104, ii. 68, 125; E. A. Cigogna, *Delle Inscrizioni veneziane* (Venice, 1824–53), iii. 10–11; *Life*, i. 322; *Tours*, i. 97 and *passim*.

[*See opposite page for n. 52*]

⌐demanding in what manner she passed the Time, & what she would do—& if she⌐ ⌐ had Read Robinson Crusoe? Charlotte coloured, & *tittered*, & answered Yes Sir, '& pray how many years *vas* he on *de* Uninhabited Island?' 'O Sir, I can't tell that—! ⌐its so long since I read it—⌐ *Vat*! don't you remember *vat* you Read? *den*, my pretty Charlotte, you might spare your Eye sight!'

'But, can you remember *vat vas de* name of Robinson Crusoe's Island?—'

'O Sir, no, that I can't indeed!'

'And could you Read all *dat* Book, & not find out, *dat* it has no Name at all?'

⌐He Enquired of me very particularly how my sister [EBB] did, whom he knew when a Child.⌐[53]

Dr. Hawkesworth, ⌐who is still in Town, & I believe will continue here for some Time,⌐ supped with us very lately, & was extremely sociable & agreeable. Yet he always seems rather to be⌐ *Reading* than *speaking*, his Language is so remarkably Elegant, & ⌐flowing.⌐ I could not but imagine that he was Reading one of his own Adventurers, in an account he gave of a school Boy's Holyday. I will endeavour to recollect it.

'His sleep, said he, the Night before, is broken & disturbed; his Anticipation of pleasure is too lively to let him rest; yet he Wakes, delighted, that the happy Day is come. If it is in his power, he ⌐lays⌐ in Bed, till he is ashamed of leaving it, & at last rises, ashamed of being ashamed. The remaining part of the morning, he passes in considering what to do; but every plan that occurs, appears unworthy employing so precious a Day. At length Evening comes, & his Recollection⌐ then tells him a thousand things which he might have done;—he spends the rest of the Night, in regretting that he wasted the Day;—& at last, goes to Bed, disgusted, wearied & disappointed.'[54]

This discription [*sic*], however, belongs rather to young men

---

[52] FBA has substituted 'whom he calls *Churlotte*, & kissed whether she will or no, always calmly saying 'Kiss-a me, *Churlotte*!' He asked if she'.

[53] Baretti had perhaps known EBB as a young prodigy on the harpsichord.

[54] Hawkesworth's impromptu is highly Johnsonian, and recalls chap. 4 of *Rasselas*. There the Prince regrets having wasted 20 months in doing nothing, passes 4 months more 'in resolving to lose no more time in idle resolves', and finally, 'for à few hours, regretted his regret' (Samuel Johnson, *The History of Rasselas Prince of Abissinia*, ed. J. P. Hardy (1968), pp. 10–12).

than to Boys, whose Childish, or boisterous, Amusements, present themselves with the light.

We went, Susan & I, to a very fine Concert lately, for Mr Fischar's[55] (the celebrated Hautbois) Benefit. [xxxxx *1 line*] ⌜Mr. Young sat with us. He [Fischer] Played incomparably, & had almost all the great Performers in London of his Band. Had Millico been one—it would have been compleat. ⌟

Never was music more lost, than upon Mrs. Young. Far from receiving pleasure, she suffered evident uneasiness. Unused to silence, whenever we were able to Escape her Tongue, she vented her *Ennui* in perpetual Gapes. She was equally irksome to herself & to us.⌟

But, can I speak of music, & not mention Miss Linley?[56] The Town has Rung of no other Name this month.

Miss Linley is Daughter to a musician[57] of Bath, a very sour, ill bred, severe & selfish man. She is believed to be very romantic. She has long been very celebrated for her singing, though never, till within this month, has she been in London.[58] She has met with a great variety of adventures, and has had more lovers & Admirers than ⌞ any Nymph of these Times. She has been addressed by men of all Ranks—I dare not pretend to say *honourably*, which, ⌜however,⌟ is doubtful; but what is certain,

---

[55] Johann Christian Fischer. His benefit concert of vocal and instrumental music took place at the Haymarket on 25 Mar. Besides Fischer (oboe), the instrumentalists were Wilhelm Cramer (1746–99), violin; Carl Friedrich Abel, viola da gamba; —— 'Weise', probably Karl Weiss (*c.*1737–95), German flute; Ernst Eichner (1741–77), bassoon; John Crosdill (1755–1825), cello; and Giovanni Punto, French horn. The singers were Cecilia Grassi and Mrs Frederica Weichsell (*c.*1745–86), English soprano (*Morning Chronicle*, 25 Mar. 1773; *New Grove*; *Die Musik in Geschichte und Gegenwart*, ed. F. Blume (Kassell, 1949–68), xiv. 444; *BUCEM* s.v. Weiss, Carl).

[56] Elizabeth Anne Linley (1754–92), soprano singer; m. (13 Apr. 1773) Richard Brinsley Sheridan.

[57] Thomas Linley (1734–95), composer, harpsichordist, concert director, and singing teacher. Linley was at times a stern and demanding father and teacher, ambitious for himself and for his children, and given to fits of despondency, but FB's description seems one-sided and exaggerated. Perhaps she had caught him in a bad mood at their meeting (see below). CB, who met Linley at Bath in 1747 ('Mem.' No. 45), praises him in Rees as a man who 'loved music', who was 'studious', 'equally versed in the theory and practice of his art', and 'the best singing master of his time, if we may judge by the specimens of his success in his own family'. See also *New Grove*, s.v. Linley.

[58] This is incorrect. Elizabeth Linley made her London début at Covent Garden in 1767 in Thomas Hull's masque *The Fairy Favour*, and sang regularly in the London oratorio seasons, 1769–73. Her first performance this year was on 26 Feb. (ibid.; *LS 4* iii. 1697).

is, that whatever were their Designs, she has rejected them all.[59]
She has long been attached to Mr Sheridan,[60] a young man of
[great talents,][61] & very well spoken of, who it is expected she
will speedily marry.

She has performed, this Lent, at the Oratorio of Drury Lane,
under Mr Stanley's Direction.[62] The Applause and Admiration
she has met with, can only be compared to what is given to M^r
Garrick. The whole Town seem distracted about her. Every
other Diversion is forsaken—Miss Linley Alone engrosses all
Eyes, Ears, Hearts.[63]

At Mrs Stanley's Invitation, Mama, Susan & myself, sat in
her Box at Alexander Balus,[64] to see & hear this Syren. Her
Voice is soft, sweet, clear & affecting, she sings with good
Expression, & has great fancy & even taste in her Cadences,
though perhaps, a finished singer would give less way to the

[59] Elizabeth Linley's 'adventures' were well known to Londoners. In 1771 Samuel
Foote had brought on stage *The Maid of Bath*, a *drame à clef* in which Kitty Linnet
(Elizabeth Linley) is saved from being married off by her mother to the wealthy old
Solomon Flint (Walter Long) by her protector Major Racket (Thomas Mathews),
whose none too pristine designs she also rejects. It played every year until 1777.
Besides Long, a Wiltshire gentleman to whom Elizabeth Linley was actually
engaged at one time, and Mathews (1743–1820), a Welsh squire living at Bath who
pursued her even after his own marriage, Miss Linley's many admirers included
Richard Sheridan's own brother, Charles, and Sir Thomas Clarges. See vol. ii;
M. Bingham, *Sheridan: The Track of a Comet* (1972), pp. 58–69; S. Trefman, *Sam. Foote,
Comedian, 1720–1777* (New York, 1971), pp. 197–201; *LS 4* iii. 1556 and *passim*; R. B.
Sheridan, *Letters*, ed. C. Price (Oxford, 1966), i. 24 n. 6, iii. 382.

[60] Richard Brinsley Sheridan (1751–1816), dramatist and politician. He had met
Elizabeth Linley in 1770 when he moved to Bath with his family. In Mar. 1772 Miss
Linley decided to run away to France to escape the unwelcome advances of Mathews,
and Sheridan accompanied her as *cavaliere-servente*. After their return (in Apr.) he
fought two highly publicized duels with Mathews. Sheridan and 'the Maid of Bath'
were married on 13 Apr. 1773 in Marylebone Church, London. FB was to meet
Sheridan in 1779 (Bingham, pp. 58–60, 65–92, 108; *DL* i. 190).

[61] Written by FBA over the original, which has not been recovered.

[62] John Stanley had taken over the direction of the Lenten oratorios at Covent
Garden (and later Drury Lane) on Handel's death in 1759. From 26 Feb. to 2 Apr. Miss
Linley sang at Drury Lane in Handel's *Judas Maccabeus*, *Alexander's Feast*, *L'Allegro ed Il
Penseroso*, *Alexander Balus*, *Samson*, and the *Messiah* (*LS 4* iii. 1697 and *seq*.; *New Grove*,
s.v. Stanley, John).

[63] The *Westminster Magazine* for Mar. 1773 (quoted *LS 4* iii. 1697) commented: 'One
of those whims by which the public are continually influenced, has made it the *ton* to
resort to . . . [Drury Lane] to hear and see Miss Linley, the syren of Bath. This young
lady . . . has drawn crowded houses incessantly; and this success has been insured by
the constant attendance of his Majesty and the Royal Family at this theatre'.

[64] Handel's oratorio (1748). This performance, 17 Mar. 1773, was by royal
command (*LS 4* iii. 1703).

former, & prefer few & select Notes. She has an exceeding good shake, & the best & most critical Judges, all pronounce her to be infinitely superiour to *all* other English singers. The Town in general give her the preference to *any* other.[65] To me, her singing was *extremely* pleasing. Perhaps, except the ⌜divine⌝ Millico, I would rather hear her (if I also saw her) than I would any other.

As Mrs Stanley's Box is very high, & I am very near-sighted, I could only perceive that Miss Linley's *figure* was | extremely genteel, & the form of her Face very elegant; I had heard from Miss Kinnaird,[66] who is acquainted with Mrs Stanley, that she always went into the Green Room after the Oratorio; & I determined to make interest for the same favour, as it had been granted to Miss Kinnaird. I had immediate success. As soon as the Performance was over, we all went into that famous Apartment, which I was surprised to see, was lined with *Red*! There was not a Creature there; but, at my request, Miss Arland, Mrs Stanley's sister, went into another Room, & asked Miss Linley, & her sister,[67] to favour us with her Company. The rest of the family, Viz, Father, mother[68] & Brother,[69] were already in the Green Room.

Had I been, for my sins, Born of the male Race, I should certainly have added one more to Miss Linley's Train;—| she is really beautiful; her Complection, a clear, lovely, Animated Brown, with a blooming colour on her Cheeks; her Nose that most elegant of shapes, Grecian; fine, luxurious, easy setting Hair, a charming Forehead, pretty mouth, & most bewitching Eyes.[70] With all this, her Carriage is modest & unassuming,

---

[65] CB, in Rees, praises 'the beauty, talents, and mental endowments of this "Sancta Cæcilia rediviva". . . . The tone of her voice and expressive manner of singing were as enchanting as her countenance and conversation. In her singing, with a mellifluous toned voice, a perfect shake and intonation, she was possessed of the double power of delighting an audience equally in pathetic strains, and songs of brilliant execution, which is allowed to very few singers.' Miss Linley had sung the principal soprano part in CB's doctoral exercise performed at the annual choral meeting at Oxford in 1771 ('Mem.' No. 115).

[66] Margaret Kinnaird (d. 1800), youngest daughter of Charles, 6th B. Kinnaird; m. (1779) Thomas Wiggens (d. 1785), MP.

[67] Mary Linley (1758–87), soprano, m. (1780) Richard Tickell (1751–93), amateur dramatist (*New Grove*).

[68] Mary Johnson (1729–1820), m. (1752) Thomas Linley (A. Wagner, 'Pedigree of the Linley Family', in C. Black, *The Linleys of Bath* (3rd edn., 1971), facing p. 292).

[69] Presumably the eldest brother, Thomas Linley, Jr.

[70] See the Reynolds and Gainsborough portraits in Bingham, Plates 4b, 6, and 9.

& her Countenance indicates diffidence, & a strong desire of pleasing; a desire in which she can never be disappointed.

I most sincerely & earnestly wish her well, safely, & happily settled. I think that so young a Woman, Gifted with such enchanting talents, & surrounded with so many Admirers, who can preserve herself, unconscious of her charms, & diffident of her powers,—has merit that entitles her to the strongest approbation, &, I hope, to the greatest happiness:—a union from affection ǀ with a man who deserves her!

Sunday, May [2][71]

I have a thousand things to Write, too many to observe method, & therefore I shall *commit* them as they occur.

Premierement—We have had, from the Cape of Good Hope, the Welcome News of my Brother's promotion. Lieutenant Shanks,[72] a young man who was on board the Adventure, one of the three sloops[73] under Capt. Cooke, was so ill, that he was obliged to leave the ship, & return to England, 'in whose place, says the Captain's Letter to Lord Sandwich, I have appointed M[r] Burney, whom I have found very deserving.'[74] This is most comfortable intelligence—& rejoices us unspeakably; he will be a Lieutenant of 3 years standing by his return. He has written to us, in very good spirits, & assures us that the Cape ǀ of Good Hope is a very agreeable place!

Lord Sandwich has interested himself ⌐much about this

---

[71] FB has incorrectly written the '3d'.

[72] Joseph Shank or Shanks, First Lieutenant of the *Adventure*, Capt. Tobias Furneaux, was subject to gout, and discharged sick at the Cape of Good Hope, 19 Nov. 1772, by order of Capt. Cook (*The Voyage of the* Resolution *and* Adventure *1772–1775*, ed. J. C. Beaglehole (Cambridge, 1961), p. 888).

[73] Originally 3 were intended for the voyage, but only 2 actually sailed: the *Adventure* and the *Resolution*.

[74] This letter, presumably mentioned by Ld. Sandwich to CB, has not been found. The content has probably been garbled somewhat; Cook's letter to the Admiralty Secretary, 18 Nov. 1772, notes that he has appointed JB Second Lieutenant of the *Adventure* in place of Arthur Kempe (d. 1823), later Admiral, who became First Lieutenant in the place of Shank (ibid. p. 687). JB himself was initially under the impression that he was taking Shank's place, noting in his private journal, 18 Nov. 1772, 'on this good day I left the Resolution being appointed 2[d] Lieutenant in the room of M[r] Shanks . . .' (*With Captain James Cook in the Antarctic and Pacific*, ed. B. Hooper (Canberra, 1975), p. 27); he probably wrote to this effect to his family (the letter is missing; see Cook's letter to JB, 18 Nov. 1772, confirming the appointment, in Manwaring, pp. 19–20).

affair, & behaved to my Father, to whom he seems really attached, in the most friendly manner. I wish he may preserve his place of first Lord of the Admiralty, to the Time of Jem's return.[75]

Mr. & Mrs. Rishton are turned absolute Hermits, for this summer, they have left Bath, & are gone to Ting Mouth[76] in Devonshire, where they have taken a *Cottage* rather than a House but the Country, she says is beautiful. They are, however, only to remain there till Stanhoe House,[77] which they have taken for 7 years, is ready for them. I hear very often from Mrs. Rishton,[78] whose friendship, affection & confidence, will, I believe, end but with our Lives.⌐

My Father's German Tour has been Published this Week.[79] In it, is inserted Proposals for printing by subscription his ⌐ History of music. If he has not 500 subscribers by next Christmas, he declares that he will not publish it at all.[80] ⌐Heaven

---

[75] Sandwich continued in the position until 1782.

[76] Teignmouth, one of the first of the English seaside resort towns and a port important in the Newfoundland trade and fisheries. MAR wrote to FB from Teignmouth, 25 Apr. 1773 (Berg): 'Here we are arrived at our little retirement which I think is one of the most beautiful Spots England affords. ... I had heard much of Devonshire but really this surpasses everything my Imagination has formd. ... I will now literally describe our dwelling ... one of the very neatest *Thatchd* Cottages you ever saw—we have it almost all that is a little parlour not much bigger than the 3ᵈ Room in Queens Square ...'

[77] In Stanhoe, Norfolk. The house, which belonged to Mrs Edmund ('Mun') Allen, is illustrated in M. Archdale, 'Buildings with the Bell Touch', *Country Life*, cxl (29 Sept. 1966), 756.

[78] MAR had also written to FB on 13 Apr. (Berg).

[79] *The Present State of Music in Germany, the Netherlands, and United Provinces, or, The Journal of a Tour through those Countries, undertaken to collect Materials for a General History of Music*, was published in 2 8vo vols. on 23 Apr. 1773 by Thomas Becket in the Strand, James Robson in New Bond St., and George Robinson in Paternoster Row (*Morning Chronicle* 23 Apr. 1773).

[80] Facing the title-page of the 2nd vol. of his *German Tour*, CB published a one-page 'Proposals for Printing by Subscription, a General History of Music, from the Earliest Ages to the Present Period', dated 'London, April 20th, 1773'. These 'Proposals' were also issued on a separate leaf in a 4to format, a unique copy of which is preserved in the Bodleian Library (shelf mark: Vet. A5 a. 15[45]). The third of the three 'Conditions' stated that 'It is the author's intention to publish the first volume in ... 1774. But, as the printing of it will be attended with too great an expence for him to risk it against the public opinion ... he cannot venture to send it to the press before *five hundred copies*, are subscribed for. ... if the number of copies specified be not ascertained by next Christmas, he will abandon the enterprize ...' By Christmas CB had a list of barely 400 subscribers, but an anonymous admirer guaranteed to bring the list up to 500. CB eventually obtained 857 subscribers for a total of 1,047 copies (Lonsdale, pp. 138–42, 180).

knows how that may be. Mr. Garrick, [Keane] Fitzgerald, Edwards,[81] & two gentlemen we do not know, are all the Names that have yet been sent in, except our Daddy Crisp, who subscribes for the set.[82] However, my father's acquaintance is so increased, that if he was at all what is called a *pushing man*, (which I thank Heaven he is not) he would have a subscription equal to Pope's for the Iliad.[83] Being that delicate & diffident man that he is, I think the Event very uncertain. "

I will, at least, hope that the German Tour will not disgrace its Brother of Italy. M͏ʳ Garrick writes that 'nothing can be more pleasing to his friends, or more agreeable to the Public; & that it is clear, interesting, instructive & delightful.'[84] |

My Father has made a prodidgious quantity of presents of this Book, "though not, as yet, half the Number he did of the Italian Tour—he sent many the Day before it was Published," viz to Messʳˢ Garrick, Colman, Woide,[85] Baretti, Strange, Hayes, Crisp, Edwards, Young; to Doctors Shepherd, Hunter,[86] Armstrong, Hawkesworth; to Mʳ Fischar, to Lord Sandwich, & to Mʳ Burney "& 5 to Norfolk Family.[87] He has sent several to his friends Abroad.[88]

---

[81] Nicholas Edwards, Esq., of Lynn, a member of the Lynn Corporation Council (subscription list to *Hist. Mus.*; 'The Poll for Members of Parliament for . . . Lynn-Regis . . . March 1768,' MS B.L.I.c., Norfolk Record Office).

[82] SC subscribed for 2 copies of the set.

[83] Pope had 574 subscribers for 653 copies.

[84] Garrick's note of acknowledgement, dated 'Wedʸ 21ˢᵗ [April]', is printed in his *Letters*, ii. 865, from the MS then in the possession of Gabriel Wells, Inc., New York City: 'My dear Burney Ten thousand thanks to you for your most kind & agreeable Present—I have, notwithstanding my present fatigue, & new Study, read a great deal of yʳ book—'tis clear, interesting, instructive & delightful—Nothing can be more pleasing to yʳ friends nor more agreeable to yᵉ Publick . . .' This time CB included as well the non-musical parts of his travel diary, insuring a wider audience and attracting the favourable notice of Dr Johnson.

[85] Charles Godfrey Woide (1725–90), oriental scholar and divine. A native of Poland, he was currently preacher or reader at the Dutch chapel royal in St James's Palace, London. He later became assistant librarian of the British Museum (1782) and FRS (1785); he also received the degrees of DD from Copenhagen and DCL from Oxford (1786).

[86] William Hunter (1718–83), MD, physician extraordinary to Queen Charlotte. As the leading obstetrician in London he had been called in by CB to attend CB's first wife during her fatal illness (in 1762). See *Mem.* i. 138, 143.

[87] He probably sent copies (one per household) to his mother-in-law Mrs Allen, Mrs Edmund Allen, the Maxey Allens, the Stephen Allens, and the Rishtons (cf. the subscription list to *Hist. Mus.*).

[88] One of these was Christoph Daniel Ebeling, who in June wrote to protest against

To Signor Millico he sent one immediately, as he had insisted on my Father's accepting two Pit Tickets at his Benefit[89] & that grateful tempered man, determined not to rest the last obliged, called her the Day after, & brought with him a Collection of Canzonettes, which he has just published.[90] Unfortunately, he was not let in; I have repined at it ever since.⁇

Captain Brydone,[91] who Mr Beckford ⎮ brought to one of our Concerts, has just Published 'A Tour to the Islands of Sicily & Malta, in Letters to William Beckford Esqr, from P. Brydone, F.R.S.' I have received very great Entertainment from this Book, it is written in an easy, natural, lively style, & is full of anecdotes, observations, & descriptions; & in many places, is very philosophical. It discovers throughout, a liveliness of Imagination, an insatiate curiosity after knowledge, & the most vehement desire of instruction. I very much wish that the Author may continue his Acquaintance with my Father, for I am sure he must be extremely Agreeable.

Dr. Goldsmith has just brought on the stage a new Comedy, called 'She Stoops to Conquer'.[92] We went to it, with Mr and Mrs Young; it is very laughable & Comic—ᵣbut, I know not

CB's 'interpolated remarks against German Genius in genere' (see above, p. 174 n. 89; Lonsdale, pp. 125–7).

[89] 25 Feb. (above, p. 244).

[90] 'Six songs, with an accompanyment for the great or small harp, forte piano or harpsichord', etc., published by Robert Bremner (*BUCEM*). A '2d set of Italian Songs for the Harp', pub. by Peter Welcker the following year, is listed in *Mus. Lib.*, p. 7.

[91] Patrick Brydone (1736–1818), traveller and author. Brydone had been travelling preceptor to William Beckford and two others on a 1767 continental tour, and the same group had travelled without Beckford to Sicily and Malta in 1770; CB met Brydone at Naples in October of that year (*Tours*, i. 258). *A Tour through Sicily and Malta: In a Series of Letters to William Beckford, Esq. of Somerly in Suffolk; from P. Brydone, F.R.S.*, was published in 2 vols. on 8 Apr. 1773 by William Strahan and Thomas Cadell (*Daily Adv.* 8 Apr. 1773). The book was to go through 7 or 8 edns. in England in the author's lifetime and was also translated into French and German. 'Captain' Brydone had been First Lieutenant in the 85th Regiment of Foot, or Royal Volunteers (Col. John Craufurd), disbanded at the end of the Seven Years' War, and was now on half pay (*AL passim*). He was made a FRS on 4 Mar. 1773 (*The Record of the Royal Society of London* (4th edn., 1940), p. 424).

[92] *She Stoops to Conquer; or, The Mistakes of a Night*, was first performed at Covent Garden 15 Mar. 1773. The *Westminster Magazine* commented: 'On the whole the Comedy has many excellent qualities; though we cannot venture to recommend it as a pattern for imitation. Still attached to the laudable intent of it, we wish it may keep possession of the stage, till a better comedy comes to relieve it' (cited *LS 4* iii. 1702). By the beginning of May it had already been repeated 14 times.

how, almost all Diversions are insipid, at present, to me, except
ᴵ the Opera.

Madame Cades,[93] the young French Harpsichord Player is
returned to Paris. I fancy her English Plan succeeded very ill,
her Husband came over for her—how they will manage his
Relations, I know not but her affection seems powerful enough
to make her happy at all events, since she is united to
M. Cades.ᵀ

Miss Linley is married to Mʳ Sheridan.[94] She has entirely
given up singing in Public, & I am very glad to find that the
Queen[95] has taken her under her protection, as private singer to
her majesty, & allows her a salary of 600. *l.* per Ann.[96] I hope
this *double* settlement will ensure her peace for Life—though
Heaven knows how many Heart it may break.

ᵀI have not seen Barsanti this Age, her Benefit is fixed for the
10ᵗʰ of this month.[97] I am very much concerned to hear from
my sister [EBB], who often sees her, thatᵀ ᴵ

[*3 leaves cut away*]

ᵀNevertheless, I returned Home with Mama, though very
reluctantly. Sukey told me that Miss Kinnaird was in Town &
had called. I was sorry I missed seeing her. It seems she gave
Susan a most ridiculous account of Mʳ Hankle[98]—that he had
gone to Bromley where Dr. Hawkesworth Lives, & beg'd of
Miss Kinnaird to give him a Note, or some pretence, for coming to our House—she told him she could only send her love—
but that, he observed, was not message sufficient to receive a
Visit—& some more flightiness of the same Nature, which I am
tempted to think owe their origin partly to her own invention,
as she is of a gay & sportive disposition, & as Mr. Hankle did
not seem to me by any means so rhodamontade and flighty a
Character. However, Miss Kinnaird has fixt it in her Fancy that

[93] Neither Madame Cades nor her husband has been traced.
[94] On 13 Apr.
[95] (Sophie) Charlotte of Mecklenburg-Strelitz (1744–1818), m. (1761) George III,
King of England.
[96] A false rumour. Miss Linley had in fact sung privately for the King and Queen at
Buckingham House on 2 Apr., when the King complimented her father on her fine
voice and presented him with a £100 banknote (*Bath Chronicle*, 13 Apr. 1773, s.v.
London, 10 April, cited in C. Black, *The Linleys of Bath*, p. 97).
[97] See below, p. 261. The reason for FB's concern about her is not known.
[98] Not further identified.

he has taken a very serious *penchant*, to a person by no means deserving it.["]99 |

My Father came Home between 4 & 5. all kindness & indulgence, he asked if we should like to go to the Opera? Mama declined it, but Susan & I were quite in raptures—To the pleasure of hearing such sweet music, was added the interest we took in its success on account of it's Composer.[1]

We called upon my sister, who was delighted at joining us. ["]There was a very *fine House*, to use the Theatric Term—the Pitt & Boxes quite full.["] Mr Harris[2] of Salisbury, famous for his Treatises on music, Happiness &c, sat just before us, & was introduced by [Mr Batt][3] a gentleman, with him, to my Father. I found he was an Enthusiast for Sacchini, whose music my Father & himself seemed endeavouring which should praise ["]it["] most. 'Such ingenious accompaniments—so much Taste—such an inexhaustible variety—' &c Mr Harris also mentioned that he was | acquainted, & consequently charmed with, the *man*, as well as the musician. ["]'How charmingly, said he, does Sacchini sing himself! I heard him this very morning in a song of his own Composition—and I never, I protest, heard a song better Composed,—better performed.

Millico's turn came next. Mr. Harris confirmed my opinion of his Judgement, by pronouncing him to be a most Capital & extraordinary singer & my Father added the most constantly & exactly in Tune of any singer he ever heard.

---

99 Presumably FB herself.

1 The opera was Sacchini's *Tamerlano* (libretto by A. Piovene), first performed 6 May 1773. The Burneys attended the 2nd performance, on Saturday, 8 May (*New Grove*; *LS 4* iii. 1720–1).

2 James Harris (1709–80) of the Close, Salisbury, Wiltshire. Harris was MP for Christchurch, 1761–80, and a former Lord of the Admiralty and of the Treasury; in 1774 he became secretary and Comptroller to the Queen. A writer on philology and philosophy and an enthusiastic musical amateur, he published in 1744 *Three Treatises: The First Concerning Art: The Second Concerning Music, Painting and Poetry: The Third Concerning Happiness* (CB's copy of the 2nd edn., 1765, listed *Lib.*, p. 23). Handel and Sacchini were his frequent guests, and his daughter Louisa (vol. ii) was a pupil of the latter. CB had met Harris through Fulke Greville in 1747, and calls him 'the most amiable, learned, & worthy of men' ('Mem.' No. 44; see also Rees, s.v. Harris; *New Grove*; Namier).

3 Inserted by FBA. This was John Thomas Batt (1746–1831) of Salisbury; barrister of Lincoln's Inn. His long friendship with the Burneys seems to date from this period. He was also a friend of Samuel Johnson, Horace Walpole, Edward Gibbon (to whom he was executor), and other notables of the day. A portrait of him by Romney was owned (in 1956) by Harris's descendant Ld. Malmesbury. See *YW* xi. 17 n. 25; Gibbon, *Letters*, ed. J. F. Norton (1956), iii. 394 and *passim*.

The Opera went off extremely well, & with great applause. I was doubly rejoiced at it as we had heard so bad an account of it's success on the first Night of Representation. The merit of the Opera remains the same that it was, but we have since heard the Coldness with which it was received at first, accounted for.[4]

Millico exerted himself Nobly—all ⌐ the other singers seemed desirous of excelling—⌐

I have never heard any Opera that has given me equal pleasure except Il Cid.

Now for ⌐Sunday [9 May].

About 7 o'clock my Father returned from Lord Grimstone's.[5] I fancy, said he, that Millico is coming immediately, for somebody has been Bowing to me from a Coach—

Just then, the Carriage stop'd. Enter Sacchini & Millico. They made their Compliments to Mama & then Sign^r Sacchini turning to my Father, desired to know if he [CB] had made his [Sacchini's] apologies to the *signorini*? which he repeated.[6]

He⌐ was in apparent high spirits, & had an animation in his Countenance that I had thought was foreign to it, as he had hitherto appeared too mild & gentle to be even lively, which, however, could meerly have been owing to his bad Health, or else his inquietude about his Operas; for this Evening he was all spirit.

He was seated next to Mama—who, when he found it in vain to address in French or Italian, he said, in a very droll voice ⌐ 'Eh bien—I *most* speak English.' Then bowing to her 'how do you do, Madam?—very well?—'

This little attempt, I believe, included almost all his English, ⌐though he exclaims that if he stays here longer, he will study it.

[4] Probably the 'Coldness' was blamed on a cabal against Sacchini and Millico. CB writes that 'the admirers of Tenducci and Guadagni, as well as the Cocchi, Guglielmi, Giardini, and Bach parties, however hostile in other particulars, all agreed in decrying every part of that opera in which their favourite had no concern. Sacchini . . . was involved in these cabals. . . . Indeed, at first both the Music and performance were frequently hissed . . .' (Mercer, ii. 878; see also above, p. 221 n. 2). However, though CB pronounced both operas 'equal, if not superior, to any musical dramas I had heard in any part of Europe' (Mercer, ii. 894), *Tamerlano* was much less successful than *Il Cid*, and was performed only 6 times (compared to 22).

[5] James Grimston (1711–73), 2nd Visc. Grimston, a neighbour of the Burneys in Queen Square. He died 'of the gout' in Dec. 1773 (*GM* xliii (1773), 622).

[6] Sacchini apparently had not recognized the Burney sisters at the opera the night before (see below, p. 258).

He has at present a master, but too little Time to profit much by him.

Millico then related the difficulty they had had in Directing the Coach-men to the House, for his servant is an Italian, & as little acquainted with English as himself.⌐ |

[*The remainder of the page is blank, except for the words* 'on *(indented and immediately following the last line above) and* stop teif *(at the bottom of the page). FB seems to have intended to insert Millico's anecdote, then failed to do so.* Stop teif *is presumably the* droll Exclamation *alluded to below.*]

⌐This droll Exclamation did not fail to make us laugh, but we concluded that he was willing to let us hear all he had learnt of our Language.⌐

My Father then told Sacchini how much he had been charmed with Tamerlano, which he had heard the Night before.

⌐'E! les *signorini*?' said he—

My Father told him that we were all there, & all equally delighted.⌐

Signor Sacchini receives Compliments with the graceful modesty of a man by Nature diffident, yet by Custom enured to them.

⌐He then again repeated his Excuses for not having known us more certainly. [xxxxx *1 line*]

'O Cried my sister

'Mais, les Chapeaus [*sic*] said he⌐7

Millico persued the Conversation concerning the Opera.—& very drolly, going to the Harpsichord, played a passage in one of the Chorusses [*sic*] | & mimicked a most terrible man, who, in spight of all the Instruction he has had, always ruins it. The Chorus is exceeding spirited, & though very indifferently performed, has a very fine effect, & is much admired. 'It shews the Composer,—said my Father in Italian,—'notwithstanding his mildness & softness,—he breaks out now & then, with all the Neapolitan Fire. He is a *Vesuvious* [*sic*] at Times!'8

---

⁷ In this obliterated passage FB has left several blank lines, presumably for additional dialogue in French which she failed to insert later.

⁸ Sacchini had spent most of his early life in Naples (*New Grove*).

ᶲ'Mais, mon Dieu, said Millico, coming from the Harpsichord with an Air *Nonchalante*—ᶲ

Mrs. & the Miss Ellerkers[9] now entered. The mother is a slow, dawdling, sleepy kind of Dame; the Daughters are accomplished, & anxious for distinction, & good & well principled; but very stiff, ᶲvain,ᶲ affected, ᶲ&ᶲ I like them, nevertheless, for their real enthusiasm for Millico & Sacchini. There is always soul with enthusiasm; though not always sense.

ᶲThen turning to my sister, he [Sacchini] demanded how the Harpsichord went on? while Millico entered ᶦ into Conversation with my Father concerning his Book, & beg'd to have his Name added to his List of subscribers.[10]

'Mais—vous chantez, Mademoiselle?—' said Sacchini, who we found knew nothing of Hetty's being married & her look is so very young, that nobody would suspect it.[11]

He told us that he had received an Invitation to go to the Feast for the sons of the clergy at St Paul's.[12] My Father told him how ill he would be entertained there, both with the music & performance—my sister added that they almost constantly sung out of Tune—

Millico advancing, she repeated what she had said & added that she supposed he might have had the pleasure already to hear ten singers out of Tune?

'O oui, said he drolly, c'est une des plaisirs ᶦ [xxxxx *3 words*] I told him that I hoped we should keep him another year in England—he said that he did not yet know himself. The managers[13] will be greatly their own Enemies, if they suffer him

---

[9] Barbara née Dixon (*c.*1720–1804), widow of Eaton Mainwaring Ellerker (*c.*1722–71) of Risby Park, Yorkshire, and her daughters: Elizabeth (1751–1831); Charlotte (1754–1802), m. (1777) George Townshend (1753–1811), Baron Ferrers, afterwards (1807) 2nd Marquess Townshend; Arabella (1755–82), m. (1776) Thomas Onslow (1754–1827), afterwards (1814) 2nd E. Onslow; and Harriet (1759–1842) (*JL* iii. 15 n. 7; iv. 327 n. 5, 340 n. 16; *GM* lxxiv¹ (1804), 600).

[10] 'Signor Millico' is in the list.

[11] Again FB has left a blank space (of 4 lines).

[12] The annual concert and feast for the benefit of this charity, dating from the mid-17th c., were held on Thursday, 13 May. The music (by Handel and Boyce) was performed in St Paul's Cathedral, and receipts were used 'for apprenticing the Sons and Daughters of necessitous Clergy'; all expenses of the concert and feast were paid by the stewards who included Ld. Sandwich (*Daily Adv.* 5, 11 May 1773; Scholes, ii. 183).

[13] The manager of the Opera (since 1769) was George Hobart (1732–1804), afterwards (1793) 3rd E. of Buckinghamshire. The treasurer, Peter Crauford (d. 1793) also seems to have had a share in the management. In Nov. of this year the Brookes and Yateses succeeded Hobart as joint managers (vol. ii; Highfill; *LS 4* i, p. lxix).

to go. I could not forbear telling him that he spoilt me for the opera for ever.

Miss Ellerker now led the way to the study.⌐ Millico, like another Orpheus, was Embracing his Harp. We all flocked about him—⌐but, he would not sing a Note till we were all seated.⌐

O *how* he did sing ⌐it⌐! his Voice with the Harp, how infinitely sweet! the delicacy of his ⌐*Diminuendo* exceeds all praise— as the brilliancy of his *Crescendo* does equally. The⌐ piano so affectingly soft! smooth, *melting* I may say—the Forte clear, well toned, exactly & nicely in Tune—the Harp alone is proper to accompany such ⌐ a Voice. He sang 4 airs, all of his own Composition & expressly made for the Harp. They are very pretty, but serve as meer outlines for him to fill up. He has lately published them:[14] he told my Father that it was not to *get*, but simply to *save* money that he Printed them,—for that where ever he played them, he found so many Ladies requested them of him, that he should have been ruined in paying Copyists.

⌐My sister was next desired to Play. She was accompanied by her Husband in a sonata of my Father's, which was very much admired, & to which Sacchini said '*Dis* pleases me *much.*' & when she took her seat, he asked her '*Will you Candle stick?*'⌐[15]

In the midst of this ⌐Lesson,⌐ two Beaus entered. Mr Grimston,[16] Eldest son of Lord Grimston, & his Brother. He is just returned from making the Grand Tour— ⌐& I did very much envy him that when he was Introduced to Signors Millico & ˙Sacchini, he Entered into an Italian Conversation with them.

Millico, to our universal satisfaction, was now again called upon to indulge us with his Harp—& he immediately Complied—he favoured us with the same Airs again, which I suppose better suited his Instrument than any others.⌐

[14] See above, p. 254. CB comments on Millico's airs in Rees, s.v. Millico: 'The canzonets of his composition, in singing which he used to accompany himself on a small harp slung over his shoulder, are still as *musica di camera*, elegant and pleasing'.

[15] i.e., 'Do you want a candle?'

[16] The Hon. James Bucknall Grimston (1747–1808). He presumably embarked on the Grand Tour after receiving his MA from Cambridge (in 1769). Upon his father's death in December he succeeded him as 3rd Visc. Grimston (Ireland); he was later (1790) cr. B. Verulam in the British peerage. Grimston had 2 brothers: William (1750–1814), admitted to Lincoln's Inn, 1767, afterwards MP; and Harbottle (1752–1823), divine.

When we had *Breathed*—which we scarse allowed ourselves to do while he sung,—Mr Burney was requested to Play.—he was animated, & never ⌐played⌐ better.

It is impossible to express the delight which his performance gave to Millico—his amazing Execution really excited in ⌐him⌐ the most hearty Laughs—the Italians cultivate Harpsichord playing so little, giving all their Time to the Voice, that Execution such as Mr Burney's appeared miraculous—& when ⌐he⌐ saw him make ˡ a fine & long shake with his 4th & little Fingers, & then change from Finger to Finger, while his left Hand kept on the subject—he was really almost Convulsed—⌐'ah! les regardez! les petits Doigts!—& insisted on Mr. Grimston's looking on—'*C'est terrible!*' said Sacchini—But if Millico had been at a Comedy he could not have been more diverted—he Laughed violently & made perpetual Exclamations—⌐ & when it was over, rising from his seat, he clapt his Hands, & cried with Emphasis & in a very droll accent '*It is terrible I really tink.*'

⌐How little did he know the common acceptation of this Expression in English.[17]

Signor Sacchini told my sister that he wished very much that he had Time to apply to Harpsichord playing, which he very much liked—Mais, said he,⌐ ˡ

[*a leaf or leaves cut away*]

We have returned the Ellerkers' visit—though they did not return their Entertainment! no music! no Millico—! no Sacchini!—every thing stupid & heavy.

Miss Barsanti's Benefit was the 10th ⌐of this month [May]. She had Macbeth as the managers[18] were of opinion that she would have a better House with a Tragedy, than a Comedy.⌐ She, ⌐however, did the⌐ Prelude, & ⌐acted⌐ Sophy in the Musical Lady.[19] I think she acquitted herself extremely well: ⌐the part of Sophy seemed to suit her exceedingly, & she did⌐ it with spirit & propriety. She had a very great House—⌐the Boxes so Crowded & hot, we could scarse support ourselves. My Father, though he could not be there, took a [xxxxx *1 word*] Box &

---

[17] Sacchini and Millico were of course using the term in its less common sense of 'formidable' or 'awesome'; the Italian *terribile* can also have this meaning.

[18] The manager of Covent Garden was George Colman the elder; his partners were Thomas Harris and Messrs. Dagge and Leake (Highfill, s.v. Colman).

[19] This was Barsanti's 1st performance of Colman's afterpiece (1762). Before the mainpiece she gave her 20th performance of his 'Occasional Prelude' (*LS 4* iii. 1721).

8 Tickets of her."⁷ I am much pleased that this Evening has proved at once so creditable & so profitable to her.²⁰ |

I do not know whether I have ever mentioned the *Breach* that happened some years since, between my Father & Mʳ Greville: occasioned by some Dispute, in which the latter conducted himself with so much Arrogance, that, Notwithstanding the very long friendship & intercourse between them, they broke off all Acquaintance: & have not met since.²¹ But, this last Week, my Father received the following curious Note.

Quʸ

[NB. I have quite forgot what the Query was.—but this followed.]²²

Lord March & Mʳ Greville had a small Bet upon this, & have both agreed to refer the matter to Dr. Burney's Decision.

They will therefore be much obliged to him, if he will send his Answer to Almack's.²³

My Father according did, but we have heard no more of it, save only a Note of | Thanks from Mʳ Greville.²⁴

---

²⁰ The account book (cited ibid.) shows a profit to Barsanti of £1 10s. 6d., plus £146 18s. from 779 tickets sold (367 box, 279 pit, and 133 gallery).

²¹ This breach seems to have occurred in late 1771 (see above, p. 32). It was caused by Greville's unexpectedly demanding back from CB the £300 he had paid Thomas Arne in 1748 to release CB from his indenture; Greville was prompted to make his demand by chronic gambling debts. In her seventies, FBA wrote an account of the quarrel, which has remained in manuscript (Barrett, BL Egerton 3696 fos. 127ᵛ–130ᵛ), as she considered it too personal to include in the published *Memoirs*. She probably based it in part on CB's memoirs, which she subsequently destroyed, and in part on a letter of CB to SC, 21 Jan. 1774 (Berg); she confusingly telescopes the quarrel to a period of several months, rather than several years. Her account of the initial breach is as follows: 'Mr. Greville [made] . . . an application, abrupt, yet composed & deliberate, to Dr. Burney, who now, he said, was "a man of easy fortune," for re-payment of the sum by which the Doctor's articles had been cancelled with Dr. Arne. . . . when Mr. Greville perceived the amazement . . . excited by this requisition, he arched his fine brow with a haughtiness he had never before exhibited to this his first favorite; &, violently ringing the Bell, ordered the Servant to enquire whether his Chair were in waiting? . . . Dr. Burney offered no opposition; & though he rose when Mr. Greville arose, suffered him to parade the room without uttering a word. When the chair was announced, Mr. Greville, with a formal, but supercilious bow, made his exit. This scene passed in a Tete à Tete in Queen Square.'   ²² Inserted by FBA.

²³ The subject of the bet was presumably musical. Almack's was the fashionable men's club in Pall Mall, established in 1764. Of the gambling there, Horace Walpole wrote to Horace Mann, 2 Feb. 1770, that it 'has taken the *pas* of White's', and 'is worthy the decline of our empire or commonwealth, which you please. The young men of the age lose five, ten, fifteen thousand pounds in an evening there' (*YW* xxiii. 187; Wheatley, i. 38–9).   ²⁴ These notes are all missing.

5. A fragmentary leaf from Fanny Burney's Journal for 1773, showing recto and verso. The bottom of the leaf has been cut away and the verso obliterated by Madame d'Arblay.

I am always concerned at the breaking off of Old friends.—I am sure that Mr Greville loves my Father, & I doubt not, wishes much to renew his intimacy—but he is a haughty man, & must be too sensible that he has acted ill, to be able to make a graceful reparation.[25]

My Father's friend, Mr Beckford, is just married. We have not seen him since—though he has *called. I should* like to be acquainted with his Bride,[26] who I think *must* be amiable. |

[*bottom of page cut away*]

^⌐[xxxxx *6 lines*]

We got admission without any difficulty & heard the whole Opera Rehearsed. Some Things in it, & indeed all the part of Orfeo,[27] were charming but Sacchini has spoiled us—in *his* Operas, like Piccini in Comic ones[28]—*every* song has some peculiar⌐ |

[*bottom of page cut away*]

^⌐Millico chanced to Catch our Eye as he was singing in the Duet—& recollected us [xxxxx *1 line*]

We were hurrying away the moment the Rehearsal was over—& as we got to the [xxxxx *1 word*] Door, it was opened beyond by Signor Sacchini—who had quitted the Harpsichord the Instant that he could, to come & speak to us. He is terribly distressed for Words in the French Language, when he first sees any who cannot speak Italian—however, he has always

[25] By Dec. FB was able to write that CB and Greville were 'at length, entirely & most cordially reconciled'. Before this happened, however, Greville seems to have renewed his demand and even threatened a law suit in Westminster Hall. See below, p. 322.

[26] Charlotte Hay (d. 1833), daughter of Thomas Hay, formerly Island Secretary of Jamaica. She m. (13 Apr. 1773) her first cousin William Beckford; the ceremony was performed in Lambeth Palace by the Abp. of Canterbury (*Daily Adv.* 14 Apr. 1773). Shortly after their marriage the Beckfords returned to Jamaica, remaining there until 1788 (F. Cundall, *Historic Jamaica* (1915), pp. 362, 366). FBA asked to be remembered to Mrs Beckford in a letter to EBB, *c.*29 Sept. 1818 (*JL* x. 929 and n. 15).

[27] The opera was evidently *Orfeo ed Euridice* by Christoph Willibald von Gluck (1714–87), libretto by Raniero de Calzabigi. First performed in Vienna in 1762 and in London in 1770, it was staged during the current season on 9 Mar. and again on Tuesday, 25 May, with further repetitions on 28 May and 8 June. Millico sang the part of Orfeo (*New Grove*; *LS 4* iii. 1699–1701, 1728, 1730, 1732). CB, who called Gluck a 'musical composer of great fire and originality' notes that the London productions of this 'famous opera' had additional music by J. C. Bach and P. Guglielmi (Rees, s.v. Gluck; Mercer, ii. 877).

[28] See above, p. 56 n. 19.

Words enough to be Polite—he Enquired after our Healths—
said he intended coming to our House very soon, & desired his
particular Compliments to my Father.

[xxxxx *5 lines*] We Had very little further Conversation, for
between my haste, & his Embarrassment, Susey was the only
Conversible of the Three.⌐ |

Mama is gone to Lynn for the summer—⌐She would not
have gone before my Father, but on account of Mrs. Allen's illness.⌐ Bessy & the sweet Dick are gone with her.

I am once more here *en maitress*, but thank heaven, my dear
Father is *en maître*. I am never half so happy as with him.

We were at the Fund play last year.[29] Garrick did King
Lear—but too well!—he has alarmed us extremely, by hinting
at a Design of leaving the stage Next year—I hope he will be
prevail[ed] upon to change his resolution.[30]

He has been here twice lately—in most excellent spirits. One
morning he called at 8 o'clock, & unfortunately, Susette & I
were not come down stairs. We hurried in vain—for he
⌐discovered our laziness, &⌐ made us monstrously ashamed,
by his raillery—

'I shall tell M[rs] Garrick, said he—that I found the Doctor
Reading Petra[r]ch[31]—in *Flannels*, | like a *young man*—but
where, says I, where [were][32] the young Ladies?—where do you
think were *my* Favourites?—why *in Bed*!—'

When he went away, he caught Charlotte in his Arms, & ran
with her down the steps, & to the Corner of the square—
protesting he intended taking her off.[33]

[29] So in the MS, but obviously a slip for 'night' or 'week'. Garrick performed Lear,
26 May 1773, as a 'Benefit for raising a Fund for the relief of those, who from their
infirmities shall be oblig'd to retire from the stage' (playbill quoted *LS 4* iii. 1728). The
poet James Beattie, who saw this performance, commented: 'Garrick's action in this
most difficult character transcends all praise. The many tears shed by the audience
bore ample testimony to his and to Shakespeare's merit' (*James Beattie's London Diary
1773*, ed. R. S. Walker (Aberdeen, 1946), p. 41).

[30] Garrick had been considering retirement ever since his return from his Grand
Tour (in 1765), but he did not quit the stage until 1776 (C. Oman, *David Garrick* (1958),
p. 307).

[31] Francesco Petrarca or Petrarch (1304–74), poet. CB was perhaps reading his 1582
Basle 4to edn. of *Le Rime del Petrarca*, with commentary by Lodovico Castelvetro (listed
in *Lib.*, p. 46).   [32] Inserted by FBA.

[33] FBA has added: 'as his own *Reynolds' Comedy*, which she looks as if she had sat for,
he says.—' The allusion is to Sir Joshua Reynolds' *Garrick between Tragedy and Comedy*,
his first picture of the actor, exhibited at the Society of Artists in 1762. See the illustrations in Highfill; Oman, facing p. 222; Stone, p. 158.

⌐I have had a most earnest & pressing Invitation from the Rishtons to pass the summer with them at Ting Mouth. My Father, however, dares not spare his *Librarian* at present—but when he goes into Norfolk, I fancy & hope I shall make a Trip to Devonshire.⌐34

Mʳ Baretti called here last Sunday. He told my Father that Dr. Johnson will be very glad to see him; has Read both his Tours with great pleasure, & has pronounced him to be *one of the First Writers of the Age* for travels! Such praise from Dr. Johnson, whom my Father reveres above All Authors, Living or Dead, has given him the highest delight.35 |

⌐The statuary, Mr. Nollekens,36 our old acquaintance, is in great favour at Court—he is now modelling the King's

---

[34] MAR made the invitation in her letter to FB, 28 May 1773 (Berg): 'If your Father can spare you to go down to Lynn he can much better spare you to come and spend the summer with me. . . . I can hardly express to you the favour it would confer on Mʳ Rishton and myself—he was so kind as to propose the scheme to me—it would be one of the greatest Conforts [*sic*] in the World to me as I am sometimes a great Confinement I am sensible on my dear Martin who woud otherwise go out oftner a fishing and shooting . . .' FB joined the Rishtons at Teignmouth in July. See below, p. 274.

[35] Dr Johnson was won over by the non-musical parts which CB included in his second *Tour*. In March 1772 he had declared to Boswell, with reference to the *Italian Tour*, that 'Dr. Burney was a very pretty kind of man; but he could not read through the book. I asked him why. He said, "Because I could not read about fiddles and fiddlestrings."' He later claimed, however, to have read the *German Tour* right through—'except, perhaps, the description of the great pipes in the organs of Germany and the Netherlands'—and he told both CB and William Seward that he had taken it as the model, for 'size and form', of his own *Journey to the Western Islands of Scotland*, published in 1775 (Lonsdale, pp. 129–30 and nn. 2–4; sources there cited). CB's close friendship with Johnson dates from this time, that is, from Johnson's first acceptance of him as a fellow man of letters, as opposed to a mere musician. Johnson's approbation was shared by the rest of London literary society. As CB later recalled, the fact that his *German Tour* had included non-musical material 'procured me many more readers than mere students and lovers of music. My publication was honoured with the approbation of the blue-stocking families at Mrs Vezey's, and Mrs. Montagu's and Sir Joshua Reynolds's, where I was constantly invited and regarded as a member . . .' (*Tours*, i. p. xxx).

[36] Joseph Nollekens (1737–1823), sculptor. CB had met Nollekens in Dec. 1770 at Calais, where they were detained for several days by bad weather. Nollekens was returning to England after 10 years of study and work in Rome. During the delay he drew a portrait in black chalk of CB, labelled by him 'Dʳ Burney at Calis in the year 1770', which is now in the Osborn Collection (see illustration). Nollekens, who became a lifelong friend of the Burneys, was already the most fashionable sculptor in London, his busts almost as sought after as Reynolds's portraits. The bust commissioned this year by George III is in the Royal Society, and is reproduced in R. Gunnis, *Dictionary of British Sculptors* (2nd edn. (1964), Plate XVIII. Nollekens's bust of CB, completed by 1803 and now in the BL, is reproduced as the frontispiece to *Tours*, ii. See ibid. i. 318; Lonsdale, pp. 414, 418; vol. ii.

Head. We have been to see it, & think it the finest Bust we ever saw.

We went the same Day to Mr. Merlin,[37] the most ingenious of mechanics, who is making an Instrument that is to have all the properties of a Harpsichord, a Piano Forte, an organ, the double & the single Harp. It is a charming Instrument—my sister tried it. He has likewise contrived a method of Roasting a Leg of mutton by a Reflector. His Genius in regard to mechanism, seems universal.

The Buona Figliuola has been done for the Benefit of Madame Syrmen,[38] who is a sweet Player on the Violin, but a very indifferent singer. She performed Cecchini tolerably, however. My sister, Susan & I went to the Rehearsal of it. Almost all the singers were new ones. ⌐ |

Sunday June 13th

This Day—Time was!—gave me birth![39] but no Bells have Rung—no Guns have Fired—I am strangely neglected!

⌐My sweet Grandmother is better.

My Father, Mr. & Mrs. Young, Susan & myself went last Friday [11 June] to Marybone Gardens intending to see the Fire Works of the celebrated Signor Torre.[40] But a violent Rain

---

[37] John Joseph Merlin (1735–1803), Flemish instrument maker and inventor. He came to England in 1760, and from 1768 to 1773 was director of Cox's Museum in Spring Gardens; he afterwards opened up a business in Prince's St., Hanover Square. The instrument referred to is presumably his 'compound harpsichord', patented in 1774, an example of which, dated 1780, is in the Deutsches Museum, Munich. CB acquired a Merlin harpsichord by 1775, and a 6-octave Merlin piano in 1777. Merlin's many ingenious inventions include an invalid chair which is still used today (*New Grove*; Scholes, ii. 202–9; *DL* i. 458 n. 4; vol. ii).

[38] Maddalena Laura Lombardini (1735–*post* 1785), m. Ludovico Sirmen; Italian violinist and composer. She made a triumphant debut at the King's Theatre in Jan. 1771, performing 'a Concerto on the Violin', presumably one of her own (*LS 4* iii. 1522). In 1772 she determined to become a singer, with disastrous consequences to her career; CB observed (in Rees, s.v. 'Sirman, Mad.') that 'she degraded herself by assuming a character, in which, though not deficient in voice or taste, she had no claim to superiority'. This benefit performance, on Tuesday, 1 June, was her last appearance on the London stage; the other singers are not named (*LS 4* iii. 1731). She subsequently returned to the Continent, still persisting in her new ambition. In 1785 she made a belated attempt to renew her career as a violinist, but by that time her style of playing had gone out of vogue. See *New Grove*; *Tours*, i. 101 n. 1, 137; Scholes, i. 166, ii. 332.

[39] This was FB's 21st birthday.

[40] Giovanni Battista Torre (d. 1780), pyrotechnist. Born in Italy, Torre was the proprietor of shops in Paris and London for the sale of scientific instruments and books. He was better known, however, for his exhibitions of fireworks and in 1772 became

came on, &, after sitting in a Box in the Gardens, almost alone, for almost an Hour—We went to sup at Mr. Young's.

Mrs. Young was insufferably impatient & disagreeable, found fault with every body—& though the scheme was of her own Planning, accused us all for bringing her there such a Night!—

Mr. Young was here last Night [12 June], with his gentle *sposa*—he was going to the Opera—Artaxerxes[41]—& endeavoured to ˩ persuade Susan or me to go with him, but I was afraid his Wife would be in a Passion—as he does not trouble him-self to wait for A *reason* for such an indulgence.—˥

Susan & I are extremely Comfortable together—& my Father, who is all kindness, ˥Monsieur Maty[42] also with us,˥ makes us truly happy. We are both studying Italian—˥I hope I shall be able to Conquer it—But the learning a Language requires great application & perseverance.˥ [43]

We are Reading [some of the][44] best French Works together not regularly, but only such parts as are adapted either to our Capacity or Inclination: we have just finished the Henriade[45]—I am not absolutely in raptures with it—I think Voltaire has made much too free with Religion, in giving Words to the *Almighty*.[46] I doat on Poetry—but cannot allow of even Poetical License giving Language human to the Divine

director of the fireworks in Marylebone Gardens. FB describes a visit to Torre's fireworks in *Evelina* (ed. E. A. Bloom (1968), pp. 231–2). The Gardens, opened in the mid-17th c., were closed in 1776. See Maxted; Garrick, *Letters*, ii. 762 n. 6; *Life*, iv. 324, 539–40.

[41] *Artaserses*, by Johann Adolf Hasse (1699–1783), libretto by Metastasio (*New Grove*; *LS 4* iii. 1733). CB, who had met Hasse the previous Sept. at Vienna, called him 'the most natural, elegant, and judicious composer of vocal music, as well as the most voluminous now alive' (*Tours*, ii. 82, 95). FB may be confusing this opera with Dr Arne's *Artaxerxes*, also performed this season.

[42] Matthew Maty (1718–76), Ph.D. and MD (Leyden), 1740; FRS, 1751; principal librarian of the British Museum, 1772; writer. FB describes him as 'a little, formal man, very civil, & very affected', 'held in the highest class for learning' (vol. ii).

[43] Just 5 years earlier Thomas Gray had observed: '. . . it is but few people in England, that read currently & with pleasure the Italian tongue; & the fine old editions of their capital Writers are sold at London for a lower price, than they bear in Italy' (to William Taylor How, 12 Jan. 1768, *Letters*, ed. P. Toynbee and L. Whibley (Oxford, 1935), iii. 995).

[44] Inserted by FBA.

[45] Voltaire's poem, the final, 10-canto version of which appeared at London in 1728. FB was perhaps reading the poem in CB's set of the 'Oeuvres, 33 tom. . . . 1757' (*Lib.*, p. 58).

[46] This occurs in Canto VII, where Voltaire gives God a 6-line speech.

Power. For which reason, | I am more attached to Poetry concerning Fabulous Times—for Jove, Minerva, Venus—may talk as much as they please—I am never hurt even at their Quarrelling—but a man pretending to belief in revealed Religion,—to presume to Dictate sentiments to his maker—I cannot think it right. Nay more, he actually makes his God so very a human Creature—as to *give up* his intended proceedings, upon the prayers of Lewis![47] It is very well for a Jove, or any other Fabulous God, to be softened, enraged, & mutable—but—an all seeing Eye—can it have any thing for another to represent?—an all wise, all Good Power—can it have any design which is *better* to be laid aside—?

But M. Voltaire is not a man of very *rigid Principles* [—at least not in Religion.][48] |

╒Susy & I walked in the Park this morning but we saw Nobody we knew, except our old Friend Prattle, Mr Pugh,[49] & that very dull but good sort of Girl, Miss Strange.

That smirking, insignificant, prating but good natured man Mr. Pugh, whenever he meets us, fastens himself to our Party most unsuitably, & we can never get away from him. I remember before my sister's marriage Miss Pascall told me that she was very certain that Mr. Pugh was really in love with—either Hetty or me—but she did not know *which*—Hetty now declares the same thing of Sue & me—& yet it is not from a *spirit of Gallantry* that he attaches himself to *the misses*, but meerly from an Insignificance & idleness of disposition, which induces him to address those who he may perhaps suppose will attend to him [xxxxx ½ *line*] Such is the vanity of the sex that I believe the most paltry of them think their [devoirs accountable to *we Fair*.][50]╛ |

[*A leaf or leaves have been cut away. Next, it appears that Signor Sacchini is repeating to FB some of the amorous English expressions he has learned.*]

╒[xxxxx 1½ *lines*] *my dear, my Heart—my sweet Heart—My Love*

---

[47] Saint Louis IX (1215–70), King of France. At the poem's end St Louis pleads successfully with God to permit Henri of Navarre's triumphant entry into Paris.

[48] Inserted by FBA.

[49] FB is comparing the Revd Mr Pugh to the gossipy apothecary, Mr Prattle, in Colman's farce *The Deuce is in Him* (1763), most recently performed at Covent Garden on 13 Apr. (*LS 4* iii. 1710).

[50] Inserted by FBA.

—*my Friend*—*my soul*—[xxxxx ½ *line*] 'Je voudrai bien, said I, parlez Italian [*sic*].'

He encouraged me very much to it, assuring me that I would find it much less difficult than French. ⌐

He told my Father, that when he first came to England, he Dined with a Person of Distinction, along with Signor Giardini; (who loves mischief better than any man alive) and Giardini gave him a Lesson, that when he wanted Wine & Water to Drink, he must ask for it in English by saying *How do do?*— accordingly, when he was ⌐Dry,⌐ he turned to a servant, & said very civilly '*How do do?*' The man made a very low Bow, & seemed very much confused—but brought him no Wine & Water! He was obliged to be patient—but took the first opportunity of saying to another of ┘ the men, '*How do do?* The man Grin'd, & Bowed, but still, no Wine & Water! He found himself extremely dry—& very much surprised—& perhaps thought he spoke ill,—but yet again repeated his demand to a third servant—upon which, *il Padrone della Casa* called out to him, 'Mr Sacchini, you are very Civil to my people—how came you to know them all?' '*Moi,*' cried he, j'ai seulement demande⌐r⌐ [*sic*] à Boire!' 'Et que dites vous pour cela?' '*How do do.*'—

Giardini's Lesson was then betrayed, the Laugh, I doubt not, was very hearty.

⌐I asked him if he was yet certain of staying another year? He said no, for a Mr. Gordon[51] is sent over to Italy, by the stupid managers with unlimited powers to engage what singers or composers they will, & Signor Sacchini cannot be either engaged or at liberty, till they hear what this man has done. ⌐┘

[*a leaf or leaves cut away*]

⌐'Monsieur'—said Mr. [Charles Rousseau] Burney.

He [Sacchini] Bowed—'je viendrai avec beaucoup de plaisir, pour vous voir, & votre jolie Femme—

'Mais quand' cried Mr. Burney.

---

[51] John Gordon (*fl.* 1744–73), violoncellist. CB describes him (in Rees) as 'an eminent performer on the violoncello, the son of a clergyman in Norfolk, and many years the first violoncello at the opera'. A manager of the Opera from 1764 to 1767, he made frequent recruiting trips to the Continent. The Theatre announced on 23 Oct. of this year that he had recently spent 2 months in Italy and had made 2 trips to Paris getting singers and dancers. No mention is made of composers, and no new ones came over for the 1773–4 season; Sacchini stayed in London until 1781 (Highfill).

'O, bientot' answered he—

'Bientot?' cried Sukey, 'Vous l'avez dit tant de fois.'

'O je vous demande pardon,' cried he, & renewed his apologies, however, Mr. Burney would not quit him, till he fix'd upon Saturday.

The Conversation was kept up with great spirit till past One o'clock, when they sent for Coaches & *en attendant*, my Father made Celestini accompany Sacchini in the Duet to Tamerlano, which they made very agreeable & afterwards Signor Sacchini sung Savoi's song of Del Fraterno e dolce amore[52]— |

We all parted then, with an agreement to meet on Saturday—”

I have now to mention a Visit from *Roscius*.[53] He came again last Wednesday before 8 o'clock. I had fortunately been up above an Hour. When I went into the study, he was playing with Charlotte.—I had, as is pretty usual with me on seeing him, something of a *Grin* upon my Face—

'O, here she comes! cried he—& resolved to look as handsome as she can—I shall run away with *her* next.—'

My Father Read to him an article he had been drawing up for a new Dictionary of Arts & Sciences, a sort of English Encyclopeidia; [*sic*]—Dr. Goldsmith is the Editor—& is to be assisted by many of the best Writers: among others, Dr. Johnson is to take Ethics:—Sir Joshua Reynolds,[54] painting, Mr Garrick *acting*.—

It was Mr Garrick who mentioned it to my Father & told him he wished to have his Name in the List, for the article music: he wrote to Dr. Goldsmith concerning it, whose answer I will Copy by memory:

To David Garrick, Esqr;

Dear Sir,

To be thought of by you obliges me; to be served still more;

---

[52] This aria of 'Sig^r Savoi' is printed in *The Favourite Songs in the Opera Tamerlano* (London: Robert Bremner, 1773), pp. 6–8.

[53] i.e., Garrick. The nickname, after Rome's most famous comic actor, was first given to him in 1742 (see C. Oman, *David Garrick*, p. 54).

[54] Sir Joshua Reynolds (1723–92). The Burneys' long friendship with the famous painter dates from this time. Mrs Thrale noted a few years later that Reynolds seemed to have 'set up as a Sort of Patron to Literature; so that no Book goes rapidly thro' a first Edition now, but the Author is at Reynolds's Table in a Trice' (*Thraliana*, i. 80). CB now found himself in this enviable position, following the success of his *German Tour* (see Lonsdale, pp. 128–9).

I am very happy that Dr. Burney thinks my plan of a Dictionary useful;[55] [still more that he will be so kind as to adorn it with anything of his own. I beg you also will accept my gratitude for procuring me so valuable an acquisition. I am

Dear Sir

Your most affec^e ser^t

Oliver Goldsmith][56]

This very Civil Note, Mr Garrick enclosed in a short one from himself

My dear Doctor,

I have just received the enclosed, Dr. Goldsmith will be proud to have your Name in the list of the Chosen; you shall have the Books very soon—.

Yours ever

D. G.

My love to your Fair Ones.[57]

My Father cannot do much in this Work, without Robbing his History, but he has Written the Article *Musician*. which he Read to Mr Garrick, who was pleased to admire it very much.[58] He also Read to him An Answer which he is preparing to

---

[55] The remainder of the MS page is blank, except for a pencilled editoral note: '(leave space for a few lines more of this letter)'. Another editorial note, on a separate leaf in the Barrett Collection (BL Add. MSS Egerton 3702-B, fo. 3) indicates that 'the remainder of Goldsmith's letter . . . M^{rs} B[arret]t can furnish from the autograph', and Mrs Barrett has copied the rest of the letter on a paste-over.

[56] The original MS of this letter is missing. FBA evidently had it among her father's papers in 1832, when she published it in *Mem.* i. 272–3, Mrs Barrett had it in the 1840s (see preceding note), and the Revd David Wauchope mentions it as being among the Burney MSS in 1885 (copy of letter to George Bell, 9 July 1885, BL). James Prior visited FBA in 1831 and secured a copy which he published in his *Life of Oliver Goldsmith* (1837), ii. 429; this version is reprinted in Goldsmith's *Letters*, ed. K. C. Balderston (Cambridge, 1928), p. 123, with the date-line 'Temple, June 10th, 1773'.

[57] This postscript is not in the extant MS, in the possession of Roger W. Barrett, Kenilworth, Illinois, printed in Garrick's *Letters*, ii. 874. FBA dates the letter 'June 11, 1773' in *Mem.* i. 272; it is addressed to 'Dr Burney, Queen Square'. The correct text of the last sentence is: 'The 2 Vol^s of Tables in Musick are bought for y^o & I will send them soon.' See Mercer, ii. 980.

[58] This may be the article on 'Musician' which CB later contributed to Rees. Goldsmith's project came to nothing. He was unable to get his publishers' backing for it, and in any event it would have been terminated by his death the following year. See A. Lytton Sells, *Oliver Goldsmith: His Life and Works* (1974), p. 179.

some Complaints made by French Writers concerning his Censure of their music.[59]

When ⌐Sukey¬ came down, & he had spoken to her, he said to my Father, 'And so you have them all about you in a morning?—'

'O yes!—'

'And so *they* prattle—& *you* rest your understanding?—'

This was monstrous.

'Quite the Contrary, cried I, my Father *exerts* his understanding to keep pace with us!—'

He understood me,[60] & getting up in a violent hurry, he came to the Table where I was making Tea—& with a thousand whimsical Gestures; he cried 'O—you quite mistake me—I meant to make you the greatest Compliment in the World!—I could not make you a greater!—what I meant was—to say that—that when you were all about him—he could then most delightfully—'

'Repose?' cried ⌐Sukey.¬

'Ay, cried he, *repose*, &—and most delightfully—do—*this*—& *that*—*& the other*'—

'Excellent! Mʳ Bayes!' cried my Father. & indeed he made it as *clear* as Mʳ Bayes could possibly have done—& with the most affected earnestness, declaring repeatedly that he meant to pay us an Amazing Compliment.

⌐Now for another day.

We had the honour of Mr. & Mrs. Young's Company at Dinner, & I was terribly afraid they would have done us the same Honour at Tea; but thank Heaven they were Engaged. They have now returned to the Country & make us most pressing Invitations, but for myself, I shall go either to Ting Mouth, or no where.

---

[59] CB wrote to C. D. Ebeling, 15 July 1773 (Osborn), that a 'M. Framery of Paris, who intends to Translate my History into French, has Criticised my account of French Music, & sent me a long, feeble & dull defence of it—even of the *Singing* A cursed *seccatura* that I *must* answer. Nothing but Panegyric will be believed: but my own feelings cannot be sacrificed to *Politesse*.' Nicolas-Étienne Framery (1745–1810), French writer, theorist, and composer, edited the *Journal de musique historique, théorique et pratique* from 1770 to 1771 (*New Grove*). Neither his letter nor CB's reply is preserved, nor did Framery accomplish the intended trans. (Lonsdale, p. 128).

[60] FB's statement is evidently a cue for Garrick to launch into the character of Bayes, the blathering and obfuscating playwright in Buckingham's *Rehearsal* (see *Garrick's Plays*, ed. H. W. Pedicord and F. L. Bergmann (Carbondale, 1980–), v. 28, 53, 313).

I went early to my sister's, as well as Susy—but my Father could not go with us, or indeed, absolutely promise to come at all, which gave me very much Concern.

The signori came about 7 o'clock.⁷ |

[*a leaf or leaves cut away*]

10   *TEIGNMOUTH JOURNAL*

[Teignmouth, 1 August–17 September 1773]

To Susanna Elizabeth Burney

AJ (paginated 361–[86], 3–[64], Berg), Teignmouth Journal.
Originally a series of journal letters gathered into a single cahier; now 31 single sheets 4to, 62 pp., inserted (following FBA's instructions) between fos. 41 and 42 of the Journal for 1773.
    Entitled (*by FBA*): Tingmouth Journal
    Annotated: 2 [*sic*] leaves missing
    This is the first of many journals, spanning nearly three decades, which FB sent to her favourite sister whenever the two were separated for any length of time (see *JL* ii. 57). SEB's reply to this initial journal (see below, p. 308) has not survived. FB joined the Rishtons at Teignmouth on 20 July. About the same time, presumably, SEB and Charlotte went to EAB at Lynn (see above, p. 265). CB had attended the Encænia at Oxford 7–9 July, journeyed from there to Worcester, returned to London for a few days, and then proceeded on to Lynn. About the beginning of August, he escaped to his friend William Bewley at Great Massingham in order to work there without interruption on *Hist. Mus.* (CB to Thomas Twining 30 Aug. 1773, BL).
    The first leaf is missing.

some repair—& I, therefore, was very late before I came in sight of Ting Mouth: half a mile from which, Mʳ and Mʳˢ Rishton walked to meet me—⁶¹

I was received with the most cordial welcome—my dear *Maria*, ⌜(as she is nowadays Called)⌝ had been quite uneasy, lest any accident had happened to me. I was very glad to find their Company were all gone.

    ⁶¹ The Rishtons had intended to meet FB at Exeter, but had lent their whisky. They sent her an apologetic note: 'Mʳ & Mʳˢ Rishton hope Miss Burney will excuse not having it in their power to fetch her. . . . Leave yʳ things to the care of Mʳˢ Tucker at the Oxford Inn, and they will come by the Carrier to morrow' (Berg).

Ting Mouth is situated the most beautifully of any Town I ever saw, or, perhaps, in England, ever can see: Mr Rishton's House is ⌜not in the Town, but⌝ on *the Den*,[62] which is the *mall* here: it is a small, neat, thatched & white Washed Cottage, niether more nor less. We are not a hundred yards from the sea, in which Mrs Rishton Bathes every morning. There is no End to the variety of delightful Walks, & rides, which this sweet spot affords.

The morning after I came, they insisted on my accompanying them to the Races,[63] & I had a very ⌜⟨polite⟩⌝ invitation from Mrs Phips, in whose Chaise & Company Mrs Rishton & myself went: Mr Rishton drove Mr Phips[64] in his *Whiskey*. |

We got a very good place in the *stand*, where there was a great deal of Company, & the Races, being quite new to me, really afforded me a good deal of Entertainment.[65] ⌜We spent the rest of the Day at Mr. Phips'. He seems a very worthy man, though not very brilliant. His wife is a pretty Woman, all good humour, chearfulness & gentleness.⌝

Mr Rishton is still more in love with Retirement than his Wife, if that is possible;—there are but two Families that he approves of keeping up acquaintance with: though I find there is at present a great deal of Company at Ting Mouth, as this is the *season* for sea Bathing, & as the rural beauties of the place become every year more known, in so much, that the Price of all Provisions, &c is actually doubled within these 3 years. The 2 Families honoured with Mr Rishton's preference, are that of the Phips, & the Hurrels, which latter consist, of Mr Hurrel,[66] a

---

[62] A long sandy tract extending to the S. of the village into the mouth of the R. Teign; the open sea is to the E.

[63] The Exeter races, held on 20, 21, and 22 July. FB attended the 2nd and 3rd days (*Baily's Racing Register* (1845), i. 372).

[64] Constantine Phipps (1745–97) of Exeter, 2nd son of Constantine Phipps (d. 1769) of St Kitts. He m. (1771, at Cheshunt, Hertfordshire) Elizabeth Tierney (*c.*1749–1832), daughter of James Tierney (d. 1781) of Theobald's (H. R. Phipps, *Notes on Phipps and Phip Families* (Lahore, 1911), pp. 33–8).

[65] The races on 21 July were for a plate of £50, for 4-year-old colts and fillies, 2-mile heats, and a 'great Sweep stakes, for the Subscription Cup, four miles' (*Baily's*, loc. cit.).

[66] The Revd Thomas Hurrel (d. 1781), Rector of Drewsteignton, Devon; Prebendary of Exeter, 1775; Rector of Tedburn St Mary, Devon, 1778 (*GM* xlviii (1778), 286, li (1781), 147). He m. (1766) Anne née Davie (1726–1804), daughter of Sir John Davie (1700–1737), 6th Bt., of Creedy, Devon; the sister was Juliana Davie (1729–97), who d. unmarried. See W. U. Reynell-Upham and H. Tapley Soper, eds., *The Registers of . . . Exeter* (Exeter, 1910), i. 268.

Clergyman of 1500 per ann. his Wife, & her sister, Miss Davy, who are Daughters of Sir John Davy.

In returning from Mrs Phips, we were met by Mr Crispen,[67] ⸢a Gentleman who⸣ has interested himself | very much in my Father's musical Plan,[68]—he is on the wrong side of an *Elderly man*, but seems to have good Health & spirits,—he has spent many years Abroad, & is perfect master of French & Italian. He is at Ting Mouth for the summer season, but I believe Bath is his usual place of Residence.

I was also Introduced the same morning to Miss Bowdler,[69] a young Woman who bears a rather singular Character: she is very sensible & clever, and possesses a great share of wit & *poignancy*, which spares neither friend or foe: she reckons herself superiour to the opinion of the World, & to all common Forms & Customs, & therefore lives exactly as she pleases, guarding herself from all real Evil, but wholly regardless & indifferent of appearances. She is about 6 & Twenty, a rather pretty little Figure, but not at all handsome, though her Countenance is very spirited & expressive. She has Father,[70] mother & sisters alive, but yet is come to Ting Mouth alone; though, ⸢at present,⸣ indeed, she is with a Miss Lockwood,[71] a rich old maid; but she will very soon be entirely *at liberty*. She, & her Family, are old Acquaintances of Mrs Rishton, & of Mama; she is therefore frequently here: ⸢but Mr. Rishton

---

[67] Daniel Crispin (b. *c.*1713). A resident of Bath, by 1780 he had moved to Clifton, where he died on 19 May 1789 (*DL* i. 330; MI, Clifton Church). He may be the 'Mr. Crispin' who showed Mrs Delany paintings by Benjamin West and Angelica Kauffmann at the Royal Academy exhibition in 1771 (*Delany Corr.* iv. 329). Earlier FBA has inserted that MAR called him 'the first person for agreeability, cultivation, pleasantry, & good breeding of their acquaintance'. He appears, however, to have become infatuated with FB, and was soon to tire her out by his playful and persistent gallantries (below, *passim*).

[68] He did not, however, subscribe to *Hist. Mus.*

[69] Frances Bowdler (*c.*1747–1835), sister of Thomas Bowdler (1754–1825), of 'bowdlerizing' fame. Miss Bowdler was a native of Bath, where FBA met her again, with her family, in 1780; the two were to become lifelong friends (*DL* i. 330 and *passim*; *JL* i. 51, ix. 14 and *passim*; dates for Miss Bowdler, which correct those in *JL*, courtesy of Warren Derry, Esq., Bath, England).

[70] Thomas Bowdler, sen. (1706–85). He m. (1742) Elizabeth Stuart Cotton (*c.*1718–97), 2nd daughter of Sir John Cotton, 5th Bt. Frances's sisters were Jane (1743–84) and Henrietta Maria, called 'Harriet' (1753–1830).

[71] Possibly identical with the 'Miss Lockwood' whom James Boswell had met at Gen. Oglethorpe's in London the past Apr., and whom he calls (perhaps in exasperation) 'a very well-behaved woman.' See *Boswell for the Defence 1769–1774*, ed. W. K. Wimsatt and F. A. Pottle (1960), pp. 188, 216.

cannot bear her—a Woman, he says, who despises the Customs & manners of the Country she Lives in, must conse⁊quently conduct herself with impropriety. For *my* part, I own myself of the same sentiment—but nevertheless, we have not any one of us the most distant shadow of doubt of Miss Bowdler's being equally innocent with those who have more Worldly Prudence, at the same Time, that her Conduct appears to me highly improper: for she finds that the Company of Gentlemen is more entertaining than that of Ladies, & therefore without any scruples or punctilio, indulges her fancy: she is perpetually at Mʳ Crispen's, notwithstanding a very young man, Mʳ Green,[72] Lives in the same House; [no]t contented with a *Call*, she very frequently *sups* with them: & though she does this in the fair face of Day, & speaks of it as openly & commonly as I should of Visiting my sister, yet I can by no means approve so great a contempt of public opinion. As to Mʳ Rishton, he almost *detests* her; but his Wife is really attached ⟨to⟩ her, which is an unfortunate circumstance. I heartily ⟨wish⟩ that she was not here, as she always drives Mʳ Rishton away when she appears; for he is delicate, or rather scrupulous, to an uncommon degree, in his Choice of Acquaintance for his Wife: ⏐ nevertheless, when she offers to entirely give Miss Bowdler up, he will not consent to it, because he knows it would be much against her Will, & because if it was not, he would not risque her Character to the *lash* of Miss Bowdler's Tongue.

'After the Races,' said Miss Bowdler in taking leave, 'I shall do myself the honour to wait on Miss Burney.'

'Ay,' cried Mʳ Rishton, when she was gone,—'they will soon make this as errant a public place as Bristol [Hotwells][73] or any other.'

Thursday [22 July] we again went to the Races, with Mʳˢ Phips, &c.

---

[72] An artist (see below, pp. 285, 286). Perhaps Amos Green (1735–1807), a water-colour painter who settled at Bath *c.*1757. He was unmarried at this time. Three landscape drawings and a watercolour landscape by him are in the British Museum. There is also a watercolour of a 'Waterfall in the Woods' in the Victoria and Albert Museum (Thieme; S. W. Fisher, *Dictionary of Watercolour Painters 1750–1900* (1972), p. 92; E. Waterhouse, *The Dictionary of British 18th Century Painters in Oils and Crayons* (1981), p. 149).

[73] Inserted by FBA.

Friday morning Mr Crispen called; ⌈he⌉ said that he should sooner *have paid his Respects* to me, but that he understood I had been engaged at the Races.

But before I talk any more of other people, let me, my dear ⌈Susy,⌉ more particularly mention my Home. And first, our dear friend *Maria*, is just the same I ever knew her: save that she is become more gentle in her manners in general, & less indulges herself in that disposition for *whim*, which Nature so lavishly gave her: but this *restraint* is more in Actions than Words, for her Conversation, except in Company very formal or old, is as flighty, as ridiculous, as uncommon, lively, comical, & truly entertaining as ever we knew it. And ⌐ her Heart, generous, frank, undisguised, admits of no alteration. We are most excessively comfortable together, & have nothing to repine at, but the impossibility of wholly avoiding visits & visitings; though she has almost all her former carelessness of what she does in this particular, to save herself the torment of seeing people she does not care for.

Her Adored Rishton improves Daily in my opinion, because I think I Daily observe in him an encrease of real affection & tenderness for his Wife. They are, indeed, most unaffectedly happy in each other; even I, who live in the House with them, should find it at present difficult to determine which of them is most Affectionately—I might say *passionately* attached to the other. Mrs Rishton's love has long admitted of no addition, though her Happiness certainly has, as Time makes her know how peculiarly fortunate her Choice has been: There is a remarkable similarity in their humours, for he is as whimsical & odd as herself,—but he is so very ⌈particular⌉ in his opinion of proper companions & acquaintance for his Wife, that he is really miserable whenever she speaks to any body but the select few of his option. Though this ⌐ exceeding *scrupulosity*, & some other things of this Nature, have perhaps, their rise from Pride,—yet he evidently proves that all his thoughts & attentions are directed towards her, & seeking to do her honour. There is a kind of generous impetuosity in his Disposition, which often hurries him beyond the bounds which *his own* cooler judgment would approve; & here again he resembles his Wife,—that he cannot at all disguise any thing that he feels.

I find myself very happy here. I am treated with the most

unbounded Confidence by Mr Rishton himself, as well as by his Wife, & I am most comfortable in finding that every thing in the Family goes on just the same as if I was away, & that I am no restraint either in their affairs or Conversation.

The rest of our Family, consists of 4 Dogs, who are prodigious favourites: two of them are spaniels, Vigo & Trump, ⌜& who are very fine ones;⌝ the third is a Newfoundland Dog, Excellent for *Diving* ⌜in the Water, & which⌝ always goes with Mr Rishton to swim or Bathe:—he is Named Ting Mouth: the fourth is most particularly for Mrs Rishton, it is called Romeo, & is a very faithful old Dog,—⌜I don't know how to distinguish his *sect*, Mr. R. gave 3 guineas for him.⌝[74] |

Mr Rishton having some Business in London, on Saturday [24 July] Mrs R. & myself accompanied him as far as Exeter in his Way. But I should mention that before we went, Mr Crispen paid us another Visit: in the course of which, he was pleased to offer himself for the most *devoted of my slaves*! but, he said, it was in all humility, & only till I met here with a *younger*: & *then*, he would resign his pretensions.

He asked Mr Rishton how long his stay here would be. 'It is quite uncertain, answered he, 'according to what News I hear from Stanhoe,—perhaps I may be kept till Christmas—if we could but keep Miss Burney.'

'O, cried Mr Crispen, if *Miss Burney* stays, *I* do!—though I intended to go in 5 or 6 Weeks, since she has accepted me for an old Lover:—but, indeed, I was in love with her before I saw her, by what I heard from *the Lamb* (a Name he has given to Mrs R.) & *now*—' &c &c—

We agreed to go again to Exeter on Thursday [29 July], which Day Mr R. had fixed upon for his return. & on Sunday Evening, Mrs R. & myself called in at Mr Crispen's, to borrow the Poem of the Minstrel.[75] |

This Mr Crispen seems attached to the fair sex in the style of

[74] FBA has inserted that Romeo was a 'Brown Pomeranian'. MAR, in her letter to FB 13 June (Berg), mentions that her husband had also bought her 'the most beautiful little mare you ever saw'. She was very fond of her animals, but the space she devotes to them in her letters reveals the poverty of her social life in the country.

[75] Presumably *The Minstrel, or the Progress of Genius* (bk. i, 1771; bk. ii, 1774) by James Beattie (1735–1803), poet and philosopher. Beattie, who lived in Aberdeen, was at this time on an extended visit to London (see *James Beattie's London Diary 1773*, ed. R. S. Walker (Aberdeen, 1946)). FB was years later to meet him at the home of Miss Reynolds, Sir Joshua's sister, and again at Windsor, in 1787 (*DL* iii. 280–1).

the old Courtiers;—I am told that he has Dulcineas without Number, though I am reigning sovereign at present. Miss Bowdler, who is on the list, & who I take for a very formidable Rival, was sitting with him. He insisted on Mrs Rishton's coming in, but demanded instantly 'have you brought my little Flame with you?'

We stayed but a few minutes, & in that Time Mr Green Entered. Mr Crispen introduced me to him, & added 'you must say every thing that is *civil*,—but nothing that is *fond*, to this young lady—for yesterday I poured forth the effusions of *my* Heart to her.'

'I will, with a great deal of pleasure, answered Mr Green, both *say* & *do* every thing that is civil that is in my power.'

'Pray, Miss Bowdler, do you allow of all this?' cried Mrs Rishton.

'O, I am obliged to it, replied she,—for *I* am but an Old Wife!'

She made no scruple of being left with the two Gentlemen, when we came away.

Mr Crispen & Mr Green were to set out the next morning [Monday, 26 July] on ⟨a⟩ Trip to Plymouth & Mount Edgecumbe,[76] with a Family who are here for the season, of the name of Colbourn; consisting of Mr Colbourn,[77] who was a Bath apothecary, but has had an immense Fortune left him, & is now enjoying it; his Wife & Daughter. They were to return on Thursday.

Monday & Tuesday, Mrs R. & myself spent in the most comfortable manner possible,—but for Wednesday—I must be more particular.

Mr Hurrel has an exceeding pretty Boat of his own here, with which he makes frequent excursions on the River Ting, &

---

[76] Seat of George Edgcumbe (1721–95), 3rd B. Edgcumbe of Mount Edgcumbe; cr. (1781) Visc. and (1789) E. of Mount Edgcumbe. Edgcumbe was a Vice-Admiral and currently Commander-in-Chief at Plymouth. FB was to visit this 'noble' seat herself in 1789 (*DL* iv. 320–1).

[77] Benjamin Colborne (*c*.1716–93). His wife presumably predeceased him, as she is not mentioned in his will (PCC, 14 May 1793, prob. 2 Nov. 1793); she has not been further traced. His daughter, Sarah Colborne (d. 1806), m. (1777) Sir Matthew White Ridley (1745–1813), 2nd Bt. Colborne's obituary notes his 'unremitted endeavors to render extensive medical benefit to mankind, which led him to devote his attention to useful discoveries, of which his mephitic alkaline water will be a lasting remembrance' (*GM* lxiii² (1793), 961).

sometimes on the sea. His Wife called here on Tuesday Evening, to invite us to be of their Party on Wednesday, when they intended sailing to Torbay, to see a Fleet under Admiral Spry,[78] which was just come from Portsmouth. We very gladly accepted the offer, & set off the next morning about 7 O'clock, our Company consisting of M^r & Mrs Hurrel, Mr Phips, a Boat-swain, another sailor, Mr Hurrel's servant & ourselves.

Mr Hurrel is quite a Poet's Priest. He is fat as Falstaff, unable to use exercise ⟨& Eke⟩ unwilling; | his love of ease is surpassed by nothing—but his love of good living, which equals whatever *detraction* has hitherto devised for a Parson's Gluttony.

Mrs Hurrel is an obliging, civil, tiresome Woman.

Our Plan was, to see the Fleet, & if possible, a man of War's *inside*,—& then to land on one of the safest & pleasantest Rocks, to Dine, as Mr Hurrel had taken special care of this particular.

But when we came near the ships, the sea grew rough, & having no invitation, we were obliged to give up the thought of entering any of them. There were 7 men of War in the Bay, & we sailed round them,—⌐Among them was the Barfleur, in which the king was in his Portsmouth Expedition.⌐[79] They are most noble Vessels. I had reason to think myself very fortunate that I was not sea sick, though I never before was on the ocean. We *put in* at ⌐Brixem,⌐ [Brixham] a most excellent fishing Town, but very dirty & disagreeable. We made but a short stay, & set sail again. ⌐Brixem⌐ is about 10 miles from Ting Mouth by sea.

The Wind was against us—& we were hardly out of the Harbour, before we found the sea terribly | rough—I own I was not very easy, as our Boat, though a large one for the Thames, was very small for the sea: but still, I considered myself as the Person of the least Consequence, whatever our danger.

However, it was no sport to me to be Danced up & down, & to find the Waves higher & rougher every instant: especially

---

[78] Richard Spry (1715–75), Rear-Admiral.

[79] The King had reviewed the fleet and fortifications at Portsmouth, 22–5 June. While there he dined and conferred various honours (including a knighthood for Admiral Spry) on board the *Barfleur*, Capt. Edward Vernon, a man-of-war of 90 guns (see the illustration in O. Warner, *Fighting Sail* (1979), p. 97; *Daily Adv.* 1 July). The *Daily Adv.* 4 Aug. reported Spry's squadron at Tor Bay on 31 July, and as expected shortly back at Spithead on 1 Aug.

when I saw Mr Hurrel, who had hitherto guided us, quit the Helm to the Boatswain, & exclaim 'We shall run foul of these Rocks!'—

The Waves foamed in little white mountains, rising above the Green surface of the sea—they dashed against the Rocks off the Coast of ꞋBrixemꞋ with monstrous fury—& really to own the truth, I felt no inclination to be Ꞌship͏Ꞌ Wrecked, however pathetic & moving a Tale our Adventure might have made.

Mrs Hurrel grasped my Hand, & looked very much frightened: her agreeable Husband repeated several Times his most comfortable Exclammation of 'We shall run foul of the Rocks!—' there followed a most terrible confusion—I don't remember, or understand, sea phrases, but | the hurrying, loud, violent manner in which they gave orders to one another was really frightful. 'Is there any danger, cried Mrs Hurrel, pray Boatswain, tell me, is there any danger?' 'No—I don't think there is, Ma'am.'

This was the most alarming sound I had heard yet—*I don't think there is*!—however, I found we were all in equal danger, for the two sailors assured us their swimming would be totally useless, as the fury of the Waves would presently swallow them up.

Mrs Hurrel grasped my Hand harder than ever—her Husband forgot his *Cloth*, & began to swear, adding '*God forgive me*!'—at length, after being tost up & down in a most terrible manner for about a ¼ of an Hour, the Boatswain said we should not reach Ting Mouth before mid night.—& just then, the Waves seemed to redouble their violence, Ꞌfor͏Ꞌ the Boat scooped one fairly over us.

I gave up the Ghost:—Mrs Hurrel burst into Tears—& cried vehemently, 'for the lord's sake—for mercy's sake—Mr Hurrel, pray let us go | back to BrixꞋeꞋm—pray do—we shall be all Drowned! O pray don't let me be Drowned!—Set me down! Set me down!' [xxxxx 1½ *lines*]

'But where are we to *Dine*?' cried he.

'O, any where, Mr Hurrel,—any where, so as we do but get a shore!—I don't mind, I assure *ee*.'

'O, that's pretty talking—answered Ꞌt͏Ꞌhe ꞋPriest,͏Ꞌ 'but that won't serve for a meal.—'

However, I believe he had no objection to prolong his Days

for when the Boatswain said that it blew *fresher* higher up, he immediately ordered that we should *tack about*:—& so we returned to Brixᵉᵐ! When we Landed, I was so very giddy, that I could hardly stand—& was obliged to go into the firṣt House, for a Glass of Water: but I am only amazed that I was not dreadfully sea sick.

How to get Home was the next consideration—Mrs Rishton had promised to meet Mr R. at Exeter the next Day, & was determined rather to Walk than disappoint him: but it is 16 miles from Ting Mouth by Land: there was no post Chaise to be had:—nor could we hear of even Horses.

We went into the best Inn of the place, & Mr Hurrel ordered Dinner. After a thousand enquiries, *pros* & *Cons*, &c—We were settled *thus*;—Mrs R. procured a Horse, Mr Phips another, on which he accompanied her "hither" [back to Tingmouth][80] & Mr Hurrel & his Wife & myself, to my great regret, were obliged to stay all night at Brixᵉᵐ⟨.⟩

"But I forgot to mention, that a sloop filled with Tingmothians, was obliged to put in at Brixem as well as us,—they were a very gay party had come out with the same view as ourselves, among them were Miss Lockwood & Miss Bowdler—I was sorry to see her in such Company: for they behaved in a most ridiculous & improper manner, Dancing about the Town, & diverting themselves in a very uncommonly easy & careless style: & though Miss Bowdler herself behaved with propriety, yet her party reflected something on her Choice, & has much added to Mr. Rishton's aversion to her."

We passed a weary Evening at Brixem, & the next mo[r]ning [Thursday, 29 July], at 3 o'clock, we got up, & set sail for Ting Mouth, intending to Breakfast in the Boat;—but, O grief of griefs! the awkward Boatswain managed to destroy all the matches, & we were obliged to give "it" up, to Mr Hurrel's very great anger & sorrow.

I will mention nothing more of our perils, though they were not inconsiderable in my opinion:—but however, we Landed at last, safe & sound, about 9 o'clock. The Hurrels' insisted on my going to Breakfast with them—after which, I came Home, & went to Bed for a Couple of Hours, having not undrest myself at Brixᵉᵐ.

[80] Inserted by FBA.

⟨B⟩ut I caught a *very* bad Cold, & know not when I shall part with it.

M^r and Mrs Rishton returned from Exeter to Dinner. & in the Evening, Mr Crispen called, just arrived from Plymouth:— protested he could not rest till he came—That this was his first Visit—and that where the *thoughts* were, there the *person* must wish itself!—&c

'But I think,' added he, 'that *my love* expressed no great Joy at seeing me?—*my* Heart went *pit a pat* all the ⟨Wa⟩y I came.—'

He sa⟨i⟩d he had rode the whole Way from Plymouth on Horseback, having given the Colbourn's *the slip*: he ⌐gave¬ a very high Character of the Daughter, both for accomplishments, & propriety of conduct. He declared that he found himself so little fatigued with his Journey, that he was ready to shew his prowess, by going on the Beach, & declaring *the Bright Burney the best of her sex*!

'*Except*,' said Mr Rishton, 'Miss Colbourn!'

'Without *any* exception!—I have a very great esteem for Miss Colbourn; & admire her greatly:—but *here*—'

'But then, Miss Bowdler?—what do you do with her?' returned Mr Rishton.

'For the little Bowdler I have indeed a most particular regard;—but still—still Miss Burney!—'

Mr Rishton mentioned some more fair Dulcineas, to all which he answered, 'O—these are but my diversion!—but Burney is my Home!' then, turning to me 'Give me your little Hand — — *I love you*!—I was prepared to love you before I saw you;—but now, I find in you so strong a resemblance to a sister[81] who was very dear to me, that I must love you more for her sake.'

The next morning [30 July], Miss Bowdler called,—she seemed in a very angry humour with her old friend, Mr Crispen: I fancy she wishes to be more *unique* with him, than she finds is in her power to be.

'He is returned quite a young man,' said Mrs Rishton '& not at all fatigued.'

'Yes,' answered she, but he droops this morning!—he must take another Journey to Plymouth to recruit. He ⌐tells¬ me that

[81] Not further traced. Mr Crispin, of course, may have invented her as a joke.

Miss Colbourne ⌐is¬ all perfection—I only laughed;—to *me* she appears the most affected, conceited Thing I ever saw: however, I am glad Perfection is so easily ⌐ob¬tained!'

'We shall hear Fanny's opinion of her to night,' said Mrs R. 'for she Drinks Tea here.'

'Well, much good may it do you!—they Extol her Painting too—but I'd lay my life all the Landscapes she has taken this Journey are from Green:—however, Crispen can afford to lavish away a multitude of Compliments, without feeling their loss: but Novelty is all in all for him.'

She said much more to the same purpose, & made me very angry with her, as Mr Crispen deserves more consideration from her.

In the Evening the Colbourns' came. The Father is a worthy kind of man, but full of that parade & bluster which constitute⌐s¬ | that sort of man we call *Purse Proud*: the mother is an insipid, good sort of Woman: the Daughter is [a] very smart Girl, some what affected, & not *too* diffident of her accomplishments: but extremely [ci]vil & obliging: & very well behaved.

I don't know when I shall come to the present [ti]me: but *Patienza*!

Saturday morning [31 July], Mrs Rishton & I walked out early [to] avoid a very disagreeable scene ⌐at Home:¬ for the Day before, Mr Rishton came Home in great haste, & perturbation; &, calling his Wife, told her that [h]e had broke Romeo's Leg!—this was occasioned by the [p]oor Dog's running after sheep, for which he has often been, in vain, very severely beat: but now, he & one of the spaniels got a poor sheep quite down, & began to tear her to Pieces: Mr R. rode up to them, & catching Romeo first, by the Leg, to prevent his biting, began to flog him violently, till he found that by the Twist, he had broke his Leg short off.—he was beyond measure concerned, & gave a man a Crown to carry him Home gently in his Arms: & the next morning he had a surgeon to set the poor animal's Leg,—which not chusing to | see, we sauntered before the Door till it was done: in which Time, Mr Crispen went by on Horseback: 'Are these *my* ladies?' cried he—'and how does *my love*? I did not see her all yesterday—th[e] Day was heavy! I felt some thing wanting!—an[d] how fares it with the Lamb?—'

'I wish you would come & hear me read Italia[n,'] cried she, 'now do, Mr Crispen, I want help extremely.'

'And does my little Burney speak it? or learn it[?']

'O yes!—' answered M^rs R.

'*Then* I'll come!—the sound of *her* Voice!—'

'Well,' returned she, I never heard any thing so genteel! upon my Word, Mr Crispen, there's no bearing all this'—

'Nay—you know I always loved the sound of your[s,'] cried he, as he rode off.

In the Evening, however, he came: but as Mr Rishton was at Home, we had no Italian: for he is too far advanced in that Language to profit by such Lessons as we want.[82] Mr Crispen brought with him some Drawings on Cards of Mr Green's performance. 2 of them were views of Ting Mouth, & he made a great *fuss* about them: asking me how I would bribe him for a sight?—I told ¦ him that I had Nothing at all to offer—

'Why, now,' said he, 'methinks 2 Drawings deserve *two* kisses—and if—'

'No, no, no, cried I, not that!' much surprised [a]t his modest request. [But he only spoke in sport, I am sure.][83]

He brought one View for Mrs Rishton, which [M]^r Green had sent her as a present; ['I wish it was for my little Burney!'

The Drawings were extremely pretty—one of [th]em I was admiring very much, it was a night [pi]ece, for it's *Coolness*—

'O,' cried Mr Crispen, [t]that is it! you would like a *cool* lover, then? *I* [a]m too *passionate* for you?—'

When we had examined the Cards, 'Come,' said M^r [R]ishton, 'won't you set down, Mr Crispen—there's a Chair [b]y Miss Burney!'

'That is where I mean to set!' answered he. Poor Romeo's misfortune then *came on the Carpet* & Mr Crispen gave Mr R. some very good & very free advice on restraining his passions, & keeping them under command;—& Mr R. who is quite afflicted for the Dog, took it very candidly & sensibly: indeed they both did themselves honour. But however, nothing could engage the old gentleman long from his gallantry to ¦ me—he

---

[82] In Apr. Rishton, through his wife and FB, had asked CB to send him 'an Italian Grammar dictionary and some book or two for young beginners' (MAR to FB 25 Apr. 1773, Berg).

[83] Inserted by FBA.

turned towards me, with a mournful air. 'I don't know how it is, but my little Burney & I don't hit it off well together!—I take all possible pains,—but I cannot please her!—Well! I can't help it!—I can only say, you would not have used me thus ⌜3⌝0 years ago!'

Thank God I *could* not, thought I.

But really I scarse knew what to say; and indeed have seldom made any other answer th[an] laughing: but I took the first opportunity of h[is] being engaged in Conversation with M[r] Rishto[n] to move off, & seat myself in the Window. He perceived it immediately, & with a reproachful Voice, called out, 'Now is this *decent*, Miss Burney, are you afraid of only *sitting* by me?' then rising, & getting his Hat, 'Well, I shall go to my little Colbourn—*She* will not use me thus!'

However, he altered his mind, & brought a Chair & placed himself before me: & the subject was changed to Miss Bowdler & the Brix⌜e⌝m Party.

Miss Bowdler might have blushed to have heard the benevolence with which he spoke of her:—he lamented in very affectionate terms that she had been ‸ unfortunately mixed with so giddy & imprudent a Party, & recommended it very strongly to M[rs] Rishton, to make it known, as much as she could, [th]at Miss Bowdler was an *Exception* when the [Co]mpany was named: he regretted her being alone [he]re, & hoped M[rs] Rishton would *extend* her friend[sh]ip to protect her, & be as much with her as [po]ssible, after Miss Lockwood's departure. He [sp]oke of her in very high terms, & said he [ow]ed her so much [regard & respect][84] that he would himself be [a]lways with her, but that he knew the People [h]ere would only sneer about it.

⌜He has a Thousand Times more delicacy for her, that she has for herself.⌝ It seems, [i]n a bad illness which M[r] Crispen had, she was his constant Nurse.

M[r] Rishton very openly blamed her for mixing with the Brix⌜e⌝m Party: M[r] Crispen could hardly justify her: 'I would not,' said he, 'have had a Daughter of mine there—or my little Burney, for the whole World!'

Then again, he renewed his discourse to me, & beg'ed me to remember an old Proverb— ‸ That—

---

[84] Inserted by FBA.

'Love burns slowest in old Veins—
But, when once Entered, long remains!'[85]

'Indeed,' said I, 'I did not come to Ting Mou[th] at all *prepared* for such fine speeches!'—
'*Fine speeches*!' exclaimed he!—'ah! that [is] always the way you answer old Bachelors!'

Now, to tell you my private opinion, my dear Susy, I am inclined to think that this gallantry is the effect of the man's taking me for a Fool;—because I hav[e] been so much surprised at it, that I have hardly ever had a Word of answer ready.—*yo*[*u*] who know how *wise* I am, must allow the injustice of such an inference! But I canno[t] write or recollect half the *fine* things he says:—but don't let all this make you think *him* a Fool:—he is much of a gentleman,—has an easy & polite address,—& is very sensible & Agreeable in Conversation,—& remarkably mild, candid & benevolent in his opinions & judgments:—but he has lived so long abroad, that I suppose he thinks it necessary to talk Nonsence to We fair sex. |

Monday, Aug. [2]

We are just going to Ting Mouth Races, which, indeed, are to be held in sight of our House. We hope for very good sport,—a great [d]eal of Company are arrived on the Den.

Augst 19th

I have not had a moment for Writing this [Ag]e—I never had less, as Mrs R. & myself are [a]lmost inseparable. The Races, however, must [b]y no means pass unrecorded.

Miss Lockwood & Miss Bowdler invited [th]emselves to accompany us to the Race [G]round: Mr Crispen also, called in & joined us. Mr. Rishton was not at all pleased, & the half Hour which we spent before we set out, he sat almost totally silent. Mr Crispen addressed himself to me with his usual particularity, which really put me quite out of Countenance, as I dreaded Miss Bowdler's opinion, & feared she would rank me with Miss Colbourne. I seated myself quietly at a distance, but

---

[85] Not found elsewhere, but compare the more familiar 'Love me little, love me long'.

Mr Crispen, determined to torment me, drew *his* [chair][86] quite close to mine, & in so particular a ⸽ manner, that I could not keep my place, but got up, & seated myself next to Mrs R. on the Window.

I then wished that I had not, for every body (except Mr R.) Laughed: I felt my Face *on Fire*: 'Do you run away from me?' cried Mr Crispen, 'to take shelter under the Lamb?'—but it wa[s] in vain, for he immediately moved after me & continued, in the same style, to complain of me. I endeavoured to change the subject, & ma[de] some enquiries concerning the Races:— but noth[ing] would do:—'Ah!' cried he, would that your Heart was to be Run for! What an effort would I make.

'Yes,' cried Miss Bowdler, (not very delicately) you would break your Wind on the occasion.

'What will they do,' said I, with the poor Pig after the Races?'

'O that my Heart,' cried Mr Crispen, 'could be as easily cured!'

'Never fear;' said Miss Bowdler: 'it has stood a good many shocks!'

'Were it now to be opened,' answered he, 'you would find Burney Engraved on it in large Characters.' ⸽

'O, cried she, 'and you would find a great many [p]retty misses there besides!'

'Ay,' said Mrs R. 'there would be Miss Colbourne.'

'But *Burney* is my sum Total!—I own, I avow [it] publickly!—I make no secret of it.'

'Yes, yes,' returned Miss Bowdler, the *Present* [is] always best!'

I just then recollected a little Dispute [whi]ch we had had with Mr Rishton, on the [pr]onounciation of some Italian Words, & giving [a] Grammar to Mr Crispen, beg'd him to decide [it]. 'Look another way, my dear little Burney, cried he, look another way!—I must take out my Reading Glass!—you have a natural antipathy to me, but don't strengthen it, by looking at me now!'

I was very glad when this Conversation was Concluded, by our being all obliged to march. We found a great deal of Company, & a great deal of Diversion. The sport began by an Ass Race. There were 16—some of them really ran extremely

[86] Inserted by FBA.

well—others were indeed | truly ridiculous:—but all of them diverting. Next followed a Pig Race. This was certainly cruel, for the poor animal had it's ⌐tale⌐ [*sic*] cu[t] to within an Inch, & then that Inch wa[s] soaped:—it was then let loose, & made run, [&] was to be property of the man who could Catch it by the ⌐Tale⌐: which, after many ridiculous attempts, was found to be impo[ssi]ble, it was so slippery: therefore, the Candidates concluded this Day's sport, by running for it themselves.

The great *sweep stakes* of the Asses, wer[e] half a Guinea: the 2^d prize a Crown, & the 3^d half a Crown. However, the whole of it was truly laughable.

The next Race Day was not till Friday [6 Aug.], which Day was also destined to a grand double Cricket match. Mr Rishton is a very good Player; & ⌐they have⌐ an Excellent Ground on the Den.

Two Gentlemen who were to be of the match, Breakfasted here in the morning. They are sons of Dr. Mills[87] Dean of Exeter. ⌐The Dean & his | [f]amily are much respected here, & seem to be [re]markably happy & amiable. His lady is Dead, [bu]t he has a Daughter & 3 sons. They were [a]ll at Eaton [*sic*] School with Mr. Rishton.[88] The Eldest wrote for the music Prize at the [la]te Installation at Oxford, & the Eldest [ha]d the honour, out of 23 which were written [to] have his chosen.[89] His Brother's was rated second.

[87] Jeremiah Milles (1714–84), DD (Oxon.), 1747; Dean of Exeter, 1762; FRS, 1742; PSA, 1768–84. He m. (1745) Edith Potter (*c*.1726–61), daughter of the Revd Dr John Potter, Abp. of Canterbury. His sons were Jeremiah Milles (*c*.1751–97), at Eton, 1763–8; BA (Oxon.), 1772; MA, 1775; barrister; Thomas Milles (*c*.1753–1830), at Eton, 1764–9; BA (Oxon.), 1773; MA, 1776; DCL, 1790; barrister (KC, 1804); and Richard Milles (*c*.1754–1823), at Eton, 1765–9; BA (Oxon.), 1774; MA, 1777; Prebendary of Exeter, 1778–1823; Vicar of Kenwyn, Cornwall, 1781–1823. He also had 2 daughters: Charlotte, the elder (d. 1777); and Amelia or Harriet (b. *c*.1758). Amelia was later described by Boswell as having a fortune of £10,000 (*Boswell Papers*, xviii. 123). She m. Richard Blake (*c*.1760–1829), a member of the Bristol Corporation. See *GM* xlvii (1777), 351; liv^1 (1784), 153; Joseph Cottle, *Early Recollections* (1837), i. 34–5; A. B. Beaven, *Bristol Lists* (Bristol, 1899), p. 279.

[88] Martin Rishton was at Eton from 1761 to 1764, so that he could not have been there with the youngest son. He may, of course, have met Richard while the latter was visiting his older brothers.

[89] The Chancellor's Prize for the best English prose composition was established in 1768 by the then Chancellor of Oxford, Lord Lichfield, along with another Chancellor's Prize for Latin verse. The English subject set for 1773 was *Ars Musica*, and the prize was won by 'Mr. [Jeremiah] Milles, eldest son of the Dean of Exeter' (*GM* xliii (1773), 153, 298). On 7 July he read his composition as part of the annual Encaenia, or Founders' Commemoration, held 7–9 July in the Sheldonian Theatre (ibid., pp. 350–

The Eldest & youngest are both very handsome, [th]e 2ᵈ is rather plain, but infinitely the [mo]st agreeable. Mr. Rishton borrowed his [O]ration, which I would have Copied for my [Fa]ther, but when I asked Mr. Rishton if he [th]ought Mr. Thomas Mills would have any [o]bjection to that he told me that in lending [i]t, he had even desired him not to shew it to me! I have, however, Read it, & with great pleasure, as it seems to me to be very clever. We have since had the *Prize* one, which, in my opinion, though very elegantly written, is by no means new or unhackneyed. Indeed the best paragraphs in it, seem to be those which are consistently taken from the | Introduction to the Italian Tour.⁷

The Cricket players Dined on the Green, where they had a Booth erected, & a Dinner from the Globe, the best Inn here, to which Mʳˢ Rishton added a *Hash*,⁹⁰ which Mʳ T. Mi[lls] assured her was most excellent, *for* Mʳ Hurrel himself Eat three Times of it! & t[hat,] he remarked, indisputably proved it's goodnes[s.]

The Cricket match was hardly over, befo[re] the *Ting Mouth Games* began. All that was [to] be done this second Day, was Wrestling, a mos[t] barbarous Diversion, & which I could not look on, & would not have gone to, if I had no[t] feared being thought affected.

A Ring was formed for the Combattants by a Rope from which we stood to see the sport. The Wrestler was to Conquer twice, one opponent immediately after another, to entitle himself to the Prize.

A strong labouring man came off Victorious in the first Battle: but, while his shins were | yet bleeding, he was obliged to attack another; [t]he Hat (their Gauntlet) was thrown by a servant of Mʳ Colbourn's. He was reckoned [by] the Judges an admirable Wrestler; & he very [f]airly beat his Adversary: A sailor directly [fl]ung his Hat: he was sworn friend of the [de]feated Labourer: he Entered the Lists in a [Pa]ssion, & attacked the servant, as all the [Ge]ntlemen said, very unfairly: &, while a [sh]ort Truce was declared for the man to have [h]is

2). Two copies of the essay, 21 and 24 pp., are in the Bodleian Library, MS. Top. Oxon. d. 163. In 1809 the same prize was won by FB's nephew Charles Parr Burney, son of CB Jr. (*Historical Register of the University of Oxford* (Oxford, 1900), pp. 158–9).

⁹⁰ See *ED* 1. 244–5 n. 2.

shoe unbuckled, he very dishonourably hit [h]im a Violent Blow: upon this, they both prepared for a *Boxing* match—& were upon the Point ⟨of⟩ Engaging, (though the whole Ring cried out shame [u]pon the sailor) when Mr Rishton, inflamed with [a] generous rage at this foul Play, rushed precipitately into the Ring, & getting between the Combattants, Colored [*sic*] the sailor, declaring he should be turned out of the Lists.

I am really amazed that he Escaped being ill treated,—but at the same Instant, two of the young Mills ran into the Ring, & catching hold of Mr Rishton, insisted on his not venturing himself against the brutality of the enraged sailor: however, he would not ¹ retire, till the sailor was Voted out of the Lists, a[s] a foul Player. Mr Rishton then returned to us, between the Mr Mills. Every body seemed in admi[r]ation of the spirit which he exerted on this occa[sion.]

The Ting Mouth Games Concluded the Day after [7 Aug.] with a Rowing match between the Women of Sha[ldon,] a Fishing Town on the other side of the Ting, & the Fair ones of this Place. For all the men are at Newfoundland every summer, & all laboriou[s] Work is done by the Women, who have a streng[th] & hardiness which I never saw equal before i[n] *our Race*.⁹¹

While Mrs R. & myself were Dressing, we recei[ved] a very civil message from M^rs & Miss Colbourne, to Invite us to see the Rowing in their Carriag[e.] Mrs R. sent word that we would come to them on the Den: but afterwards, we recollected that we were Engaged to Tea at Mrs Phips. This put us in a Dilemma—but as Mrs Phips was the prior Engagement, we were obliged to march to Mr Colbourne's Coach on the Den, to make our apologies. The first Object I saw, was Mr Crispen— he Expressed himself prodigiously charmed at seeing ¹ us—I said we were obliged to go—He said he had heard of our not being Well—'I could ill bear, he added, 'to hear of the Lambs

---

⁹¹ Cf. MAR to FB 25 Apr. 1773 (Berg): 'You see nothing here but women in the summer their Husbands all go out to the Newfoundland fishery for 8 or 9 Months in the [year]—so the women do all the laborious business Such as *rowing* and *Towing* the boats and go out a fishing yet I never saw Cleaner Cottages nor healthier finer Children—the Women are in general Handsome none plain tho tall and *Strapping* owing [to] their robust work—their Husbands come home about November or December—consequently the winter is their time for Mirth and Jollity—they are very poor yet no signs of poverty Appear nor have I seen a Beggar since I came . . .'

illness—*but*, when they told me that *you* was not well!—I should not have been so long without seeing you, but from having had a violent Cold & Fever myself—& I thought, in my confinement, that *one* half Hour's Conversation with *you*, would have compleatly recovered me.'

'If I had known, said I, 'my miraculous power—'

'O,' cried he, taking my Hand, 'it is not yet too late!'

We made our apologies as well as we could, & they insisted on setting us down at Mr Phips'. Mrs Colbourne & Mr Crispen on one side, & we 3 Lasses on the other. All the way we went Mr Crispen amused himself with holding the same kind of Language to me — —

The Women Rowed with astonishing dexterity & quickness—there were 5 Boats of them. The Prizes which they Won, were shifts with Pink Ribban[ds.]

I must now miss a whole Week, having no Time to recollect any thing which passed. Last Sunday [15 Aug.] M^r & Mrs Western[92] arrived here, to make a Week's visit. Mrs Western is Cousin to Mr Rishton, being sister to Mr Martin Folkes. She is infinitely the most agreeable of her Family: good tempered, lively, well bred & obliging. Mr Western is a very sensible man, but has an Oddity in him which I know not how to Characterize. He has a good deal of drollery—but I ⌜fear⌝ makes a very uncomfortable Companion,—I think he has the *remains* of a very agreeable man, as strongly marked in his looks & manners, as I have ever seen the *remains* of a celebrated Beauty visible in a Countenance: he is still a young man, but has such very indifferent Health, that it imbitters every moment of his life.—Mrs Western was most violently in love with him when they married, though their Fortunes on each side, were too considerable to make either of them be styled *romantic*;[93]—but I think at present, she seems to have the most perfect, the Coldest Indifference for him, that ever Wife had: Mr Western is still reckoned a very *gay* man, in ⟨no⟩ very *constant* ⟨sen⟩se of

[92] Maximilian Western (*c.*1739–1801), of Cokethorpe, Oxfordshire; m. (1763) Elizabeth Folkes (*c.*1746–1804), daughter of William Folkes (d. 1773) of Hillington Hall, Norfolk and Queen Square, by his first wife, Ursula née Taylor; Mrs Western was a half-sister of Martin Browne Folkes (1749–1821), cr. (1774) Bt., and a first cousin of Martin Rishton's *mother*, Mrs Dorothy (Folkes) Rishton.

[93] Mr Western was the only son of Maximilian sen. (d. 1764), a director of the East India Company (*GM* xxxiv (1764), 198).

that Word: he may therefore, have trifled away her Affection, while his ⟨ow⟩n for her appears still continued. O what bad policy in men, to accustom their Wives to their fickleness, till ⟨ev⟩en their love becomes a matter of indifferency! Ind⟨ee⟩d I am sorry for them both; as each of them seem formed for a degree of happiness to which they really seem to deny each other.

Mrs Western has, in the politest manner, invited me to accompany M^r & Mrs R. to Oxfordshire, when they return this Visit. As to Mr Western—he & I are particularly good friends: Indeed, Mrs R. & myself are as free from restrai⟨nt⟩ or ceremony, as before they came, for, fortunately, they neither of them have the least grain of it in their Compositions.

We all went on Monday Evening [16 Aug.] to the sea shore, to see the *scene* [seine] Drawn: this is a most curious Work: & all done by Women. They have a very long Net, so considerable as to Cost them 13 or 16 pounds—this they first draw into a Boat, which they go off the shore in, & Row in a kind of semi Circle, till they Land at some distance: all the way, they spread this Net, one side of which is kept above ⏐ Water by Corks. Then they Land, & divide Forces; half of them return to the beginning of the Net, & half remain at the End: & then, with amazing strength, they both *divisions*, at the same Time, pull the Net in, by the two Ends: whatever Fish they Catch, are always encircled in the middle of the Net, which comes out of the Water the last; &, as they draw towards each other, they all join in getting their prey: when once they perceive that there is Fish in their Nets, they set up a loud shout, & make an almost unintelligible Noise, in ⌜quarreling,⌝ their joy, & in disputing at the same Time upon their shares, & on what Fish Escaped them. They are all robust & well made, & have remarkably beautiful Teeth: & some of them are really very fine Women: their Dress is barbarous: they have stays half Laced, & some thing by way of Handkerchiefs about their Necks, they wear ⌜one⌝ colored Flannel, or stuff petticoat;—no shoes or stockings; notwithstanding the hard Pebbles & stones all along the Beach:—& their Coat is Pin'd up in the shape of a pair of ⌜⟨Bree⟩ches,⌝ leaving them wholly Naked to the knee. ⏐

Mr Western declares he could not have imagined such a Race of Females existed in a Civilized Country—& had he come hither by sea, he should have almost fancied he had been Cast on a new discovered Coast. They caught, this Evening, at one Time 9 large salmon, a John Dory, & a Gurnet: on Tuesday Evening, we went again, & saw them Catch 4 dozen of mackeral at a Haul. After this was over, we Crost the Ting in a Ferry Boat, to Shaldon, & took a most delightful Walk up a high Hill, from whence the Prospects both by sea & Land, are inconceivably beautiful. We had the 3 Dogs with us: poor Romeo is still Confined, & being an old Dog, I fear will never recover:[94] we returned by the same Boat: the Dogs have always swum across—& they Jump'd into the Water as usual—but the Tide was very high;—& we were obliged to go a quarter of a mile about, before we could Land: M[r] Rishton hallowed to the Dogs, & whistled, all the Way, to encourage them.—however, the Current was so strong at the Point where we Landed, that they could not stem it:—M[rs] Western, R. & myself Walked Home, & left the Gentlemen to watch the Dogs— | Ting Mouth, [the] Newfoundland Dog, [af]ter a hard struggle, by his excellence in swimming, at length got safe on shore: Trump, who is a ver⟨y *c*⟩*unning* Brute, found out a shorter Cut, & arrived safe;—his fellow Spaniel, Vigo, they could see nothing of—M[r] Rishton sent after him—but he did not appear all night—& the next morning, we found that he was Drowned! This has been a great concern to us all—"the Brace of spaniels cost Mr. R. 5 guineas."

Yesterday [18 Aug.] was settled for a Grand Cricket match—but it proved so miserable a Day, that the Gentlemen "found" it "impossible:" we went, out of curiosity, to the Beach, as the sea was extremely rough, & the Waves uncommonly high: as we stood, looking at it, a Wave came suddenly, with such amazing force, that though we all Ran away full speed, M[rs] Western & M[rs] Rishton were Wetted all over—I had happened not to be so near. We hurried Home, & they were obliged to entirely new Dress themselves.

In the Evening, the M[r] Mills called, to settle on to Day for Cricket. They brought with them 2 Gentlemen, (who were on a Visit at the Dean's, on purpose to be of the Party) Captain Salter[95] & M[r] Gibbs.[96] | The latter of them is esteemed one of

---

[94] Romeo did recover, though slowly (MAR to FB 2 Oct. 1773, 17 Feb. 1774, Berg).
[95] Probably Elliot Salter (1743–90); Lt. (RN), 1765; Commander, 1769; Capt.,

[*See p. 296 for n. 95 cont. and n. 96*]

the most learned young men Alive, having Won the [Craven][97] Prize at Cambridge. Our little parlour was quite filled.

M[r] T. Mills beg'd me to remark the beauties of our Chimney Piece; on each side of which was placed, just opposite to each other, a Dog & a Cat: 'I am sorry, said he, to see these Animals here, for I fancy they are meant as an Emblem of Husband & Wife;—now no two Creatures disagree so much as Dog & Cat' — — 'And Husband & Wife?' cried I—'O no, I beg your pardon, Ma'am,' cried he, 'I am only sorry *these people* have ⌈ill⌉ judged them so!'

To Day has been but very *so*, *so*—nevertheless, the Cricket match could be no longer defer'd. M[rs] Western, ⌈R.⌉ & I went on the Green at Noon, ⌈to look on.⌉ M[r] T. Mills, not being then Engaged [in play],[98] met us, & got 3 Chairs out of their Booth, for us to ⌈see⌉, without danger [of the Ball:][98] but it was too Cold ⌈to sit.⌉ Capt. Salter & M[r] Gibbs ⌈came &⌉ walked round with us—M[r] Gibbs came on my side pretending to screen [m]e from the Wind, & Entered into small Talk with [a] facility that would not have led me to supposing [ho]w high his Character stood at the university. |

M[rs] Rishton was in one of her provoking humours. She came behind me every now & then, & whispered, '*fie, Child!*'—& then shaking her Head, & walking off, added 'upon my Word, the Girls of this Age!—there is no more respect for a married Woman than if—well, I'd rather be whip'd than married, I declare! really, M[rs] Western, we matrons are no more regarded by these Chits, than so many Pepper Corns.—'

Then, in a few minutes, she returned to me again, 'Really, Miss Fanny Burney, I don't know what you *mean* by this behaviour!—O Girls! Girls! Girls!'

1776. Like the Milles brothers, their father, Martin Rishton, and also Mr Gibbs, Elliot Salter was an old Etonian (1753–9). See D. B. Smith, *The Commissioned Sea Officers of the Royal Navy 1660–1815* (Greenwich, 1954), iii. 806.

[96] Vicary Gibbs (1751–1820). A native of Exeter, he went to Eton in 1764, where he gained distinction for his compositions in Latin verse. Proceeding to Cambridge in 1771, he greatly distinguished himself there in Greek studies, and was elected a Craven university scholar in 1772. Elected a fellow of King's College in 1774, he received his BA in 1775 and MA in 1778. In 1769 Gibbs had been admitted as a student of Lincoln's Inn, and he was called to the Bar in 1783. Resigning his fellowship at King's in 1784, he subsequently had a notable career as a judge. In 1805 he was knighted, and in 1814 he was named Chief Justice of the Common Pleas.

[97] Left blank by FB.   [98] Inserted by FBA.

When the Wind grew more violent, we went into the Booth, for shelter—soon after, Captain Salter called out 'Take care, Ladies, ⌐&¬ hurried me suddenly out—for the Cricket Ball came over the Booth.—Mrs Rishton, with one of her droll looks of sternness, came behind me, & in a half whisper, cried 'very well, Miss Fanny Burney! very well! I shall write to Dr. Burney to-morrow morning.'

They have all diverted themselves with me, not a little, ever since, except Mr Rishton, who does not approve these sort of ⌐Jokes.¬ However, his Wife suffice[s] for *two*, at least! She & Mrs Western have talked of t[he] *Captain* ever since: Mr Western has been very *dry* ab[out] the Mr Mills—'They are very agreeable young me[n] ^| said he, 'but I think he that sat by Miss Burney (Mr T.) is much the *most* agreeable. What do *you* think, Miss Burney!' 'O yes!' answered I.—Then again at supper, Yesterday, he said 'A very Agreeable Evening, upon my Word—don't you think so, Miss Burney?' And to Day, after Dinner, he said he was going to the Cricket Ground, to see how they went on—'I shall acquaint the Gentlemen, said he, how industrious you all are, (we were picking sea Weeds) and that Tea will be made in the same Corner it was yesterday—hay, Miss Burney?'

Friday, Aug^st [20]

We have been taking a most delightful Walk on the Top of the Rocks & Cliffs by the sea shore. Mrs Western is so charmed with this Country, that she endeavours to prevail with her Husband to Buy an Estate & reside here:—indeed it is a most tempting spot—

Sunday, Aug: [22]

Yesterday morning we went to Ugbrook, the seat of Lord Clifford,[99] about 5 miles from here: the Gentlemen on Horseback, & we 3 in Mr Western's Chaise.

What is most remarkable in the House, is a Bed, of [ex]quisite Workmanship, done under the direction of [th]e Dutchess of

---

[99] Hugh Clifford (1726–83), 4th B. Clifford of Chudleigh. His seat was Ugbrooke Hall, near Chudleigh, Devon. CB had met Ld. Clifford's mother, the Dowager Lady Clifford née Elizabeth Blount (d. 1778), at Paris in 1764 and again in 1770 ('Mem.' No. 104; *Tours*, i. 12, 20, 23).

Norfolk:[1] it is on a beautiful Pink [Gro]und, & Worked in Birds
& natural Flowers, with such | glowing Colours, & so exact a
resemblance to Nature, that it is reckoned the most finished
piece of Work in the kingdom. The House is situated in a
delightful Park, filled with Deer,—We went 5 miles round his
Lordship's Grounds, & took a view of the Rocks at Chudleigh,
which are the most romantic & beautiful imaginable.[2]

This morning, M^r & Mrs Western left us,—which we are all
sorry for,—we passed a very gay Week with them, being all of
us perfectly intimate & easy. Mr Western is really a very agreeable man, & his Wife is a charming Woman. Mr Rishton is
quite melancholy, at their departure, as they are prodigious
favourites with him. Indeed, this has been the dullest Day we
have spent yet. Mrs Western has, very particularly, repeated her
Invitation to me, which I fancy, as Mrs Rishton is extremely
earnest with me for it, I shall accept.[3]

We seem to have quite dropt Mr Crispen—he cannot but
have perceived Mr Rishton's Coldness, as he never Calls.—M^r
Rishton has an uncommon aversion to every thing that leads
towards Flirtation; & Mr Crispen, from being much regarded
by him, is become almost odious. I fancy that his friendship for
Miss Bowdler has much contributed to make Mr Rishton
disli[ke] him. However, whenever I meet him, he assures me of|
the constancy of his *passion*, though I really endeavour to shun
him, to avoid Mr Rishton's disapprobation.

It is not possible for a man to make a better Husband than
Mr Rishton does: he spends almost every moment of his Time

[1] The Dowager Lady Clifford's younger sister Mary Blount (*c.*1702–27 May 1773),
who m. (1727) Edward Howard (1686–1777), 8th D. of Norfolk. Lady Clifford and the
Duchess were daughters of Pope's friend Edward Blount, of Blagden, Devon. The
curtains of the State Bedroom at Ugbrooke were of silk damask, 'exquisitely wrought in
needle-work with birds, flowers, and fruit, under the direction of the late Duchess of
Norfolk. In a poem, descriptive of Ugbrooke, the decorations of this celebrated bed are
thus elegantly described: "See, on the silken ground, how flora pours / Her various
dyes, an opulence of flowers; / How, blended with the foliage of the rose, / And rich
carnation, the streak'd tulip glows . . ."' (J. Britton and E. W. Brayley, *A Topographical
and Historical Description of . . . Devon*, [1804], p. 105).

[2] '*Chudleigh Rock*, about half a mile from the town, is . . . "one of the most striking
inland rocks in the Island." Viewed from the west, it exhibits a bold, broad, and almost
perpendicular front, apparently one solid mass of marble; from the south-east, a hollow
opens to the view, with an impetuous stream rushing over the rude stones that impede
its passage, and forming in one part of its course a romantic water-fall . . .' (ibid.,
p. 102).

[3] See below, p. 313.

with his Wife, & is all attention & kindness to her. He is Reading Spencer's [*sic*] Fairy Queen to us—[in][4] which he is extremely delicate, omitting whatever, to the Poet's great disgrace, has crept in that is improper for a Woman's Ear. I receive very great pleasure from this Poem: in which there is an endless fund of Invention & Fancy.

Mrs R. & I study Italian together, though very slowly. Indeed we go out so much, either Walking or in the whiskey, that we have hardly any Time.

There are not above 3 Houses here, which have not Thatched Roofs. One of the 3 is Sir John Davy's,[5] which we have been to see: it is delightfully situated on the River Ting.

⌐I have heard nothing of my dear Father since I have been here, nor dare I much flatter myself that I should. Mr. Rishton is extremely warm about his [s]ubscription. He has absolutely insisted on having a set to himself—& 3 or 4 Gentlemen have subscribed [with] him, among them, Mr. Phips & Mr. Colbourne.⌐[6] |

Mr T. Mills has told Mr Rishton that he was in the same College with my Father when he was at Oxford last, at the Installation;[7] & that no man has been received with so much honour there, as *Dr. Burney*, since it was a University. Hearing Mr Rishton Name him, 'Pray, said the Dean, 'are you talking of *the* Dr. Burney?'

⌐The Eldest of these Youths has subscribed to Mr. Rishton.⌐[8]

Wednesday—Augst [25]

On Monday the three Brothers Dined here. They are really very agreeable & amiable young men. I add the latter Clause, presuming upon the Harmony & affection which seems to

---

[4] Inserted by FBA.

[5] Sir John Davie (1734–92), 7th Bt.

[6] Martin Rishton and MAR subscribed for a total of 20 copies, and Constantine Phipps and Benjamin Colborne for one copy each.

[7] CB had attended the Encaenia held at Oxford, 7–9 July. Thomas Milles was a student at Queen's College, and CB was presumably one of the numerous 'genteel Company' put up there for the occasion, beginning 4 July (*Oxford Journal*, 10 July 1773). The Chancellor of Oxford, Ld. North, was also in Queen's. CB no doubt was present at the 'sumptuous entertainment' held there on 7 July, besides going to the Chancellor's levees in Queen's, 6–9 July (ibid.) CB took the opportunity to insert advertisements for his subscription in the *Oxford Journal*, 3 and 10 July.

[8] Jeremiah Milles subscribed for one copy.

reign among them; & they appear to regard their Father only as an Elder Brother, to whom they owe more respect, but not less Openness.

After Dinner, Mrs R. & I took a Walk, & the Gentlemen went on the Den to play at quoits. We returned first, & were just seated, when we heard a Rap at the Parlour Door—'Come in,' cried I, 'whoever you are['—]the Door opened, & Mr Crispen Entered—'Whose sweet Voice bid me Come in'? Cried he, 'may I hope that my love Welcomes me?'—he came in immediately & drew ⌐his⌐ chair before m[e] as I sat on the Window, & began to relate his suffering[s] from his long Absence,—I told him I thought it rathe[r] ˥ an Affront that he was Alive.—he complained very much of my usage of him, which he said was extremely ungenerous, as I took advantage of his *fondness*, to treat him with cruelty.

To say the truth, he has of late grown rather more ⌐free⌐ than I wish, ⌐or chuse to submit to,⌐ having taken it into his Head to pay me many Compliments of too ridiculous a Nature to bear Writing; besides, he is somewhat troublesome in taking, or rather *making*, perpetual opportunities of taking my Hand. I was very glad that his attention was just called off, to look at a particular kind of Cane, which he moved away from me to examine, as the Gentlemen returned. Mr Rishton made him a very Cold Bow, and the Eldest Mr Mills came & seated himself in the Chair which he had left Vacant, & entered into Conversation—

Mr Crispen was obliged to seat himself at some distance: the first *interval* he could Catch, he said to me 'I observe that my sweet friend is not without ambition; for I have taken notice that she always seats herself as high as possible.' 'It is only, answered I, because I require some Assistance to my Height.'

Tea & Coffee were now brought in—Mr Crispen presented my Cup, & then hastily ⌐took⌐ his Exit. I fancy [tha]t his reception was such as will by no means speed ˥ another visit from him. Miss Bowdler too, was with us all the morning, & if she is not determined to be blind, *must* perceive Mr Rishton's Coldness to her.

⌐Yesterday Mr. Rishton was out all the morning, with the Mills, shooting—at 2 he came Home, in a great hurry, to Dine, having Engaged to join them again in the afternoon. Mrs.

Rishton upbraided him for spending a *whole day* thus away from her & being in a ridiculous humour, as soon as the Cloth &c. were removed she left her place, & insisted on sitting on his Lap—indeed, this is an action she is by no means averse to: notwithstanding Mr. Rishton expostulates on my presence, & assures her that she makes me Blush every Hour of the Day. For my part, I say nothing, as I know that if I remonstrated, she would find double sport in it.

'So you go out again this afternoon? cried she—well, I have no notion of such behaviour—Women & Cats stay at Home!— Dogs & men go out—give me Leave to tell you Mr. Martin, you are a very bad man!'—

'Well, my dear, do but go to your seat, & you shall tell me what you will—'

'O Rudeness! Fanny, Fanny, never marry—never tru[st] the men!—Give me my wine, Mar[tin] Folkes—"|

[*A leaf or leaves have been cut away. Next, FB and presumably MAR encounter a party, a few of whom are apparently amusing themselves with some kind of fisherman's work.*]

"[xxxxx *3 words*] that employment from the Fish[er]men, & were amusing themselves with that work [xxxxx *2 words*] their party was Miss Honeywood,[9] Miss [xxxxx *1 word*], a young lady who is of a similar disposition, [& M]iss Honeywood's most intimate friend, Captain [Sal]ter, & the youngest Miss Mills,[10] a girl of 15, & Mr. Tom Mills. We stood some Time looking [at] them,—they endeavoured in vain to persuade [Mi]ss Mills to join them but it grew Dark, & we left [the]m to their Enterprize as we knew Mr. Rishton [wou]ld by no means approve our being of such a [Par]ty—late he is as good as a Duenna.

Thursday, Aug. [26]

Another Cricket match was held this morning. Mrs. R. & I walked to the Gentlemen's Booth, where [we] saw the Miss

[9] Annabella Christiana Honywood (*c.*1755–1808), only daughter of William Honywood (1731–64) of Malling Abbey, Kent; m. (1775) Robert Gorges Dobyns Yate (*c.*1752–85) of Bromesberrow, Gloucestershire (*GM* xlv (1775), 406; lxxviii[1] (1808), 463). She was sister of Sir John Honywood (*c.*1757–1806), 4th Bt., and of the Revd Edward Honywood (*c.*1753–1812), DCL (Oxon.), 1793, later Rector of Honiton, Devon, and Prebendary of Exeter. She was also a niece of William Courtenay (1742–88), 8th Visc. Courtenay. FB met her again in 1777, on a visit to Gloucester (vol. ii).

[10] Amelia or Harriet (b. *c.*1758), afterwards Mrs Blake.

Mills & their Cousin,[11] & Miss Honeywood: [I w]ill say nothing of these ladies, unless I see more [of] them, which is not probable, as they make it a [ru]le to never Visit at Ting Mouth.

At Night the Youngest Mills Drank Tea here. [We] are teaching Mr. Rishton to play at Back Gammon [fo]r which we make a Pool every Evening. It is [th]e only Game in the World that gives me any [pl]easure,—at Cards, I can never keep awake.ॸ

Friday—Augst [27]

To Day, for the first Time, I Bathed. Ever since [I w]ent to Torbay, I have been tormented with a [dre]adful Cold, till within this Day or two; and ˡM^r Rishton very much advised me to sea Bathi[ng] in order to *harden* me. The Women here are so poor, & this place till lately was so very obscur[e] & retired, that they wheel the Bathing machi[ne] into the sea themselves, & have never heard of [?Horses]. I was terribly frightened, & really thought I shou[ld] never have recovered from the Plunge—I had n[ot] Breath enough to speak for a minute or tw[o,] the shock was beyond expression great—but aft[er] I got back to the machine, I presently felt myself in a Glow that was delightful—it [is] the finest feeling in the World,—& will induc[e] me to Bathe as often as will be safe.

Saturday, Aug^s[ᵗ 28]

ॸMr. Rishton was out the whole Day with the Dean & his Family, at sea, on a shooting Party. Mr. T. Mills called in in the morning, to beg Mrs. R. would not be uneasy if they kept her Husband out till late, as all water Expeditions are uncer[tain—] however, in the Evening, we Walked on the Beach hoping to see them Land, but growing tired of para[d]ing up & down we were returning Home, when a voi[ce] behind stop'd us—it belonged to the Eldest Mills who, with Miss Casal, his Cousin, were running, alm[ost] after us—'What cried he, & was you looking after [him?] ˡ never fear, he won't be lost. We have a greater trust at stake than you have,—5 of us are gone'—

'But why, said Mrs. R. did you not go?'

'Because, answered he, my Cousin & I are very economical

---

¹¹ Miss Casal (below). Not further identified.

young people—& as soon as venture out at sea, we Cast up our accounts—Besides we are always willing to take care of the *Family*—therefore we two stay at Home in case the Boat should be lost.'

We then turned Back, & walked with them for near an Hour upon the Beach, every now & then looking out with a Glass which Mr. Mills had with him—His Cousin is a very ordinary Girl, but seems to be sensible & good tempered.

Mr. Mills talked nonsense with her very fluently, [saying that the *man in the moon* was her Lover &c.]¹²

Mrs. Rishton grew once again tired, & we came Home,—& very soon after, Mr. Rishton returned.˥

Sunday, Augˢᵗ [29]

This morning *all the World* was at Church, as the Dean of Exeter Preached. He gave us an excellent Discourse, which he delivered extremely well. We met all the Family as we came out, & Mʳ T. Mills joined our party: the morning was lovely, & we took a very pleasant Walk. Mʳ Rishton proposes going to Ivy Bridge or Staverton ˥ in a short Time, for a few Days, in order to Fish: Mʳ T. Mills invited himself to be of our Party.

We had again the pleasure to hear the Dean in the After-noon, who gave us a most admirable sermon on moral Duties. The singing here is the most extraordinary I ever heard,—there is no Instrument, but the People attempt to sing in Parts—with such Voices! such expression & such Composition! They to Day, in honour, I presume, of the Dean, performed an Anthem. It was really too much to be borne decently—it was set by a Weaver,—& so very unlike any thing that was ever before imagined, so truly barbarous, that, with the addition of the singers trilling & squalling,—no Comedy could have afforded more Diversion: Mʳˢ Rishton & I Laughed ourselves sick—though we very much endeavoured to be grave—Mʳ Rishton was quite offended, & told his Wife that the Eyes of the whole Congregation were on her—but nothing could restrain us, till the Dean began his prayer—& there is a something *commanding* in his Voice, that immediately gained all our Attention.˥

¹² Inserted by FBA.

Monday, Augst 30th

This morning, Mr Rishton being out, his Wife & I were studying Italian, when we received a Visit from Mr Crispen.

He was scarse seated, when turning to me 'Now did I not behave very well t'other Day?' said he,—when the Mills were here?—I told you that when a *young* Lover offered, I would retire—And really, the Eldest Mills—took to my little Burney just as—indeed he is a very pretty young man—and I think—'

I interrupted him with very warm expostulations—letting him know, as well as I could, that this Discourse was quite too ridiculous. Mrs Rishton got the Peruvienne Lettres,[13] & beg'd him to hear her Read—which when he had done, he insisted on giving *me* a Lesson—I was extremely shy of receiving one, but he would take no denial—'Don't mind *me*, said he, what am *I*?—if it was Mr Mills, indeed,—'

To silence him, I then began. He paid me prodigious Compliments, & concluded with modestly saying—'Yes—I will follow you to London, and give you a Lesson a Day, for 3 kisses Entrance, and 2 kisses a Lesson.'

Really I believe the man is mad; or thinks me a Fool,—for he has perpetually proposed this payment to himself for different things. I was very grave with him: but he was only the more provoking.—

'Why now, said he, you think this a high price for *me*—but it would be nothing for Mr Mills!—'

In short, I believe he has determined to say any & every thing to me that occurs to him.

When he was going, he turned to me *pathetically*[—]'This was a most imprudent Visit!—I feel it *here* stronger than ever—I must tear myself away!—'

Seating myself, however, again, the Conversation I know not by what means, between Mrs R. & him turned on ill proportioned marriages, on which he talked very sensibly—but concluded with saying 'Had I—come into the World 35 years later—*here* I had been fixed!' taking my Hand—& then he went on in a strain of Complimenting till he took his leave.

As soon as he was gone, We went to pay a Visit to Miss Bowdler—& here again we found Mr Crispen.

[13] *Lettres d'une Péruvienne* (1747), by Madame Françoise de Graffigny (1695–1758).

We both remarked that she was most excessively Cold in her reception & behaviour—perhaps Mr Rishton has infected her—& perhaps Mr Crispen's unexpected perseverance in his devoirs to me offends her, for she would be his Eloisë [*sic*]—a Character she beyond all others, admires[—]at least her behaviour has that appearance.

Mr Crispen said I looked very like a Picture he had seen of Ione[14]—I never saw it, & could therefore make no speeches: I told him I had never before been compared to any picture but that of the goddess of Dullness in the Dunciad. His usual strain was renewed — — Mrs Rishton observed that he *must* make love to *me*—

'Ay,' cried Miss Bowdler, 'or to any body!'

'No, no,' cried he—'*if* I had but been born 35 years later—I had certainly fixed here for life!'—

'Or else with Miss Colbourne,' cried Mrs Rishton—

'Never did Miss Colbourne hear such a Declaration'—said he—'no, never!'

'Ay, but the little Bowdler!' returned Mrs R.—

'No, nor the little Bowdler niether,' answered he.

'O,' cried she, '*I* am quite out of the Question *now*.'

'And *always*,' said he, 'in regard to *love*, *always* out of the Question!—'

'Why yes—replied Miss Bowdler, colouring,—'to give him his due, he never talked that nonsense to *me*.'—

Tuesday Aug. 31st

We Dined at Mr Hurrel's, & met there M^r & Mrs Onslow:[15] the latter is a sister of Mr Phips. They are the handsomest Couple I ever saw: Mrs Onslow has suffered very much from illness, but must have been quite beautiful: they are well bred & sensible.

I cannot imagine what whim has induced Mr Rishton, so lively, so entertaining as he himself is, to take a fancy to the Hurrels, who are, Mrs R. & I both think, most truly stupid and

[14] One of the Nereids, daughters of the sea god Nereus. She is named with her sister sea nymphs in Spenser's *Faerie Queene*, IV. xi. 48–51 (see above, p. 299).

[15] Arthur Onslow (1746–1817), 3rd son of Lt.-Gen. Richard Onslow (*c.*1697–1760), Governor of Plymouth; at Eton, 1760–3; MA (Oxon.), 1771; DD, 1781; Vicar of Kidderminster, 1795; Dean of Worcester, 1795; m. (1772) Frances Phipps (d. 1810).

tiresome. Miss Davy, the sister, is a well bred conversible old maid, & I much prefer her.

Wednesday, Septr 1st

I was never before at the House of a sportsman on this most Critical Day[16]—& really it is not bad Diversion.—

Mr Onslow & Mr T. Mills agreed to be of Mr Rishton's Company this morning, in shooting—at 4 o'Clock the commotion in the House awoke ⌐ me—I heard a thousand different Noises—the Horses Prancing—the Dogs called—the Gentlemen Hallowing—[Messrs][17] Onslow & Mills were here before Mr Rishton was up—the House was in an uproar—& it was by no means light, though they were so eager for sport.

⌐They have been out the whole Day. & it has rained incessantly.

Friday, Septr 3^d

They came Home, at 8 o'clock, like Drowned Rats. I never before saw such miserable Figures. Yesterday Mr. Rishton was obliged to go to Exeter. Mr. T. Mills & Mr. Onslow went out shooting by themselves—indeed they have all resolved never to go 3 together again—they are too fond of *sport* to make these Excuses for ⟨vani⟩ity.

The Eldest Mr. Mills called here just as we had finished a late Dinner, for Mr. Rishton did not return till 6 o'clock. He sat with us for some Time & in the Evening his Brother Tom Called, to settle this Day's sport with Mr. Rishton.⌐

Nothing is now talked or thought of but shooting & Game— Mr R. is just now set off with Mr T. Mills,—Dressed such Figures! really sportsmen have no regard to even common appearances—⌐

They complain very much of Poachers here—for my part, I have no great compassion for their injuries.—Mr Hurrel, who is too fat & too lazy to shoot, is also too great a *Gourmand* to deny himself Game, & is therefore suspected to be a very great encourager of Poachers. They Live but next Door to us, & came out this morning, as well as Mrs R. & me, to see the

---

[16] The opening of the hunting season for partridge (see below, p. 307).
[17] Corrected by FBA from 'Mrs.'

sportsmen set off—Mr T. Mills, very slyly, began to entertain them with discoursing on the injuries they received from Poachers—& added 'it is not for the Birds—we sportsmen do not much value them—but for the pleasure of *finding* them, that we quarrel with Poachers about—and, (turning to me) I am sorry to say—for the pleasure of *killing* them!'—

'I had some intention, said I, of sending an Ode on the 31st of August, with the Partridges complaint, to every sportsman in the Country.'

'I am sure I should have been very happy,' cried he Bowing *with an Air*, to have received it from you:—and I would have given it—'

Here he stop'd,—checked, I presume, by Conscience from making any promissory professions.

^rI find myself obliged to mention these Brothers, so after I have attempted a sketch of their Characters, such as they appear to me.

Mr. Mills, the Eldest, is almost 24 years of age—a very good Figure & extremely handsome, but rather too much of the *embonpoint*—he seems polite, mild, sensible & amiable.

Mr. Tom Mills is very plain, but Tall & genteel; has an excellent address, great readiness of Conversation, is universally admired by the Ladies, & in short, is a very agreeable young man.

Dick Mills, the youngest, is quite a beautiful youth—a clear & glowing Complection, a sleepy Eye & exceeding fine hair—he has a degree of bluntness, that, in one so young, denotes an honest Heart—his manners & expressions are *naif*—free, & easy.

The whole Family are much esteemed here, & universally remarked for the Harmony which reigns amongst them. They come to Ting Mouth every summer from the Deanery at Exeter.ⁿ

Sunday, Sept^r [5]

This morning we heard Mr Onslow preach. He says he always Travels with a Brace of sermons, that he may be ready to give occasional assistance to his Brother Clergymen, ^rmuchⁿ requested. I did not at all admire him, as he seems to be conceited: & indeed, the Dean has at present made me difficult.

After service, the two youngest Mills, & Mr Onslow Called in, to settle their next shooting party with Mr Rishton. It is amazing what a laborious business this is: they go out before Breakfast,—after two or 3 Hours shooting, they get what they can at any Farm House—then toil till 3 or 4 o'Clock, when sometimes they return Home, but if they have any prospect of more sport, they take *pot luck* at some Cottage, and stay out till 8 or 9 o'Clock. The Weather makes no alteration in their pursuits,—a sportsman defies Wind, Rain, & all inclemencies of either heat or Cold. As to Mr Rishton, he seems bent on being proof against every thing; he seeks all kinds of manly Exercise & grows sun Burnt, strong & hardy.

We went to Dinner at Star Cross, a little Town about 8 miles off—Mrs Rishton, as usual, Driving me in the whiskey, & Mr Rishton & the man on Horseback. We Dined at an Inn, in a Room which overlooked the River Ex. We were very unfortunate in the Evening, and were overtaken by Rain, wind & Darkness—and as these Roads are very narrow, very steep, & very Craggy, [|] we should really have been in a very dangerous situation, after it grew too Dark for Mrs R. to see to Drive, had not her Husband made the man lead his Horse, ⌐&,¬ in the midst of the Wet & Dirt, led the Whiskey himself. On these occasions he is very uncommonly good natured & attentive.

Thursday, Sept^r [9]

⌐I doubt, my dear Susan, if you will receive this pacquet before we meet—however, I will Continue to Write, in hopes of some opportunity of sending it you. After many disappointments I have at length heard from you, but as I shall send you a Letter on this subject, will drop it now[18]—only repeating that I am extremely rejoiced that Signor Sacchini remains with us another year. The Opera will be Composed of [xxxxx *1 word*] *Friends*.¬

Mr Tom Mills Breakfasted with us this morning at 6 o'Clock; & then set out with Mr Rishton on a shooting Party: Mrs. R. & I went in the Whiskey to Dawlish, a mighty pretty Village on the sea Coast. We had the Hurrels with us in the Evening—that

---

[18] Both letters are missing. FB presumably scolded SEB at length for not replying sooner to her journal letters.

stupid Couple, to whom Mr Rishton has taken a most un-accountable liking, *ennui* both his Wife & me to Death: her good Nature is so tiresome & officious, that I would prefer even a bad Temper, with a little portion of understanding.

We see Mrs Phips but seldom since her | sister in Law, Mrs Onslow, has been here. She is a sweet Woman, & has pretty blue Eyes, like my dear Susan's.

Septr 15th

I must give you this last Week all in a *lump*—for I have no Time for Daily Datings.

We have been to Staverton—⌐& without Mr. Tom Mills, who was otherwise engaged at the Time—we went on Sunday [12 Sept.] & returned on the Monday Evening.⌐ It was a very agreeable Excursion. We slept at Ashburnham,[19] & went in the Whiskey many miles round,—the Country of Devonshire is inexhaustible in the variety of its rural beauties. Hills, Valleys, Rivers, plains, Woods, lanes, meadows—every thing is beyond all Description romantic & beautiful. The River Dart, which is the boundary of the Staverton manor, is the most rapid, clear & delightful one I ever saw,—there are Walks along the Banks that are delicious. The whole manor belongs to the Miss Folkes,[20] & their married sisters. The richness of the Land is astonishing—plenty & abundance riegn [*sic*] *partout*—but I have niether Time or talents to describe this most charming Country. There are places about Ting Mouth which do all together, exceed every other, as all the pros⟨pe⟩cts have some view of the sea, which is so noble ⟨an⟩ object, that it enlivens & beautifies all others. |

Thursday, Septr 16

We leave Ting Mouth to-morrow.

It will not be without regret that I shall quit this incomparable

---

[19] FB's slip for Ashburton.

[20] Ursula Folkes (d. 1797), eldest daughter of William Folkes of Hillington Hall and Queen Square; m. (1775) Capt. (later Admiral) John Macbride (d. 1800) of Plympton, Devon; and Mary Folkes (d. 1813), the 3rd daughter, m. John Balchen West (d. 1793) of Woodcock Lodge, Herts (*GM* xlv (1775), 350; lxiii² (1793), 1061, 1151; lxvii¹ (1797), 171; lxxxiii¹ (1813), 289). Their married sisters were Mrs Western, the youngest daughter, and Dorothy Folkes (living 1796), the 2nd daughter, who m. (1764) Edmund Rolfe (1738–1817) of Heacham, Norfolk (V. Berry, *The Rolfe Papers* ... (Norwich, 1979), p. x; subscription list to *Camilla*).

Country—ᴦI speak of it only as incomparable in England, which is universally allowed. [xxxxx ½ *line*]ᴎ

Mʳ Crispen went yesterday. We have seen very little of him lately; Mʳ Rishton's extreme coldness has been too visible to be unnoticed;—We were not returned from Staverton when he went, & so took no leave of him: by which mea[ns] I dare say I lost an abundance of fine speeches: though I believe he thought himself Laughed at by Mʳˢ Rishton, as well as slighted by her Husband,—for of late, he has contented himself with insisting on my never marrying *without his Consent*, & on my letting him give me away—this he has been *vehement* about [and he earnestly and very *seriously* solicited me to write him, that he might prepare himself for his office, &c.][21]

ᴦMr. Mills called here on Saturday, *pour prendre Congé*,—he was going to spend some Time at his ⟨Gorge⟩,[22] or nigh, & from there to his studies at Oxford.

Mr. Tom Mills, contrary to all expectations from his Character, has left Ting Mouth without paying his devoirs to the fair sex—he must never ⟨set up⟩ as a man of gallantry henceforth—ᴎ |

ᴦDick Mills has behaved in the [xxxxx *1 line*] ⟨his⟩ motto to be Ease & carelessness. The Dean & his Daughters remain here some Time longer.ᴎ

Miss Bowdler, who goes to Bath to Day, called this morning: we have all parted upon very civil terms, though I am sure her penetration is too great to have suffered Mʳ Rishton's dislike ᴦofᴎ her to escape her. ᴦMr. Rishton is now gone to take·his leave of shooting in the Country, with Mr. Onslow, who Breakfasted with us. This Mr. Onslow is Brother to the Captain[23] who was formerly so obliging as to disgrace my Brother!

[21] Inserted by FBA.

[22] Reading uncertain; perhaps the well-known scenic gorge on the River Avon near Bristol.

[23] Richard Onslow (1741–1817) cr. (1797), Bt.; Capt. (RN), 1762; Admiral of the Red, 1805 (D. B. Smith, *The Commissioned Sea Officers of the Royal Navy 1660–1815*, iii. 684). Onslow had been captain of the *Aquilon*, on which JB served, 1766–9, and had evidently disciplined the young sailor for some offence (see above, p. 83 n. 10). FB was to meet him at Saltram in 1789, while on a royal tour. 'He told me he had brought up a Brother of mine for the sea. I did not refresh his memory with the cruel severities he practiced in that marine Education!' (Court Journal, 26 Aug. 1789, Berg, printed *DL* iv. 323).

Friday Sept[r] [17] 6 o'Clock [a.m.]

I have h⟨urrie⟩d myself to preserve Time to ⟨write to you⟩ for the last Time from Ting Mouth.⌐

We spent yesterday between Packing & leave taking.—We only found Time to go down to the Beach, to take a last view of the sea. M[r] Rishton was in *monstrous* spirits all Day,—I am afraid he was grown somewhat tired of Ting Mouth, where he has been 6 months.

M[rs] R. & I went to sit with the Hurrels & Miss Davy, in the Evening—Lady Davy,[24] who is a great fright, in every sense of that Word, was there. They took a very affectionate leave of us. We then went to M[rs] Phips, ⌐where we met Mr. Rishton Drinking Tea—we stayed there till ⟨4⟩ o'clock—the Onslows were with them.⌐

I wish it may happen that I may ever see M[rs] Phips again—[25]

[*The Journal for 1773 resumes. The Rishtons took FB back to Queen Square, whence they departed on Saturday, 18 Sept., to pay a visit to the Westerns at Cokethorpe (MAR to FB, [19 Sept. 1773], Berg).*]

Oct[r] [16]

M[r] Garrick, to my great confusion, has again surprised the House before we were up. But really my Father keeps such late Hours at Night, that I have not resolution to rise before Eight in the morning.

My Father himself was only on the stairs—when this Early, industrious, active, charming man Came: I Dressed my self immediately, but found he was going as I entered the study— he stop'd short, & with his accustom'd drollery, exclaimed— 'Why now, why are *you* come down, now, to keep me? — — But this will never do! (looking at his Watch) upon my Word, young ladies, this will never do!—You must never marry at this rate!—to keep such Hours—no, I shall keep all the young men from you—'

He invited my Father, in Lord Shelbournes[26] Name, to go

[24] Catherine Stokes (d. 1776), daughter of John Stokes, Esq., of Ryll, Devon and Lincoln's Inn Fields; m. (1763) Sir John Davie, 7th Bt. (*GM* xxxiii (1763), 362).

[25] There is no record of their having met again.

[26] William Petty (1737–1805), 2nd E. of Shelburne; cr. (1784) M. of Lansdowne; statesman and patron of literature and the arts. His town residence was Shelburne

with him to Dine at his Lordship's, as he has a fine statue lately
come from Italy, which has a musical Instrument, & which he
wishes to shew my Father. ⌐

My Father asked him for his Box for us at night, to see the
Mask of Alfred,[27] which is revived. But he insisted upon our
going to the Front Boxes—'You shall have my Box, said he,
⌐an⌐other Time that you please—but you will *see* nothing of
the new scenes up there:—now you shall have my Box to see
me,—or the *old new* play that is coming out,[28] with all my
Heart.'

'O don't say that! cried I—don't say to see *you*—you don't
know what you promise!—'

He laughed—but I determined not to let such an offer be
made with *impunity*.

He took much notice, as usual, of Charlotte—he seems,
indeed, to love all that belong to my Father—of whom he is
really very fond—nay, as he went out, he said, with a very
comical Face, to me—'I like you!—I like you all! I like your
looks!—I like your manner!—'

⌐In the Evening, accordingly we went to Alfred—Mr. Garrick had secured us 8 places in the ⌐ Centre Box, the first 2
second Row. We took with us my sister [EBB], Miss Humphreys[29] & my Aunt Anne. It is a charming Drama to *Read*—but I
think it acts very badly.[30]

(afterwards Lansdowne) House, on the S. side of Berkeley Square. The statue
mentioned was presumably one of the ancient marbles purchased by Shelburne from
the painters and excavators Gavin Hamilton (1723–98) and Thomas Jenkins (d. 1798).
Shelburne exhibited the marbles in a special gallery in Shelburne House. See Hamilton's letters to Shelburne about these marbles, 1771–3, printed in *The Academy*, xiv
(1878), 142–3, 168–9, 192–3; also, *Catalogue of the* . . . *[Lansdowne] Marbles* . . . (1930),
p. 45.

[27] *The Masque of Alfred*, which contains the famous chorus of 'Rule Britannia', was
originally a heroic drama with musical scenes, the libretto by David Mallet and James
Thomson, the music by Dr Arne. First performed in 1740, it underwent numerous revisions and revivals (including a version of 1751 with the music mostly by CB). The
current revival opened at Drury Lane on Saturday, 9 Oct., with additional music by
Augustus Smith. William Hopkins noted that it had 'New Scenes, Machines, Decorations &c.' (MS Diary, 1769–76, cited *LS 4* iii. 1750; see also *LS 3* ii. 1161; *LS 4* ii. 922;
Highfill, s.v. Arne, Thomas; *New Grove*, s.v. Arne; Lonsdale, pp. 34–6).

[28] Garrick presumably refers to *The Alchemist* (see below, p. 313).

[29] Miss H. Humphreys or Humphries (*c.*1724–96), sister-in-law of Richard Burney
of Barborne Lodge ('Worcester Mem.', pp. 10, 43 and *passim*; below, p. 315; vol. ii).

[30] 'The piece is very dull' (Hopkins, loc. cit.). It closed on 1 Nov., after 8 performances, and was not revived again (*LS 4* iii. 1758).

My dear Rishton came from Oxfordshire last Wednesday
[13 Oct.], & stayed a Day or two in' Town. It seems Mr. Western had written a Letter of very civil Invitation for *me*, which
was left at Stapleton's Coffee House, & not received by Mr.
Rishton till he returned to Town. However I am not sorry that I
stayed away, as Mrs. R. has owned to me that she was not
remarkably comfortable.[31] It is, indeed, easier to be agreeable
out, than it is to be so *at Home*: at least so Mr. Rishton was.
They are now gone into Norfolk for 3 weeks, after which they
will return to Town."[32]

Dr. Hawkesworth Dined here the same Day [Wednesday,
13 Oct.]; his Wife & Miss Kinnaird were to have accompanied
him, but were disappointed.[33] I was *very* sorry at not seeing
Miss Kinnaird, who is a sweet Girl;—I find that she is ¦ sister to
Lord Kinnaird,[34] a young Scotch Nobleman, just come of age.

Dr. Hawkesworth looks very ill; he has had very bad Health
lately. Indeed I believe that the abuse so illiberally cast on him,
since he obtained 6.000 pounds for writing the Voyages Round
the World, has really affected his Health, by preying upon his
mind. It is a terrible alternative, that an Author must either
starve, & be esteemed, or be vilified, & get money.[35]

Seeing in the Papers on Thursday [14 Oct.] Abel Drugger
by Mr Garrick[36]—I prevailed with my dear Father to Write

---

[31] The Rishtons were guests of the Westerns at Cokethorpe from 21 Sept. to about
10 Oct. MAR wrote to FB from there, 2 Oct. (Berg): 'I don't think M^r W[estern] near so
agreable in his own house as he was at Tingmouth—is continually saying sharp dis-
agreable things to his Wife—& is angry with her for indulging ye Child [their daughter
Elizabeth (Bessy) Western] . . . there is a want of hospitality in M^r W[estern] in several
things—he lets the fires go out as if by Chance—but they are never lighted again—My
fingers are now benumbd with Cold . . . There is a meanness likewise in their Table . . .
This house is a good one and a park very well laid out but their [*sic*] is an Air of Melan-
cholly reigns thro' the Whole that I should be sorry to be immurd in it with such a help
mate as Mr Western.'

[32] They intended to go to Lynn by way of Enfield, and visit, among others, Mrs John
Towers Allen (ibid.).

[33] Mrs Hawkesworth and Miss Kinnaird had hoped to come to town to dine with
Miss Kinnaird's uncle, Col. Johnstone (Hawkesworth to CB 8 Oct. 1773, National
Library of Australia, Canberra).

[34] George Kinnaird (*c*.1752–1805), 7th B. Kinnaird of Inchture.

[35] A month later Hawkesworth was dead. FB recounts this last dinner party in more
detail in a letter to SC, below, pp. 325–7.

[36] e.g., *The Morning Chronicle*, 14 Oct.: 'Drury-Lane, by His Majesty's Company . . .
This Day will be presented *The Alchymist* [by Ben Jonson]. Abel Drugger, Mr. Garrick
. . .'. Garrick played the role a total of 80 times in his career (Stone, pp. 277, 487).

him a Note,[37] which he did very drolly, claiming his promise, but begging for only *two* places: he sent immediately this answer—

My dear D^r

I had rather have your Family in ⌜the Front⌝ Box, than all the Lords and Commons — — yours ever　　　　　　　D.G. ⌐

⌜& enclosed was—

Admit [xxxxx *1 word*] to the front BOX [xxxxx *1 line*]　D.G.

He is really too good—it is *so* difficult to get places when he acts, that I am almost ashamed of his good nature. We found that he had secured us the same places as at Alfred.⌝

Never could I have imagined such a metamorphose as I saw! the extreme meanness—the vulgarity—the low wit—the vacancy of Countenance—the appearance of *unlicked Nature* in all his motions.—

In short, never was Character so well entered into, yet so opposite to his own.[38]

We have had a Visit from Miss Ford, & her Companion Miss Mills.[39]—She lent us her Box yesterday [15 Oct.] to see Miss Barsanti in the part of Charlotte Rusport in the West Indian.[40] She did it with great ease, sprightliness & propriety, ⌜was extremely elegantly Dressed,⌝ ⌐ & looked exceeding well. I am very glad that she has succeeded in so genteel a part.

⌜She called here this morning [16 Oct.], & sat with me two Hours. I am quite happy to find her as good & worthy, as well

[37] Both CB's note and the original MS of Garrick's answer are missing.

[38] The moment Garrick came upon the stage 'he discovered such awkward simplicity, and his looks so happily bespoke the ignorant, selfish, and absurd merchant, that it was a contest not easily to be decided, whether the burst of laughter or applause were loudest' (Thomas Davies, *Memoirs of . . . Garrick*, ed. S. Jones (1808), i. 61, cited Stone, p. 487; see also other contemporary appreciations quoted ibid., pp. 485–90).

[39] Theodosia Mills (*fl.* 1748–?94), actress. She was probably the Miss Mills who appeared at the James Street Theatre on 31 Oct. 1748 as Lucy in *The London Merchant*. She was a close friend of the Colmans, Miss Ford's parents, and at some point became George Colman's mistress. This probably occurred after the death of Mrs Colman (in 1771) and may account for her leaving the stage permanently after the 1770–1 season. She is named in Colman's will, dated 30 Apr. 1789 and proved 8 Dec. 1794; Colman left her £20. See Highfill; R. B. Peake, *Memoirs of the Colman Family . . .* (1841), i. 107; Garrick, *Letters*, iii. 1053.

[40] By Cumberland. This was Barsanti's 1st time in that role and the play's 1st performance at Covent Garden (*LS 4* iii. 1752).

as agreeable and entertaining a Girl as ever. I would it was in my power to keep a constant & steady intimacy with her. I find she has received two very provoking & insolent offers, to both of which she has given answers that are spirited & praiseworthy. I grieve at the probability there is of these dreadful propositions being frequently made to her. But she is a good Girl, & I hope will always retain the sentiments which have hitherto guided her Conduct. She is [again][41] in favour with Mr Colman, & gains Ground at the Theatre [Covent Garden]. I will see as much as I can of her. I am really happy to be able to continue my good^ ⌐ |

[*a leaf or leaves cut away*]

[?My grandmother Burney][42] ⌐finds Miss Humphries of in-finite comfort to her. We have some hope of seeing my Cousin Anne[43] in Town soon.

Our way of life is prodigiously altered—our Family is now very large[44] [xxxxx *2 lines*]^⌐

[Nov^r][45] 9th
3 in the morn^g

My poor mother is extremely ill, of a Bilious Fever—this is the third Night that I have sit up with her—but I hope to Heaven that she is now in a way to recover.

She has been most exceeding kind to us ⌐ever^ since her return to Town—which makes me the more sensibly feel her illness. [xxxxx *2 lines*] She is now sleeping—so is her Nurse—& *I* write to avoid the Contagion—⌐Mrs Allen had insisted on our having an hired Nurse, but Mama has an | absolute aversion to her, & is kind enough to accept of my services with pleasure and preference. I have not quitted her since her illness (except

[41] Inserted by FBA. This suggests a temporary breach with her manager. Colman may have been the source of one of the 'provoking & insolent offers'.

[42] Conjecturally supplied. Miss Humphreys may have been helping to nurse the old lady through an illness. 'Worcester Mem.', p. 43, notes that the early part of Miss Humphrey's life 'consisted in active services'; in 1778 she came to town from Worcester to nurse Richard Gustavus Burney (*ED* i. 214).

[43] FB's 'amiable' Worcester cousin Ann ('Nancy') Burney (1749–1819), who m. (1781) the Revd John Hawkins (d. 1804), of Nash Court, Kent. See below, p. 319; vol. ii.

[44] Not counting the absent JB, and CB Jr. (in the Charterhouse), there were currently 8 in the Burney household, including the infant Sarah Harriet.

[45] Corrected by FBA from 'Oct^r'.

when I have slept) till this morning, when I was obliged to go in search of lodging for Mr. & Mrs. Rishton, who have sent me that Commission, being wholly ignorant of my situation. My dear Susy would very fain take my place, but I dread her Health so much, that I will not suffer her.ᵀ

Dr. Fothergal,⁴⁶ the celebrated Quaker, is Mama's physician. I doubt not his being a man of great skill,—but his manners are stiff, set, & unpleasant: his Conversation consists of sentences, spoken with the utmost solemnity, conciseness & importance. He is an upright, stern, formal looking Old man. He Enters the Room & makes his Address, with his Hat always on, & lest that mark of his sect should pass unnoticed, the Hat which he Wears is ofᴵ the most enormous size I ever beheld.

Nevertheless, this old prig sometim⟨es⟩ affects something bordering upon gallantry—The first Time he came, after he had been with Mʳˢ Allen to the Bed side, & spoken to Mama—& then wrote her prescription;—he stalked up to me, & endeavouring to arrange his rigid Features to something which resembled a smile, 'And what, cried he, must we do for this young lady's Cough?' Then he insisted on feeling my pulse, & with a kind of dry pleasantry, said—'Well—we will wait till to-morrow:—we won't lose any blood to-night!'

| 11 | Queen Square, 13 November [1773] |

To Stephen Allen

ALS (Houghton), 13 November 1773
Double sheet 4to, 4 pp. *pmk* 15 NO red wax seal
Addressed: Stephen Allen Esqʳ, | Lynn Regis, | Norfolk
Annotated (in an unknown hand): Frances Burney | (Dtʳ of Charles Burney Dʳ of Music, FRS.) | the ingenious Author of | Evelina | & | Cecilia | Keeper of the Robes to the Queen
FB's cool formality in this letter reflects her continuing disapproval of her reckless stepbrother, who had eloped with Susanna Sharpin the previous

---

⁴⁶ John Fothergill (1712–80), MD (Edinburgh), 1736; FRS, 1763; botanist, philanthropist, friend of Benjamin Franklin.

year. Her relationship with Stephen and his wife was to remain always distant.

Queen's Square
Novr 13th

Dear Sir,

It makes me extremely happy to find it in my power, at the same Time that I thank you for your Letter,[47] to acquaint you of Mama's amendment. It is not for a *few Days* to secure her recovery—but we have Dr. Fothergal's Word that she goes on in the *right way*, though Time, as well as care will be requisite to restore her entirely to Health. She desires her blessing & love to you, & rejoices to hear you are better; she particularly hopes that you continue to use Daily Exercise on Horse-back.

M^r & Mrs Rishton came to Town this Evening—your sister had the shock of finding Mama ill, without having any preparation, as I had not, for this last Week, known where to direct to her. I thank Heaven that they did not come some Days sooner, when my mother was so much worse, that the shock would have been still greater. We have been a good deal disappointed to Night in not seeing Miss [Dorothy] Young, which Mama had flattered herself she should have done.

Mrs Allen begs her love to you, & that you will be so kind as to acquaint Mr Allen[48] with the good News of my mother's being, (we hope) much better.

I beg to be remembered to Mrs Allen,[49] & that you will believe me ever

Your Affectionate humble ser^t
Frances Burney.

[*The Journal for 1773 resumes.*]

Novr 24th
2 in the morn^g

Though it is now a Fortnight since I wrote last, I take up my pen exactly in the same situation, & with the same view,[50] as

---

[47] Missing. [48] EAB's brother Maxey Allen of Lynn.

[49] Susanna Sharpin (1755–1816), daughter of Edward Sharpin (*c.*1712–82), physician, of East Dereham, Norfolk; m. (28 Oct. 1772, at Gretna Green) Stephen Allen. Despite the inauspicious start of their marriage, she settled down to a life of eminent respectability with her husband, giving him 12 children.

[*See p. 318 for n. 50*]

I then did,—save that Mama is exceedingly recovered, & thank God, nearly well.

Since I wrote last, I have myself been ill with a sore Throat, which I believe was the effect of overrating my strength. Dr. Fothergill has been my very good friend, & that whether I would or not; he immediately perceived when I was taken ill, &, after seeing Mama, said to me 'I am afraid Thee art not well thyself?' On Examining my Throat, he advised me to be very careful for that it was Catching, the sort which I had, which was the putrid, though in a slight degree.[51] He told me what to take, &c, & was most exceeding Attentive to me the whole Time & really, for him, has been amazingly civil & polite to me. But yesterday, after complaining of his fatigue & great business, he turned suddenly to me, & taking my Hand, cried 'My dear, never marry a Physician! if he has but little to do, he may be distressed; if he has much—it is a very uncomfortable life for his Companion.'[52]

He came here several Times before he saw my Father, who, when at Home, is always shut up in his study; but one Evening, when Mama was very ill, being anxious to hear the Doctor's opinion, he came up stairs. He addressed himself, like a man of the World, to the Doctor,—who rose, & with great solemnity said 'I suppose it is Dr. Burney that I see?' My Father Bowed, & said he was happy in being known to him—'I never, answered he, had the satisfaction of seeing Dr. Burney before!' 'No, Sir, said my Father, I have always been so unfortunate as to be out when you have been here.' '*Most commonly,*' answered the old Quaker, with a dryness that seemed not to give implicit faith to the assertion. But since this, they have had many Conversations, & are very good friends. And really, with all his stiffness & solemnity, he appears to be as humane as he is skillful.[53]

Mama has so good a Night, that I fancy this will be the last of

[50] i.e., to stay awake.

[51] Fothergill's most important writing was the *Account of the Sore Throat attended with Ulcers* (1748; 6th edn., 1777), which was trans. into several European languages and which *DNB* calls 'a model of clinical description'.

[52] Fothergill did not marry.

[53] Benjamin Franklin said of Dr Fothergill, 'I can hardly conceive that a better man has ever existed' (letter of 1782, cited in R. H. Fox, *Dr. John Fothergill and His Friends* (1919), p. 362).

my Nocturnal communications. While she was ill, she desired me to Write for Miss Young, who is now here. I had not seen her some years.[54] She is exactly the same she was—sensible, intelligent, bashful, shy, aukward, affectionate, feeling & truly worthy. I love her much.—& hope we shall keep her some Time.

⌐I have been obliged to Enter into Correspondence with Mr. Stephen Allen, upon Mama's illness. He writes me very civil letters,—but rather different to former ones—[xxxxx *5 lines*]⌐[55]

[*The tops and bottoms of the next 2 pages have been cut away.*]

⌐Mama is perfectly recovered. She has been twice to Bradmore (Mr. Young's) & is now as well as ever I knew her.

We have had a month's Visit from our Cousin Anne Burney of Worcester, whose very amiable qualities have engaged the friendship & esteem of us all, in the highest degree. Her visit was but uncomfortable, as Mama's Illness, my sister's Confinement[56] & [xxxxx *3 lines*]⌐

I have, ⌐also⌐, entered into a very particular Correspondence with M⌐ Crisp: I write really ⌐a⌐ Journal to him. & in answer, he sends me most delightful long, ⌐& incomparably clever⌐ Letters: Animadverting upon all the facts, &c which I acquaint him with, & dealing with the utmost sincerity in stating his opinion, & giving his Advice. I am infinitely charmed with this Correspondance—*ant* I mean—which is not more agreeable, than it may prove instructive.

[*At this point FBA has inserted the original fragmentary MS, double sheet 4to, 4 pp., of the following AL from SC, probably written in early Dec. 1773. The letter is paginated continuously with the rest of the Journal for 1773, from 399 to 402.*]

[54] Their last recorded meeting was in 1768, but FB probably saw Dorothy Young again at Lynn the summers of 1769 and 1770. Her letter is missing.

[55] For this obliterated passage FBA has substituted: 'Mama is almost recovered. Dr. Fothergill makes his visits very seldom. He says he always knows when his Patients are really recovering by these signs: if men, he finds their Beds covered with News Papers: if Women, he sees them with new Top Knots, or hears them exclaim "Dear me! what a figure I am!"'

[56] On 22 Oct. EBB had given birth to her eldest son, Richard Allen Burney (see vol. ii), who was christened in St Paul's, Covent Garden, on 22 Nov. (*Registers of St. Paul's Church, Covent Garden* (1906–9), ii. 70; 'Worcester Mem.', p. 14).

My Dear Fanny

In consequence of our Agreement, I shall now begin with an instance of the most pure & genuine sincerity, when I declare to You that I was delighted with your letter[57] throughout—a proof of which (that perhaps, You would have excus'd) is this immediate answer, with a demand for *more*—the horse-leech hath two Daughters (saith the Wise man) saying *give, give* ![58]—I find myself nearly related to them on this Occasion—I profess there is not a single word or expression, or thought in your whole letter, that I do not relish—not that in our Correspondence, I shall set up for a Critic, or schoolmaster, or Observer of Composition—⌐Damn it⌐ all! — — I hate ⌐it⌐ if once You set about framing ⟨s⟩tudied letters, that are to be correct, nicely grammatical & run in smooth Periods, I shall mind them as no others than newspapers of intelligence; I make this preface because You have needlessly enjoin'd me to deal sincerely, & to tell You of your faults; & so let this *declaration serve* once for all, that there is no fault in an Epistolary Correspondence, like stiffness, & study—Dash away, whatever comes uppermost—the sudden sallies of imagination, clap'd down on paper, just as they arise, are worth Folios, & have all the warmth & merit of that sort of Nonsense, that is Eloqu[ent] in Love—never think of being correct, when You write to me—so I conclude this Topic, & proceed to be sorry & glad, that Y⟨ou⟩ | & your Mammy have been ill, & are better—Y^r Dr Fothergill I am well acquainted with by Character, & pronounce You a very able Portrait Painter; I find he has taken to You, & I observe we old Fellows are inclinable to be very fond of You—You'll say, what care I for old Fellows?—give me a young One!—well, we don't hinder You of young Ones; & we judge more coolly & disinterestedly than they do; so, dont turn up your Nose even at our Approbation—Now Fan, I do by no means allow of your reconsideration, & revocation of your Tingmouth Journal; on the contrary,—I demand it, & claim your promise, & confirm my own; Viz. to return it safe, to Charley Burneys, well & carefully seald up, & the contents lodg'd in my own snowy Bosom—your Pleas, frivolous ones they are; I reject them

---

[57] Missing.
[58] Cf. Proverbs 30: 15.

all[59]—ꝏsend the book by the Express Post addressed for me at Mr. ⟨Pevey's⟩[60] shoemaker at Epsom—ꝏ as to that Rogue your Father, if I did not know him to be incorrigible, I should say something of that regular Course of Irregularity he persists in— 2, 3, 4, 5 o'Clock in the morning—sup at 12!—is it impossible for him to get the better of his Constitution?—has he forgot the Condition he was in, the Winter after his first return to England?[61] Perhaps he is like a season'd old Drinker, whose inside is so lin'd with a Coat of Tartar, that his Brandy only goes in ꝏat one End, & out at the other,ꝏ like a Worm in a still, without affecting the Vessel it passes thro'—certain it is, that he Uses his thin Carcass most abominably, & if it takes it at his [hands,] it is the most passive, submissive slave ˡ [of a carcass in] Europe—I am greatly pleas'd with the growing reputation of his Tours; of which I never had the least doubt; & no less so, with those marks of Favor & Esteem from the Great & the Eminent; & only wish him to make that *worldly* Use of them, which he ought; in which particulars he has hitherto been so deficient—& desire you would transmit to him the enclos'd quotation, which I have lately read in a letter from his Friend Petrarch to Mainard Accurse.[62]

Now if Petrarch (for whom all the Princes & geniuses of Europe were contending for 50 years together) could find out this severe & mortifying Truth; surely 'tis a lesson to all future Candidates for Fame & Favor, to make that *Bienveillance*,

[59] FB overcame her diffidence and sent the Teignmouth Journal to SC. He still had it in Dec. 1774, when FB wrote to reclaim it (see vol. ii).

[60] Not further identified.

[61] CB returned from his Italian tour in Dec. 1770, exhausted and in poor health. Nevertheless, he worked strenuously on his journal of the tour until it was sent to the press, after which he collapsed and was confined to bed for several weeks (see above, p. 198 n. 39).

[62] See above, p. 265. Mainardo Accursio (d. 1349) of Florence was one of Petrarch's earliest friends. The enclosed quotation, which is missing, may have been the following, in the *Rerum familiarum*, Book VIII, Letter 4 ('an exhortation for moderate goals, and for not deferring plans for a better life'): 'Nor is it now indeed a matter of superiors whose kindness may be considerable but whose presence can hardly be counted upon, for there stands in the way of mutual intimacy a disparity of fortune and that poison of friendship, pride, which prompts such superiors to be fearful of demeaning themselves, and to expect to be worshipped rather than loved' (Francesco Petrarca, *Rerum familiarum libri* I–VIII, trans. A. S. Bernardo (Albany, 1975), pp. 396, 401, 406; see also E. H. Wilkins, *Life of Petrarch* (Chicago, 1961), p. 84). SC presumably sent the original Latin quotation or his own trans. of it; there was not yet an English edn. of the familiar letters.

(which at bottom is all self, & Vanity) turn to some account, & make Hay while the sun shines— ⌐

[*bottom of page cut away*]

I am quite comforted to hear he is so full [of business, which][63] if it does not improve & increase, 'tis his own fault—on my blessing I charge him, not for any consideration, to neglect *that*; which at last, & at the long run, will prove his surest, firmest, best, perhaps his *only* Friend—mark that—while he preserves that, it will prove his best security for holding fast other friends—I cannot too much inculcate, beat, drive, hammer, this saving Doctrine into him; which makes me dwell so long on this•Article. [xxxxx *6 lines*] ⌐

[*The bottom of the page is cut away and the remainder of SC's letter missing. The quarrel between CB and Garrick, mentioned next, seems to have been over CB's nephew Charles Rousseau Burney and was not finally made up until early 1775. See vol. ii.*]

⌐[?Mr. Garrick,] indeed, by no means acted as he ought. Yet it is ever a subject of grief to me when there is any Coldness raised between old friends but, with all my partiality for Mr. Garrick, I cannot help ⟨noti⟩cing, that he has by no means the Virtue of *Steadiness* in his attachment, &, indeed, is almost perpetually giving offence to some of his friends.[64] Dr. Johnson told my Father, that he attributes almost all the ill errors of Mr. Garrick's Life, to the [xxxxx *1 word*] *fire* & hastiness of his Temper, which is continually misleading him.[65]

However,⌐ I am glad that my Father has recovered an old friend, with whom he had a Breach: he is at length, entirely & most cordially reconciled to Mr Greville, who has been here 2 or 3 Times, in his old way, without fuss or Ceremony.[66]

[63] The MS is torn here; reading supplied by Mrs Ellis (*The Early Diary of Frances Burney 1768–1778* (1889 [1890]), i. 260).

[64] Oliver Goldsmith alludes to this aspect of Garrick's personality in his mock epitaph in *Retaliation* (1774): 'He cast off his friends, as a huntsman his pack; / For he knew when he pleased he could whistle them back . . .' (cited in Highfill).

[65] Garrick's temper was no doubt tried by his constant dealings with egocentric actors and authors, and in later years especially it was aggravated by overwork and ill health.

[66] Before this reconciliation took place, Greville seems to have renewed his demand for the £300 he had paid to release CB from his indenture in 1748 (see above, p. 262). CB, writing to SC, 21 Jan. 1774 (Berg), recalls a letter he had received from Greville several months earlier threatening a lawsuit in Westminster Hall over the matter. CB

┌My Father's subscription fills apace. It is to be kept open till the first Vol. is published.⁶⁷ ┘

The charming Barsanti — — for she is a most truly charming Girl, spent a whole Day with Susy & me, while the family were at Bradmore. She rises in my esteem by the continuance of her good Conduct—but Mᵣ Crisp sometimes terrifies me, as he asserts that, sooner or later, she *must* fall.—but I hope *he Can* be mistaken. He is very fond of her, notwithstanding he passes so cruel a doom. I answered that her intentions are All good, & I flatter myself with the hope of seeing her pass through life an Exception to the *infallibility* of our Prophet, whose wisdom & judgement nevertheless give me fears whether I will or not.┐⁶⁸

I have had, lately, a very long, & very strange Conversation with Mᵣ Young: we happened to be alone in the parlour—&, either from confidence in my prudence, ┌ or from an entire, & unaccountable carelessness of consequences, he told me 'that

had sent Greville's letter to SC, asking his advice about what to do; SC, writing back, counselled him to ignore the threat and give Greville time to return to his senses. But even before CB received SC's counsel, Greville 'was in Town & we had an Interview together 1ˢᵗ at his House in Brook street & 2 Nights after he supped wᵗʰ me & family in Queen Square!!!' CB then mentions to SC a series of letters between himself and Greville in which Greville proffers his friendship again, and CB makes clear his unequivocal stand against paying back the £300. 'We met after this at his Lodgings & at the opera, & all smooth and well . . . in abᵗ 10 Days he went out of Town; but before his Departure he came to my House with a large Bundle of Papers . . . The Contents I must not tell . . . it was a strong Mark of his Confidence . . .' Greville, the man of leisure, was now prepared once more to make large demands on CB's time, as he had in the old days, when his patron. CB, however, extremely busy with his teaching and musical researches and by this time thoroughly tired of Greville and his 'constitutional inconstancy' (SC's phrase) refused to permit this return to the old status quo, and henceforth he avoided Greville as much as possible (see *Mem*. iii. 134–6). All the correspondence mentioned by CB in his letter to SC is missing; in 1812 he and FBA destroyed all but a few of Greville's letters to him, 'all of which were clever, but many disputative, quarrelsome, & highly disagreeable' (FBA to EBB, [25–]8 Nov. 1820, *JL* xi. 186).

⁶⁷ See above, p. 252 and n. 80. CB inserted the following advertisement in the *Public Advertiser*, 6 Jan. 1774 (cited Lonsdale, p. 141):

The time being now elapsed when Dr. Burney promised either to send his History of Music to the Press, or return the Subscription Money that had been deposited, finding that he has ascertained nearly the stipulated Number of Subscribers, he has the Honour to acquaint those who have favoured him with their Names, and those who may be inclined to encourage the Work in Future, that he has determined to print it with all possible Expedition, and to keep the Subscription open till the First Volume is published, which the Author still hopes will be in the Course of the ensuing Year, 1774.

⁶⁸ Barsanti kept her virtue, and in 1777 married the young Irish aristocrat John Richard Kirwan Lyster (d. 1779).

he was the most miserable fellow breathing, & almost *directly* said that his *Connections* made him so,—& most vehemently added, that if he was to begin the World again, no Earthly thing should ever prevail with him to marry! That now, he was never easy, but when he was litterally in a plow Cart,—but that *happy* he never could be!

[I a]m sorry for him—but cannot wonder

[*middle of page cut away*]

I am truly concerned, as we all are, at the untimely Death of Dr. Hawkesworth,[69]—he had not strength to support the abuse he has most unjustly been loaded with—I cannot help attributing his Death to the uneasiness of his mind,—which brought on a slow Fever, that proved mortal.

When he was last here, he told us his plan of Defence, which he was then preparing for the press, as soon as a Law suit then depending, was decided. I am doubly sorry that he left this plan unaccomplished, & his fame & reputation at the mercy of his Enemies: who have, however, been wholly silent since his Death. The World has lost one of its best ornaments,—a man of Letters, who was Worthy & honest. Poor Mrs Hawkesworth is in great affliction;

[*The middle of the page has been cut away. The remainder of it seems to be about the Hawkesworths' friend Miss Kinnaird. After Hawkesworth's death Miss Kinnaird visited 'her Sister. . . . somewhere N. Westward about 140 miles from London', after which she went to her grandmother in Edinburgh (James Hutton to FB 16 May 1774, Berg; vol. ii). The sister was Helen née Kinnaird (d. 1795), wife of the Revd Edmund Dana (c.1737–1823), Vicar of Wroxeter in Shropshire.*]

⌐[?Miss Kinnaird, who with her compassion]ate Heart must have suffered very much, is gone to Shropshire, to some friends. I never expect to have the pleasure of seeing her again, which gives me a good deal of Concern. [xxxxx *2 lines*]¬

---

[69] 17 Nov. See FB's fuller account in her letter to SC, following.

[Queen Square, ?December 1773]

To Samuel Crisp

AL (Berg), *n.d.*
Single sheet 4to, 2 pp.
Docketed and annotated (by FBA): remnant of an old Letter to Mr. Crisp ✷
FBA has placed this fragment at the end of the Journal for 1773.

The Death of poor Dr. Hawkesworth is mos[t] sincerely
lamented by us all. the more so, as we do really attribute it to
the Abuse he has of late met with from the news papers: his
6000 l. was dearly purchased, at the price of his Character &
peace—& those envious & malignant Witlings who persecuted
him, from his gaining money, are now satisfied & silent.[70] You
may perhaps doubt of this—but indeed if you had known him
more, you would not. He Dined with us about a month before
he died[71]—& we all agreed that we never saw a man more
Altered—thin, livid—harrassed! He conversed very freely upon
the affair of his Book & abuse: my Father told him that there
was hardly a man in the kingdom who had ever had a Pen in
his Hand, who did not think that he could have done it with
more propriety—& that his Enemies were all occasioned by his

[70] See above, p. 173 and n. 88. Dr Hawkesworth died on 17 Nov., 'of a slow fever', at
the house of his friend Dr William Grant in Lime St. (*GM* xliii (1773), 582; Abbott,
p. 190). According to Edmond Malone, he was 'supposed to have put an end to his life
by intentionally taking an immoderate dose of opium', a rumour which gained wide
currency afterwards; Professor Abbott, however, considers a suicide unlikely (Sir James
Prior, *Life of Edmond Malone* (1860), p. 441; Abbott, pp. 187–8).
  Hawkesworth had published, on 9 June, *An Account of the Voyages Undertaken . . . by
Commodore Byron, Captain Wallis, Captain Carteret, and Captain Cook . . . Drawn up from the
Journals which were kept by the several Commanders, and from the Papers of Joseph Banks, Esq.*,
3 vols. 4to (*Public Advertiser*). Even before its publication Hawkesworth was attacked (by
'Candour', in the *Morning Chronicle*, 15 May 1773) for the 'extortionate' sum of £6,000
paid him for the copyright by William Strahan and Thomas Cadell (cited Abbott,
p. 160). After the work's appearance he was savaged in the newspapers, particularly in
letters signed 'A Christian' (in the *Public Advertiser*, 14 June–28 Aug.) for his 'impious'
refusal to attribute to divine providence the various escapes from danger he had
recorded (see *Account*, i, pp. xix–xxi). He was also attacked for factual and textual exag-
gerations and inaccuracies; Capt. Cook and Capt. Carteret themselves later complained about his free literary reworking of their journals. Lastly, the frank passages
describing the sexual habits of the South Sea islanders offended the moral delicacy of
many. See Abbott, pp. 137–86 *passim*.
[71] See above, p. 313.

success, for that if he had failed, every one would have said
'Poor man! 'tis an ingenious, well written Book—he deserved
more encouragement.' Dr. Hawkesworth said that he had not
yet made any answer to the torrent poured upon him—except
to Dalrymple,[72] who had attacked him by Name—he added
that he was extremely sorry when any of his friends had vindi-
cated him in print[73]—for that a Law suit | was then depending
upon Parkinson's[74] publicatio[n,] & that he would take no
methods of influencing justice, but as soon as it was decided, he
should publish at once a full & general answer to the invidious,
calumniating & most unjust aspersions which had been so
cruelly & wantonly cast on him.—He has not lived to accomplish his Plan!—he told my Father, that he had earned every
thing he possessed by dint of labour & industry, except the last
6.000 l.—that he had had no Education or advantage but what
he had given himself: but that he had preserved an unblem-
ished Character & reputat[ion] till his last year.—since when, I
believe, he has had reason to detest the Fortune which only

[72] Alexander Dalrymple (1737–1808), hydrographer to the Admiralty. He published
*A Letter from Mr. Dalrymple to Dr. Hawkesworth, Occasioned by Some Groundless and Illiberal
Imputations in his Account of the Late Voyages to the South*; the 35-page pamphlet is dated
22 June 1773. Hawkesworth replied in a preface to the 2nd edn. of his work. See H. T.
Fry, 'Alexander Dalrymple and Captain Cook: The Creative Interplay of Two
Careers', in *Captain James Cook and His Times*, ed. R. Fisher and H. Johnston (1979),
pp. 50–1 and nn. 36, 37; Abbott, pp. 157–8.

[73] These 'friends' have not been identified. Hawkesworth was defended by corre-
spondents to the *Public Advertiser* signing themselves 'J.H.', 'L.O.', and 'Atticus alter'
(ibid., pp. 162–3).

[74] Sydney Parkinson (?1745–71), draughtsman. Parkinson was natural-history
draughtsman to Joseph Banks on Cook's first voyage to the South Seas. Before reaching
England again he died of fever and dysentery. In a suit filed in Chancery on 26 Jan.
1773, Hawkesworth claimed that Joseph Banks had purchased all the papers and notes
of Sydney from his brother and executor Stanfield Parkinson. Stanfield had then
borrowed the papers from Banks, allegedly just to scan them, but had surreptitiously
made copies and was preparing them for publication. The Court granted Hawkesworth an injunction against this publication, but after hearing Stanfield's answer
(5 May) ordered, on 12 May, that the injunction be 'dissolv[e]d ... unless the
pl[ain]t[iff] ... shew unto this Court good Cause to the contrary' (Court of Chancery,
Entry Books of Decrees and Orders, 1544–1875, PRO. C33/439, fo. 256). Hawkesworth
filed a rejoinder on 10 June, and on 14 June Stanfield was ordered by the Court to pro-
duce witnesses in support of his case. With the suit still pending, he went ahead with
the publication, and his brother's papers appeared in July as *A Journal of a Voyage to the
South Seas, in his Majesty's Ship, the Endeavour: Faithfully transcribed from the Papers of the
late Sydney Parkinson, Draughtsman to Joseph Banks, Esq.*, 4to, 212 pp. Hawkesworth's
death, of course, terminated the suit. See *Chain of Friendship: Selected Letters of Dr. John
Fothergill*, ed. B. C. Corner and C. C. Booth (Cambridge, Mass., 1971), p. 458 n. 4;
Abbott, pp. 149–50, 160, 222–3 n. 25.

preceded detraction & defamation. He Died of a lingering Fever—which had begun to prey upon him when we last saw him. My Father read to him a good deal of his History,[75] with which he appeared much pleased, & only objected to *one* word all the way. He candidly declared it was all new to him—& that though he had never studdied or cared for music, he found it easy to understand, & very entertaining. He expressed much curiosity about the remainder; & made my Father explain his Designs & intentions. |

[75] 'Dr. Burney read to him the dissertation,—then but roughly sketched,—on the Music of the Ancients, by which the History opens' (*Mem.* i. 277).

APPENDIX 1

FANNY BURNEY'S FIRST POEM

THIS is FB's earliest known writing. It is on the recto and verso of a ragged 12mo leaf in the Berg Collection, Accession Number 208271B. At the top of the recto is *FBA's note*: composed & Written as now remaining on this vile paper at Eleven Years of age.

Line divisions and indentations have been mostly normalized. Words inserted above lines have been brought down into the lines. The final version of the poem is given, with first thoughts in half brackets.

> Content! thou real, only Bliss,
>   Best reviver of the soul
> Greatest cordial of Distress
>   Ever surest to Console:
> Oh thou, who to the Heart oppress'd with grie[f]
> With resignation sweetly give relief.
> Oh thou, who drivest away despair
>   Who can the Wretches anguish heal
> Make misery misfortune bear
>   Lig[h]ten what th'unhappy feel:
> Content alone does happiness bestow
> Content! our sole felicity ⌜only happiness⌝ below
> It is not the unmeaning Noise
>   of sable pomp, or empty spor[t]
> Nor yet is it the flatt'ring Joy[s]
>   The glitt'ring folly of a Court
> 'Tis not in these alone
>   Content we find
> Content! the balmy soother
>   of the mind.
> Ah! what are riches? what is power
>   And what is Grandeur's boast ⌜gain⌝
> Employers of the misspent hour
>   When Ev'ry Moments lost ⌜folly⌝
> These homage bring—for blessing[s] sure not meant
> For Ah, does servile Homage give
>   Content?

APPENDIX 2

FANNY BURNEY'S VERSES TO MARIA ALLEN

FB may have composed these verses about the time of MA's jilt by Martin Rishton (see above, p. 142). They are reproduced here from the original on two leaves, 8vo and 4to, BL Add. MSS Egerton 3696, fos. 79–80.

Female Caution.
Addressed to Miss Allen.

Ah why in faithless man repose
The peace & safety of your mind?
   Why should ye seek a World of Woes,
To Prudence and to Wisdom blind?

Few of mankind confess your worth,
Fewer reward it with their own:
   To Doubt and Terror Love gives birth;
To Fear and Anguish makes ye known.

The roseate Cheeks, the sparkling Eyes
Which bright in liquid lustre swim,
   Love views but as his destin'd prize
Those Cheeks to fade, those Eyes to dim.

Your minds, ingenuous, open, just,
To Love, to Tenderness inclin'd,
   Unguarded, the Deceivers Trust,
Nor, till too late, the error find.

While They, inur'd to specious art
Seek but their vanity to feed;
   Complete the conquest of the Heart
Then leave that wretched heart to bleed.

In vain the Inconstant are accus'd;
In vain the Injur'd may upbraid,
   Mourn their credulity abus'd,
Their sensibility betray'd!

The lovely Harriet, gay and fair,
Possest the happiest power to please;
   Her sparkling Eye, her smile, her air,
All sportive, spoke a mind at ease:

   Till false Alcanor saw the maid,
And aim'd the conquest of her heart:
   With fatal excellence he play'd
A vile, insinuating part. [|]

   Adieu to Freedom, & to Ease!
The breast that Love admits they leave:
   The wayward swain's attentions cease;
'Tis His to rove—'tis Her's to grieve.

   O, Wiser, learn to guard the heart,
Nor let it's softness be its bane!
   Teach it to act a nobler part;
What Love shall lose, let Friendship gain.

   Hail, Friendship, hail! To Thee my soul
Shall undivided homage own;
   No Time thy influence shall controll;
And Love and I—shall ne'er be known

APPENDIX 3

MARIA ALLEN'S FIRST LETTER
TO FANNY BURNEY

THIS is MA's earliest surviving letter to FB, on two leaves 4to, in the Berg Collection. It is *dated* 1768 *by FBA and addressed* To | Miss Fanny Burney

FBA later described her stepsister's letters as 'flighty, ridiculous, uncommon, lively, comical, entertaining, frank, and undisguised' (*ED* i. 106). All these qualities are present in this first specimen, besides a penchant for the slightly indecent, a trait MA shared with her mother, EAB. The letter is also interesting for its references to FB's 'delicasy of constitution' and to her girlish attempts at the 'sublime' style in her (missing) letters to MA.

The letter is reproduced literally with MA's characteristic misspellings and oddities of punctuation. The lack of punctuation here is soon succeeded by a heavy use of dashes; these stylistic quirks reflect MA's impulsive nature and contribute to the 'flighty' and impetuous quality of the letters.

Come Fan Psa'w your a good Girl and Ill write to you first Thats what I will. & I'll say all my clever things to you Miss— and Hetty shant hear One Aa—ah Well I do Love you dearly for Loving me well Enough to write to me: but I always said Fanny was a *very fine Girl indeed* and she has proved it I really Pity your distress but think the stile you purpose figuring in is *great* I have no doubt of your Letters being so Much above our Comprehension that we shall adore you for A Divinity for you know *People* always have a much greater opinion of a thing they dont understand that [*sic*] what is as plain and as simple as the nose in their faces. Now hettys Letters and your Papas Lord why they are common Entertaining Lively witty | Letters such as d[r] Swift might write or People who prefer the beautiful to the sublime. but *you now*! Why I dare say will talk of *Corporeal* Machines. *Negation fluid*, *Matter* and *Motion* and all those pretty things Well Well fannys Letters for my Money—I like your Plan immensely of Extirpating that vile race of beings call[d] man but I (who you know am clever (VÈRRÉE) clever) have thought of an improvement in the sistim suppose we were to

Cut of [*sic*] their *prominent members* and by that means render them Harmless innofencive Little Creatures; We might have such charming *vocal* Music Every house might be Qualified to get up an opera and Piccinis Music would be still more in vogue than it is & we might make such usefull ¦ Animals of them in other Respects Consider Well this scheme. Liddy [Miss Lidderdale] raves about Mr Gresham *and y* *silence* but desires her Love to you &c. &c. &c. I tell you no News I refer you to my *very Entertaining* Little history of anecdotes which will arrive in Poland in a short time. You will be *amazed* at the Brilliancy of Sentment [*sic*] Elegance of Ex[pression] Depth of thought and reasoning *containd in* the *hole* [*sic*] I prepare you lest the surprise shoud be too great for one of your delicasy of constitution.

Light of my Soul!
Apple of My Eye!
Pillar of My Existence!
ADIEU!
I remain your *FRIEND*
Maria Allen

INDEX

This is an index of proper names in Fanny Burney's text and of the more significant or interesting occurrences of names in the main introductory sections, annotations, and appendices. In selecting names of marginal significance from the editorial matter the editor has tended to concentrate on those relatively obscure figures who were none the less important or well-known to FB. In general, women are given under their married names unless they first appear under their maiden names. Similarly, peers are given under their titles unless they are first mentioned before their elevation. For the most part, works are cited under the author (translator, editor), composer, or artist. Main biographical notes are indicated in boldface.